THE NEW

Our Right To Love

A LESBIAN RESOURCE BOOK

Ginny Vida, Editor

Karol D. Lightner, Assistant Editor

Tanya Viger, Assistant Editor

A Touchstone Book

Published by Simon & Schuster

TOUCHSTONE
Rockefeller Center
1230 Avenue of the Americas
New York, NY 10020

TOUCHSTONE and colophon are registered trademarks of Simon & Schuster Inc.

Designed by Jaye Zimet

Manufactured in the United States of America

1   3   5   7   9   10   8   6   4   2

Library of Congress Cataloging-in-Publication Data

The New our right to love / Ginny Vida, editor ; Karol D. Lightner,
assistant editor, Tany Viger, assistant editor.
p.   cm.
Includes bibliographical references and index.
1. Lesbianism—United States. 2. Lesbians—United States.
I. Vida, Ginny, 1939-   . II. Lightner, Karol D.   III. Viger, Tanya.
HQ75.6.U5N48   1996   96-3833
306.76'63—dc20   CIP

ISBN 0-684-80682-7

This publication contains the opinions and ideas of its editor and contributors and is designed to provide useful advice in regard to
the subject matter covered. The book is sold with the understanding that the editor, contributors, and publisher are not engaged in rendering
financial, legal, medical, or other professional services in this publication, and it is not intended to replace professional, individual advice. Laws
vary from state to state, and if the reader requires expert assistance or legal or medical advice, a competent professional should be consulted.

The editor, contributors, and publishers specifically disclaim any responsibility for any liability, loss, or risk, personal or otherwise,
which is incurred as a consequence, directly or indirectly, of the use of any of the ideas in this book.

Contents

Contributors

Virginia M. Apuzzo is a commissioner of the New York State Civil Service Commission. Until recently she also served as president of the commission, and prior to that post, as deputy executive director of the New York State Consumer Protection Board. Ms. Apuzzo previously served as executive director of the National Gay Task Force, and of the Fund for Human Dignity, NGTF's educational affiliate. A national spokesperson for the lesbian and gay community, she has been instrumental in persuading the Democratic party to broaden its commitment to lesbian and gay rights.

Cory Baca lives a quiet life in a Southern California beach community. She shares a cottage with two dogs and multiple cats and enjoys an active life with many, many friends.

Miriam Ben-Shalom was a staff sergeant/drill sergeant/instructor in the U.S. Army Reserve. She serves as chairperson of the Gay, Lesbian, and Bisexual Veterans of America, and works with other groups to challenge and eliminate discrimination in the military.

Dr. Betty Berzon is a psychotherapist in private practice in Los Angeles, specializing in work with lesbians and gay men since 1972. She is the editor of the anthology *Positively Gay*, and the author of *Permanent Partners: Building Gay and Lesbian Relationships that Last*.

Terry Boggis is director of communications at the Lesbian and Gay Services Center in New York City. She is also a member of the steering committee for the center's family project, Center Kids.

Rita Mae Brown is the author of seventeen novels, the most recent of which is *Dolley* (1994). She is also a screenwriter who has received two Emmy nominations. In addition, she is a farmer—and a Mother of the Movement.

Victoria A. Brownworth is a columnist for the *Philadelphia Daily News* and *Deneuve*. She writes for over sixty mainstream and queer publications, including *Out, Ms., The Nation, The Village Voice,* and *Spin*. She is the author of seven books and is most recently the editor of *Night Bites: Vampire Stories by Women*. Her forthcoming books include *Too Queer: Essays from a Radical Life* and *A Revolution of Women*. She lives with her partner, filmmaker Judith M. Redding, in Philadelphia.

Barbara Cameron Nation Shield is the founder of the Institute on Native American Health and Wellness; its first project is a press for Native American women and girl writers. She resides in San Francisco with her partner Linda, son Rhys, cats Della Zizila and Mahto, and dog Shelby. Playing bridge is a favorite activity. She is currently writing a screenplay, "Long Time No See."

Colonel Margarethe Cammermeyer is completing her thirty years of military duty after being reinstated into the military. She challenged the policy barring gays and lesbians from serving in the military, was separated from the military in 1992, and reinstated by the courts in 1994. She is the coauthor of *Serving in Silence* (with Chris Fisher, Viking Press, 1994), elucidating that battle. The book is also the basis of the made-for-TV movie with the same name. Dr. Cammermeyer is a nurse scientist and neuroscience clinical nurse specialist at American Lake Veterans Affairs Medical Center, Tacoma, Washington.

Wendy Caster is the author of *The Lesbian Sex Book*. Her short stories have appeared in *Bushfire, Lesbian Bedtime Stories 2, Cats (and Their Dykes),* and *Silver-Tongued Sapphistry*. She has had over three hundred opinion columns published in lesbian and gay newspapers.

Karen Clark was elected to the Minnesota House of Representatives in 1980 on a platform of economic and social justice and neighborhood priorities. She was reelected in 1982, 1984, 1986, 1988, 1990, 1992, and 1994. Prior to her election she was active in numerous South Minneapolis neighborhood housing, health, human rights, labor, women's, peace, and child care organizations. A former public health nurse, she was raised on a farm in Southwest Minnesota.

Jan Crawford is a feminist self-psychologist in private practice in New York City. She is cofounder of the Center for Integrative Approaches in Psychotherapy and has been involved in spiritual practice for many years.

Margaret Cruikshank teaches English, women's studies, and gay/lesbian studies at the City College of San Francisco. She edited several lesbian anthologies and an anthology of literature about aging titled *Fierce with Reality*. She is the author of *The Gay and Lesbian Liberation Movement*, a college text.

Gloria Donadello has practiced psychotherapy for thirty years, working with individuals, groups, and families, predominantly gays and lesbians. She has an MSW from the University of Pennsylvania and Ph.D. from Smith College in clinical social work. Dr. Donadello recently retired from her practice and teaching. She is professor emeritus, Fordham University, School of Social Work, where she taught in the clinical sequence. She now resides in Santa Fe, New Mexico.

Buffy Dunker (Elizabeth Dennison Dunker), now deceased, lived in Cambridge, Massachusetts. A graduate of Vassar, she taught music for twenty-three years at Woodstock Country School in Vermont. She was involved in counseling women and in lesbian activities and was a contributor and editor of *Lesbian Psychologies* (University of Illinois Press, 1987). She had three children, nineteen grandchildren, and seventeen great-grandchildren.

Deborah Edel is a cofounder of the Lesbian Herstory Archives. She has made an enormous commitment of time and energy to building what she believes is an important grassroots cultural institution for the lesbian community. Professionally, she works as an educational psychologist with children with learning disabilities and their families, and as a social worker with children with behavioral and emotional problems.

Paula L. Ettelbrick is currently the legislative counsel for the Empire State Pride Agenda, New York's lesbian and gay political organization, and an adjunct professor of law at New York Law School. She is a longtime activist in the feminist and lesbian/gay rights movement, having served for many years as the legal director for Lambda Legal Defense and Education Fund, where she was responsible for bringing test cases to expand the rights of lesbians and gay men through courts around the country. She also served as the director of public policy for the National Center for Lesbian Rights. Paula has written and spoken extensively about the legal rights of lesbians and gay men.

Judith Blazer Foster is a writer who is currently working on a novel that explores the journey of the soul, patriarchy versus partnership, and the collective unconscious. Judy lives in a lesbian community and loves it.

Sally Miller Gearhart is a lesbian feminist professor of speech communication at San Francisco State University and author of *The Wanderground* and *A Feminist Tarot*. She appeared in the film *Word Is Out* and in the Academy Award–winning documentary, *The Times of Harvey Milk*. Her commitment to political action (particularly to animal rights) outstrips her love of two-stepping and barbershop harmony, but only by an inch or two.

May Glazer, Esq., has practiced law for twenty-six years in New York City. She and Wilma Gottlieb have been partners in the firm Glazer and Gottlieb since 1983, specializing in estates and trusts, wills and estate planning, matrimonial and family law, and elder law.

Jewelle L. Gomez is a poet and literary critic. She has written for *The Village Voice*, Wellesley's *Women's Review of Books*, and *Essence* magazine. She is the author of a novel, *The Gilda Stories* (Firebrand Books, 1991).

Beth Gorman was born and raised in Western Pennsylvania. She has been a Catholic school educator for about eighteen years, both on the east and west coasts. She has been a member of the Conference of Catholic Lesbians, the Women's Ordination Conference, and previously served as vice president of Dignity, USA. She has lived in San Francisco since 1987.

Barbara Grier, an activist for more than forty years in the lesbian movement, is an author, bibliographer, lecturer, editor, and CEO of Naiad Press, the oldest and largest lesbian publishing company in the world. Self-described as a garden-variety lesbian in keeping with the seed packet explanation of "resistant to blight and guaranteed to grow."

Pat Griffin is associate professor, social justice education, at the University of Massachusetts, Amherst. She is a former college swim coach, former high school field hockey and basketball coach, and former high school and college athlete. A bronze medal winner in the biathlon in Gay Games IV, she currently plays third base in a lesbian feminist softball league and is a recreational racquetball player. She is also a workshop leader for homophobia in athletics and physical education.

Anne Harris is a playwright and journalist, a teaching artist in the New York City public schools, and the founder and artistic director of LEND, International (Lesbian Exchange of New Drama), an advocacy and resource organization for lesbian theater arts. Her plays have been performed at the Public Theater and at regional theaters throughout the country.

Elise Harris is associate editor at *Out* magazine. She teaches current events at the Harvey Milk School in New York City. A contributor to *The Village Voice*, *The Nation*, and *Mademoiselle*, she also works with Apocalypse Now, a New York–based collective of gay men and lesbians formed to counter the momentum of the Christian right.

Marjorie J. Hill, Ph.D, is a public health advocate and has been an activist in the lesbian, gay, and progressive communities for over fifteen years. A licensed clinical psychologist, she has worked extensively with lesbian and gay families, couples and individuals. Dr. Hill currently serves as vice chair of the New York State Workers' Compensation Board and is on the boards of the Black Leadership Commission on AIDS and Gay Men's Health Crisis.

Lee Hudson served in the administration of Mayor Edward I. Koch as mayoral liaison to the gay and lesbian community from 1984 to 1988. She became assistant to the mayor and the first director of the Mayor's Office for the Lesbian and Gay Community in 1989.

Nancy Johnson is a psychic healer practicing in the United States and Europe. She is also raising two young children adopted at infancy. This new challenge has increased her interest in pediatric health, and she is sharing the principles of self-healing with the children.

Joan Jubela is an award-winning independent videomaker specializing in experimental cinema vérité documentaries, including *Bombs Aren't Cool*, which won the Nagasaki Mayor's Prize at the 1987 Hiroshima International Film Festival. Other award-winning productions include *Crack Clouds Over Hell's Kitchen*, and *Hard to Get: AIDS in the Workplace*, starring Ruby Dee.

Irena Klepfisz is the author of *A Few Words in the Mother Tongue: Poems Selected and New* and *Dreams of an Insomniac: Jewish Feminist Essays, Speeches and Diatribes.* An activist in the lesbian, feminist, and Jewish communities, she has taught Yiddish, creative writing, and Women's/Judaic Studies and, for two years, served as executive director of New Jewish Agenda. She is currently a member of the collective Hemshekh: Feminist Institute for Secular Jewish Cultural Continuity.

Michele Kort is a writer who has long specialized in women's sports and fitness. She won the Miller Lite Women's Sports Foundation and Journalism Award in 1993. She is currently senior editor for *Living Fit* and *Fit Pregnancy* magazines.

Karen Krahulik is getting her Ph.D. in American history at New York University, with an emphasis on gender and the history of sexuality.

Karol D. Lightner has worked as an editor, teacher, actress, and social worker in her long and colorful career. A longtime activist, she is both a writer and performance artist, and frequently gives readings of her work and testimony to lesbian audiences. She is featured in *Tomboys* (Alyson Publication, 1995).

Beverly Little Thunder is a forty-seven-year-old Lakota lesbian mother who was active in the American Indian movement until coming out in 1985. She is currently active in the Native American Two Spirit movement. She lives in a small ghost town in Arizona with her partner of five years, three dogs, five cats, four birds, and a ferret. A proud grandmother of four, she is a caseworker for HIV/AIDS clients. She continues to sponsor all-women's Sun Dance ceremonies.

Audre Lorde, Black Lesbian Feminist Warrior Poet, was a professor of English, retired from the City University of New York. Author of thirteen books of poetry and prose, and holder of two honorary doctorates, she lived in St. Croix, Virgin Islands. She died of breast cancer in 1992.

JoAnn Loulan, a licensed marriage, family, and child counselor and sex therapist, is in private practice in Palo Alto, California. Her numerous public speaking engagements have varied in content from human sexuality to self-esteem. She is the author of *Lesbian Sex* (1984) and *Lesbian Passion: Loving Ourselves and Each Other* (1987, with Mariah Burton Nelson), both published by Spinsters Book

Company. She is the coauthor of *Period* (1979), a book for girls on menstruation, published by Volcano Press.

Phyllis Lyon, Ed.D., was one of the founders of the Daughters of Bilitis (1955), first editor of its magazine *The Ladder* (1956–60), and coauthor of *Lesbian/Woman*. She served as commissioner on San Francisco's Human Rights Commission from 1976 to 1987, and is professor emeritus of the Institute for Advanced Study of Human Sexuality. Active in the lesbian, gay, and feminist movements, she is currently involved with Old Lesbians Organizing for Change and was a delegate to the 1995 White House Conference on Aging.

Del Martin was founding president of the Daughters of Bilitis (1955) and first "out" lesbian elected to the national board of the National Organization for Women (1973). She served on San Francisco's Commission on the Status of Women (1976–79) and California's Commission on Crime Control and Violence Prevention (1980–83). She is coauthor of *Lesbian/Woman* (1972; with a twenty-year update, 1991) and author of *Battered Wives* (1976). Del was one of three "out" lesbians out of 2,217 delegates to the White House Conference on Aging.

Sharane Merial-Judith is a senior at Gonzaga University in Spokane, Washington, studying sociology and women's spirituality. She is outspoken in everyday situations, bringing a lesbian perspective to every class. A lesbian activist since 1987, she formerly served as eastern vice president of Washington Privacy Lobby and president of the local Dorian Group. She hopes to teach women's studies in the future. Right now, her main focus is raising her children.

Virginia Ramey Mollenkott is professor of English at the William Paterson College of New Jersey. With Letha Scanzoni, she coauthored *Is the Homosexual My Neighbor? Another Christian View* (1978). Her more recent books include *The Divine Feminine: Biblical Imagery of God as Female; Women of Faith in Dialogue; Godding: the Bible and Human Responsibility;* and *Women, Men and the Bible.* With her partner, Debra Marrison, she resides in Hewitt, New Jersey.

Nathalie N. Nevins served in the U.S. Air Force three and a half years. A resident of New York City, she is a founding member of Senior Action in a Gay Environment and a former vice president of the Hetrick-Martin Institute for the Protection of Lesbian and Gay Youth. Ms. Nevins is currently a candidate for an M.A. in management.

R. Elaine Noble, in 1974, was the first gay person elected to statewide office. She served in the Massachusetts legislature until 1978 and now works as a health care consultant and lobbyist to support herself, her two dogs, and two horses. She continues to serve as a spokesperson on behalf of gay/lesbian issues.

Jean O'Leary is former executive director of the National Gay and Lesbian Task Force and of National Gay Rights Advocates. She is currently a member of the executive committee of the Democratic National Committee (DNC), the governing body of the National Democratic party. Ms. O'Leary was this country's first openly gay presidential appointee, serving on the National Commission on the Observance of the International Women's Year and on the National Advisory Committee for Women. A business owner and political consultant, Ms. O'Leary is cofounder of National Coming Out Day.

Torie Osborn has been a social change activist for thirty years, twenty-three as an out lesbian feminist. She has been executive director of the National Gay and Lesbian Task Force and the Los Angeles Gay and Lesbian Community Services Center. She currently is a "movement management consultant" for several national and local groups and is a regular columnist for *The Advocate.* Her book, *Coming Home to America,* was published by Putnam Books in June 1995.

Val C. Phoenix is a New York–born freelance writer focusing on lesbian politics and arts. She lives in San Francisco.

Barbara Raboy is founder and executive director of the Sperm Bank of California, and a consultant specializing in health care needs assessments. A former health educator and public relations director for Women's Choice Clinic in Oakland, she received her graduate degree in public health from the University of California at Berkeley. She has lectured extensively on technologically assisted reproduction and public policy. She lives in the Bay Area with her son.

Liza Rankow PA-C, MHS, is a lesbian health researcher, educator, and activist. She offers training to health care practitioners on lesbian issues, adolescent health, and cultural sensitivity. She is the compiler of *The Lesbian Health Bibliography,* published by the National Center for Lesbian Rights.

The Reverend Sandra Lynn Robinson is president and chief executive officer of Samaritan College, the professional school of the Universal Fellowship of Metropolitan Community churches (UFMCC), which trains pastors and laity for ministry and provides a nonhomophobic theological education for those interested in religion. She has also served as the executive director of the Department of People of Color at UFMCC.

Barbara E. Sang, a psychologist in private practice in New York City, has been active in the lesbian/gay and women's movements since the 1960s. She currently serves as metropolitan New York coordinator for the Association for Women in Psychology. A painter, nature photographer, hiker, and biker, Sang is the coeditor, with Joyce Warshow and Adrienne Smith, of *Lesbians at Midlife: The Creative Transition.*

Tatiana Schreiber is a freelance print and radio journalist focusing on women, health, and the environment. She has contributed to *Gay Community News* since 1984, and to *Sojourner* and other forums. Her coauthored article, "Breast Cancer: The Environmental Connection," was published in *Confronting Cancer, Constructing Change*, Third Side Press. She is currently working to bring back *Gay Community News,* which ceased publishing in 1992, and is a member of the Lesbian and Gay Prisoners Project of *GCN* and Gay and Lesbians in Public Radio. She lives in Jamaica Plain, Massachusetts, with her dog and cat.

Katherine D. Seelman has long been active in the lesbian and gay communities in New York and Washington, D.C. She is one of the founders of the Passages Conference, an annual Washington, D.C., event that routinely draws over five hundred women. Seelman is also active in disability rights and is an open lesbian appointee serving in the Clinton Administration.

Adrienne J. Smith, Ph.D., was a clinical psychologist in private practice in Chicago. One of the founding members of the Feminist Therapy Institute, she was a past-president of the Society for the Psychological Study of Lesbian and Gay Issues, Division 44 of the American Psychological Association. She was also a coeditor (with Barbara Sang and Joyce Warshow) of *Lesbians at Midlife: The Creative Transition*, published in January 1991 by Spinsters Book Company. Dr. Smith died in 1992.

Barbara Smith is a black feminist writer and activist. She is the editor of *Home Girls: A Black Feminist Anthology*. She is cofounder and publisher of Kitchen Table: Women of Color Press.

tatiana de la tierra lives with a lower-case mentality, on the edge of herself in Mayami. Armed with a Colombian soul and an honorary degree from Marimacha University, she is cofounder and editor of *conmoción, revista y red revolucionaria de lesbianas latinas*. She writes poetry, political manifestos, pungent social commentary, and journalistic pieces that keep latina lesbians visible, all in the name of transformation.

Nancy Toder, Ph.D., is a clinical psychologist and psychoanalyst specializing in therapy with lesbians. She is the author of *Choices*, a novel that explores relationships between women and the development of lesbian identity. Active in the feminist and lesbian movements since 1971, she has a chapter on lesbian couples in *Positively Gay*.

Kitty Tsui is the author of *The Words of a Woman Who Breathes Fire*. Her work appears in over twenty-five anthologies, including *Lesbian Erotics, Pearls of Passion, Chloe Plus Olivia, The Very Inside, Lesbian Cultures and Philosophies,* and *Gay and Lesbian Poetry in Our Time*. A bodybuilder, Tsui has won gold and bronze medals at Gay Games II and III. She has appeared on the covers of *On Our Backs* and *The Village Voice*. She has just completed a historical novel, *Bai Sze, White Snake*.

Robin Tyler, the first openly gay or lesbian comic in America, is also one of the leading activists, as well as a speaker and producer, in the lesbian/gay, progressive, and women's movements. She was the main stage producer of the 1979, 1988, and 1993 Marches on Washington for Lesbian and Gay Rights, as well as a keynote speaker at the 1989 NOW Washington Pro-Choice Rally. In 1994 she starred in and coproduced the First International Gay & Lesbian Comedy Festival in Sydney, Australia.

Dr. Virginia Uribe, the founder of Project 10, is a veteran teacher and counselor for the Los Angeles Unified School District. She has been on the staff of Fairfax High School since 1959.

Ginny Vida is investigator-auditor for the San Francisco Ethics Commission. She formerly served as director of the Office of Sexual Harassment Issues at the New York State Division of Human Rights, deputy director of the New York City Commission on the Status of Women, and media director of the National Gay Task Force (now the National Gay and Lesbian Task Force), which cooperated in the first edition of *Our Right To Love.* A former English teacher and textbook editor, she is an avid tennis buff. She has an M.A. in English linguistics from New York University.

H. Joan Waitkevicz, M.D. is an internist in private practice in New York City. She was one of the founders of the St. Mark's Women's Health Collective in 1973.

Eleanor F. Wedge is a freelance writer and editor. She has worked on several reference book projects within the last fifteen years and has specialized as a writer of biographical material.

Janet Weinberg has been an occupational therapist for thirteen years. She is on the board of directors of the Lesbian and Gay Community Center in New York City and has also served on the board of Education in a Disabled Gay Environment (EDGE) and the Center of Independence for Disability in New York (CIDNY). Janet has participated in twenty lesbian and gay pride marches in New York City and won medals at Gay Games IV. Her relationship with Rosalyn Richter has added great joy to her life. She and Rosalyn have registered as domestic partners.

Rabbi Nancy H. Wiener was ordained at Hebrew Union College–Jewish Institute of Religion where she now serves as fieldwork coordinator and instructor in pastoral counseling. For her doctoral project, she developed a model for clergy to use when working with gay and lesbian couples who are preparing for religious ceremonies of commitment. Rabbi Wiener is a member of the Ad Hoc Committee on Human Sexuality of the Central Conference of American Rabbis. She sits on a national committee that is compiling practical guidelines for the inclusion of gay and lesbian members in congregations of the Reform movement. She and her life partner reside in New York City.

Bonnie Zimmerman teaches women's studies at San Diego State University. She is the author of *The Safe Sea of Women: Lesbian Fiction 1969–1989* (Beacon Press, 1990), and of numerous articles in lesbian and feminist journals and anthologies.

Acknowledgments

The New Our Right To Love has been made possible through the cooperation of numerous contributors, photographers, editors, and consultants who have devoted many hours to this project. Although I am grateful to everyone who contributed in any way, I would like to mention the names of a few individuals whose participation has been essential.

First, I am grateful to my agents, Charlotte Sheedy and Ellen Geiger, for their guidance, persistence, and wise counsel. I am also much indebted to Caroline Sutton, Senior Editor at Simon & Schuster, for her thoughtful review of the manuscript, her genuine appreciation of the contents, and for moving this project forward. Rob Henderson also provided a careful copyedit and proofing of the manuscript.

The book's two assistant editors, Karol D. Lightner and Tanya Viger, devoted hundreds of hours working closely with me on developing the manuscript; communicating with the contributors; preparing resource lists; conducting, transcribing, and editing interviews; and identifying and recruiting authors with expertise on particular subjects. Both Karol and Tanya provided crucial editorial assistance. For their hard work, patience, and moral support, they have my enduring appreciation. Brian Grant, Judith D. Lee, Marge Paules, and Jane Rubin also provided valuable assistance.

As I was embarking on this project, Charlotte Bunch met with me to suggest essential topics to be covered in the book and identified a number of women who could be approached to write about them. Her vast knowledge of the lesbian feminist movement, including politics, theory, and literature, was extremely valuable in helping me establish a basic framework for this book.

Though the work of several photographers is represented here, I especially wish to thank Natt Nevins, Donna Gray, Shoshana Rothaizer, Morgan Gwenwald, Ginny Briggs, Bettye Lane, Joan Biren, and Ann Meredith, who devoted much time going out on assignment to photograph particular women and/or taking time to give me a tour of their photo files. I also appreciate the many photos submitted by mail by lesbian photographers from across the country.

To all contributors of *The New Our Right To Love,* I proudly offer my thanks for sharing your expertise and personal experiences with the lesbian community through this project.

Foreword II

or Tempus Fugit

Rita Mae Brown

Nearly twenty years have passed since I wrote the forward to *Our Right To Love*—passed, hell, they flew by with the speed of light. It's reassuring to know that the bell tolls for everyone, straight or lesbian. Ask not for whom the bell tolls, it tolls for thee.

I wonder how often you have heard that quote and considered what it really means. I'll spare you the literary analysis and get to the point: It means we are all part of one another.

Simple as that concept is to write it seems quite difficult to live. The human race apparently relishes argument and lesbians have raised it to an art form. Put two lesbians in a room and you'll get five opinions. Occasionally this habit is amusing; more often than not, it is trying. I think of it as the narcissism of small differences and I have had ample melancholy occasion to observe its debilitating effects.

Politically the pendulum has lurched to the right and we can't afford such narcissism. These are not the best of times, but then again since tempus fugit, they won't last forever, although they may last long enough to make you and me reconsider our political direction.

First let's consider our political direction. Do we have one? I know we continually respond to crisis (for example, a mother loses her children in a child custody case) but that's hardly the same as a unified political program. I also know that for the last fifteen years we have given generously, nay, even foolishly to other causes. We poured body and soul into the feminist movement and we marched right alongside gay men. This is not to say we shouldn't make common cause with other people but it is a political reality that common cause should be reciprocated. The brutal question we must now ask ourselves is: Has it? If not, why do we continue coalitions that sap our strength? Are we so desper-ate to be "liked," to be "legitimized" that we will allow ourselves to be used? These questions may be unsettling to you but someone's got to finally ask them and it might as well be me. I'm accustomed to the fuss so what's a little more?

If we are going to move ahead politically, maybe even survive politically, I think we have a perfect right to say to any other group, "We will do this for you but then you must do this for us." It's time to start asking, sisters.

The question of political direction is crucial because are we to be a reactive movement or an active movement? If we stay reactive then we never define the program and we're always on the defensive. A lesbian gets thrown out of the service. We respond. It's all very well and good that we respond on an ad hoc basis but it's no way to make political gain. The way you gain is to create a program and then press for it. Keep your enemies on the defensive. I know it's quite hard for some of you polite ladies to think

Rita Mae Brown.

in terms of offense, but I'm not saying that you be personally offensive, only that you push politically and part of pushing is touching the sensitive nerves of your political enemies. It doesn't mean you're a bad person, it means you're a smart politician. Look my dears, we can't change the rules of the game. You can only do that when you win. We are a long way from winning so take off the gloves and start slugging.

I can't give you a political program in an introduction. But we must find it. I can give you one point of a political program which I think is utterly critical: equal pay for equal work. What good is the right to love if you can't eat or pay rent? Obviously, that one political point would mean that we would work with any person who agrees. We can make a coalition. Another point of our program should be the right of a mother to keep her children regardless of sexual preference. A woman should also have the right to serve in the military regardless of sexual preference.

Many other issues need to be considered before we do generate that program but remember this: The conundrum of oppression is that while you fight your oppression you lose the time to fight for other issues—a balanced budget, a reduction of the defense budget, a reduction of nuclear arms, the promotion of agriculture, and the enforcement of reasonable environmental protection laws. The horrible truth is that as long as we stay "in our place" the white men controlling our government will never be challenged. We can win a few of our lesbian issues and still lose the war, if you get my drift.

My suggestion is that we first understand what our program is. Then some of us must dedicate ourselves to that program exclusively. Others of us will be in our professions, some even in political office, addressing other issues of importance to us but keeping in our minds the lesbian agenda and helping when we can.

All of this is easier said than done, but without some clarity about our goals it's a sure bet we aren't going to do Jack Shit.

Now consider yourself. What do you want to do with your life? If you aren't happy with the work you do, find what you do like, reclaim it, and get on with it. Do what you love and the money will follow. I know you've heard that before, too, but it is absolutely true. You may not get what you want but you will get what you need.

When you find your work I don't mean to imply that you won't feel pain, but you will be far better able to put that pain in perspective and to use it to grow. Pain isn't the enemy; rigidity is the enemy.

I used to think that I could reason with rigid people but time has taught me this is not so. People are rigid out of fear and anger, and since the basis is irrational there's not much you can do with them. In contrast to the way I thought in my youth, I now realize that people are stupid, foolish, and fragile. That still doesn't give me the right to hurt them. I avoid them when I can and fight them when I must, even when they are within our own ranks.

I've also come to realize that a true individual is a frightening figure to many people. When you're young and you must confront homophobia it's easy to think that you're fighting for your right to love. Not necessarily. What you are fighting is homophobia. If you and I were really fighting for the right to love then we would welcome love in whatever guise it appeared. How many lesbians you can think of would rejoice if one of their lesbian friends found deep love with a man? Chances are they would be as censorious of her as the general culture is of the lesbian. Curious, isn't it, this endless cycle of judgment and rejection? I suggest we be true revolutionaries and stop the cycle today.

I shall assume if you are reading this introduction that you have some interest in lesbianism and perhaps are a lesbian yourself (congratulations). If you truly believe in love, then allow people to find it however they can: love of work, love of place, love of friends, love of a woman, love of a man, of a child, of animals, whatever. The issue is no longer our right to love but everyone's right to love. The only people who are queer are the people who don't love anybody.

Yours, as ever,
Rita Mae Brown

Introduction

Ginny Vida

The first edition of *Our Right To Love* was published in 1978, at a time when there was a dearth of literature celebrating lesbian lives. Over the years many lesbians have told me how much the original edition meant to them as they were coming to terms with their sexual identity, seeking positive role models, and trying to shed internalized homophobia. Especially important, they said, were the articles addressing personal issues: coming out to families, friends, and employers; dealing with relationships; sexuality; breakups; role-playing; and integrating feminist principles into their personal lives. It was with great pride that I accepted the American Library Association's 1978 Gay Book Award on behalf of *Our Right To Love* and its many contributors.

This edition has been revised and expanded to include over sixty articles and interviews (the first edition had forty). It reflects dramatic headline-producing events in our lives as well as many barely perceptible, behind-the-scenes acts of courage and conviction that caused our community, and our culture, to evolve over the years.

Much has changed since *Our Right To Love* was first published. And some things have not changed. On the one hand, many more lesbians and gay men are open about their sexual orientation, having come out to their parents, children, friends, and even to their employers. This has helped produce a positive change in public opinion and in our social climate, especially as heterosexuals have begun to realize that people they know, and people they love, are lesbian or gay.

On a political level, the lesbian and gay movement has made significant strides in terms of strategy, professional expertise, and voting power. In 1978 there was only one publicly acknowledged lesbian elected official, Elaine Noble in Massachusetts. Today there are several, mostly at the municipal and state levels. Dozens more have been appointed by mayors and governors, and even by the president, to high positions in government agencies. Lesbians are prominent among those elected and appointed to public office. State legislators include Deborah Glick (New York), Karen Clark (Minnesota), Liz Stefanics (New Mexico), Kate Brown (Oregon), Sheila Kuehl (California), Cynthia Wooten (Oregon), Tammy Baldwin (Wisconsin), Susan Farnsworth (Maine), Dale McCormick (Maine), Hedy Rijksen (Oregon), and Gail Shibley (Oregon). Elected municipal officeholders include Kathleen Triantifillow (Cambridge), Carole Migden (San Francisco), Susan Leal (San Francisco), Christine Kehoe (San Diego), Sherry Harris (Seattle), Jackie Goldberg (Los Angeles), Susan Hyde (Hartford), Roslyn Garfield (Provincetown), and Irene Rabinowitz (Provincetown). Roberta Achtenberg, appointed by President Bill Clinton as assistant secretary for Fair Housing and Equal Opportunity, was confirmed by the U.S. Senate to serve in that post. We even have one mayor, Judy Abdo, of Santa Monica, California.

Currently eight states and more than a hundred counties and municipalities have gay rights laws on the books. In 1978 there were no states and only forty counties or municipalities with such protections, and domestic partnership laws and policies were a distant dream. Today, a number of municipalities, state governments, and individual corporations such as Apple Computer offer benefits to employees of domestic partners.

Complementing these political gains, both the broadcast and print media have begun to pay more attention to us. It is no longer an oddity to see a positive article in the newspaper about what local lesbians are doing. *Roseanne,* one of television's most popular shows, has a recurring lesbian character played by Sandra Bernhard. Lesbian comics have appeared on Comedy Central. The media, spurred by movement activists who spent years clamoring for access and fair coverage, has helped us educate the public, with the result that the act of coming out does not produce the shock waves it once did. In some ways, coming out is probably a more realistic choice for lesbians today than ever before, carrying with it fewer risks of rejection by loved ones or loss of employment. More and more, the public reaction is "So what?" when the issue of sexual orientation is raised.

Still, despite measurable progress, homophobia is alive and well in certain quarters. Campaigns against lesbian and gay rights laws are still being mounted, as reactionary forces try to persuade voters, with notable successes and failures, to repeal protective legislation. In Oregon and Idaho, voters rejected initiatives in 1994 that would have banned or overturned local gay rights ordinances, although backers of both measures vowed to try again. Certain conservative religious leaders, forever quoting biblical passages about Sodom and Gomorrah, still characterize lesbians as child molesters and evildoers. Persons with HIV, in the midst of dealing with life-threatening illness, are said to have incurred the wrath of God in the form of disease because of their sexual conduct. Congress, stonewalling attempts to lift the military's ban on lesbians and gays, has written into law a "don't ask, don't tell" policy that can only be described as insulting and oppressive. And conservative forces in Congress want to reinstate the witch-hunts of the past that routed lesbians and gays from the armed forces.

Lesbian and gay candidates for public office have been charged with promoting a "gay agenda," as if they had no interest in the public welfare as a whole. Karen Burstein, who had enjoyed a double-digit lead in the polls in the 1994 race for attorney general in New York, was defeated for statewide office by 2 percentage points following homophobic attacks by one public official who questioned her fitness for office because of her acknowledged lesbianism. Unfortunately, voters were persuaded to consider this factor more important than her twenty-one years of distinguished public service as state senator, judge, and government agency head. Nonetheless, her courageous campaign helped to lay the groundwork for what will eventually be statewide—and national—victories for our community.

Despite the negative forces in our midst, we have much to celebrate: the everyday opening of closet doors and the proliferation of organizations that represent our rights and provide critical social outlets and services for our community. Today there are thousands of lesbian and lesbian/gay groups appealing to our most varied interests: jogging, chamber music, politics, rock-climbing, tennis, twelve-step recovery programs, religious affiliations, theater-going, card playing, and career-oriented groups in every profession, every line of work. It is also a notable achievement that increased political ties have been forged with women's groups and rainbow coalitions with people of all races and ethnic backgrounds. National figures such as Jesse Jackson have done much to pave the way for a politics embracing full diversity. In 1978 national leaders of color who supported lesbian and gay rights were few and far between.

With this edition of *Our Right To Love* we pay tribute to the rich and emerging literature of lesbian writers and poets, with especially notable contributions from African American, Latina, and Asian American lesbians. We recognize lesbian publishers who translate lesbian voices to the printed page. And we also honor notable lesbian performing artists and athletes who, like k. d. lang, Melissa Etheridge, and Martina Navratilova, have publicly acknowledged their sexual orientation and serve as open, positive role models for our community. (In 1978 we had no "out" lesbian celebrities.) Amazing. You even hear of "lesbian chic" nowadays. Indeed, some folks think it's downright trendy to be a lesbian.

Our Right To Love celebrates the lives of early lesbian activists who confronted the ignorance pervading all of society's institutions—who were interviewed by hostile talk show hosts and arrested in street demonstrations when legislatures and the media failed to respond to our needs, and who pressured our country's libraries to stock the shelves with intelligent information about lesbians

Ginny Vida.

and gay men. We honor those lesbian "herstorians" who preserved for posterity the positive contributions to history of our lesbian foremothers, and who researched and brought to light the history of our culture's persecution of lesbians and gay men. The Lesbian Herstory Archives, which now has its own building in New York, is a prime example of a volunteer research and archiving effort that blossomed into a precious national repository of lesbian lore.

We also rejoice in the lives of lesbian mothers—and their children, some the product of heterosexual marriages, and more recently, those born to lesbians in same-sex relationships, those born to single lesbians, and those adopted by lesbians. When the first edition of *Our Right To Love* was published, the surprising news that lesbians could be mothers at all, let alone good mothers, was just finding its way to the printed page. Our own community understood that lesbians had become mothers through heterosexual marriage. Lesbian motherhood via sperm donation and adoption was almost unheard of. Today, it's a way of life for thousands of lesbians, lesbian partners, and their children who are pioneering new avenues of family life, and giving "family values" new meaning.

Yet as we count our blessings, we remember those who, in the past, took their own lives rather than live in the face of homophobia, hostility, and rejection by family, friends, and employers. And we mourn the passing of untold thousands of our lesbian sisters who have died of breast cancer, and many thousands of gay brothers who have succumbed to HIV. None of us who were active in the movement in the early 1970s, when our vision was full of hope and promise, could have imagined that one day, so many of our contemporaries in the struggle for justice would die in their youth or their midlife years. The loss and the tragedy are incomprehensible.

The HIV era has transformed the sexual lives of gay men, and although there is little evidence to date that woman-to-woman transmission of the disease is a serious health threat, some lesbians, too, have become more cautious in their sexual practices and more discriminating in their choice of sexual partners. The age of HIV has also affected lesbians in that many have become employed as HIV-related health care advocates and health care and social service providers. Others have donated many volunteer hours to AIDS-related service organizations outside their regular jobs.

The new and revised edition of *Our Right To Love* presents nearly all fresh material, covering many new areas and issues affecting lesbian lives. Some of the original subjects, such as surviving a breakup, are covered by new authors with a fresh perspective. And the community's greatly accentuated interest in certain areas such as lesbian parenting is reflected in an expanded series of new articles dealing with strategies for getting pregnant through donor insemination, as well as raising children in a positive environment created by lesbians with support from friends and, where possible, from family members.

New perspectives on sexuality—including sexual technique, safer sex, sexual style, and butch-femme roles, are explored here. Coverage of lesbian health issues has also been extended in this edition to include articles on breast cancer, spiritual healing, and lesbians with AIDS. Dealing with the illness and death of one's life partner is addressed here for the first time.

This edition's lesbian activism section now includes an interview with Minnesota State Representative Karen Clark. One of the lesbian community's greatest political success stories, Karen has been elected and reelected to office for six successive terms. Another highlight of this section is a brand-new remembrance of things past by our movement's national treasures, Del Martin and Phyllis Lyon.

The education section presents all-new material reflecting the stormy controversies in our schools over the "rainbow curriculum," a multicultural approach that recognizes the contributions of lesbians and gays to society as well as those of women and persons of color. Also, addressed for the first time in the new edition is the subject of lesbians in sports, in a memorable article by Pat Griffin, who has done pioneering work on confronting homophobia in this context.

The subject of religion has received expanded coverage with all-new pieces on lesbian Catholics, Protestants, Jews, and the Metropolitan Community churches. To these have been added contributions on Witchcraft and Native American spirituality, alternative spiritual pursuits that have attracted the interest of thousands of lesbians in the New Age.

Our Right To Love's discussion of lesbian legal rights includes a basic overview of this developing area of the law by Paula Ettelbrick, followed by Miriam Ben-Shalom's report on lesbians in the military. Also featured in this section is an interview with Colonel Margarethe Cammermeyer, a highly decorated army nurse whose 1994 book, *Serving in Silence,* was transformed into a made-for-TV movie. The legal section also includes Lee Hudson's fifteen-year history of the lobbying effort to pass this country's first proposed gay rights bill (in New York City), followed by May Glazer's excellent discussion of, and helpful tips on, legal planning for lesbian life partners.

Covered for the first time in the Spectrum of Lesbian Experience are contributions from lesbians with disabilities, as well as African American, Latina, Asian–Pacific American, Native American, Jewish, younger, older, and midlife lesbians. Lesbians in prison, an often forgotten population, are also represented here.

The discussion of lesbian culture has been enriched with Bonnie Zimmerman's new review of lesbian literature, Karen Krahulik's discussion of lesbian history, and Deborah Edel's tribute to the Lesbian Herstory Archives. Also highlighted here is an interview with performing artist Melissa Etheridge, followed by articles on lesbian music festivals and lesbians in the arts.

The book concludes with an updated directory of national lesbian organizations, compiled by Karol Lightner, and Wendy Caster's annotated bibiography of lesbian literature.

The revised edition of *Our Right To Love,* like the 1978 edition, has been a labor of love. There were many times when I thought I would never finish it; this edition took much longer than the first edition to complete. It is a project close to my heart, and one I never could have completed without the assistance of Charlotte Sheedy, Ellen Geiger, Caroline Sutton, Rob Henderson, Charlotte Bunch, Karol Lightner, and Tanya Viger.

On behalf of this edition of *Our Right To Love* and all of its contributors, I hope that you will find the contents of this book helpful, informative, and invigorating. It is my hope that these articles and interviews will help lesbians understand and appreciate where we've traveled as a community, what our struggles and issues have been, what our activist sisters have achieved for us and themselves, so that, with our spirits renewed, we may rededicate ourselves to building a society that ensures justice for all.

I

Relationships

Therapy as Support for Relationships:

An Interview with Gloria

Donadello, Ph.D., and

Marjorie Hill, Ph.D.

(Editor's Note: The following interview was conducted with two psychotherapists who have worked extensively with lesbian and gay families, couples, and individuals. Dr. Gloria Donadello, now retired after thirty years of teaching and private practice, has an MSW and a Ph.D. in clinical social work. Dr. Marjorie Hill, an experienced licensed clinical psychologist, is also a public health advocate and has been an activist in the lesbian, gay, and progressive communities for over fifteen years. Their biographies appear on pp. 10 and 11. We discussed the uses of psychotherapy in dealing with problems in relationships.)

How do cultural attitudes affect lesbian relationships?

GD: Lesbians live in a culture where they suffer from oppression—from sexism, homophobia, and racism. This influences how they experience issues of trust and communication in relationships.

MH: That's particularly important in terms of how couples get support. In traditional relationships, families rally around the relationships and buy wedding presents, and so on. Or even if straight couples are just living together, it's "Bring your boyfriend over." But many families of lesbians, even when they feel supportive, relate to the lesbian's lover as a good friend or buddy in a way that is nonsexual. I think that this impacts on lesbian relationships—they have less support.

GD: Straight people have structures and rituals that validate their relationships. Even when the family feels okay about the relationship, they don't know *how* to feel okay about it. Do they tell other members of the family? Their best friends? How do they deal with this?

MH: Yes, when this couple shows up at the sister's wedding, what do they say? "This is my daughter's ...???" It's a courageous act for some parents to say "partner" or "lover." With some families the resolution is to discourage the lover from coming, or to have her come but keep it toned down.

Given the lack of societal supports, how do lesbians manage to form lasting relationships?

GD: When I'm asked this question, I'm reminded of Evelyn Hooker's research. She found that, given the oppression that lesbians have to endure, it was astonishing just how healthy they were. We mustn't assume that because people are lesbian or gay, their behavior tends to be pathological. There is still a prevailing myth out there about this.

MH: It's a struggle not to internalize society's message that "You're sick, you're perverted, there must be something wrong with you." It's similar to what African Americans experience. It's a wonder, given how pervasive racism is in our society, that *any* African American is successful, that *any* African American children grow up with any iota of self-esteem, that people don't just internalize the prevailing message of the culture. However, through pride and cultural awareness, individuals are able to successfully struggle against racism.

And I think that what makes the difference in lesbian relationships—in terms of dealing with homophobia—is developing supports. Some of these supports are in the community, where couples establish long-term relationships with other couples. Let's say, for example, they identify with people who are also raising children. They share experiences with people who don't regard them as oddities.

GD: What Marjorie says is very much to the point. When I was younger, we didn't have the same kinds of communities that we have now. There were only bars. The quality of my relationships then was very different from the quality of my current relationship. We have other couples who are friends. We're both active in the community, and we're both out. This makes a huge difference.

MH: Therapy is also a support. If you're in a disenfranchised group and in situations where you're being oppressed, therapy is a way of giving you an additional support. It's like taking vitamins.

What motivates lesbian clients to seek the help of a therapist?

MH: I see a number of women between the ages of twenty-five and forty, and if I had to identify the number-one concern, it's relationships—the desire for a reciprocal, nurturing, satisfying relationship. I feel that part of the problem is developmental. We don't teach our children to form good relationships. We teach girls to be nice, and we teach boys to be entitled. If you have two women together who have been taught just to be nice, it's problematic. We need to teach children how to negotiate.

GD: I think we can translate "nice" into a kind of passivity, including feelings of helplessness about what to do when we meet someone. So if you want something, you have to think actively about how to reach and achieve it. That's an active stance, as opposed to a passive one. When you get two women together who have been socialized in these passive modes, you have problems.

The other role that women are socialized into is the role of the arbitrator, the person who makes peace all the time. So when conflict comes up, it's like, "Oh my God, the world is coming to an end." Conflict becomes earth-shattering. This is something that women can deal with in therapy.

When couples come to you for counseling, what do they ask you to help them with?

MH: Couples come into counseling because they're in trouble; the relationship isn't working. And often, therapy is viewed as a last resort. Couples, in my opinion, are the most reluctant subset of people to enter treatment. They'll say, "We've tried everything, and *you're it.*" And you, as therapist, have two weeks to solve it all.

GD: Marjorie's right. It's not only that therapy may be a last resort, but one of the partners has her bags packed and is going to leave *next week* if something doesn't happen. The most difficult couples are those

Patty Hazeldine and Annie Bandler.

where one member sees no problem, and the other is crawling the walls. These couples are in crisis. They're hurt and angry; they're defensive. So before you can identify the issues and begin working on them, you've got to diffuse the anger. Then you try to help them clarify what the issues are.

MH: When they decide, "Okay—I'm not going to leave; you're not going to leave," it still takes time before enough of the hurt and anger is vented before they can think, "How are we going to understand how we got off track and how we get back on track?"

GD: Let's look again at what it means to be part of a culture where you meet oppression almost every day, and how that impacts on communication in relationships. You learn to communicate indirectly because often your survival depends on it. If you then continue to communicate in this way with your partner, problems arise because this kind of communication leads to confusion, misunderstandings, and no understanding. If, in addition, you internalize the devaluation of lesbian relationships, that may lead to feelings of ambivalence about the relationship. These behaviors, some of which are unconscious, can promote acting out in the relationship, which leads to further problems. The impact on the relationship is negative and destructive.

What are some other examples of problems you deal with in a therapy situation?

GD: Holidays create a special kind of stress because of the expectations people have: Everybody is supposed to be happy between Thanksgiving and January 15. It doesn't happen that way, and that creates stress in and of itself.

MH: There are also heightened expectations about families of origin being accepting. It's like, "This year they're going to invite my lover to the seder" or "Christmas dinner." And when it doesn't happen, there's disappointment.

GD: You know, it's amazing how often we forget that people bring years of experience into relationships that are outside the knowledge of the other person. We make the assumption that the other person will *know* about the strong feelings we have around such events, when, of course, the other person *doesn't* know.

MH: Sometimes it's something that someone has held onto for a very long time, and couldn't hold onto it any longer. The therapist can help people feel it's safe enough to say, "I'm mad at you because three Valentine's Days ago, you didn't do such-and-such."

GD: But you see, just in the process of talking in a safe place with a third person present, the process begins to teach communication skills. For example, the therapist might interject at one point and say, "That's important for you, but how would she have known that?"

MH: Yes, and one lover might say, "I don't know what you mean." And the other will often say, "You don't *want* to know. You always say that when we start to talk about something difficult." But if the therapist says objectively and in a supportive way, "I need you to explain that a little better," it be-

Mary Kaminsky

Michelle and Linda at Heart-to Heart Dog Grooming, Cleveland.

comes clearer to the other lover: "Oh, is *that* what you mean? Why didn't you just tell me?"

Having a safe space and having someone facilitate difficult moments provides a framework in which conflicts can be resolved. It is my responsibility as a therapist to make sure that the communication is ongoing. We're there to encourage dialogue, to facilitate a process; we're not there to be judge and jury, to see who's right or wrong. Once people develop trust and confidence in us, we can engage in that process.

GD: Growing in relationships is a lifelong process. You don't come to therapy to learn it, once and forever. Therapy is a learning process, and the therapist is a facilitator in that process. What you hope to accomplish is that people acquire some tools they didn't have before in learning how to communicate and negotiate differences. And it's an experience where the person's self-esteem has an opportunity to develop out of the respect that is inherent in the therapist-client relationship. I don't think it's so unusual that so many lesbians find themselves in therapy, given the oppressive experiences they've had.

MH: People are attracted to differences, but my experience has been that after the initial infatuation and the couple settles into the relationship, those differences become apparent. So it's "Yes, I know that you eat meat, but don't you understand what that *means*? And you really want to bring that into the *house*?"

In relationships, people are always unfolding to themselves as well as to their partners. Issues around family, politics, and "outness" are reflections of some fundamental personal principles we have developed over time, and continue to develop. People don't necessarily inquire about these issues when they first meet, however. "How do you relate to your mother?" is probably not a bad question.

GD: It's remarkable how we take for granted the excitement of being with somebody who is different, and yet how difficult it can be to bridge those differences, to negotiate them. I always love to tell about this couple, one of whom is very laid back. She has a built-in clock that enables her to get to the airport just as the doors of the plane are closing. And the other partner travels all over, is very organized, and she gets to the airport an hour early. After many bitter fights over this, they hit on a

solution: They never went to the airport in the same car together. The car service would send two cars, one for Judy and one for Lisa. And it worked.

But the fantasy for many couples is that because we got along so well for the first six months, we are going to get along forever. Women tend to come to a place of acceptance and understanding about differences in friendships more easily than they do in intimate relationships. And sometimes there is the expectation that "You ought to be more like me; if you were more like me, we wouldn't have this kind of difficulty."

MH: Actually, it's more like, "I thought you *were* like me, which is why we're in therapy now, because you misled me." I really feel that our society has not dealt with the issue of differences—there's this myth, this melting pot sameness. But we're not the same. We're equal, but we're not the same. And to learn to dialogue and appreciate and negotiate with those differences is very important. It's no wonder that couples have this sometimes unconscious assumption that we're going to be alike in every way.

GD: Sometimes I wonder if, because as lesbians, as women, frequently as minority women, we deal so much with differences outside our relationships, we want people who are more like us to be intimate with.

MH: There's also this sense that sexual, intimate attractions are above and beyond consciousness, beyond our control. So "I'm drawn to you and here I am." There's a mystique where sexuality is involved, about not having control.

GD: And I think that carries over into other areas of communication: expectations of "You know what I want." The other thing is that women bond very quickly, and we often equate having a satisfying sexual relationship with "This person is right for me." Sex and love are very much intertwined in how women approach relationships. But some of the literature I've seen troubles me, because it suggests that this bonding has the makings of pathological relationships. Because women bond differently, they are apt to set up house perhaps a bit more precipitously, without really giving each other an opportunity to really get to know one another. But that bonding is just a difference, and brings with it different sets of coping that people have to do. It's not pathological.

What about dealing with sexual problems?

MH: When there's an attraction, people bond around that, and when there is disappointment, sex often ends up reflecting that disappointment. And because we as women are not encouraged to talk about sex, or to be sexual, there is some reluctance to say, "Well, you know, it's not like it used to be." I find that I really have to push people to talk about sex even when it turns out that it's a major concern, either on the part of one partner or both.

GD: This is so true. It used to come up in the lesbian group that I ran. One group member would sort of hesitantly say, "Sometimes I wish we could get around to talking about sex." And everyone would say, "That's a great idea." And then—total silence. And I think it's very difficult for women in a relationship to talk not only about sexual issues that might be coming up, but also about sexual behaviors—who would like whom to do what to whom. One study I looked at last year—and it looked like a valid study—reported that lesbians tend to have sex less frequently than a control group of heterosexual women. But when you think that you've got two women, both socialized to think that they shouldn't be concerned with sexual matters, you see the groundwork for some difficulties.

Any final observations about the uses of therapy?

MH: I think it's important for people to see therapy not as a last resort. It is clearly a strong source of support rather than something to do while one is packing to leave.

GD: There is a sort of mentality about "one fix." If you get the right kind of fix, if you visit the right therapist, everything will be okay. But in fact, life is a series of problems to be solved. Therapy can't solve them all, but it can help people to identify the important ones so they can be worked on.

MH: I would really encourage lesbians who are either looking to be or who are already in relationships to talk to people who've been together for five or more years. Many of the couples I've seen have the attitude that lesbian relationships don't last. Talking to people who have been together for a long time is a source of support and will help dispel the myth that there's no longevity in lesbian relationships.

GD: I'd personally like to see some of our organizations sponsor groups that deal in a more informal way with some of these relationship issues. I see a lot of people go to twelve-step programs, and some of them go not necessarily because they have addictions but because these groups offer something that is not available elsewhere. As I come to the end of my professional life, if I had it to do over again, I think that I would invest heavily in developing groups like this—relationship groups, couples groups, where the emphasis is not necessarily on therapy but on learning how to cope as special people with special problems in a world that is so hostile to them. There's a lot of displaced anger that lesbians take out on each other. These are things that get handled in therapy, but not everybody wants to come to therapy, and not everybody needs to.

Surviving the Breakup of a Lesbian Relationship

Adrienne J. Smith, Ph.D.

Breakups can occur at any point in a lesbian relationship: after three months, three years, or thirty years. There is no guarantee that a relationship will last forever or even that it is in the best interests of each woman that it does. There are, however, ways to enable each of us to gain the most growth and sense of self-worth possible from the painful experience of breaking up. Some of these ways are defined by the type of relationship and the reason for the breakup; others are involved in any breakup.

There are three general reasons for relationships to end: growth, dishonesty, and betrayal. The growth of either partner will lead to a breakup unless both partners are able to change and to acknowledge her own and the other's growth. Relationships in which there has been a major change of status, such as one partner or the other changing from student to professional, becoming sober, developing a successful career, will end if the basis of the interaction has been the difference in status. This is also true if the relationship had been one of "mentor-protégé" and the "protégé" partner begins to grow into an autonomous, independent person. This often happens, paradoxically, because the "mentor" partner has done such a good job of mentoring. Again, if either partner cannot deal with the change in status, the relationship will end.

Often, the "mentor" partner feels that she is being deserted, abandoned without any appreciation for what she has done for her "protégé" lover. The lover who needs to grow may feel guilt for leaving her lover, fear of "making it on her own," but also the excitement of the challenge. These feelings may be much more intense than the present circumstances warrant.

This intensity suggests the added impact of the reenactment of past feelings based on childhood and adolescent experiences. If each partner can become aware of the "leftover" feelings from childhood and adolescence and deal with them and one another honestly, this type of breakup has the best prognosis for continued growth and may lead to long-term friendship between the ex-lovers, a phenomenon which is very common among lesbians.

The second type of breakup is the inevitable result of a lesbian relationship built on dishonesty. During their time together one or both of the partners has disguised her true feelings, sometimes even from herself, in the interest of avoiding conflict or of maintaining a particular kind of image. Those of us who are dishonest with ourselves and our lovers are often caught in caretaker or hero roles. We believe we must be nice or accommodating at all times; we are terrified of the possible consequences of expressing any negative thoughts or of even displaying any needs of our own.

Inevitably, the "good" one finds that her needs are not being met and often redoubles her efforts to be accommodating, expecting that after she has given enough it will be her turn and her partner, the recipient, will become the giver.

When this does not happen (as it never does) she becomes enraged, feels cheated, and explodes. Sometimes she becomes so frightened by the strength of her anger that she ends the relationship rather than confront and express her feelings. Her partner is often stunned by the sudden radical change in her formerly quiet, gentle lover and may feel betrayed or tricked, since the assumptions on which the relationship had been built have been proven false. Each may be furious at the other for perpetrating this duplicity.

Again, each partner may find herself repeating childhood patterns, perhaps that of the "good" child hoping, through her goodness, to earn the love of an unavailable parent. The other partner may find herself caught up in repeating her pattern of desperately fighting to maintain her integrity against what she sees as tremendous pressure to change. To the extent that these newly understood differences can be named and discussed honestly, the ex-lovers have the opportunity to develop a friendship on a new and more realistic basis.

Betrayal, the third major reason for breaking up, applies to all the relationships in which one partner believes something about the other that proves to be false. When we deceive ourselves into thinking we can change our lover's bad habits or help her heal from a drinking problem, a bad relationship, or the inability to hold a job, for example, we are simply putting off the day when we will have to face the fact that no adult can change another unless that person wants to change. The recognition of that fact is often accompanied by a sense of betrayal and disillusionment.

I also use the term *betrayal* in referring to relationships in which one partner is an alcoholic or drug user, is physically or emotionally abusive, or has secret affairs. All these behaviors, whether or not under conscious control, constitute betrayals of an implicit pact made between lovers that each will treat the other with care and "be there" for her. In couples such as these, while it may seem that one partner is doing more active and visible damage to the relationship, the other partner is cooperating in the sense that she tolerates the destructive behavior while convincing herself that her lover will change.

The breakup usually occurs when the more tolerant partner (currently known as the "enabler") finally realizes that her partner's behavior is not changing.

When a sense of betrayal results in a breakup, healing can be affected through increasing honesty with ourselves about our feelings and needs, about our part in the breakup, and our current state of being. Childhood memories may be stirred up, either of trying to ignore or to fix a dysfunctional parent or of a woman repeating old patterns of handling stress.

There are no villains or victims in relationships between two adults. Even in couples in which one is abusive or betraying a trust, the other is responsible for tolerating the behavior. However, it is clear in such relationships that one woman is being more actively hurt; and we have a right to protect ourselves from abuse or injury.

During the early stages of breaking up, we are continually in touch with, sometimes almost overwhelmed by, a wide range of feelings: anger, hurt, remorse, grief, relief, loss, joy, even hatred. It is essential to our growth and healing that we validate our right to have feelings and to *verbally* express all our feelings. Most of us are more comfortable with one style of emotional expression, usually either anger or hurt, and have learned to suppress the other. We may need help and encouragement to express feelings we have been taught to consider "unacceptable." Since one's feelings alone cannot harm someone else, there cannot be a "wrong" or "unacceptable" feeling. Only actions can be judged good or bad, acceptable or unacceptable.

We may also need help to stop blaming our former partners. Blame is a natural and often essential part of separation. Especially in relationships that ended as a result of betrayal or self-delusion, it is imperative that the "injured" party is able to recognize and blame her partner for hurting her or for violating her trust. Blaming others, however, no matter how well justified, can too easily become a self-indulgent way of avoiding responsibility for our own actions. If assigning blame to others, whether the offending ex-partner, a boss, or the outside world in general, becomes our only mechanism for understanding our lives, then we are establishing ourselves as helpless victims with no control over the course of our own lives. While it may be painful to acknowledge our part in breakups, we must do so in order to recognize that we have some control over what happens to us. Taking responsibility for our role in our relationships also allows us to become aware of repetitive patterns, which eventually enables us to change them.

Perhaps the most important single lesson we can learn from an honest appraisal of a breakup is that people treat us the way we allow them to treat us. By acknowledging the ways in which *we* interact with others, we can become aware of the unconscious messages we are sending and decide whether we want to change them. Then we can begin to answer the question, "Why do I always attract women who are _____ (takers, mothers, drinkers, abusers, etc.)?"

Each of us will react to the ending of a relationship in a manner consistent with our style of reaction to any life stress. Some of us will turn to religion, some will convert our feelings into data to be studied, some will become immersed in work or political activities, some will withdraw from social contact, and some will seek out friends and even strangers so as not to be alone. Many of us flee from one relationship to another and do not deal with any of the breakups until after the fifth, tenth, or fiftieth repetition of the same pattern with different partners. Whatever our particular style happens to be, growth and learning will not begin until we allow ourselves to feel the feelings and accept the responsibility for our contribution to a breakup.

The growth process that can occur after a breakup takes time and cannot be done alone. The extent to which we are in or out of the closet will determine how many of the details of our relationships we can share and with whom. There are still couples, hopefully many fewer than in the past, who have never shared their lesbianism with anyone and who, when they break up or when one partner dies, cannot talk with anyone about their pain. Fortunately, since the advent of the gay rights movement we have been much more able to share our lives with friends and, for some, family. Thus, we will turn for support to the network we have already built for ourselves.

Connecting, or reconnecting, with friends can be complicated by the separation. Some friends may side with one member of the couple and against the other. Others may try to remain friends with both women and either maintain a strict neutrality or want to carry messages between the estranged partners. Some coupled friends may be threatened by our newly single status and become distant or hostile.

It is important to honor our perceptions, that is, "stay in touch with our gut" and not deal with "friends" who do not have our best interests at heart. It is equally important to honor our own needs and not to try to cover hurt with a facade of invulnerability or fear with bravado. It is essential that we learn to ask for what we need and to determine who can fulfill those needs.

Lesbians often have a hard time watching a friend going through pain and anxiety. They may try to reassure us before we've truly grieved, or become so angry at the former partner on our behalf that they do not allow us our ambivalence and sorrow. We may be pressured to meet someone new and "forget her" without finishing the process of mourning. Some friends may feel we are "dwelling on" our pain, others may want to hear all the gory details repeated endlessly. We may feel pressure to break up before we are ready or to stay longer than we should. To deal with such a mixed bag of motivations we must be able to keep our own needs in mind at all times and to separate our needs from those of the lesbian community.

At times seeking professional help may be advisable. Most obviously, if there are no friends with whom we can honestly share all our feelings we may need a "paid friend." A therapist may be extremely useful in helping us to become aware of repetition patterns in our relationships and their endings, or when we appear to be "stuck" in one of the stages of mourning; when we cannot get beyond anger and blaming or cannot stop being depressed.

Finding the right therapist is one of the most important tasks we will face at this point. It is essential that the therapist be either lesbian or lesbian-affirmative, that is, that she recognize lesbian love as being of equal value with heterosexual love and that she be knowledgeable about the struggle for gay rights and the lesbian community. Once such a therapist has been found, we need to ascertain that she will validate our feelings without taking sides. Then we will be free to explore our responsibilities within a relationship and to learn to more honestly take control of our own lives.

Recognizing our needs, honoring our feelings, and accepting our responsibility will enable us to gradually heal from a breakup. By allowing ourselves the time to hurt, be angry, and grieve, we, with the help of friends and/or a therapist, can turn the pain of a breakup into a growth experience.

Further Reading

The following two books have excellent discussions of lesbian relationships, although neither is specifically directed toward the issues around breaking up.

Berzon, Betty. *Permanent Partners*. New York: E. P. Dutton, 1988.
Clunis, D. Merilee, and G. Dorsey Green. *Lesbian Couples*. Seattle, Wash.: Seal Press, 1988.

Love and Adoption

Sharane Merial-Judith

When I was growing up, I loved my girlfriend. I would have done anything for her. I picked flowers for her and wrote poetry to her graces. I had read romantic tales of Best Friends in centuries past, when women held hands and kissed each other without a second thought. I knew I was the best Best Friend any girl could possibly want. I thought I was just a hopeless romantic.

When I was twenty-three, my school chum and I parted ways. I was crushed. After twelve years, I felt all at loose ends. I began looking for a new Best Friend. I tried on friends like one tries on shoes. None fit quite right. Until I met Celeste.

I had scoffed at love at first sight, and still have my reservations, but there was a "first time I laid eyes on her" magic to the way I encountered Celeste. I must have seen her before; for six months my husband and I had been attending the church at which Celeste and I met. But one electric moment—"*Who* is *she?*"—stands out in my memory as the beginning of an era of my life.

I was married and had two children. I was looking for a friend with whom to have coffee, go shopping, and talk on the phone. My heart beat hard in Celeste's presence, I so wanted a Best Friend.

Even so, it took over a year to get to know Celeste. I admired her and genuinely cared about her, but she was so surrounded by friends that I just couldn't get close enough to talk to her. Finally, in 1982, we began to be friends. I was in heaven.

In June 1983, after enduring my effusive overtures of friendship in spite of herself, Celeste fell in love with me. Again, it was a case of sudden revelation. And I didn't even know what had happened. Celeste did. She'd been 'round the block before with women and knew she was in love. She did not clue me in to the import of the occasion.

The joy we shared as friends lit the skies for us. Colors were brighter, the air was sweeter, the babies were cuter. Work was light, time together was long, and our husbands tried to be patient.

Physical affection came as easily as water flows downhill. We touched—just touched. We wrestled and held hands and kissed. The contact moved my being like no other had done. "At last," I thought, "I've found another romantic Best Friend."

But this Best Friend was connected to more. She was an open door, an ancient hidden door that led to a whole world of beauty and knowledge. We had the capacity to share so much more than I'd ever known before. I had dreamed romantic dreams of confidences and intimacy. "At last!" I thought. As we poured ourselves into each other, as our souls reached out to and for each other, our bodies met. I wanted to give all of myself to Celeste and to experience all of her, her past hurts and joys, her hopes and dreams, fears and doubts for the future, her pain and delight alike in the present. Though a picture is worth a thousand words, a loving embrace expresses what words alone can never convey.

At last, too, I had discovered a loving that didn't violate my body. I had been married to a good man for six years; I had not missed lesbian love because I had not known it existed. Once I knew, there was no going back to the unnatural sexual relationship of my marriage with my husband.

I tried to go back, but God let both Celeste and me out of bondage through the painful process of splitting with our church. We were told God hated our loving.

I couldn't buy it. In my relationship with God, I couldn't find the disgust the church leaders said was there. God is love. Love is good. My prayers for deliverance were met with compassion and tenderness on God's part, not judgment and discipline. I came to understand that I was to respect Celeste's marriage, but our gender was not prohibitive to our love relationship.

Some time after we were both divorced, an incident occurred that put the pieces together for us. Celeste, my two children, and I were living in Boise, far away from our past. We were working hard to live up to our standards of behavior as Christian Best Friends.

Then Celeste's ex-husband invited her to visit him in Colorado, and I got jealous. Not "roommate" jealous, not "Best Friend" envious, I got JEALOUS! I realized that what was threatened was my Primary Relationship. I didn't love her like a mere Best Friend. I would never leave her and marry a man, like Best Friends did in the romantic books. Living next door would never be enough. I realized I was a lesbian.

Celeste was afraid of losing her church family. She tried to flee. Desperately, I gave her space. I knew her to be a person who must seek the truth and live in it. The children and I went back to Spokane, leaving Celeste in God's loving hands.

A lesbian couple we met through the Metropolitan Community church in Boise became our God-Mothers, together with a traveling minister of MCC. Ten days after the ceremony, Celeste called me in Spokane. She loved me. She wanted me in her life, intimately, always. No matter what it was labeled—gay, lesbian or Martian—that was the truth. I came home.

Once we figured out we had a valid relationship, we put it in the context of our Christian faith and got married. First, we married one another before God alone. Then we had a Holy Union celebration, replete with flowers and music, preacher and vows, cake and (nonalcoholic) bubbly, and friends. The children carried flowers and exchanged vows with Celeste, too. It was June 25, 1986. Exactly two years had passed since Celeste had fallen in love with me. I was twenty-nine, Celeste was twenty-five. Daisy was six and Marianne was just three. Celeste and I both expected that our marriage would last forever.

A year after our Holy Union, the idea arose that Celeste would adopt the girls from their father, step-parent style. I camped in the Gonzaga University Law Library until I knew such an adoption was not forbidden by law. Still, to our knowledge, no two same-sex, openly gay parents had adopted a child in Washington State. (Later we learned that there had been two cases before us, but they did not share their triumph with the public.)

It was not a snap decision. Each person had to adjust to the idea. I had to understand that the confirmation of Celeste's parenthood did not diminish my motherhood. As the girls say, they have two moms, but only one Mama.

Celeste had to understand that, though the adoption would legalize her parenthood, she had already committed herself to raising two children. Likewise, the children's father, who lived in another city, had to realize that his relationship with the girls was no more dependent on state papers than was Celeste's and my marriage. We assured him, and the children, that he would always be "Daddy." (Later, he told us he would not have let a man adopt the kids; he agreed to it because Celeste was a woman, not competing for "Dad.")

Raising the money for the lawyer and the court-required home study was the hardest part. Since the adoption would benefit the gay community, we thought it would not be inappropriate to solicit funds. Some people were eager to help, some thought we were crazy.

The legal process actually went very smoothly. With a lot of casting about and good karma, we

The Glatzmaiermace family: (back) Celeste and Sharane (parents); Daisy and Marianne, 1988.

Gerry Wood

found the ideal professionals. Our lawyer was an elderly woman, well-respected in the legal community. The woman who did our home study and was appointed guardian *ad litem* (to represent the children in court) could not have been better qualified. And she was with P-FLAG (Parents and Friends of Lesbians and Gays). The adoption rested primarily on her report.

By law, an adoption is a closed (private) hearing held in the county superior court. Ours was brief and informal. It was one of the most exciting moments of my life! And it was June 23, 1988, only two days from our anniversary.

Another lesbian couple completed their adoption in 1989. They had started before we did, but because of complications their victory came later.

Upon adoption, the adoptee is issued a new birth certificate from the state of birth naming the new legal parents. With the added impetus of a second adoption, Washington State was persuaded to adjust the birth certificate form to accommodate same-sex parents. I am "mother," Celeste is "parent." (Vital Statistics is where we discovered the two previous adoptions.)

Our story was published in the local city newspaper in April 1989. Reaction to it ran two-to-one in our favor. With the other adoptive family, we appeared on TV. I am preparing to devote my life to the pursuit of justice and equality; I want to be a lobbyist.

Here we are, in 1990. Celeste enjoys a good job in the field in which she trained. I'm enjoying college. The children are in an alternative education program within the public school system. We live in quiet truth with our friends and community. The success of the adoption inspires us to be open and proud. We want it to empower gay men and lesbians everywhere to live fully in what freedom we already have, and to hope and plan and persist until we have attained true equality.

(Editor's Note: Sharane and Celeste's adoption was followed by five more adoptions in Spokane alone over the next two years. Families sent the two women pictures of themselves and their children, and a new family invited Sharane and Celeste to their adoption celebration.

Then in 1992, Sharane and Celeste painfully parted ways. Although their expectations of a permanent marriage were not met, they are still very much a part of each others' lives. Today Daisy, age fourteen, lives with Celeste and her new partner, and Marianne, age eleven, lives with Sharane. There is lots of visitation back and forth. The parents get along well and work together to keep the children going in a positive, empowered direction.

First Love at Sweet Briar

Sally Miller Gearhart

Daylight was fading, but from my desk by the window on the second floor of Randolph Hall I could see Lakey begin stripping the moment she stepped off the Lynchburg bus. By the time she crossed the quadrangle and reached the arcade she had removed her hat, replaced the hatpin, crammed her short gloves into her linen purse, and begun unbuttoning both her suit jacket and her blouse, all this while juggling an overburdened shopping bag. When she flung open the door to our room moments later, her feet were free of the linen pumps and the waistband to her skirt was opened, the placket unzipped.

"I finally found Ayn Rand," she announced, dumping shopping bag, hat, purse, jacket, and shoes on the bed, "but nobody had *Lost in the Stars*." Her monologue, fired by the intensity of her disrobing, ebbed and flowed with the range of resistance offered by her clothes. Her words sped with the sliding of her skirt to the floor and the shrugging off of the silk blouse. They stopped altogether as she stepped out of the skirt and lifted her slip so she could begin unhooking her nylons. Her discourse gathered speed again and volume as she stood first on one foot and then on the other, recklessly peeling the stockings down her legs, over her ankles and feet.

"I wound up getting Silly Putty for Bobby and a book for Arlene," she burbled, undoing her garter belt and whipping it out of her panties. She slowed perceptibly to separate the straps of her slip from the straps of her bra, pulling them down over her arms and sending the slip to the floor alongside her skirt. While she hoisted on her faded rolled-leg jeans, her voice rose again, and when she slid her bare feet into the rundown white penny loafers, it dropped to a quiet ending.

"Lookie-here!" She tossed me a small bag. "Cotton beauties. Five pair for a dollar." She swung into the ample folds of her brother's cast-off shirt, leaving the tail to hang out mid-thigh over her jeans, and buttoned herself at last into a satisfied silence.

Thus the proper vision of The Sweet Briar Girl, Girl of Grace and Beauty, Girl of Good Taste and Good Judgment, stood revested in the comfort of clothes that the college tolerated only in the privacy of dorm rooms or under the protection of long coats. She was beautiful and I loved her.

I think now that we were both making a memory of that moment, Lakey standing there transfixed as our eyes met, me sitting there clutching a bag of white panties. We did that a lot—when we were alone, of course—looking at each other in breath-stilled silences, as if we understood in some part of ourselves that we could not hold the joy forever, and that somewhere, ages and ages hence, we would need to believe again in the incredible fullness of all we were finding in each other.

Lakey broke the spell by diving into the shopping bag. "Close your eyes and hold out your hands." I did so. I could hear her move toward me. Then I felt her lean over me as the window shade spooled down and the desk light snapped off. "Not even a silhouette," I thought. We'd learned to be so careful.

I waited. Then instead of some schmoo-doll or a box of tampons (latest craze for the "modern woman") I felt her strong hands over mine, raising me to my feet. Softly, like a mother taking up a sleeping babe, she drew me into her arms. I rested my head on top of her shoulder. She buried her face in my neck. We stood holding each other, laughing softly and sighing in the sheer contentment of our full-body contact, rocking back and forth, there in the twilight of a Virginia springtime.

Her gift was Franck's D-Minor Symphony. We put the record on the phonograph, turned the volume low, and set a straight chair casually against our lockless door—not to block it but to provide at least some flimsy obstacle, a second or two of warning in case some friend burst in upon us. Then we stretched out on our wide bed, made up of our two single beds thrust together—"to save space," we always explained to those who had the nerve to ask. We doused the lamp, prayed that no one would call us to the phone, and settled in each other's arms to listen and to love.

It was long past dinner, long past vespers, long past the ten o'clock closing down of the campus, when we emerged into the moonlight of the second floor arcade. Two of our classmates sat on the single bench, smoking and huddled together against the night's chill. We knew they were holding hands beneath the light blanket that covered their knees.

Mariana Romo-Carmona and June Chan.

And we knew that in their room two beds had been thrust together to make the one large one. We knew, they knew we knew, we knew that they knew we knew, and we all worked tirelessly to avoid any acknowledgment of that knowing.

We returned their soft greeting and then leaned into our own separate conversation, speaking in low voices and lighting up Lakey's Chesterfield, my Pall Mall. We had homework to discuss, books to compare, papers to write.

It was 1951. We were suspended in an isolated pocket of leisure and privilege, far from the war stirring in Korea or the witch-hunts in Congress. We were third-year students at one of the nation's finest women's colleges, daily discovering vast new intellectual horizons, sounding the depths of astounding inner oceans of creativity. And in the spring of the previous year we had unexpectedly found in each other a passion that had almost blown our lives asunder.

My small rural "class C" high school had given me very little of the background necessary for admission to Sweet Briar, and it was not at all clear that I could handle even the first year of that college's courses. The admissions director allowed me to enter as a kind experiment in "underprepared students."

It took me six weeks to discover that I was out of my intellectual league, out of my social class, and probably out of my mind. I found no friends, I could not communicate with my roommate, I understood little of what textbooks and professors said, I was appalled by the weekend dating frenzy, and I hated the food which, moreover, had to be eaten at least twice a week in hose and heels. I've never been so lonely, homesick, and miserable, before or since.

Two things saved me. First, the theater reached out and claimed me for her own. I was hooked by her timeless magic, and as I settled into roles for the winter and spring productions my days became tolerable. Second, Lakey entered my life. On a warm afternoon on the steps of the dormitory, I was rolling up my jeans so they would not show beneath my raincoat. I bumped Lakey, also rolling up her jeans. We both grinned, apologized, and then began a conversation about one of her books that went on over coffee and hot plate chili until three the following morning.

Throughout that spring and our following sophomore year, we spent time together almost every day. Since we dated only occasionally, we spent long weekends traipsing over the campus's hills and forests, exploring trails, bridle paths, and the beer joint two miles down the main highway. I was an unapologetic Galatea to Lakey's Pygmalion: an eager, unschooled, undisciplined, diamond-in-the-rough whose thirst for information and ideas must have astonished even her wise heart. With Lakey I discovered how to take a thesis apart and put it back together, how to listen to messages from myself that would take me into worlds I had never dreamed existed. I see her even now in my memory, flinging open door after intellectual door, leading me by the hand to treasure troves of history, music, and poetry.

When I discovered to my delight that Lakey could handle a football, we'd often fill the West Dell with whoops of joy as we perfected our passing. We sang a lot, laughed a lot, read to each other, indulged in highly competitive contests of mumblety-peg and bridge, sparred verbally with our professors and classmates, pounded out papers on our Underwoods, and studied all night in the smoking room. We exhausted our bodies on the hockey field and our minds in the library. I discovered how to organize my ideas and my time. Toward the end of my second year, it dawned on me that I was passing my courses with more than Ds. And to boot, I had Lakey and a growing circle of friends. I remember skipping to class one bleak rainy morning, alive with the new sweet knowledge that I was happy.

That year, 1949–50, Lakey and I each lived in a "single." Since each of us tired of having to trudge back to our own room after an evening of studying or talking, we planned to be roommates the following year. But for now, the night before we'd both be leaving for the summer, I stood in my room looking at the piled-up bed filled with clothes, packing boxes, suitcases, books. Lakey had followed me down the hall. "Leave it," she said, looking over my shoulder and picking up my pillow. "Come sleep with me. We can squeeze together." I nodded, exhausted and relieved.

We did our nightly libations, miraculously found our pajamas in the chaos of our packing, opened the window in hopes of some breeze, and fell into Lakey's narrow bed, dousing the light and covering ourselves only with a sheet. She faced the wall and I lay inches from her so as not to crowd her or make the warm night more uncomfortable. I fitted my body into a shadow of her contours, not touching her and keeping my arms between us. She reached over to pat my buttocks goodnight. I patted her hand patting my buttocks and then we each withdrew into our own bubble.

Sleep was not an option for me. I lay there suddenly aware of Lakey's body, its warmth and softness. I'd not allowed myself to think about how I would miss her over the summer. Our separation at Christmas and spring breaks hadn't been a problem. But now she was heading for Europe with her family and I'd be with my summer stock company. We'd have an ocean between us.

Tears welled up inside me and began clogging my throat and nose. I tried to swallow softly and breathe evenly. A huge loneliness washed over me, a desolation. My life, which just yesterday had teemed with joy and excitement, was all at once dry, tasteless, meaningless. I didn't want her in Europe. I wanted her with me.

I risked a long, controlled inhalation, trying to hold back a sob. Then, as if bestowing a gift, my nose cleared and I was drenched with the Johnson & Johnson shampoo smell of Lakey's hair. Some crazy notion entered my mind that at least I could carry that with me over the summer, the smell of her hair. I just wouldn't exhale, that's all. Just hold it in, right there inside me.

I was wondering if you could die holding your breath that way when a slow realization overtook me. Lakey wasn't breathing either. In fact, Lakey's body was tense, rigid, very much like my own. I held my breath for another eternity, not daring to disturb the silence. Then to my horror I felt my arm revving up to put itself around Lakey's waist. I mentally reprimanded it, only to feel it resist me. I focused on it, incredulous that it was disobeying me. But it was no longer my arm. It was somebody else's arm. Or just some dissociated independent member, hell-bent on reaching out now toward Lakey.

That rebellious arm never got to make its move. Instead, at that moment Lakey's taut body began slowly turning, turning up and around to face me and, without hesitation or haste, moving artlessly into my own waiting arms. The cry that was bursting from her and the release of my own explosive breath must surely have roused the whole sleeping quadrangle.

I understood with a clarity I've rarely experienced since then that my entire life until that moment—every decision, every activity, every pain, every happiness—had been a preparation for that embrace. I was a wanderer at last come home, a skeleton at last enfleshed, an orchard at last in flower. I couldn't hold her tight enough. We lay shaking and crying and laughing in a delirium of release and joy, stunned and exuberant at what was happening, understanding it not at all, and incredulous that we had waited so long to express a love that now seemed so obvious and so total. Most of all we agonized with the knowledge that in a few hours just having found each other we would have to part.

There was no doubt that the energy between us was sexual, so far outdistancing any that we had ever felt with men that it was in another category altogether: intense, exhilarating, profound, and full of a million delicious possibilities. Yet we didn't touch each other genitally in any way. Instead we spent the night alternating between glory and peace, on the one hand kissing and stroking and tumbling in breathless excitement as we marvelled at the new world that so suddenly had burst upon us, and on the other simply holding and rocking each other in a soft, sweet, new-found comfort. Nothing in Lakey's experience or in mine had prepared us for the power and meaning of that encounter.

As advertised, the summer was one long ache of missing each other and counting the days until we could return to Sweet Briar in the fall. Elizabeth and Essex, Anthony and Cleopatra, Romeo and Juliet—

their passion was a mere ember when set beside our reunion. We arrived early, closed the door to our room, and barricaded it with heavy bureaus—we would explain that we were trying out various furniture arrangements. For two days we emerged from that room only to eat and use the bathroom. And even then, even with the breathless catching up and the all-over-again amazement at the depth and intensity of our feelings, even then we never touched each other sexually. In fact, we embarked on what I now am convinced was the longest sexual foreplay in the history of lesbianism. Maybe some unconscious sophistication was telling us, "Go slow and the pleasure will be exponentially enhanced," or, since we were both brand new to it all, maybe we were just plain scared.

Whatever the case, the time we spent together in bed that semester was an agony (and an ecstasy) of restraint. The first week back we held and kissed, fully clothed. By the end of the second week we were unabashedly touching each other's breasts— still with clothes. When we at last slipped our hands under the pajama tops (week three) we found such delight that we lingered there a month. By Thanksgiving we were titillating each other with the verbal and even tactile prospect of "touching below the waist" (first with and only then without clothes, of course), and by the middle of December, motivated no doubt by the prospect of a separation at Christmas, we had actually made genital contact and discovered that our bodies not only knew what to do but did it superbly.

We slept very little, grew very thin, and moved around campus in a glow of secret satisfaction. How we managed to contain our joy at the astounding transformations that were overtaking us I will never know. Not only were we carrying on a clandestine relationship but our days were exploding with activity. It was as if life's floodgates had been flung wide. We studied less (but better), wrote masterpiece academic papers, engineered complicated and brilliant term projects. Our grades soared, our circle of friends expanded, we joined in more campus activities, and spent untold hours in song and laughter. Once in a while just for looks we went out on a date with a Virginia Man, always returning to each other's arms with a sign of relief and renewed gratitude for the miracle we were experiencing.

We pretty much pooh-poohed the notion of hus-

Amy and Pam.

© Shoshana Rothaizer

bands and decided early on to run away to Samarkand together after graduation. Only occasionally did a shadow suggest to us that even our remarkable love could someday break under the demands of the world. And we were wise enough to know that the joy we had together would be punished if it were discovered. Thus the cost of our happiness was measured in units of fear and dishonesty, in the little pretenses to friends and the bigger lies to our families.

Sweet Briar's homophobia was hardly unique in the fifties, for nothing existed in the world at large to support same-sex love as a natural expression of affection. Yet Sweet Briar, that women's college of such excellent quality, gave a special spin to society's heterosexual assumption. It called up the best and most blessed of our hearts and minds and yet it made very clear the fact that we would use that fine education not for ourselves but for our husbands and children—and maybe for a charity or two. As one of my Marxist friends put it later, we were expected to bear and raise the sons and daughters of the ruling class.

Lakey and I stayed together for a year after graduation, getting our master's degrees at an Ohio university. When I entered the doctoral program at the University of Illinois, we carried on a long-distance relationship for two years.

Then Lakey got married.

My consummate act of masochism was to be a bridesmaid in her wedding, a classy three-day affair where I felt like the proverbial bull in the china shop—wrong clothes, wrong hairdo, wrong smile, wrong stance, wrong gait, wrong words, and certainly the wrong desires. I knew even as I arrived for the final dress fittings that my motives were not pure. I had wisely decided not to kidnap the bride but I wanted to see if Lakey really would go through with such a charade. And, frankly, I wanted to rattle her parents who must have thought she was rid of me by then.

In a tearful scene in her bedroom the day before the wedding, Lakey admitted she was marrying to appease her family, and that she had been shocked when I agreed to be a bridesmaid. "You are the air I breathe," she said, "and I know that by doing this I am cutting off life itself. But the price of loving you is just too high. I can't hide that way anymore." I was wild. I ranted and raved, oblivious to her attempts to keep me from being heard in other parts of the house. When none of my pleas reached her I stormed out of her room and down the stairs, heading I knew not where, but somewhere out of that pain.

At the foot of the staircase, waiting for me, stood a woman I had mentally labeled "Mrs. Amazon." She was the mother of one of the other bridesmaids and herself a good friend of the family. She was a big woman whose impeccable dress and demeanor nevertheless hinted that she had acquired them only at great psychological cost, perhaps after years of conscious and determined practice. She held out a set of keys.

"Take my car. It's the blue Caddy. And don't come back until you can handle all this." She put the keys in my hand and very gently touched my shoulder. Then she vanished, back to the solarium where she was seeing to the proper display of the wedding gifts.

I drove the turnpike at breakneck speeds that afternoon, shouting and sobbing my rage and indignation. It was almost dusk when I came back to the house, subdued, resolute, and still unapprehended by the highway patrol. I made it through the stiff rehearsal without incident and endured the huge dinner seated uncomfortably beside "my" groomsman. I was garbed like a matron in an ill-fitting dress that I had borrowed from Mrs. Amazon. I danced with the requisite number of men of the party including the groom, made light chatter, and returned the polite enmity of Lakey's parents, until I could escape to the bedroom I shared with the other bridesmaids. No further words passed between Lakey and me, nor did I respond to her efforts to catch my eye.

I had decided to leave her to heaven, to get through the formalities, and then shake the dust of her world forever from my feet. I wavered only once the following day when in the ceremony before a packed church the minister said, "If any man knows any reason why these two should not be united in holy matrimony, let him speak now or forever hold his peace." In the pause before the minister proceeded, I knew there were at least four people—Lakey, her parents, and Mrs. Amazon—whose hearts were in their throats. I could have made history that moment. It's to my credit, I suppose, that I declined the opportunity, rationalizing even with no feminist theory to back me up that the word "man" had excluded me from the ranks of potential objectors.

At the reception I dutifully hugged Lakey and wished her well. I made a feeble pretense at reaching for her bouquet when she threw it, musing even as I did so that marriage was already deteriorating the force and accuracy of her passing arm. She and her man took off in a shower of rice and I went inside to call a taxi. In the bridesmaids' room I peeled out of the frilly dress and sighed into my rolled-up jeans and penny loafers. I covered myself with my trenchcoat so as not to offend my hosts, and cast a parting look at the reception celebration still in progress in the back of the house. As I waited with my suitcase at the curb I picked up a few grains of rice and put them in my pocket. The cab pulled up at exactly the same place the happy couple had departed from.

"Greyhound Bus Depot," I said, putting my bag in the seat beside me.

I never saw Lakey again. In 1980 her husband's letter found me. He said that she had died, the result of a fall and a concussion. He said that she would have wanted me to know.

In the fifties and sixties, my dark closet years, I never felt sick, never felt sinful, and never took my criminal status to be more than the unfortunate result of society's ignorance and bigotry. I credit Lakey with a lot of that self-love, for though our paths had separated, she had clearly been the agent of my greatest self-discovery, and in her hands I had learned my true identity. Thank you, Lakey.

A Love Story

Katherine D. Seelman

During the last years of her life, Chris Cowap was supported by a network of sustaining love. As Chris's lifetime partner, I offer this narrative to you, as a gift from Chris and from her support group to inspire others who wish to live and die as she did, held in the arms of a caring community.

The story of the last years of her life—and indeed the last years of our relationship—is a love story. We met in 1976 and eventually moved into a New York City Upper West Side apartment with two Siamese cats, one German shepherd, and one mixed-breed dog. Even so, in the two years preceding the diagnosis of cancer, Chris and I had drifted apart. The cancer diagnosis, in 1980, set off an extraordinary healing process.

I remember the day she was diagnosed. The doctor was no stranger: She had been my physician for many years and knew about our relationship. Together, Chris and I received the doctor's report. Chris had oat cell lung cancer. The doctor and Chris would have to wage a formidable battle to cure it. I instantly joined the battle. That is the point I identify as the beginning of the healing in our relationship.

Of course, there were tears. But Chris responded with grace and grit. She wanted to live, and she had guts in her fight for life and in her response to pain. Chris's chemotherapy and radiation treatments began almost immediately. At the same time, Nancy Johnson, a healer in our community, began working with Chris. They organized an international network of friends who joined together during a fifteen-minute period to concentrate white light on Chris. Shortly afterward, the lung cancer disappeared. However, chemotherapy continued for seventeen months and with it, the punishing side effects of hair loss, weight loss, and constant bouts of nausea. During this period, what would become a formidable community of support began to form. This group included former lovers and very close friends, our animals, co-workers, residents of our co-op, members of our families, the medical team, and the legal team.

Ironically, the years between the diagnosis of Chris's first cancer in 1980 and her second cancer in 1987 were the best of my life. We traveled, we laughed, and we loved. We did not focus on the illness even with the knowledge that a formidable enemy was in our midst. As a precautionary legal measure, we had our wills, medical power of attorney, and "no extraordinary treatment" documents prepared. These papers were invaluable later when Chris was diagnosed with her second cancer.

She was very sick during that last year of her life. I, and the other members of her support group, were thankful not to have to explain to ambulance attendants and hospital intensive care personnel why we, not her family, were making life and death decisions.

Chris and I were fairly open about our relationship and active in the lesbian community. I think this contributed significantly to the care she was given. Our lawyer, a lesbian, worked with Chris at her hospital bed, and her healer, also a lesbian, visited the hospital and our home consistently through those eight years. Our physician, who was aware of our relationship, was certainly accepting and supportive. Additional support came from Chris's colleagues at the National Council of Churches, and from our co-op apartment building, where Chris had served as president of the board. Some of our family members, while not totally accepting of our relationship, had long grown accustomed to it and recognized and supported the special bond between us.

People from each of these groups joined the caring circle which was vital to us, especially during the last year of Chris's life.

Before going on to describe the emotional turmoil of that last year, I must mention some practical issues, especially health insurance. Ironically, Chris had been instrumental in the effort at her workplace to secure comprehensive medical coverage. Her eventual success became the basis for our financial security and our ability to transform our vision of caregiving into reality.

It allowed Chris to have her need for quality of life and empowerment met by loved ones, rather than be cared for by strangers or leave this life from an impersonal hospital bed instead of our home. Her health insurance policy was sufficiently comprehensive so that options such as home hospice care were covered. The policy covered most of the costs of her illness, perhaps over $500,000, and we did not have to "spend down" or turn to drastic financial measures to finance medical care.

During Chris's second cancer, when quality of life, especially pain management, became a major issue, her medical team at Sloan Kettering Memorial Hospital in New York used the health insurance policy to provide holistic health care, with emphasis on warm human relationships, nutrition, and counseling.

In 1986, when Chris began to experience severe pain again, test after test returned without explanation of why. Finally, almost a year later, in February 1987, a bone biopsy showed that she had squamous cell cancer. With that diagnosis and the subsequent medical judgment that neither surgery nor radiation were treatment options, Chris began to hedge her bets.

On the one hand, she purchased an expensive camera so that retirement from her job might be followed by a reentry into the job market as a professional photographer. On the other hand, she began saying good-bye and mending a few slightly worn fences. She visited old friends and lovers, went on a splendid camping trip in the Sierras, and sent a second letter to her many friends saying that she again had cancer and that she again intended to beat it. However, by September 1987 she was quite ill.

We had just returned from the Hebrides where, in Iona, Chris and I, both secular people, had written her name in a book in the old church so that the healers of Iona might help us. Throughout the trip, I had been attending to an abscess on her back where the cancer had pushed out from the bone, erupting into an ugly festering cavern. Our doctor had retired during this time, and her new doctor was an oncologist. Although they bonded closely, he simply did not know what to make of this angry sore other than to prevent infection.

The months from September 1987 to February 1988 were a miracle of coordination and support from people who had full-time jobs and full-time lives. Chris was in and out of the hospital many times. It was a period when I wished to be more skilled in helping to mobilize and coordinate a very diverse group of people, all of whom loved her. These people included members of her family of origin and her family of choice. I was commuting on weekends from my job—first from Washington, then Boston. The dogs were at home with Chris.

Our vision of modern community became manifest—a vision of the interweaving of lives into ever-changing circles. People came to our home to care for her when she no longer was able to be alone. When one could not come, another filled in the gap. With one short exception, she was never cared for by strangers. Her sister left her family in Boston to be with Chris; her friends Ginny, Peggy, Mary Lou, and Marilyn, and her niece Heather canceled their engagements. The circle extended even further to include her friends Joanna from Rochester, New York, and Ann, from Oklahoma. My sister spent her entire academic break with Chris, though she herself was ill.

Chris, in the meantime, was fighting for her life, taking chemo when the chances were close to nil. She continued to inspire us with her courage and sense of humor. But the traumas began piling up. One evening a caregiver arrived to find Chris in a confused state. Her speech was slurred. An ambulance carried them to Sloan Kettering intensive care. The hospital called me in Boston for permission to do certain procedures. Afterward, I rushed to New York to find all that I loved hooked up to a hundred tubes and blinking lights.

The next week, after Chris was transferred to another hospital, there were signs that she was not receiving adequate care. Her bandages had not been changed and her food tray had been left at the end of the bed where she could not reach it. After numerous civilized requests for care, I walked into the nurses' station and staged a tantrum. I was summarily kicked out. I called the hospital administrator and explained the situation. Later, Chris's sister-in-law went to their board of trustees.

During this period, the head nurse at the pain unit at Sloan Kettering visited me to gently share what the next few months would be like. I explained that I wanted Chris at home as much as possible. She said that someone would have to be at home with her, and that medical paraphernalia such as a respirator and hospital bed, and twenty-four-hour pharmaceutical delivery would have to be provided.

People took weeks off to live in the apartment. Our den overlooking the Hudson River was converted to a second bedroom, and Chris moved, able to view the activity on the Hudson and to welcome guests in her favorite room. At this point our little group of caregivers were given a bit of rest. Twenty-four-hour-a-day nursing care began in late December, and with it another gift, our nurses. One nurse in particular, Nel, bonded with Chris and with all of us. Like Chris, Nel was generous and had a sophisticated understanding of life and, of no small importance, had spent a period of her life in England. Nel shared her poetry and her life with us. She and all the other nurses came from the finest tradition of the healing sciences, which tends to the spirit as well as the body.

On one of the last weekends of Chris's life, Marilyn, Chris, and I had a wonderful Chinese dinner. Chris, who so loved the opera, watched *Der Rosenkavelier* at home, surrounded by her dogs, her people, her nurse, and all the medical paraphernalia. Folks in the co-op who owned an extra apartment offered it to Chris's family and other guests. Many people came to say good-bye.

Chris died at home, holding the hands of her friend Joanna and her nurse, Nel, and with our dogs nearby. She said, "Please let me go now." Then she left. Later, waves of police officers arrived to investigate the unusual occurrence of a person dying at home with loved ones. Before releasing the body, they had to be assured that homicide was not the cause of death. The apartment would have been sealed off had Marilyn not reminded me that even though Chris was dead, this was still my home. Assured that Chris had died of natural causes, the police released the body. The funeral home people put Chris's body into a bag and carried it away.

In her life, Chris had drawn together so many gifted people. At her death, they designed a marvelous celebration of her life. Our friend Ann compiled a booklet of testimonials by Chris's family and many friends. Her photo was on the cover with one of her favorite social activist quotes: "Never retract, never retreat, never apologize. Get the thing done and let them howl." The morning of the celebration of her life began with a service at the Episcopal Cathedral of St. John the Divine. In the afternoon a feminist service was held in a chapel—our dogs attended as well as the dog sitters, and the neighbors, friends, and family. The service provided a graceful blend of faith and feminism. Carol Etzler and Bren Chambers performed original songs; we all sang "Blue Birds Over . . ." Ginny read Chris's coming out remarks to the National Council of Churches presented at the time the council was considering the application of the Metropolitan Community church for membership. Chris's nurse Nel spoke eloquently of Chris's "legacy of love." Peggy, Chris's closest friend, reminded us—with humor—of her faults. But Peggy concluded by observing, "Chris did no less than learn to live ethically with dis-ease." After the celebration, R-SAC, an organization of church women that Chris had helped to found, provided a Shalom dinner. If Chris had been looking over our shoulders, she would have said we had done well.

Sharing Your Lesbian Identity with Your Children:

A Case for Openness

Betty Berzon, Ph.D.

The handsome, bright, professioLand in the Ozarksnal woman sat in my office shaking her head, saying over and over again, "I just can't. I just can't see any reason that makes sense for telling the children that I'm a lesbian."

Her children were in early adolescence. We talked about the possibilities of their learning about lesbianism from sources less considerate of their sensibilities than she was, their ill-informed peers, pornographic literature, comedians' jokes, a variety of homophobic adults. Yes, she could see that it would be better if they heard positive, accurate personalized information from her. But, still, she wasn't sure . . . How might it affect their own sexual identity? How would they feel about her? Whom might they tell? What kind of an experience would that be for them? Important questions. We dealt with them one by one. Still, she didn't know . . .

She had recently ended her marriage and become involved with a lover who was about to move into the house with her and her children. I asked if something happened to her, an accident or a sudden illness, would the children call her lover. "No, they wouldn't. They'd call their father, some of my relatives. They'd have no reason to call ———." I asked how she felt about that. "I don't like it. That would be terrible."

I pointed out that she could hardly blame her children for not calling her lover, whom they'd been led to believe was just a friend. She pondered that a long time. We probed more deeply into her fears about disclosing her gayness to her children, and her own ambivalent feelings about her identity began to emerge. Telling her children was like looking into a mirror for her, in which there would be reflected the final undeniable image of herself as a lesbian. It was that image she was not ready to face. As she began to sort out the various elements of her dilemma she was soon able to work them through sufficiently to reach a decision to disclose herself to her daughter and son. She did, effectively, and that created a new potential for depth in her relationship with her children.

This woman's concern about the sexual identity of her children being affected by her own sexual orientation is shared by many lesbian mothers. This concern is reinforced by popular notions of appropriate gender behavior and what affects it, same-sex role models being considered critical to the development of properly feminine/masculine identity. Sex researchers agree, however, that the essentials of gender identity are established very early in childhood and by a process that is complex and so far unyielding to explanation. There is even speculation now that prenatal programming plays an important part in the determination of gender identity.

A more productive concern, I believe, would be for the young person's orientation to sexuality itself. That is strongly affected by parental attitudes and behavior.

If there is secrecy and tension around the topic of sexuality in the home, the children may grow up believing that sex is something to be frightened of and to keep hidden. Homosexuality is not contagious. Fear and shame are. Children are especially sensitive to the feelings underlying communication by adults.

Of course the children's age should make a difference in how they are approached. Preschool children are likely to be concerned with changes in mother's behavior or in the household routine primarily as it might directly affect the attention they are getting.

After a child starts school there is likely to be a new interest in comparing the family situation with those of classmates. The interest, however, is not likely to be in the sexual arrangement but in how similar or different the situation is to that of other children. This might be a good time to talk to the children about the many differences there are among people and how they live. The important thing is not to be defensive or apologetic about a lifestyle that is different, but to present it matter-of-factly as a reasonable expression of the needs and preferences of given persons.

The time for particular alertness to the effect of disclosure should be during early adolescence when a youngster is forming her/his own personal orientation to sexuality and to life. Emphasis here should be on establishing a clear separation of the youngster's sexual development from that of the mother. A matter-of-fact attitude toward all variants of sexual preference is recommended. One should not be judged more desirable than another. What should be valued is the individual's right to follow the path that is most personally suitable.

The mother should keep in mind that adolescence is a time when peer approval is of great importance to youngsters. This might mean being prepared to deal with some initial rejection of anything that might threaten disapproval from peers, in this instance, her own sexual orientation and life style.

Another concern lesbian mothers often have is whether or not they should give some special attention to their male children. I do think there is a basis for making sure it is communicated that Mother's noninvolvement with a male partner does not reflect a rejection of her son as a male person. The origin of the concern is probably of more importance. It is usually other adults in the mother's environment who fear the son won't have sufficient male influence in his life to counterbalance the influence of the women around him.

I believe the lesbian mother should not make this her special burden to bear. People have the same concerns about sons of divorced, nongay mothers. But homosexuality bothers people more than divorce, so the expressions of concern might be louder and stronger and taken more seriously by the woman who is a lesbian in addition to being divorced. The action I recommend is to put this matter in proper perspective. Strong expressions of concern here usually reflect an overinvestment in sex-role stereotypes and an underinformed protest against homosexuality. They should be dealt with as such.

Needless to say, the woman who has been openly gay around her children since they were infants will have worked through most of these dilemmas. It is to the woman who is just evolving into a gay lifestyle or just connecting with the possibilities for more openness with her children that these remarks are mainly addressed.

I am a strong advocate of *planning* for disclosure events about important subject matter. All too often the decision for disclosure of a mother's lesbianism is made by default.

There is a sudden and unexpected confrontation by the children, or by a relative or friend or ex-spouse in the children's presence. The disclosure is made, without preparation, without the important working through to a conviction that this is the right thing to do and the right time to do it. There has not been an opportunity to choose the time, the place, the conditions, or the supporting cast. Mother is in the high-speed lane of the freeway during rush hour, the car is full of her children and their friends. Her son asks if sleeping every night with the same woman the way she does makes you a lesbian, and is she one?

On the other hand, a decision to disclose, followed by careful preparation with the help of a friend or professional person, thinking through what, how, when, and where can make the difference between a constuctive experience and a calamity.

I am most hopeful for positive outcome of disclosure when I hear reasons for the decision like the following:

I value my emotional life enough to want to share it with my children. I want them to learn to trust and value their emotional life and I want to help them do that, by example. I want there to be as much honesty and truth as possible in my relationship with my children. I want them to understand that a relationship with a woman lover is a special, close, and serious one for me. I want them to understand why I choose to spend so much time with such a person, especially when it might mean excluding them in the process.

For most people making the decision is just the beginning. How, when, where, what, and "what can I expect" come next. Let's take these questions one at a time.

Shall I Wait Until I'm Asked or Shall I Take the Initiative?

I believe it is important, whenever possible, to take the initiative in order to be able to exercise some control over the conditions of disclosure. It is best if the children can be prepared ahead of time. "I have something I want to talk to you about that is important to you and to me." And, incidentally, a long face foreshadowing doom is not the best introduction to a discussion of your gay identity. Assuming that you will have worked through much of your own ambivalence about your sexuality, your attitude should be upbeat and positive. Hopefully, you are sharing something with your children that you prize and they should be given the best possible chance to do that also.

A related matter is that of avoiding the act of disclosure by forcing the children to tell *you* what you are trying to tell *them.* The nervous mother, unable to get the words out, might ask, "You know what I'm trying to tell you, don't you?" Unfair. The disclosure of your lesbianism is an act of faith in your children. Give them and yourself the best chance for a successful outcome by participating as *fully* as possible in this personal affirmation of your relationship with them.

Shall I Tell Them One at a Time or All Together?

If there is a large difference in your children's ages, you might want to tell them in different ways. In addition, telling your children separately might give them a special feeling that will enhance the experience you have with them. If you tell them separately, you should not let too long a period elapse between the times you tell each of them. If your children are close in age and it is a usual event in your family to talk things over as a group, it is probably best to tell them together. However you choose to do this, your own judgment is your best guide. You know how each of your children reacts to you and to the others. You are the final expert on this matter.

Is There Anything Important About When and Where They Should Be Told?

Yes, I think it's important to arrange for a place that is quiet and private and a time in which you won't be interrupted or distracted. It is particularly important to have plenty of time planned in for explanations and expression of feelings.

What Do I Say?

In working with lesbian mothers struggling with the coming-out process I have been surprised, at times, to see extremely bright, articulate, sometimes eloquent women at such a total loss for the words to use with their children. There are, of course, no universally applicable guidelines. And there are no magic words. However, planning gives you time to think through some possibilities and decide what feels best for you. I present below a device to help with such preparation. It is a questionnaire including some of the basic questions children ask, allowing for age differences and levels of sophistication, of course. Following each question I have listed some possibilities for answers, again to be adjusted for age and sophistication level. I suggest you try to answer each question for yourself, modifying or adding to what I have offered. It has been my experience that women who are particularly troubled by what to say are able to approach disclosure much more easily once they have gone through this kind of exercise.

Question 1. What does being gay mean? What is a lesbian? Being gay means being attracted to a person who is the same sex you are. It means being attracted in such a way that you might fall in love with the person. You might want to be very close to the person, as people are when they're married, or when they love each other and live together as though they were married. A lesbian is a woman who feels this way about another woman.

Many children of school age will have heard the words "gay" and "lesbian" already. They may think they know what they mean and tell you there's no need to explain them. It is, however, very important that you do supply your own explanation. The odds are that what your children have heard already is derogatory, riciduling, or frightening. They have probably learned that lesbians and gay men are people to be wary of, to feel sorry for, or to laugh about. How fortunate that you have an opportunity to correct those impressions.

Question 2. What make a person gay? No one knows exactly what makes a person choose one kind of a partner to love and be close to rather than another kind. It's probably for a lot of different reasons. I wonder if your question might really be, "Will I be gay?"

©JEB (Joan E. Biren)

Evelyn Torton Beck and Nina Rachel Beck.

Question 3. Will I be gay? You won't be gay just because I am. You have a different makeup and different life experiences from mine. You are a separate person. You'll be whatever you are going to be because of your own makeup and your own experiences. What I hope is that you'll be a person who has interesting and loving relationships with people, and who is open to whatever life has to offer. Whatever you are I hope you'll be a happy and self-fulfilled person.

Question 4. How can you tell if someone's gay? You can't just by looking at them. All kinds of people are gay. Gay people are women and men, young and old, skinny and fat, poor and rich, mothers and fathers, daughters and sons, athletes and bankers and teachers and doctors and lawyers and farmers and

businesspeople. So many different kinds of people are gay they couldn't possibly all look alike.

Question 5. Are there a lot of gay people? Yes, millions in the United States and millions more all over the world.

Question 6. Where are all the gay people? A lot of lesbians and gay men *hide* the fact that they are gay. They hide it because there are still many people who don't really understand what being gay means. Because they don't understand it they think there's something bad about it and they make life difficult for those people who are gay. But that's changing now. In the last few years gay people have started talking about themselves a lot more, so there is beginning to be better understanding. As more and more people understand what being gay is about there is not so much need for gay people to hide.

Question 7. What do you think I should tell my friends about this? First of all, remember that a lot of people don't understand what it means to be gay and they put it down. Some of your friends may find it interesting. Some may want to make jokes or say critical things about it. That's the way it is with their parents and that's probably the way it will be with them. If there are friends you'd really like to tell, who you think would understand, try it out. If you have a bad experience, let's talk about it. We can learn together about the best ways of talking to people about it.

There are additional questions that children frequently ask that are best answered, I believe, from an entirely personal point of view. For instance, *"How can you tell if you're gay?"* You would do well to inquire into the personal meaning of the question for your child because the question is more likely, *"How will I know if I'm gay?"* I think that is best answered by the mother discussing her own experience, perhaps then leading into the abstractions offered above in answer to the question "Will I be gay?"

Other questions often asked are:

"Why did you marry and have children if you are a lesbian?"

"Do you hate men?" ("Do you hate me?" your son might be asking.)

"Is this why you got divorced?"

If you are introducing a lover into your household for the first time, you should be careful about not causing it to appear as if this development (your gayness) is purely a function of your relationship with *this* woman. In this event, your children might come to regard her as the "villain" who turned their mother into a lesbian. It is sometimes easy for women to disclose their lesbianism to their children strictly in terms of their relationship with a particular lover. It might be very important to their acceptance of this person to understand that your gayness is a function of *your* needs and preferences, not something that's being done to you by an outsider.

What Can I Expect?

The answer to this question, of course, depends entirely on the kind of relationship you have with your children to begin with, how old and how sophisticated the children are, and how comfortable you are with your lesbian identity. If all of those systems are "go," your disclosure will probably be relatively trouble-free and a good experience. If, however, there are reasons for a child to react negatively, that reaction might come in the form of name-calling, expression of angry feelings, or total silence. You should be prepared for any of the three.

Name-calling and Angry Feelings. "You're a *queer!*"

"Dyke!"

"You *lesbian*." (angrily)

Terrible to hear? Stirs up your own anger? Want to retaliate? Or is your inclination to deal with the *words*? "I don't want to hear that kind of language from you!!"

What is the real issue to be dealt with? This young person has been given a hot potato to handle and is saying, "Ouch!!" You wouldn't object to your child's emotional response if it was a *physical* discomfort being experienced. It would seem a "natural" reaction. So is this one. If you can hold onto that idea and not cut off the reaction through retaliatory anger of refocusing on the words being used, you will be opening an important channel for expression of feelings around this touchy subject. It is infinitely better for your daughter or son to express these feelings with you than to turn them inward or act them out destructively. You can help further by recognizing that these words are a way of giving voice to the strong feelings that have been touched off. And you can say so. "This is making you pretty angry right now."

Total Silence. If your child meets your disclosure in total silence, it is best to recognize, again, that s(he) is having a difficult time with this information. You might try to gently draw feelings out, or if that seems unworkable to invite further discussion as soon as possible. At least make it clear that you are available any time and want very much to hear whatever feelings or questions there are.

Others in the Family

What about others in the family? Your ex-husband. Does he know you are gay? If not, that is something you should take care of, if at all possible, before you make your disclosure to the children. If your ex-husband knows you are gay but you're not sure how he is feeling about it, talk with him again, if possible. Try to assure yourself, insofar as you can, that there will be support and understanding from this source if your children choose to use it. If that is an impossible dream, as is sometimes the case, unfortunately, at least you will know where you stand and what you are getting into, and you can then prepare the children.

What about other family members, grandparents, the children's aunts and uncles, and so on? If your children are close to any of these family members, you should, again if possible, be sure that (1) they know you are gay, (2) they understand what that means to you, and (3) they are supportive of you. It is particularly helpful if these relatives can accept and reinforce the positive attitudes your children develop toward your gayness.

Finally . . .

Finally, there are two things to remember.

First, keep the channels of communication open with your children. Continue to talk about the topic of your lesbian identity as often as seems appropriate. Hopefully you will be able to do this comfortably and it will become a natural subject for conversation in your household.

Second, trust yourself. You are the world's leading expert on *your* mother-child relationship. The real clues for the decision on disclosure to your children—how, when, where, what to say—are in your intimate knowledge of that relationship. Use it to put the suggestions of this writer, and everyone else offering help in this important personal matter, in perspective.

Turning the Beat Around:

Lesbian Parenting 1986

Audre Lorde

(Editor's Note: The following article, excerpted from A Burst of Light, *by Audre Lorde, was written in 1986, six years before the author's death in 1992. In her discussion of lesbian parenting, Lorde alludes or refers to certain events and conditions current at that time: the appointment of William Rehnquist as chief justice of the U.S. Supreme Court, a South Africa whose apartheid policy had not yet begun to change, and an Idaho lynching that the local media had failed to acknowledge as racially motivated.)*

These days it seems like everywhere I turn somebody is either having a baby or talking about having a baby, and on one level that feels quite benign because I love babies. At the same time, I can't help asking myself what it means in terms of where we are as a country, as well as where we are as people of Color within a white racist system. And when infants begin to appear with noticeable regularity within the Gay and Lesbian community, I find this occurrence even more worthy of close and unsentimental scrutiny.

We are Lesbians and Gays of Color surviving in a country that defines human—when it concerns itself with the question at all—as straight and white. We are Gays and Lesbians of Color at a time in that country's history when its domestic and international policies, as well as its posture toward those developing nations with which we share heritage, are so reactionary that self-preservation demands we involve ourselves actively in those policies and postures. And we must have some input and effect upon those policies if we are ever to take a responsible place within the international community of peoples of Color, a human community which includes two-thirds of the world's population. It is a time when the increase in conservatism upon every front affecting our lives as people of Color is oppressively obvious, from the recent appointment of a Supreme Court chief justice [William Rehnquist] in flagrant disregard of his history of racial intolerance, to the largely unprotested rise in racial stereotypes and demeaning images saturating our popular media—radio, television, videos, movies, music.

We are Gays and Lesbians of Color at a time when the advent of a new and uncontrolled disease has carved wrenching inroads into the ranks of our comrades, our lovers, our friends. And the connection between these two facts—the rise in social and political conservatism and the appearance of what has become known in the general public's mind as the *gay* disease, AIDS—has not been sufficiently scrutinized. But we certainly see their unholy wedding in the increase of sanctioned and self-righteous acts of heterosexlsm and homophobia, from queer-bashing in our streets to the legal invasion of our bedrooms. Should we miss these connections between racism and homophobia, we are also asked to believe that this monstrously convenient disease—and I use *convenient* here in the sense of *convenient for extermination*—originated spontaneously and mysteriously in Africa. Yet, for all the public hysteria surrounding AIDS, almost nothing is heard of the growing incidence of CAIDS—along the Mexican border, in the Near East, and in the other areas of industrial imperialism. Chemically Acquired Immune Deficiency Syndrome is an industrial disease caused by prolonged exposure to trichloroethylene. TCE is a chemical in wholesale use in the electronic sweatshops of the world, where workers are primarily people of Color, in Malaysia, Sri Lanka, the Philippines, and Mexico.

It is a time when we, Lesbians and Gays of Color, cannot ignore our position as citizens of a country that stands on the wrong side of every liberation struggle on this globe; a country that publicly condones and connives with the most vicious and systematic program for genocide since Nazi Germany—apartheid South Africa.

How do we raise children to deal with these realities? For if we do not, we only disarm them, send them out into the jaws of the dragon unprepared. If we raise our children in the absence of an accurate picture of the world as we know it, then we blunt their most effective weapons for survival and growth, as well as their motivation for social change.

We are Gays and Lesbians of Color in a time when race-war is being fought in a small Idaho town, Coeur D'Alene. It is a time when the lynching of two Black people in California within twenty miles of each other is called nonracial and coincidental by the local media. One of the two victims was a Black Gay man, Timothy Lee; the other was a Black woman reporter investigating his death, Jacqueline Peters.

It is a time when local and national funds for day care and other programs that offer help to poor and working-class families are being cut, a time when even the definition of family is growing more and more restrictive.

But we are having babies! And I say, thank the goddess. As members of ethnic and racial communities historically under siege, every Gay and Lesbian of Color knows deep down inside that the question of children is not merely an academic one, nor do our children represent a theoretical hold upon some vague immortality. Our parents are examples of survival as a living pursuit, and no matter how different from them we may now find ourselves, we have built their example into our definitions of self—which is why we can be here, naming ourselves. We know that all our work upon this planet is not going to be done in our lifetimes, and maybe not even in our children's lifetimes. But if we do what we came to do, our children will carry it on through their own living. And if we can keep this earth spinning and remain upon it long enough, the future belongs to us and our children because we are fashioning it with a vision rooted in human possibility and growth, a vision that does not shrivel before adversity.

There are those who say the urge to have children is a reaction to encroaching despair, a last desperate outcry before the leap into the void. I disagree. I believe that raising children is one way of participating in the future, in social change. On the other hand, it would be dangerous as well as sentimental to think that childrearing alone is enough to bring about a livable future in the absence of any definition of that future. For unless we develop some cohesive vision of that world in which we hope these children will participate, and some sense of our own responsibilities in the shaping of that world, we will only raise new performers in the master's sorry drama.

So what does this all have to do with Lesbian parenting? Well, when I talk about mothering, I do so with an urgency born of my consciousness as a Lesbian and a Black African Caribbean american woman staked out in white racist sexist homophobic america.

I gave birth to two children. I have a daughter and a son. The memory of their childhood years, storms and all, remains a joy to me. Those years were the most chaotic as well as the most creative of my life. Raising two children together with my lover, Frances, balancing the intricacies of relationship within that four-person interracial family, taught me invaluable measurements for my self, my capacities, my real agendas. It gave me tangible and sometimes painful lessons about difference, about power, and about purpose.

We were a Black and a white Lesbian in our forties, raising two Black children. Making do was not going to be a safe way to live our lives, nor was pretense, nor euphemism. *Lesbian* is a name for women who love each other. *Black* means of African ancestry. Our lives would never be simple. We had to learn and to teach what works while we lived, always, with a cautionary awareness of the social forces aligned against us—at the same time there was laundry to be done, dental appointments to be kept, and no you can't watch cartoons because we think they rot your feelings and we pay the electricity.

I knew, for example, that the rage I felt and kept carefully under lock and key would one day be matched by a similar rage in my children: the rage of Black survival within the daily trivializations of white racism. I had to discover ways to own and use that rage if I was to teach them how to own and use theirs, so that we did not wind up torturing ourselves by turning our rage against each other. It was not restraint I had to learn, but ways to use my rage to fuel actions, actions that could alter the very circumstances of oppression feeding my rage.

Screaming at my daughter's childish banter instead of standing up to a racist bus driver was misplacing my anger, making her its innocent victim. Getting a migraine headache instead of injecting my Black woman's voice into the smug whiteness of a women's studies meeting was swallowing that anger, turning it against myself. Neither one of these actions offered solutions I wanted to give my children for dealing with relationships or racism. Learning to recognize and label my angers, and to put them where they belonged in some effec-tive way, became crucial—not only for my own survival, but also for my children's. So that when I was justifiably angry with one of them—and no one short of sainthood can live around growing children and not get angry at one time or another—I could express the anger appropriate to the situation and not have that anger magnified and distorted by all my other unexpressed and unused furies. I was not always successful in achieving that distinction, but trying kept me conscious of the difference.

If I could not learn to handle my anger, how could I expect the children to learn to handle theirs in some constructive way—not deny it or hide it or self-destruct upon it? As a Black Lesbian mother I came to realize I could not afford the energy drains of denial and still be open to my own growth. And if we do not grow with our children, they cannot learn.

Audre Lorde.

Dagmar Schultze

That was a long and sometimes arduous journey toward self-possession. And that journey was sweetened by an increasing ability to stretch far beyond what I had previously thought possible—in understanding, in seeing common events in a new perspective, in trusting my own perceptions. It was an exciting journey, sweetened also by the sounds of their laughter in the street and the endearing beauty of the bodies of children sleeping. My daughter and my son made issues of survival daily questions, the answers to which had to be scrutinized as well as practiced. And what our children learned about using their own power and difference within our family, I hope they will someday use to save the world. I can hope for no less. I know that I am constantly learning from them. Still.

Like getting used to looking up instead of down. How looking up all the time gives you a slight ache in the back of the neck. Jonathan, at seventeen, asking, "Hey Ma, how come you never hit us until we were bigger'n you?" At that moment realizing I guess I never hit my kids when they were little for the same reason my father never hit me: because we were afraid that our rage at the world in which we lived might leak out to contaminate and destroy someone we loved. But my father never learned to express his anger beyond imaginary conversations behind closed doors. Instead, he stoppered it, denying me his image, and he died of inchoate rage at fifty-one. My mother, on the other hand, would beat me until she wept from weariness. But it was not me, the overly rambunctious child, who sold her rotting food and spat upon her and her children in the street.

Frances and I wanted the children to know who we were and who they were, and that we were proud of them and of ourselves, and we hoped they would be proud of themselves and of us, too. But I remember Beth's fifteen-year-old angry coolness: "You think just because you're lesbians you're so different from the rest of them, but you're not, you're just like all the other parents . . ." Then she launched into a fairly accurate record of our disciplines, our demands, our errors.

What I remember most of all now is that we were not just like all the other parents. Our family was not just like all the other families. That did not keep us from being a family any more than our being Lesbians kept Frances and me from being parents. But we did not have to be just like all the rest in order to be valid. We were an interracial Lesbian family with radical parents in the most conservative borough of New York City. Exploring the meaning of those differences kept us all stretching and learning, and we used that exploration to get us from Friday to Thursday, from toothache through homework to who was going to babysit when we both worked late and did Frances go to PTA meetings.

There are certain basic requirements of any child—food, clothing, shelter, love. So what makes our children different? We do. Gays and Lesbians of Color are different because we are embattled by reason of our sexuality and our Color, and if there is any lesson we must teach our children, it is that difference is a creative force for change, that survival and struggle for the future is not a theoretical issue. It is the very texture of our lives, just as revolution is the texture of the lives of the children who stuff their pockets with stones in Soweto and quickstep all the way to Johannesburg to fall in the streets from tear gas and rubber bullets in front of Anglo-American Corporation. Those children did not choose to die little heroes. They did not ask their mothers and fathers for permission to run in the streets and die. They do it because somewhere their parents gave them an example of what can be paid for survival, and these children carry on the same work by redefining their roles in an inhuman environment.

The children of Lesbians of Color did not choose their Color nor their mamas. But these are the facts of their lives, and the power as well as the peril of these realities must not be hidden from them as they seek self-definition.

And, yes, sometimes our daughter and son did pay a price for our insisting upon the articulation of our differences—political, racial, sexual. That is difficult for me to say, because it hurts to raise your children knowing they may be sacrificed to your vision, your beliefs. But as children of Color, Lesbian parents or no, our children are programmed to be sacrifices to the vision of white racist profit-oriented sexist homophobic america, and that we cannot allow. So if we must raise our children to be warriors rather than cannon fodder, at least let us be very clear in what war we are fighting and what inevitable shape victory will wear. Then our children will choose their own battles.

Lesbians and Gays of Color and the children of Lesbians and Gays of Color are in the forefront of every struggle for human dignity in this country today, and that is not by accident. At the same time, we must remember when they are children that they are children, and need love, protection, and direction. From the beginning, Frances and I tried to teach the children that they each had a right to define herself and himself and to feel his own and her own feelings. They also had to take responsibility for the actions which arose out of those feelings. In order to do this teaching, we had to make sure that Beth and Jonathan had access to information from which to form those definitions—true information, no matter how uncomfortable it might be for us. We also had to provide them with sufficient space within which to feel anger, fear, rebellion, joy.

We were very lucky to have the love and support of other Lesbians, most of whom did not have children of their own, but who loved us and our son and daughter. That support was particularly important at those times when some apparently insurmountable breach left us feeling isolated and alone as Lesbian parents. Another source of support and connection came from other Black women who were raising children alone. Even so, there were times when it seemed to Frances and me that we would not survive neighborhood disapproval, a double case of chicken pox, or escalating teenage rebellion. It is really scary when your children take what they have learned about self-assertion and nonviolent power and decide to test it in confrontations with you. But that is a necessary part of learning themselves, and the primary question is, have they learned to use it well?

Our daughter and son are in their twenties now. They are both warriors, and the battlefields shift: The war is the same. It stretches from the brothels of Southeast Asia to the blood-ridden alleys of Capetown to the incinerated Lesbian in Berlin to Michael Stewart's purloined eyes and grandmother Eleanor Bumpurs shot dead in the projects of New York. It stretches from the classroom where our daughter teaches Black and Latino third graders to chant, "I am somebody beautiful," to the college campus where our son replaced the Stars and Stripes with the flag of South Africa to protest his school's refusal to divest. They are in the process of choosing their own weapons, and no doubt some of those weapons will feel completely alien to me. Yet I trust them, deeply, because they were raised to be their own woman, their own man, in struggle, and in the service of all of our futures.

Lesbian Parenting 1994

Terry Boggis, Center Kids,

New York City

Let me begin with an apology. There are many ways for lesbians to create and define their families. Our way is only one of them. My apologies to the many lesbians who have created their families through adoption, or those who have struggled with infertility, or those who have merged families, or all the other variations and vagaries of family life and constructs. My family's story is not representative of any other's. I hope it will still prove helpful.

My lover and I began discussing the possibility of having a child almost as soon as we began sleeping together. I remember her saying, at the very beginning, "It's a good thing we aren't really involved, because I'd be pressuring you to have a child." As she continued to speak compellingly about the sanctity of conceiving and bearing children, I felt my own urge to have a baby, tabled for several years in a relationship with a woman who had no interest, reawaken. I was thirty-two years old—it was time at least to think about it.

My lover and I spent several years together as an unencumbered couple, and during that time, we returned to the issue of kids with increasing frequency and seriousness, conducting research as lesbians (and gay men) do before they have children together. We spoke to the few lesbian parents we knew, we read what little there was to read, we attended workshops and forums that were offered with increasing frequency in New York. These are some of the things we learned.

Our options were limited, but we had them. Never had I felt so empowered as a woman as I did entering into the Baby Project. Finances permitting, I could go to any one of dozens of sperm stores, comparative shop for donors, and buy what I needed to construct, in the privacy of my home or gynecologist's office, our baby. I witnessed the gay men I knew who wanted children struggling to come to terms with the virtual impossibility of having them biologically. A few were able to arrive at coparenting agreements with lesbians (on the lesbians' terms), a very few were able to afford surrogacy arrangements, and the rest faced the adoption minefields, wrestling with the issues of being out and proud as gay people entitled to and capable of raising children versus homophobic statutes, agencies, nations, and international adoption policies.

We explored foster care as an avenue, with eventual adoption as the goal. As much as I wanted a child, I was not enamored of the idea of pregnancy, of the possible difficulty in achieving it, and the havoc it can wreak on a girl's figure. But we quickly concluded that the State-with-a-capital-"S" could threaten our custody rights far less if our child was ours biologically.

My lover had borne two daughters during her marriage, so I was to be the one to attempt pregnancy. Our first choice for a sperm donor was my lover's cousin, her closest male relative. We wanted, however remotely, to have Rosemary biologically connected to our child. Her cousin, a gay man, considered, consented, and then withdrew from the process during the early stages, discovering during the physical examination, to everyone's great grief, that he was HIV-positive.

Our next approach was to seek interested candidates for sperm donation through classified ads. We felt it would be best for the child to have an identifiable father figure, although we would want to raise the baby without interference from the donor.

I'm amazed at our naïveté when I remember how we anticipated dozens of phone calls in response to our advertisement. I guess I thought many men would be flattered into donation, or that they would be motivated by a longing for their own immortality, or because they felt like doing a lesbian a big favor. We placed ads in two papers, and received exactly two responses, both male couples wanting more than a sperm drop, but to be, to whatever degree we'd agree, involved parents. We "dated" both couples several times, all parties presenting our most appealing faces as we tried to uncover each others' true motives and intentions.

In the end, we turned the men down, believing it would be difficult enough to agree between ourselves on decisions for this baby, and seeing how much more difficult it would be for four people to have input. We wanted to be free to move to another state, determine our child's religious upbringing, and never have to consider sharing the baby with assorted grandparents and other extended

Mothers and children, Washington, D. C., 1987.

families on holidays. We decided on an anonymous donor, for simplicity's sake.

At this point, in the mid-1980s, there were fewer sperm banks than there are currently. Still, there were many to choose from, but only one that offered an option we found overwhelmingly appealing. The Sperm Bank of Northern California in Oakland, which at the time was affiliated with the feminist Oakland Women's Health Collective, was not only an outspoken advocate for lesbian insemination (anything but the case at many other sperm banks, where lesbian candidates for insemination had to remain closeted, and those who didn't were sometimes given "psychological" examinations and deemed unfit), but also was the only bank where some donors agree to be identified to the children after they reach their maturity.

There is little available data on the emotional development of children of sperm donors, but my lover and I suspected that they must go through a process similar to children who have been adopted,

that is, that they become at the very least curious about their biological parents, regardless of the degree of their love for and identification with the families who raise them. So we chose a donor from the Northern California bank, who agreed to allow his identity to be disclosed.

The sperm was shipped to us overnight express on dry ice after my gynecologist announced to the bank that I was about to ovulate. It looked like nothing—two tiny glass vials with a very tiny amount of white fluid, packed in a picnic cooler. It was impossible to fathom how a human being could come from this, but in the second month of trying, following inseminations both in the doctor's office and at home, one miraculously began to grow.

My pregnancy passed uneventfully. We built a house in the country during that time, completing it in April 1988. I chose to have chorionic villus sampling, a prenatal test conducted between the ninth and eleventh weeks of pregnancy, rather than wait until the sixteenth week for amniocentesis. Not only was I eager to make sure the baby was healthy before I allowed myself to love it, but I was also eager to know the gender.

Seventy to 80 percent of donor insemination babies are boys. I had never been a tomboy kind of dyke. I had loved my dolls and dress-up clothes, loved my Tinkerbell toilet water, my jacks, the Bobbsey Twins, and toe shoes. I had always thought boys and their activities were rough, mean, dangerous, loud, violent, boring, ridiculous, and a little scary. I had to have time to adjust to the idea of a son.

In July, Ned was born. The minute he was placed on my chest, my concerns fell away. He was my baby, and I was as overjoyed with him as I could be. Since the first day of his life, I have been, and continue to be, utterly enchanted by the sweetness of little boys, and as we've contemplated a second child, I've been certain I'd be equally enthusiastic with a second son as I would be with a daughter. (I find the "girls" aisle in toy stores, dripping in pink and lavender and turquoise Barbies with platinum hair to their ankles, pastel toy kitchens and ironing boards and heart-shaped makeup kits, every bit as obnoxious as Mighty Max and Ninja Turtles.)

Once Ned was out of the gate and we entered into the parenting process, we realized we'd spent years focusing on how we would get a baby, and not much time on how we, as a lesbian couple, would raise him. We immediately discovered that lesbian parenting has its own specific pitfalls.

Most painful and pointed was the division of labor, responsibility, and identity as two mothers. I had been through the insemination, the pregnancy, the labor, and was now into the breast-feeding. It was a very exclusive biological process. Our fantasy had been that we would quickly wean Ned from full-time breast to part-time breast-and-bottle, in order for Rosemary to participate in the key, rewarding responsibility of infant parenting: feeding. We didn't anticipate a baby who refused the bottle. It caused friction between us, with Rosemary resenting the secondary "daddy" role of work (there was no "paternity" leave), errands, and holding a crying baby who could only be comforted by sucking on the other parent's breasts. I was sore, exhausted, locked in an abusive relationship with postpartum hormones, stuck in a non-air-conditioned New York City apartment in one of the hottest Julys ever recorded.

I wouldn't recommend this. I would recommend help from maternal-type, doting relatives, or in their absence, the hired kind, or friends. More than anything, I'd beseech candidates for comothering to talk these issues to death before the baby comes: Try to anticipate the built-in imbalance in roles, realize you are not the same as a man and a woman going through this, that the nonbiological parent will have strong needs for parallel involvement, and consider how that need can be accommodated.

We have friends who have divided the responsibilities by having the biological parent work outside the home, while the nonbiological mom stayed home to bond with the baby. Others have restored balance to their households by each mom bearing a child biologically, and each experiencing the "coparent" role. Some households have been untroubled by the power and proximity dynamic, simply because one mother admits to being less nurturing and less interested in the day-to-day baby care work, and is happier to work outside the home and play a supportive, secondary role. But I've seen couple after couple hurt, at least on occasion, by the unequal affection of the child, who clearly prefers one mother over the other.

There is plenty of room in a child's heart for two loving parents, but lesbians are both women and both expect to be "mommy." There are no models for achieving this. It requires planning, patience, and compassion, and dedication to pioneering new definitions of family and the roles within it.

Although we'd come out in our all-hetero labor coaching class and to our obstetrician (a straight man who, after delivering thousands of babies, continues to be moved at the appearance of each and at the fortitude of the women who bear them—in short, a miracle of manhood), as we moved past early infancy, we encountered full force the challenge of coming out every day in straight institutions—pediatricians' offices, insurance companies, nurseries and preschools, babysitting services, and as the child becomes more verbal, public rest rooms, drugstores, supermarkets, playgrounds, bus stops—any place public, where you can count on your kid to introduce his two mommies with great enthusiasm and at top volume.

It is impossible to remain closeted as a parent and not communicate to your child that you are ashamed to be gay. Out lesbian parents present a model of courage, honesty, pride, and forthrightness for their children that offspring from conventional households do not get to experience. Every time we come out in the presence of our children, we convey to them the fundamental, matter-of-fact right of our families to live openly and partake fully in American society. To do otherwise is to communicate furtiveness, dissonance, secrecy, shame—a terrible lesson, a terrible disservice to our kids, raising them to be as homophobic as our enemies. In fact (and I'm not unmindful we live in Greenwich Village, not Wichita or Idaho Falls or Chattanooga), response to our family difference has been met sometimes with bewilderment, but more often with a surprised kind of interest.

Now that we are participants in the public school system, other challenges have arisen. Beginning in 1992 in New York City, a recommended multicultural curriculum for first graders entitled "Children of the Rainbow" included children of lesbian and gay parents, and mention of lesbian and gay people. The books about lesbian and gay families on the recommended reading list were not required reading, but were simply provided to assist teachers in preparing lessons that teach the value of diversity in society, and respect and appreciation for difference.

The public outcry against the inclusion of these books revealed the homophobia that is every bit as ugly and menacing here in liberal New York as anywhere else. Lesbian and gay parents attending local school board meetings to come out and speak out in support of an accurate, evenhanded depiction of our families in school curricula were taunted, threatened, and refused the opportunity to speak. Neighborhoods and neighbors were divided, the issue dominated school board elections and prompted an unheard-of turnout for a school board vote, and eventually proved the undoing of a highly principled and progressive New York City school chancellor. In the end, the curriculum was rewritten in such an adulterated way as to, once again, render lesbian and gay people virtually invisible. The battle was lost.

Parenting mainstreams lesbians and gay men to a far higher and more threatening degree than any other move we make. With children in hand, we march into sacred and forbidden zones such as classrooms, playgrounds, pediatricians' offices, the PTA, Brownie troop meetings, Gymboree, and all of suburbia. We're no longer confining ourselves to Christopher Street and the Castro, to Fire Island,

Provincetown, Northampton, Gurneville, and Key West. We've embraced this last, most holy institution of the heterosexual world—we're raising kids. There we are, breast-feeding on the park bench alongside our straight sisters. We're obsessing about sleep schedules and birthday party themes. We're wearing maternity smocks as easily as we've sported black leather. We're rupturing stereotypes—if we're active in the PTA, we're not sitting in bars, we're not having nonstop sex, we're not living on the fringe. We're harder to identify, more difficult to distance from. Being parents makes it much tougher for us to be outplaced as "other." And this, we've learned, makes people mad.

The Children of the Rainbow struggle made warriors of its survivors. The war continues to be fought, classroom by classroom, by parents coming out every day, assuming responsibilities as class parents and in parents' associations, initiating discussions on the issue of nontraditional families in our own schools with local faculty and parents and administrators, offering ourselves as models and sources of information, buying books on lesbian and gay families out of our own pockets to stock our children's school library and classroom shelves, breaking down resistance by revealing ourselves as lesbian and gay parents who are also excellent parents, committed parents, loving and involved parents. Our progress is not spectacular, not a news story, but incremental, slow and steady. The effort is essential, as any lesbian mother who has felt her heart stop when she realizes that her sexual orientation puts her child at risk would agree.

Sources of support as we pioneer new family structures are few and far between. It pains me to say that the larger lesbian community is not necessarily likely to be there for lesbian moms.

Our lesbian friends who do not have kids have been warm and supportive. But as soon as the arrival our baby removed any semblance of spontaneity in our lives, made us unavailable for Sunday brunch, tea dance, cocktail and dinner parties, and all the other things we used to do with friends, our lives veered apart. Lesbian institutions, regardless of the professed and certainly politically correct support of lesbians' right to choose, have little in their structure to support family life—events and organizations for gay people still presume childlessness in their planning and design.

In the end, lesbian mothers have each other. Four months after our son was born, my lover and I found a support group of lesbian and gay parents, founded the same month he was born. Center Kids, the family project of New York's Lesbian and Gay Community Services Center, has given us many new and valued friends, friends who make us feel shored up and strong, or at the very least, confused and exhausted in the best company. The extraordinary worth of a supportive and organized community of gay parents can't be overstated, both for the parents and for their children.

I once moderated a panel discussion for Center Kids that consisted of four college-age kids who had been raised in gay households. They agreed across the board that the greatest difficulty growing up had been the feeling that they were alone in their difference, the only ones. It's a sense lesbian moms can recollect from their own early lives, and it's a pain that's never completely left behind. If any of us can relieve our children of that kind of sorrow, we do. And finding or creating a support group of lesbian moms not only provides a source of profound strength and connection for the adults, but a community from the cradle for our children. They will always know children who come from homes like theirs, who are different in the same way, whose existence validates each other's lives.

Ned is five now (or "five and five-sixths!" as he would say). He is the dearest, most difficult, most challenging and enriching part of our lives. By joining us, he has forced us to be better people than we were before, to confront our own limitations, to be more out, more outspoken, more ferocious advocates for our rights to create a family, and for our son's right to be clear and proud and happy about his origins and his home.

Ned's presence has initiated a sea change in our relationship, and not all of it positive. We have lost some of the intimacy that defines a couples-only household. We can't stay in bed reading the paper, drinking coffee, making love, and catching up until early Sunday afternoon like the old days. We can't read aloud to each other and fall asleep on the beach like we used to. We can't stay up as late, or prepare nothing but popcorn for dinner, or take a walk at 11 P.M. But we can integrate our lives as lesbians and as mothers more than women ever could before. We can use our bodies to make babies our way, our wisdom to create and define our families our way, and contribute as lesbians to the generation of new life. And that's been, for me, the deepest joy.

Resources

For those residing in the New York metropolitan area, Center Kids may be reached by calling 212-620-7310, or by writing Center Kids, Lesbian and Gay Community Services Center, 208 W. 13th Street, New York, NY 10011 (fax: 212-924-2657). In other areas, the Gay and Lesbian Parents Coalition International, based in Washington, D.C., has member parenting groups in hundreds of locations across the country. Call 202-583-8029 for further information, or write GLPCI, P.O. Box 50360, Washington, DC 20091.

Lesbians in the Workplace

Ginny Vida

In 1979, after working for the National Gay Task Force for four years, I decided to explore opportunities in publishing, a field in which I had previously worked as an editor of children's textbooks. I remember going to see a counselor ("Sam") at an employment agency that specialized in editorial jobs. Sam looked at my resume and said, "I can get you a job in publishing, but not with this resume." He was referring, of course, to my most recent employer, listed prominently in my job history. In offering me this advice, Sam revealed that he was gay himself and wanted to be helpful.

"But I could never misrepresent myself in an interview," I declared.

"You can tell them once you get into the interview, but let them meet you, let them fall in love with you first," he replied. He advised me to go home, revise the resume (delete the National Gay Task Force), and come back the following day. Sam feared that my "out" resume would conjure up stereotypes and deprive me of an interview.

As it turned out, I went home, picked up the phone and started calling my lesbian/gay movement contacts—an initiative that led to my getting a job in the mayor's office. But my conversation with Sam had served to remind me of a sad reality: The world of work was, at best, only partially safe for lesbians and gays.

Today, fifteen years later, there are lots of "out" lesbians in editorial jobs. There are, in fact, more and more of us in nearly every line of work. The climate has become more lesbian-friendly. Today, more than twice as many cities have ordinances

Dale Rosenberg, Special Assistant, Federal Reserve Bank of New York.

DALE ROSENBERG

Natt Nevins

protecting lesbians and gays in employment, housing, and public accommodations than there were twenty years ago. More businesses have voluntarily adopted nondiscriminatory policies; some have even granted health benefits to domestic partners of unmarried employees. Some employers, such as Levi Strauss, have "out" lesbian and gay caucuses. Some employers address homophobia in diversity training. No doubt these protections and benefits are helping to create a more tolerant climate in today's world of work.

Then, too, occasional newspaper stories and talk shows featuring "respectable" lesbians, and the presence of sympathetic lesbian characters on a few TV sitcoms and dramas, have also educated the public and contributed to an employment atmosphere of increasing tolerance and safety.

Perhaps most importantly, tens of thousands of lesbians and gay men have come out on the job, encouraging others to follow suit. When I went to work for the New York City mayor's office in 1980, there were four or five openly gay men and just one open lesbian in city government—me. When I left eleven years later, there were well over a hundred, with lesbians well represented. The initial handful of us made our presence visible and persuaded the mayor to host events celebrating the lesbian-gay community: receptions at City Hall, a historical photo exhibit, the first-ever lesbian program sponsored by the mayor's office. The word got around to closeted lesbian and gay employees that this administration welcomed and appreciated them. By the time I left, we even had our first gay commissioner heading up a city agency.

The mayor's office may not be a typical workplace, but in many employment sites, if a few brave souls venture out, it won't be long before others will say to themselves, "They're out, and they're still here. The sky didn't fall. So-and-so even got promoted. What am I doing in the closet?"

The Lesbian-Friendly Workplace

One of the first groups to come out professionally were self-employed lesbians who provide services to the lesbian and gay community or to a progressive clientele. There are legions of lesbian attorneys, physicians, psychotherapists, dentists, printers, and accountants who have built an entire practice serving the lesbian and gay community, advertising in movement publications, or getting referrals from the lesbian network. (Is it my imagination, or it is really true that 80 percent of lesbian activists, in particular, have become lawyers, psychotherapists, and massage therapists—and that the rest of us lesbians are regularly *visiting* these lawyers, psychotherapists, and massage therapists?)

Lesbian/gay business groups and networks are thriving in most major U.S. cities. One thing about being your own employer is that you don't have to worry what the boss thinks about your sexual orientation: You're the boss! If you are so inclined—and many are—you can also hire from your own community, surrounding yourself with kindred spirits. (Bear in mind, however, that where there are laws banning discrimination on the basis of sexual orientation, it's illegal to discriminate against straight folks.)

A second group of out and emerging lesbians has gained a real foothold in state and local government. For some lesbian activists with a credible record of

Anne Miller, letter carrier.

© JEB (Joan E. Biren)

volunteer service, opportunities are opening up, as progressive elected officials become eager to demonstrate that they employ diverse people as members of their staffs. The greater the person's prominence in the lesbian/gay community, the greater the prospects of employment. Why? Politicians want to employ someone with credibility, someone with positive name recognition in the community. This person can successfully advise the public official on how to address the needs of that community, and the appointment may translate into votes in the next election, as the lesbian appointee helps garner her community's support of her employer/candidate.

Working in political campaigns for public office can also enhance the likelihood of this type of appointment. The "down" side, of course, is that if the public official gets defeated in the next election, you may be bumped from your job to make room for another political appointee when the new administration takes over. (In this event, your outstanding performance evaluations may count for little or nothing.)

Working as a movement volunteer can also lead to employment opportunities in both the public and private sectors simply because your professional network will be greatly expanded. You'll hear about jobs before they're even advertised, and if you're a really skilled and dependable volunteer, you'll meet and work with people who can rave about you to a prospective employer. You know what they say about getting a job—that it's not just what you know but *who* you know. Of course it's important to have the skills and credentials for a job, but you may not be able to get in the door for an interview unless you *know someone*. In my early years of working for the lesbian/gay and women's movement, I met and worked closely with hundreds of people. It was those contacts that led to my first paid position—at the National Gay Task Force. People whom I had worked with at the Gay Activists Alliance and Lesbian Feminist Liberation established NGTF and asked me to serve on the board. Several months later they called me in and asked me to accept the media director's position. I didn't even have to apply!

In the job at NGTF I met hundreds more people, broadened and refined my skills, and four years later, through the movement grapevine, heard about a position at the Commission on the Status of Women, where I applied, interviewed successfully, was hired, and worked for more than eleven years. A couple of years after I left that job, a dear activist friend I'd known since the early 1970s told me about an opening at the state agency where she worked. I applied, called my contacts (people to recommend me), got in for an interview, made a successful pitch to the interview committee, and was hired. It's not always as easy as all that, but make no mistake, contacts are critical—and no one is more eager to help you than members of your own community.

Progressive nonprofits tend to provide another lesbian-friendly workplace, especially those organizations providing services to the poor and disenfranchised—agencies that see themselves as promoting a world where social justice will be the order of the day. Our own lesbian/gay political advocacy and social service organizations are also employing more and more lesbians, as are HIV/AIDS-related service organizations. When I went to work for the NGTF in 1976, paid employment in lesbian/gay agencies was practically unheard of, whereas today many of these agencies have sufficient funding to employ a paid (though often not handsomely paid) staff.

The publishing world has become a very comfortable place for lesbians to work. Today many mainstream houses employ lesbian or gay editors to acquire and handle books targeted at the lesbian/gay community—a very significant market. And, as you'll see from reading Barbara Grier's article in this anthology, there are a number of small publishers that specialize in lesbian, gay, and feminist literature. No doubt lesbians are well represented among their employees.

The arts and entertainment industry, of course, has long attracted and employed lesbians and gay men, and it's becoming more possible to be out in these fields. Although most lesbian actresses, artists, and entertainers haven't proclaimed their sexuality in public for fear of damaging their professional opportunities (in terms of fewer opportunities to perform, being typecast, etc.), nonetheless they're out to many of the people they work with. And a growing number of lesbian singer/songwriters like k. d. lang and Melissa Etheridge are coming out in public. Then, too, some lesbian performing artists—especially singers and comics—who established their careers performing for women's (mostly lesbian) audiences, have now found their audiences widening beyond their own community.

The Lesbian-Unfriendly Workplace

But, hey, let's face it: For all the improvements in public attitude, there are few (if any) publicly acknowledged lesbians serving as coanchors of the evening news, Wall Street financiers, or vice presidents of Fortune 500 corporations. Where are the open lesbians endorsing products on TV? (Yes, I did see Martina Navratilova in a *New York Times* commercial, a welcome breakthrough.) But, alas, certain jobs still seem to require a straight image. Where public image translates into megadollars for an employer, you've probably noticed that "out" lesbians are scarce as hen's teeth. The perhaps well-grounded fear is that if closeted lesbian celebrities proclaim themselves, opportunities and endorsements will evaporate.

Lesbians who work with children—for example, teachers and day care workers—are very vulnerable in most communities. Out lesbian and gay teachers may be subject to attack by homophobes who don't want kids to be exposed to positive lesbian/gay role models. The homophobes carry on about recruitment of innocent youth, but what they really fear is giving kids a choice of whether to act on their sexuality. Given these pressures, the vast majority of lesbian teachers remain in the closet, although gay and lesbian teachers' groups have been in existence since the 1970s and are becoming more visible.

The uniformed services are another example of a workplace that is visibly hostile toward lesbians—and in fact all women. Although lesbian/gay police officer groups have emerged, most lesbian officers remain closeted, fearful that they'll be viewed negatively by their colleagues and superiors. As for lesbians in the military, coming out is likely to result in automatic dismissal from the armed services under current policy.

Even some self-employed lesbians like my friend Noreen, a former lesbian activist who now manages her family's store in an ultra-conservative ethnic neighborhood, have chosen not to come out to customers for fear of losing their business. The bottom line is that those of us who aren't independently wealthy have to provide for ourselves. It's easy for some folks to say that everyone should come out. But who's going to support me if I lose my job? Who's going to compensate me if I'm denied a promotion or my business goes belly up?

Coming Out on the Job

Some lesbians come out to everyone on the job from day one—as a matter of personal integrity and personal comfort. Others move more slowly and selectively. Some seek out a trusted co-worker or two with whom to confide their otherwise closeted identity. They may cultivate the friendship of other women or men in the workplace whom they think might also be gay or at least sympathetic, and when they get enough positive signals from such a colleague, take a leap of faith and declare themselves. Many reveal themselves to their supervisors over a period of time.

Karol works for a social services agency in San Diego. As someone who has always dressed for comfort and considers herself "dykey" in appearance, she feels that her colleagues probably assume she's a lesbian. But Karol doesn't announce her sexual orientation to everyone. "I prefer to lay low, let people get to know me—then come out slowly. After awhile they see that I do good work, that I'm thoughtful. It's better not to frighten people. I like to worm my way into their hearts. Even people who think they aren't supposed to like gays may find themselves saying, 'But she's so nice.'"

Still others never tell a soul at work, fearful that this revelation will come back to haunt them. Sure, it may be okay for the person who just wants to stay in her present job. But what about someone who is ambitious? What if she is passed over for a promotion to the sales force or some other image-important job, or is concerned that she won't be seen as part of the employer's inner circle—or is just plain unsure how the terms and conditions of her employment might be affected? During times of recession, when jobs are scarce, people may be even more cautious about making irrevocable statements about themselves. After all, if the fallout is bad, there may be no place to go in a tight job market, where 150 people may be applying for every decent job. The problem is that we never can be sure that some bigot won't be in a position to wield influence over us—even after we leave the workplace. There's always a concern that the person we'll have to depend on to serve as a reference in applying for our next job might be less than enthusiastic if we come out.

Dress Codes

Many lesbians, especially those in jobs where a professional image is important, wear skirts, heels, pantyhose, and makeup to the office. For some this comes naturally, but many others heave a sigh of relief when they get home in the evening and can throw off the trappings of a straight image. "The first thing I do when I come home—even before feeding my hungry cats—is change into my jeans," said one friend of mine. "And on weekends I never wear makeup. What I do during the week is all part of making it in the world of work." Karol, on the other hand, dresses in pants every day, unwilling to compromise her sense of identity and comfort level. For some lesbians, dressing in a way that makes them feel unnecessarily vulnerable (skirts, heels, pantyhose) and artificial in appearance (makeup) is simply not an option, no matter what the professional sacrifice.

The Costs of Keeping Up Appearances

Balanced against the "safety" of staying in the closet are the costs of doing so. Homophobic pressure that keeps lesbians from being themselves is a daily insult. It may keep you from putting a picture of your partner on your desk the way married folks do, even though you've been together seventeen years. It forces you to remain silent when straight folks talk about what they and their significant others did over the weekend. It's the excuse you manufacture when a well-meaning co-worker tries to fix you up with a date. Perhaps it's feigning interest in the opposite sex to appear straight. For some, it's even bringing a gay male "date" to the office party to keep up appearances.

These are all acts of self-denial. As such, they can take a toll on our sense of integrity and self-respect. Then there's the anxiety about being discovered, the constant worry about who may discover our secret. Of course, the fact that it's a secret implies some-

thing negative, and while we may tell ourselves we're only closeted for practical reasons, it's hard not to feel some internalized homophobia ourselves, as if our participation in the cover-up confirms some negative reality—that under these appearances, we're not acceptable. Playing into the conspiracy of silence is damaging to our sense of self.

There's also a cost to our community and to straight society. Our silence deprives our own community of role models and the visibility we need to find and recognize each other. The closet also deprives us of the opportunity to educate straight society and reduce homophobia. If everyone came out, we could speed up the transformation of societal attitudes and the passage of gay rights laws.

The In's and Out's of a Job Search

Most lesbians have a "straight" resume. Certainly if you've never volunteered or worked for a lesbian or gay organization, there's no reason why your resume would be anything else, and no reason why you would come out in an interview if you're applying for a straight job.

But growing numbers of lesbians work for lesbian/gay organizations—either as volunteers or paid employees—and then conduct a job hunt aimed at the "straight" workforce. The experience you gained as a board member of your local lesbian/gay community services center might well be related to the job you're applying for—as executive director of a nonprofit, where you'll be working with a board—but do you put it on your resume? I'd say yes, but you should find out as much as possible about the "climate" and the attitudes of the agency's leadership before making this decision.

Certainly, if you're applying to work in a government office on HIV/AIDS policy and services, your experience as lesbian board member could be a real asset. If you're applying for a high-profile job with a conservative bank, then maybe not.

Some folks have an "in" resume and an "out" resume, depending on the job. Others will apply with the "in" resume and then come out during the interview—or wait until after they're hired and have been at the job long enough to pass probation with flying colors.

The Benefits—and Ethics—of Coming Out

Assuming you don't suffer adverse professional consequences, the benefits of coming out are tremendous. Obviously you won't announce your sexuality to everyone you interact with on a daily basis; it wouldn't be relevant. But people will know who you are, and you'll be relieved and even proud that they know. I do think straight people respect the courage of lesbian co-workers who come out to them, and they may in fact feel flattered that you trusted them with this information about you.

You'll be free of anxiety about being discovered, and you'll know that you're being visible is helping to reach out to other lesbians and educate and transform society. You'll be part of the solution.

One final word—about the ethics of coming out. Once you're out, other lesbians in the workplace may come out to you. Unless they specifically give you permission to share that information with others, I believe it is unethical to "out" them to anyone else. No matter how public we ourselves may be, and no matter how much we would like others to join us, we must respect everyone's decision to be as private or public as she chooses.

In the meantime, those of us who work for large employers can form a caucus in our company and approach management about posting a nondiscrimination policy, publicizing the lesbian/gay caucus in the newsletter, addressing our issues in diversity training, offering benefits for domestic partners, and testifying in support of gay rights legislation.

In the meantime, we await, and work to bring about, a world of work where sexual orientation is no longer an issue.

An Interview with Ruth:

A Lesbian on the Job

I'm a vice president at a major money center bank on Wall Street that has about ten thousand employees. I've been working there for five years; I manage a group of about fifty people in operations. At times, being a lesbian doesn't affect me at all. But at times, when the business relationship gets into the personal realm, as it often does during lunchtime discussions, I play the pronoun game, which is talking about what I'm doing, who I live with, without mentioning any pronouns. I talk about my partner, my friend, the person I live with. Sometimes I feel schizophrenic because I go back and forth between "I do this" and "We do that." "I bought an apartment, we bought an apartment."

Working in operations means I don't go out and talk with the clients. I really like working in the back office and producing a product—it's the factory part of the bank. If I had to work with clients it would be different because I'd have to entertain them and their spouses. That would be a lot more awkward. My father was a lawyer who was always tending to clients, so I think that definitely influenced my decision not to get into a client-related field. I didn't want to be entertaining them as a single woman, which could be difficult. And I didn't want to make up a man or drag a man along. And I really didn't think bringing my *lover* along would help the client relationship—though in a few cases it probably would have!

When I first started working at the bank I had decided that out of the ten thousand people there I was the only lesbian, and I didn't look for any others—because the women all look alike in their business suits. Then I joined a group of gay bankers, the New York Bankers Group. And I spotted a man from my training class at a social function. He told me about someone else from my training class, so out of thirty in the class there were three of us—we hit the national statistic of 10 percent. It was interesting for me to realize that even at a very conservative institution like this one, gay people are 10 percent, more or less. That made the bank feel much different to me, and since then we have a network of gay men and lesbians who work there. We get together for lunch and talk, and it's fun to have a place where your work and your life overlap.

Some of us are out to friends at the bank, but not to our managers. Actually, though, through a family circumstance I am out to one of the heads of the bank because he's my mother's neighbor. The more I stay at the bank, the less I am afraid of a boss finding out. I think my reputation gets more solid the longer I'm there. So I'm not really nervous about hiding, but that's very different from coming out—a much more active role—and that's something I'm not quite prepared for.

Out of 250 members of the New York Bankers Group, only a few are out on their jobs. I think people's fear of coming out ranges from the fear of being fired to the fear of a stymied career. Some of our most open members have been fired from jobs. They suspect it was because they are gay, although that was not the stated reason. On the other hand, other open members have not seen any negative effect on their careers.

You'll also find that a lot of the people—including gay people—who are attracted to financial services jobs are generally conservative people themselves. Being gay has kind of made them shift on their social views, but they're still very conservative on many of their economic and political views. Many of them think that being gay is a private matter and no one's business. They don't necessarily realize how much it affects them day to day, what a price they pay for hiding.

There definitely are compromises in this field, and sometimes it feels like it's not worth it. I don't know how much longer I want to put up with juggling pronouns. The feeling of isolation is also worse for lesbians, because there are fewer women in this line of work and it's difficult to spot other lesbians. The gay men have better networks. Then, too, there's the inconvenience of having to dress up: the business suit, the nylons, the requisite set of fake pearls. I draw the line at wearing heels, though. I wear flats. Actually I've gotten somewhat comfortable in dressing this way because it feels like a uniform that I put on. But it is very different from the clothes I'd like to wear.

Having pointed out all the negatives, there are important compensations in this line of work. I like the resources that one has at her disposal in a large corporation. There are lots of people I can learn from, I can get computers, and I also like being able to affect the lives of the people who work for me. A lot of people started at the bank after high school, and right now I have a lot of women who work for me. I like working with them and trying to empower them in the hierarchy. In one sense being a lesbian enhances my work. I'm attuned to the career paths of these women and take them seriously; many of the men don't. And then, of course, there are the financial rewards—I get paid very well, and that's nothing that I can put aside lightly. As one works longer and longer, one gets used to pulling in a fairly good salary; that's definitely a piece of it.

Being in a gay professional group has helped a lot. Actually, it's a very brave group; 250 members sounds like a lot, but when I think of all the gay people in financial services it's really a small number. It takes a lot for people to even contact a gay group when they're in such a conservative profession. It took me seven months before I ever got up the nerve to call after I heard about the organization. People hear about it through friends, and we advertise in some gay and feminist publications. One third of our members are women. We have separate women's brunches every other month so that the women know each other, and our board of directors is half women. Not many of the other professional groups have as many women. That's unique, and one of the things that makes the New York Bankers Group very special.

(Ruth lives in New York City with her lover of fourteen years and their numerous pets. She is active in New York gay and lesbian professional groups and fund-raising activities.)

Land in the Ozarks

Judith Blazer Foster

Just before solstice 1980, word went out in the lesbian community that womyn interested in living on land were invited to meet together. By May 1981 twenty of us had agreed we wanted to make a commitment to buy 240 acres in the Ozarks. Nearly eight years later there are still twenty of us in the land association, ten of whom are from the original cluster of womyn.

Though we come from different backgrounds, our collective vision has always been to find a balance between the needs of the land, the community, and each womon as an individual. At present we're separatists and nonseparatists, come mostly from white working- and middle-class backgrounds and range in age from thirty-three to fifty-nine. Some of us have disabilities. None of us is in a wheel chair. We are planning to make our main house wheel chair accessible in the not-too-distant future.

Our particular piece of land cost $100,000. With it came two wells, a pond, several springs, one very large house, a barn, some out buildings, and in my opinion, one of the most wonderful places on earth to live. One of our members paid the $40,000 down payment—half of which she donated; the other half we paid back over a five-year period.

We live in an economically depressed area, especially for womyn. (The year we bought our land, 83 percent of the womyn in this state earned under ten thousand dollars, compared with 62 percent of men.) Because one womon had the means and desire to make the down payment, and because collectively there are twenty of us to meet the bank note, our original payments were sixty-seven dollars a month. This helped us keep the land more affordable to womyn with low incomes. The payments have subsequently dropped to fifty-one dollars per month due to the pay-down of one bank note and payback of the down payment.

Each of us has a lifetime lease on a five-acre plot. The other 140 acres we hold in common. That is, we share the pastures, wood lots, and pond. All water is held in common no matter whose land it's on. We determined that the land could support twenty parcels of five acres each. Our system allows us to live in a community as private individuals.

For womyn who do not have the resources to build or buy a structure to live in, or who are in the process of doing just that, we have what is called the main house. Though some rooms are still unfinished, it has a flush toilet and shower, kitchen facilities with running water from a dug well, a wood stove for heat, and several separate bedrooms. I specify a flush toilet because it is the only one on the land. One of our ecological agreements is that we won't have flush toilets in individual homes because of the amount of water they use. I personally have a commercially purchased composting toilet. Other womyn have designed their own system for composting or disposing of waste.

My house was close enough to an existing well so that I could use a gravity flow system and pipe the water into my bathroom and kitchen. Other womyn have set up guttering systems to collect rain water, which they then divert to storage tanks and pump into their homes. Some womyn haul their water.

We've limited conventional electricity to areas where it existed when we moved here. Our electric company won't bury their lines, and they require a fifteen-foot easement, which means they cut all trees in their path. About six individual parcels are accessible to conventional electricity. We also have two workshops, one considered "noisy" because it uses power tools and the other considered "quiet." Both of these have access to electricity, though one has always used alternative energy. Two homes use solar panels.

Some of us were anxious to live on this land and did whatever we could to get here. One womon bought a school bus for eight hundred dollars and drove it onto the land. Another bought a trailer, which she lived in for several years before adding a large room onto the front. Two womyn built one-room cabins.

I hired a womon carpenter and started building my house with a savings of about two thousand dollars. I was a truck driver then and worked a week on the road while the carpenter worked on my house. Then I'd come home and work with her for a week and then go back on the road. After about three-and-a-half months, I moved in. My house was

Judith Foster at home with Mr. Bosley, her cat.

far from finished, but it had a roof and windows, and though the siding then was Celatex, I could call it mine.

At one point there were eight of us living here. But the numbers have gone up and down. Since we each have individual space, womyn can choose to come and go without affecting the choices of other womyn. Womyn are committed to paying their financial share whether they live here or not. In fact, we are set up so that nonpayment over a three-month period may result in a womon forfeiting her share. That's never actually happened. But it does insure that the community won't lose the land if a womon decides, for whatever reason, not to pay.

At this writing there are seven of us on the land: One womon is an artist and makes her income primarily from a lesbian greeting card business, another is a writer/artist, two womyn have retired from jobs in New York and moved here to live, two womyn are residents—nonmembers who live on a member's parcel—one is a black womon who makes and sells African-inspired jewelry and earns additional income working for lesbians only, the other resident is changing professions from carpentry to healing, and I am a writer and work as a transportation manager for a food co-op.

Some womyn plan to build homes here as soon as they can work out the financial details, while others see this as a place to retire. Womyn who don't live on the land earn their money as a copier supervisor/technician, a researcher for educational resources, a bookkeeper, a small engines mechanic, an architect, nurse, pharmacist, house painter, and so on. Two are carpenters.

Living on the land or not, we have all worked together to develop the bylaws, land contract, and ecological agreements—the decisions we live by on these 240 acres. And, of course, that includes womyn who are no longer members of our land holding association. Our ideal remains to work for integration of the needs of the land, the community, and individual womyn.

At the beginning our meetings were held every week or two. Now those of us who live in the area have meetings every two months. Our meeting process is an important part of how we function. Our decisions are based on consensus-minus-one. We feel strongly in this form because it allows us to disagree on an issue and still move forward. But it is our discussion process that sets the tone. We do work to reach decisions that all of us can live with. If a womon has passionate objections, she often gets support to block consensus, and we either work further for a compromise or table the discussion until we can find a way to satisfy all objections.

We don't operate as a social club, but neither would we welcome a womon to join us whom we did not feel safe with. We have chosen not to have open womyn's land here. A visitor must be invited. We've formed deep bonds over the years, and as in all relationships, we sometimes get upset with each other. But we're there to help when a car gets stuck in a mud hole or when one of us needs to anguish over a lost love. We are fiercely proud of our successes. We believe in our process, though there are still sensitive questions, such as male children on the land, to be answered fully.

Every year in May we have our annual membership meeting and workday. We invite womyn from our area who are not members to come celebrate another birthday with us. We spend the daylight hours fencing the community garden, repairing the door on the barn, crowning trees in the pasture, clearing the easement under the electric lines so men won't spray chemicals, and doing general maintenance and repair on the main house. At lunch we provide gazpacho, an array of Mexican dishes, and gallons of sun tea. In the evening we gather again to eat and talk and then to dance. On Sunday we have our meeting.

This annual event seems to symbolize what we're about. As each year passes and we grow older

Deb Bryan and Deb Robey; building forms for composting outhouse at the Land Project, collectively owned land in Pennsylvania.

Louise Luczak

with each other, it becomes more clear that our dream of living in the country with lesbians is a reality. Our land is now paid for, and it's comforting to look back at the last nine years and see the progress. Knowing that we continue to deal with our differences, struggle with sensitive issues, and care for the land is one of the most satisfying things I've ever known. What we do here works for us. We continue to struggle, change, and grow. It's a good feeling.

1. *Editor's Note: The spelling of woman as "womon" and women as "womyn" is the author's choice.*

II

Sexuality

Sexual Problems of Lesbians

Nancy Toder, Ph.D.

When I told a friend that I had been asked to write an article on sexual problems of lesbians and that I had a three-week deadline, my friend replied, "Oh, that's plenty of time; lesbians don't have many sexual problems." I find this attitude, that all lesbians have great sex all the tme, to be one of the most popular and destructive myths in the lesbian community. The result of this myth is, on the one hand, an implict lack of permission for women to acknowledge, let alone talk about, the real sexual problems they may be experiencing, while on the other hand, women whose sex lives are quite satisfying may be convinced that they have a sexual problem just because sex isn't dynamite every single time. These illusions survive because although there is much bantering about sexuality, it has been my experience, both professionally and personally, that outside of the joking, teasing, and flirting, there are few opportunities for lesbians to talk freely and seriously with each other about sexuality.

In this article, I want first to place women's sexual problems in a societal perspective and to deal with the basic issues of defining a sexual problem. Then I will describe specific sexual problems of lesbians and will discuss the causes and treatments of these problems.

As most women are filled with insecurities about their sexual adequacy, a state of mind created and perpetuated by the mass media and other institutions in our society, they are always looking outside themselves to see whether they have sexual problems. Given the lack of honest communication among women about sexuality, women have no reference points to judge their own sexuality. In the absence of real norms, women's insecurities create unrealistic norms based on misinformation spread by male authorities (the professions, media, religions, etc.). It is my opinion that women's sharing their experiences and generating reality-based norms of female sexual response can be very helpful, by giving us knowledge about the diversity and range of female response, as well as by providing support from the recognition that other women have experiences similar to our own. This support from sisters has been helpful in all aspects of our exploration of our identities and our growing solidarity as women.

Some feminists object to talking about sexual norms, because they are fearful of the ways that norms can be (mis)used, primarily to label someone as abnormal. As lesbians, we know that this fear is reality-based; our culture is very judgmental, and most of us have experienced great conformity pressures in all aspects of our lives. However, I feel that knowledge of the true norms and range of female response (based on our own observations and data, not the interpretations and conclusions of men) is likely to be comforting to most women.

This discussion raises more fundamental questions: Who defines what a sexual problem is? Are there clear-cut objective standards for determining which behaviors, feelings, and inhibitions are problems? Are these standards determined by certain values or assumptions, or are they simply based on a statistical concept of normality?

In my opinion, a woman has a sexual problem if she herself feels frustrated with her sexuality. What one woman may define as a problem, another woman will be totally comfortable with. For example, one woman may feel she has a problem if she doesn't like oral sex, whereas a different woman may feel that this inhibition is perfectly fine, that there are plenty of other sexual behaviors that she can and does enjoy, and that her pleasure is not significantly affected by this one inhibition. However, a problem can still arise if this woman is in a relationship that is important to her, and her lover is frustrated by the limitations imposed on their lovemaking.

At one time, women were expected not to enjoy sex; sex was supposed to be something a woman submitted to for functional reasons. Now, women are pressured to be turned on all the time, to have orgasms every time they make love, to have and enjoy sex with any partner, and to be able to engage in any sexual practice, anywhere, anytime. No one lives that way, of course, but all of us are affected by these myths and pressures. This means that many women who previously might not have labeled themselves as having a sexual problem, now would.

The information that most women are capable of multiple orgasms or that most women have orgasms at all can be very intimidating for a woman who has never had an orgasm but enjoys sexual contact. This woman would be more likely today to define herself as having a sexual problem than she would have been twenty years ago. But on the other hand, twenty years ago many straight women didn't think they were capable of or had the right to demand an orgasm for themselves, and so many women settled for less sexual pleasure than they could have had. In fact, orgasms are a very pleasant part of sexual satisfaction.

We need to be able to express our desires and to feel we have the right to fulfillment, yet it seems that our desires and expectations have been shaped and elevated by the latest Madison Avenue type. Madison Avenue and Hollywood keep us insecure all the time—we're not sexy enough or turned on enough—and set standards for our sexual response that are outside of ourselves and don't take our particular uniquenesses into account.

How can a woman know when a particular need or expectation is truly her own, rather than an internalization of a societal pressure? This is a very difficult question. All I can say is that there is a difference between knowing that your body isn't getting what it wants and is frustrated, and the feeling of inferiority and inadequacy that results from knowing you're not living up to some mythological norm. It is likely that a woman's sense of self must be fairly developed and stable before she can easily feel that difference.

Sexual Problems

What are some of the common problems that lesbians experience? One category of sexual problems is sexual dysfunctions; these are inhibitions of sexual response that block the natural flow of sexual arousal and release.

Sexual dysfunctions in women are commonly divided into three syndromes: orgasmic dysfunction, general sexual dysfunction, and vaginismus. Lesbians experience many of the same sexual dysfunctions as heterosexual women; however, there are also some noticeable differences. For example, it is very rare (I have never heard of a case) for a lesbian to complain of vaginismus—the tightening of the muscles surrounding the vaginal entrance and preventing

vaginal penetration—whereas this is a more common, yet still relatively infrequent, complaint of heterosexual women who are unable to have intercourse. Obviously (although it wasn't obvious to me until I had done some thinking about it), the differences between the ways lesbian commonly make love and the ways heterosexual women commonly make love place a different emphasis on what is likely to be seen or experienced as a problem, as well as possibly causing differences in the incidence of different dysfunctions. At this time, there is no research to indicate whether lesbians simply do not have vaginismus (a definite possibility, as the insertion of a finger is unlikely to arouse the same degree of fear and muscular tension as the insertion of a penis), or whether some lesbians do suffer from vaginismus but do not define this as a problem, simply refraining from vaginal penetration while making love. There may be differences in the likelihood of vaginismus between lesbians who have had recent sexual experiences with men (especially unpleasant experiences) and those women who have been lesbians for a long time. Again, this is speculation on my part. The sample of women I've worked with is too small to draw any conclusions, and no research has been done in this area.

Perhaps the most common sexual complaint among women is orgasmic difficulties. The term *orgasmic dysfunction* refers to the specific inhibition of the orgasmic component of the sexual response. Masters and Johnson have suggested that female sexual response is divided into four phases: *excitement,* when a woman first becomes sexually aroused and begins to lubricate, the vagina expands and lengthens, and blood accumulates in the pelvic area; *plateau,* when a woman reaches a high level of stimulation, the vaginal opening narrows from the engorging of the outer third of the vagina with blood (this process is known as the orgasmic platform), the inner two thirds of the vagina continues to expand, the uterus elevates fully, and the clitoris retracts under its hood; *orgasm,* when the sexual tension is released by a body reflex characterized by involuntary vaginal, uterine, and anal contractions; and *resolution,* when muscle tension and blood congestion disappear from the pelvic area and the entire body returns to its nonaroused state.

The woman with orgasmic dysfunction does not go beyond the plateau phase. Masters and Johnson have refined the concept of orgasmic dysfunction by subdividing it into two diagnostic categories—

primary and secondary—and then further subdividing these categories into absolute and situational. A woman has primary orgasmic dysfunction if she has never experienced an orgasm, whereas a secondary orgasmic dysfunction develops after a period of time in which the woman was orgasmic. In absolute orgasmic dysfunction, a woman is unable to have an orgasm under any circumstances of stimulation, whereas a woman has situational orgasmic dysfunction if she can have an orgasm, but only under specific circumstances. In the most common situational dysfunction, a woman is able to masturbate to orgasm, but is unable to have an orgasm with a partner.

Masters and Johnson report that primary orgasmic dysfunction is frequently related to a corresponding dysfunction in the woman's partner (assumed by Masters and Johnson to be male). In other words, a woman may never have experienced an orgasm because she has never been stimulated adequately during lovemaking. In my clinical experience, this is rarely true for lesbians—which may suggest a lower incidence of orgasmic dysfunction among lesbians than among heterosexual women. The role of the clitoris in lovemaking may have surprised the heterosexual world in the last ten years, but it is not news to lesbians.

The third sexual dysfunction commonly ascribed to women is labeled general sexual dysfunction. A woman who is generally dysfunctional experiences little if any erotic arousal from sexual stimulation. Physiologically, she is suffering from an inhibition of the vasocongestive (engorging of blood) component of the sexual response: She does not lubricate, her vagina does not expand, and no orgasmic platform is formed. She may also be inorgasmic, but not necessarily. My hunch (again there is no research) is that general dysfunction is less common among lesbians than among heterosexual women. Certainly it is more rare for lesbians to present general dysfunction as a problem.

A problem that seems more common in the lesbian community is the fear of some women of being touched in a sexual way. These women are comfortable about making love to a woman, but refuse to allow a woman to make love to them. It is possible that some of these women are generally sexually dysfunctional and are better able to protect themselves from unpleasurable sexual stimulation in the context of a lesbian relationship. (It is not unheard-of for a problem of this sort to be accepted in a lesbian relationship for long periods of time, whereas I imagine that few men would accept this behavior for any length of time, as it would preclude intercourse.) For other women, the refusal to allow women to make love to them may reflect "old gay" notions of appropriate roles. A woman who is playing butch to the hilt, who identifies herself as the man or husband in the relationship, is likely to be very uncomfortable with her surprisingly very female genitals. This woman might also be uncomfortable about being fully naked with her lover, thus dispelling the illusion of her maleness, as well as horrified by the notion of her lover playing an "aggressive" role in bed. It is likely that for many of the women in this predicament, the alienation that they feel from their genitals is expressed in general sexual dysfunction, but again, not necessarily. My impression is that as the feminist and lesbian movements have grown, the number of women who adhere to rigid role-playing has diminished, and that role-playing is becoming a somewhat archaic form in the American lesbian world.

Another problem unique to the lesbian community is the reverse of the above: the refusal of some women to make love to their partners. This passivity may be a function of intrapsychic conflict and/or societal conditioning (factors to be discussed later in more detail), but is more likely to be a reflection of the woman's ambivalence toward the lesbian relationship. Some women who are involved in sexual relationships with women continue to identify themselves as primarily or exclusively heterosexual. This is justified in their minds by the fact that *they* are not making love to a woman, and therefore they think they are not engaging in homosexual behaviors. Negative consequences for the committed lesbian involved in such a relationship may be many. The continual rejection of her sexuality and her body by her "lover" may result in an internalization of intense negative feelings about her own desirability, and these feelings may in turn precipitate sexual dysfunction in future relationships. The imbalance of such a relationship is also likely to produce lowered self-esteem. Thus, a woman who enters into such a one-way sexual relationship feeling relatively good about her body and herself may not leave the relationship in as good a state of mind.

A different type of sexual problem is sexual inhibitions; these include sexual phobias and rigid or restrictive lovemaking patterns. With lesbian couples, the most common presenting problem of this sort is that one woman in the couple dislikes or fears oral sex. If both partners dislike or are indifferent to oral sex, and they enjoy other sexual behaviors, there is no problem. However, if oral sex is very pleasurable and important to one woman and aversive to the other, then there is a relationship problem.

It is interesting that lesbian couples are more likely to define a woman's dislike of oral sex as a problem than are heterosexual couples. Colleagues who work with heterosexual couples tell me that these couples very rarely seek sex therapy because of one or both partners' discomfort with oral sex. In contrast, many lesbians clearly feel that oral sex is an important part of sexual fulfillment, as lesbians are frequently motivated to seek therapy to overcome an oral sex inhibition, even when the rest of the sexual relationship is in many respects highly satisfying. In other less positive instances, a woman may feel pressured into working on her "problem with oral sex" because her lover is defining this problem for her. The lover may feel deprived of a very pleasurable type of lovemaking, and/or she may have internalized some distinctly lesbian myths that can be very destructive when used against a lover. A prime example is, "A woman is not a *real* lesbian if she doesn't like oral sex." Variations on the same theme are, "Any lesbian who is not into oral sex is clearly not capable of deep passion for another woman," and the more catastrophic assertion, "If you don't want to go down on me, it's obvious you don't really love me." The above statements are examples of ways in which we intimidate each other sexually and set narrow definitions of acceptable erotic behavior.

Some lesbians have developed phobic reactions to different parts of their bodies. The most common areas of the body affected seem to be the breasts, anus, and vagina. Women who have such phobic reactions may prohibit touching of these areas or may only allow them to be touched under very special conditions and in very special ways. Additionally, some women complain that they are able to enjoy sex and/or be orgasmic only if they engage in a particular sequence or type of lovemaking or fantasy. These women often feel frustrated by the rigidity and limitations imposed on their sexual response.

A difference in desire for frequency of sex is a very common problem for which lesbian couples seek help. The woman with greater needs often feels frustrated, rejected, and resentful, while the woman with less frequent desire often feels pressured, inadequate, and resentful. The longer the discrepancy in demand for sex, the greater the likelihood of hostility and dysfunctional behavior patterns.

In a large proportion of lesbian couples complaining of different needs for frequency of sex, both partners report that when they do have sex, the sex is good to fantastic. My clinical impression is that a higher proportion of lesbians than of heterosexuals have both high-quality sex and frequency problems; heterosexual couples with quantity problems are more likely to have quality problems, too. In fact, among heterosexual couples, poor quality of sex for one of the partners (usually the woman) often results in that partner's avoiding sexual contact. In contrast, my work with lesbians indicates that discrepancies in demand for sex are likely to be a function of a real difference in needs or a reflection of other relationship problems. Similarly, many heterosexual women complain that their partner is unwilling to be affectionate and that sex is too goal-oriented. This complaint is rarely heard from lesbians. Many lesbians in long-term relationships report plenty of hugs and kisses, but not enough nitty-gritty sex.

Causes of Problems

Before moving on to issues in the treatment of sexual problems, it will be helpful to look at some of the causes of sexual dysfunction in individuals and in relationships, as treatment decisions are often based on the causes of the dysfunction, as well as on its specific nature.

Sexual dysfunctions in women are rarely a product of pathology in the sex organs. In a clear-cut situational pattern of dysfunction, the physical soundness of a woman's sex organs is established, indicating that the cause of the dysfunction is most likely psychological. However, if a woman is experiencing discomfort or a dampening of sexual excitement during sexual contact, then the first step should be a complete medical examination to rule out the possibility of organic complications, such as vaginal infections or clitoral adhesions. (Many gynecologists not only are insensitive to women who experience sexual problems but also are not up to date on the various organic factors that can affect sexual satisfaction. Thus, a woman who wants a sexological examination should either get a referral from a sex clinic or go to a gynecologist she knows and trusts.)

General loss of interest in or responsiveness to sex may be the product of fatigue, depression, illness, or drug use. However, orgasmic functioning is not likely to be affected by such factors.

The great majority of sexual problems are psychologically determined. Helen Kaplan, in her excellent book *The New Sex Therapy,* suggests that these psychological factors may be a function of both immediate and remote causes. Common immediate causes are the failure of lovers to communicate honestly their genuine feelings and desires; misinformation about the normal range of female sexuality; and sexual anxieties stemming from fear of failure, pressure to perform, an excessive need to please the partner (which prevents a woman from focusing on her own satisfaction), or fear of rejection. The fear of losing control, of fainting, screaming, or urinating while having an orgasm, is common among preorgasmic women. These various conflicts and fears may create defenses that interfere with a woman's ability to abandon herself to the sexual experience. Another common reaction, labeled by Masters and Johnson as "spectatoring," refers to the experience of observing one's own lovemaking, usually as a response to performance fears.

On the other hand, sexual anxieties, guilts, and fears may derive from deeply ingrained intrapsychic conflicts. These conflicts may have arisen from early family experiences, such as religious orthodoxy or constrictive upbringing, or they may have come from a more general exposure to our antisexual and antifemale culture. From religious doctrine and general attitudes that permeate our entire society, we learn that our genitals are dirty; that our primary task in life is to make some man happy, including "servicing" him sexually; and that our own sexuality somehow is both a trifle not worth bothering about and an overwhelming, insatiable force that must be suppressed, lest it make us unfit for our holy roles as wife, mother, and guardian of society's "morality."

It is not surprising, then, that many women experience intense conflicts, often unconscious, between enjoyment of sex, and fear of punishment (learned from childhood experiences) or feelings of guilt (associated with "sinful" or "unnatural" behavior). For the lesbian, the fear and guilt are compounded by the fact that she is stepping totally out of the realm of acceptable sexual feelings and behaviors. Her experience is likely to be condemned as anti-God, anti-Man, anti-Nature, and anti-Life. And on some level, even the youngest and most sheltered of women experiencing lesbian feelings knows the degree to which the expression of her feelings will violate the most basic of society's rules. Not exactly a healthy or supportive atmosphere for getting it on!

Sexual dysfunctions are also acquired through behavioral conditioning and reinforcement. In contrast with dysfunctions caused by learned attitudes toward sexuality, behaviorally conditioned dysfunctions do not involve the same degree of intrapsychic conflict; instead, they are a response to certain specific experiences. The most common of these experiences are childhood sexual traumas, such as rape or incestuous seductions, or negative sexual experiences as a young woman, which may range from mild (setting certain patterns of sexual response) to severe (rape). One uniquely lesbian set of experiences involves young women in all-women environments, such as all-girl schools, convents, and the military. The consequences of getting caught making love in such situations are severe, and the likelihood great, so that the lovemaking is often rushed and accompanied by fear and guilt. With time, these experiences may result in orgasmic dysfunction, avoidance of foreplay, and an inhibition of movement and sounds during lovemaking.

Finally, sexual difficulties may be not an expression of one person's intrapsychic conflict, but rather may reflect sexual or more general problems in a relationship. Sexual problems in a relationship may be due to a destructive sexual system between the two lovers that encourages and perpetuates anxieties about sexual performance and failure. Communication difficulties may exacerbate the problem; these may arise from culturally induced shame and guilt about talking openly about sexual matters, or they may reflect a more deeply rooted communication problem of the couple. Often in couples that seem sexually incompatible, underlying ambivalences, hostilities, and anxieties are being acted out in the sexual relationship; women are often unaware of the subtle forces that have turned them off to each other sexually. Sometimes, a woman who is generally unassertive and who feels intimidated by her lover will choose sex as a way to express resentments, because she is afraid to express her anger in more direct ways. Kaplan suggests some dynamic explanations for rage at a lover and fear of abandonment (two feelings that can affect the couple's sexual relationship adversely), including failure to establish trust and intimacy, unresolved conflicts with parents that are acted out on the lover (transferences), power struggles, unrealistic expectations of the lover or the relationship, and excessive dependency and demands. The anger or fear may directly inhibit the sexual response (for example, secondary orgasmic dysfunction), or it may be acted out in different maneuvers aimed at sabotage of the sexual interaction (for example, choosing to make love when both partners are too tired).

Treatment

If you feel that you do have a sexual problem, and maybe have some idea of why you're having the problem, your first decision is whether you can deal with the problem alone (or with a lover) or whether you should seek help. Sometimes just recognizing the problem and talking about it with your lover or a friend can help. For most sexual dysfunctions, therapy, is your best bet. (Some additional options are available if you are preorgasmic; I will discuss these later.) Therapy is also in order if your problem is in the context of a relationship, and if you and your lover have exhausted your own resources for trying to solve the problem.

In some of the larger cities, you may be able to locate lesbian therapists who have expertise in working with sexual problems. In a greater number of areas, you may have access to straight feminist therapists, who are unlikely to have antilesbian attitudes and who should have more liberated and less sterotypic notions of female sexuality than their more traditional colleagues.

In my opinion, the therapist's knowledge of and experience in working with sexual problems are as important as her feminist "credentials." A therapist who knows nothing about behavioral sex therapy techniques may focus attention on the remote causes of sexual problems and ignore the immediate causes. This exclusive focus on remote causes can result in many years of therapy, huge costs, and little progress in solving the sexual problem. In general, the rapid-treatment behavioral approach has been much more successful in treating sexual problems. The ideal sex therapist is flexible enough to use behavioral techniques for treating the immediate causes, and more insight-oriented strategies for dealing with the deeper elements of the problem when necessary.

How to find a therapist? Your friends may be your best resource. If a therapist comes highly recommended by a lesbian friend, that's a good start. Other resources are local women's organizations, many of which keep lists of feminist therapists with notes on their particular expertise. If you live near a university or medical school, you can call the psychology or psychiatry department and ask whether the school has a sex clinic. If you go to a sex clinic, ask for a female therapist, preferably one with some experience in working with lesbians. (A competent and imaginative sex therapist, however, can generally work successfully with a lesbian or a lesbian couple even without prior experience.)

You may want to make one appointment each with several prospective therapists, and then choose the one you like best. In these initial appointments, ask each therapist about her therapeutic orientation and her training and qualifications in both general and sexual therapy, tell her what you want out of therapy, and ask her what you can expect in therapy with her. Don't be afraid to ask specific questions, and trust your judgment: If you don't feel good about the prospect of working with a certain therapist, probably your instincts are telling you something important.

Once you go into sex therapy, you can expect the course of treatment to be something like this: First, you and the therapist will define your problem. Next, the therapist will ask you for a detailed sex history (including your experiences, feelings, and expectations). Do not be surprised if the sex history takes several sessions; this time investment will pay off by enabling the therapist to develop a specific and suitable treatment plan for you. After the sex history is complete, the therapist will summarize for you the aspects of the history that clarify the nature and origin of your sexual problem, and she and you will set goals for the treatment. The treatment will probably include both sex education (to counter myths, misinformation, and unrealistic expectations) and structured homework assignments. These assignments will be sexual and erotic experiences designed to reduce performance anxieties, to provide a relaxed and supportive atmosphere for you to explore your sexuality, and to relieve your specific problems.

Whatever the nature of your sexual problem, if you are involved in a primary relationship, then it is most helpful for both women to participate in the therapy together. This permits the couple to deal with the inevitable frustrations and misunderstandings that have resulted from the problem, and ensures the cooperative and active participation of both women in the problem-solving process. Conjoint sex therapy examines the myths and misconceptions about each other's behaviors and feelings, delineates the problem situations, and finds more adaptive ways to deal with these situations.

Sex therapists make a distinction between sexual problems that seem to be a function of anxiety and those that seem to arise from anger. If anxiety is the primary cause of the problem, then sex therapy from a behavioral perspective, with some attention to changing destructive sexual attitudes, is appropriate. However, if the sexual problem is arising from underlying hostilities and resentments in the relationship, then a more traditional therapy, which will help identify dynamic problems in the relationship and provide a safe outlet for expressing feelings and solving the problems, is needed.

One way to help determine whether the sexual problem is stemming from anxiety or anger is to see when the problem began. If you have always had the problem, then it is likely to be caused by anxiety. If the problem is specific to your present relationship, then it may be either anxiety or anger. If, however, you and your lover had good sex for a while, and then a problem arose—say, after one of you had an affair, or after you began to fight frequently—then the sex problem is more likely to be caused by anger.

Often a couple will identify one of the two women as having the problem: She doesn't have orgasms, or she rarely wants to make love. Again, let me stress that even if only one woman is dysfunctional or inhibited, the problem is still a relationship problem, and it is important for both women to be involved in the process of therapy. When both women are involved, not only will their sex life together be enhanced, but their communication and intimacy in all areas of their relationship are likely to improve.

If you are preorgasmic and live in a large city, you may be able to find a therapist who offers groups for preorgasmic women. The advantages of such a group over individual or couple therapy are that the group provides additional support and more varied viewpoints, and costs less. On the other hand, you get more of the therapist's time and attention in individual therapy, and your lover cannot participate in the therapy if it takes place in a group. If you can't imagine talking about the intimate details of your sexuality in a group, then you may be more comfortable in individual therapy.

Two books are now available to help women expand their sexual awareness and become orgasmic: Lonnie Barbach's *For Yourself: The Fulfillment of Female Sexuality,* and Julie Heiman, Leslie LoPiccolo, and Joseph LoPiccolo's *Becoming Orgasmic: A Sexual Growth Program for Women.* I prefer Barbach's book, as it is firmly entrenched in a woman's perspective, has a little more awareness of lesbian realities, and effectively stresses individual differences by including the reactions and responses of many women to the different stages of the treatment program. If you feel optimistic about your ability to solve the problem on your own with some guidance, or if therapy is a financial impossibility, get one or both of the books and give it a try.

Men

In conclusion, I want to mention a topic that is taboo in the lesbian community—a topic about which women are filled with shame, anxiety, and fear—namely, the experience of sexual feelings, fantasies, or dreams about men, or the actual experience of having sex with a man. As lesbians almost never talk about these experiences, many lesbians assume that other lesbians never have them, and literally panic when they have a sexual fantasy or dream that includes men. Many women immediately begin to question their identity: Am I really a lesbian? Does this mean that I should pick up a man and go to bed with him?

In my work with lesbians, I have found that many women have sexual feelings or dreams about men, or engage in sexual contact with men, for many different reasons. Women who are still insecure about their lesbian identity (and how many of us aren't at one time or another, given the societal pressures we face daily?) will sometimes go to bed with a man to prove to themselves that they still can do it, or that their lesbianism is a choice and not (as society says) a rejection by men. This often happens to women when they visit their parents; isolated from lesbian supports and realities, women sometimes succumb to pressure to be heterosexual.

Some lesbians engage in sexual fantasies about or behaviors with men out of curiosity. For those women who have never had sex with men, it is a new experience; for women who once were actively heterosexual and who have been lesbians for some time, sex with men is an old forgotten experience. Sometimes women who live relatively separatist lives find themselves missing men; a dream may communicate this message to a woman, or quick sex may be an easy way to make limited contact. Other times, a woman may decide to sleep with a man because of anger: One woman with whom I was working was angry with the women's community because she was having a hard time finding a lover, and a big part of her desire to sleep with a man was really a desire to say "fuck you" to her lesbian friends.

I bring up this taboo subject in order to reassure women that many lesbians share these feelings and experiences, and to make a plea for recognition and acceptance of *all* parts of ourselves. Until we recognize those parts of ourselves that are disquieting and inconsistent, until we respect our individual differences, the unity we build is false. More fundamentally, when we limit ourselves by imposing rigid and punitive rules for acceptable sexual feelings and behaviors, we are in fact capitulating to the same forces that we struggle against in asserting our lesbianism.

Further Reading

The following books provide accurate factual information on female sexual response and sexual dysfunction. Unfortunately, all of these books are heterosexual in orientation.

Barbach, Lonnie Garfield. *For Yourself.* New York: Doubleday, 1975. Excellent description of a group therapy program for preorgasmic women. Also includes a chapter on the anatomy and physiology of female sexuality.

Belliveau, Fred, and Lin Richter. *Understanding Human Sexual Inadequacy.* New York: Bantam Book/Little Brown, 1970. A readable discussion of the therapy principles and techniques used by Masters and Johnson in their treatment of sexual dysfunctions.

Boston Lesbian Psychologies Collective. *Lesbian Psychologies: Explorations and Challenges.* Urbana: University of Illinois Press, 1987. An inclusive book written by feminist writers, therapists, and academics. Focuses on lesbian identity, relationships, therapies, and community. Many excellent articles on sexuality, problems in lesbian couples, race and culture, homophobia, and other important topics relevant to the lesbian experience.

Boston Women's Health Book Collective. *The New Our Bodies, Ourselves.* New York: Touchstone, 1992. Written from a feminist perspective. Includes a well-written chapter on the anatomy and physiology of sexuality, with excellent photographs and drawings of female pelvic organs.

Clunis, D. Merilee, and G. Dorsey Green. *Lesbian Couples.* Seattle: Seal Press, 1988. An important guide for lesbians presenting the pleasures and challenges of being in a coupled relationship. Discusses the stages that most couples go through and other issues such as work, sex, money, coming out, monogamy/nonmonogamy, children, recovery, disability, and aging.

Heiman, Julia, Leslie LoPiccolo, and Joseph LoPiccolo. *Becoming Orgasmic: A Sexual Growth Program for Women.* Englewood Cliffs, N.J.: Prentice-Hall, 1976. An individual program for preorgasmic women. Very heterosexual in assumptions, but contains some useful information and techniques.

Kaplan, Helen Singer. *The New Sex Therapy.* New York: Quadrangle Books, 1974. Highly informative and useful. Technical but accessible. Focuses on sexual dysfunction, but includes excellent chapters on the anatomy and physiology of sexual response and on the effects of illness, drugs, and age on sexuality.

Loulan, JoAnn. *Lesbian Sex.* San Francisco: Spinsters Book Company, 1984. Excellent presentation on the basics of lesbian sexuality, written in a warm and funny style with practical suggestions and exercises to explore one's sexuality alone or with a partner. Contains important chapters on long-term couples, disability, motherhood, sobriety, aging, and youth.

Loulan, JoAnn. *Lesbian Passion: Loving Ourselves and Each Other.* San Francisco: Spinsters Book Company, 1987. Another excellent exploration, written in a similar style to the first book, expanding on topics such as passionate friendships, dating, sex toys, enhancing long-term sexual relationships, and lesbians and AIDS.

Loulan, JoAnn. *The Lesbian Erotic Dance: Butch Femme, Androgyny, and Other Rhythms.* San Francisco: Spinsters, 1990.

A Sexual Odyssey

Karol

I felt I was the only lesbian in Des Moines, and I finally moved to Iowa City with the express purpose of either coming out or trying to compromise something. I went into therapy, and took my mother's advice and tried men first. It was "so-so"! I ran across a woman who seemed to be coming on to me and I found myself coming on to her. We began to have feelings for each other, but she was not very far out—she'd had a couple of minor experiences, and I had no experience with women.

We got to the point where we would get more affectionate—we would hug, and the hugs got longer. One night we started kissing each other on the cheek and our mouths brushed together for half an instant. I was afraid. I'd never kissed a woman like that before. We finally slept together. Neither of us had any idea what we would do. It's strange to come out with someone who is also coming out, but it's also very sweet and spontaneous.

Neither of us had any expectations, except that we both knew we wanted to please each other. After a very jittery dinner together we began to hug and kiss and I confessed I had been so nervous that day that I had taken *two* baths; she told me she was so scared, she had taken *three!* That broke the ice. We began to undress each other slowly. I was shaking like a leaf. I wasn't sure what to do and so began to do just what I wanted to do. There she was, naked—and she wanted me. I began to touch and stroke her all over, especially her breasts and parts I had never been able to touch. We kissed and touched for some time and then I got on top of her. We moved our bodies together (the clinical term is "tribadize") and she was quite receptive to that.

I fell to her side and began to explore her with my hands. She told me earlier she had never had an orgasm: I manipulated her clitoris very gently, put my fingers inside of her, following the same rhythmic patterns she was doing with her body. She moved around quite a bit, reminding me of ocean waves. She would slow down and then start up again. At one point her breathing stopped and her face tensed up, but then it stopped. She said, "I think that was *it*," but I noticed she still wanted to move around and her clitoris was not that sensitive to my touch, as it is immediately after a woman has had an orgasm. We let it go at that, temporarily. She made love to me, next, in the same way. Her hands explored, it was really nice! We did that all night long and on the second time around, when I again made love to her, all of a sudden her breathing got very heavy, almost panting, and she began to moan. I knew, I just *knew* she was coming. She gasped, "Oh, my God—what is *that!*" and I said, "That's *it*, honey!" She went off like a rocket . . .

We were very pleased that not only had we brought each other out, but she had experienced her first orgasm. It was very rewarding for both of us. Oddly enough, I did not have an orgasm that night. I had experienced them before, both in masturbation and with men. They came to me easily, from the beginning. Ironically, before this affair, I had been trying to repress my feelings for women via therapy at a university outpatient clinic; the shrinks there had given me a prescription to help me curb my sexual fantasies and appetites. Two weeks before we first slept together, I had thrown out the pills, but they were still in my system and I was not able to experience orgasm for a couple of weeks into the affair.

As for oral sex, I found the Midwest was not the best place to learn about it. Most of the midwestern dykes I ran across were into digital sex. I experimented with oral sex, but I didn't know what I was doing and there was no one to teach me. The first time I had an orgasm with oral sex, my lover and I were in a motel and she was exploring down there. She accidentally managed to cover my clitoris with her mouth and slightly stroked it with her tongue. It was a *weird* feeling, like some sort of "liquid force" was enveloping me, and the sensation was so new and wild that I had a very sudden climax.

I never really got into oral sex until I came East. Lucky for me, the first woman I ran into there had a Ph.D. in the Oral Arts. She knew *all* the strokes— and I learned from her. I learned that not only could I do all sorts of innovative things when I went down on a woman, but I could stay down there almost indefinitely. I could use any number of different tongue-strokes, patterns, etc., and penetrate inside with my tongue. I love oral sex—I like doing it to other women and I enjoy being gone down on, too, especially by someone who knows what she is doing; that will send me into space faster than anything else!

The fourth lover I had in the Midwest liked to be penetrated, even to the point where I could get my whole hand inside her, and she would get so worked up, just go crazy, almost. This woman was not yet "out." We got into bed and I was all ready to show her the ropes, you know, the "big butch" act. I was on top of her when she suddenly pitched me off, rolled me over on my back, and began to make love to me. I said, "Wait a minute. I'm supposed to be bringing *you* out—let me go first and show you." She stuck her lower lip out and said, "*I* want to go first!" I said, "Oh, . . . okay." She was quite good for someone who'd never slept with a woman before. She likes to initiate things; she always "goes first."

On my thirty-first birthday, I had a brief affair with a woman who was quite an adept lover, and she and I discovered that I was able to have multiple orgasms. She was good with her hands, also with oral sex, and she knew how to combine them. I had been curious about anal sex before I met her and had discovered, through masturbation, that I could experience orgasm by inserting a tiny vibrator into my anus. I found that the sensations caused me to feel excited. I had thought only men could have anal orgasms, and then *I* had one; I liked it and told my new lover about it. She did something to me that I really dug; first, she went down on me and, at the same time, put three or four fingers inside of me, then she took her other hand and inserted one finger into my anus. So there were three things going on at once. Talk about an orgasm!

After that, she withdrew her fingers, but did not take her mouth from my clitoris: She stayed stock-still for a minute, and then very slowly, gently, began to manipulate my clitoris with her tongue, again. I thought, "Oh, I won't be able to *bear* this." I was always very sensitive in that area after climaxing. I wondered if I was going to be able to ride out the feeling of irritation in the clitoral area and, sure enough, within a minute the irritation passed and I went right back up again. And again, and again!

I don't feel that someone should do anything she doesn't feel comfortable doing. I don't like to "trick"—I enjoy getting to know a woman first. I like a bit of courtship. I have never gone home with a woman I have met the same night, and rarely anyone I've seen only once or twice. The one time I came closest to a "trick" was such a bad experience that I was glad to go in the morning.

I enjoy being with a woman who knows how to use her hands and fingers, all silky-smooth and gentle—I don't like people to be rough with their hands. I enjoy lots of affection and cuddling, tons of foreplay. I appreciate, most of all, a woman who knows how to go down on me. No matter what my state of mind, even if I were dead, I think I could have an orgasm if she went down on me and knew what to do.

Once in a while, I might get into a 69 position, but it's not a comfortable position for me, top or bottom, or sides, even. I find it hard to concentrate on what I am doing when I am being done at the same time, and I usually "lose it." I finally was able to slightly master mutual lovemaking—that is, when both partners touch each other's clitorises at the same time and experience simultaneous orgasm. This takes concentration, but it can be done.

I have also initiated a situation where, as I lay on my back, the other woman knelt and I slipped my head underneath her. I don't go down on her—she "comes down" on me. I've done both positions, but if I'm over her I find I need something to lean against. I have trouble with orgasm if I am standing, sitting up or kneeling—I just get spacey and fall over. One lover went down on me while we were in the shower together, and I fell over in the tub.

I've also experienced ménage-à-trois. And this was not an overnight encounter; it went on for a whole summer. Because I didn't like the French term, which reminded me of a soft-porn movie (usually with two men and a woman), I called it instead a "triad," or a loving trinity. The triad, which consisted of me, my lover, and a third woman my lover and I found extremely attractive, was emotionally a bit difficult, but the sex—oh my dears—the sex was exquisite. Use your imagination!

Imagine oral sex, if you can, and that universal complaint about it being isolating because you cannot embrace someone going down on you. Well, *no problem:* One woman holds you, strokes you, touches and kisses you, your breasts, your body, while the other woman goes down on you—and you don't know whose name to cry out! Imagine two women tribadizing, one on top of the other, while the third, after watching a few minutes, quietly slips down and penetrates them both. They experience simultaneous orgasms.

Imagine one woman has breasts so sensitive that she can sometimes come from having her nipples sucked. Now she has *two* lovers—one at each breast!

The drawback is obviously this: It can spoil you. You get to the point where you can't imagine yourself in bed with just one woman. And I'd recommend it only for those who can transcend possessiveness and most kinds of jealousy, who will not feel left out if the other two drift off for awhile by themselves. For the record, I'd do it again.

And, in a "kink" world ranging in ice cream flavors from brick vanilla to rocky road, I am, for the record, vanilla—make that French vanilla, with perhaps a smattering of chocolate nuts. I am obviously not opposed to acting out someone's fantasy, and have enjoyed mild bondage—being tied up with silk scarves, hand and foot to the bed, and made love to slowly and methodically. I had a most delicious fantasy of being a large jungle cat that needed to be restrained because I was so wild and ferocious.

In earlier years, I wrote about my anal sex experiences. I don't anymore. I also don't practice it, not since the early days of the AIDS crisis. I figure if anything is at the top of the list for unsafe sex, anal sex is—along with penetrating hard and/or fisting until you or your partner bleeds inside; or going down on a woman when she is having her period. I've done these things in the past; I don't now.

However, I've gotten more into sex toys in recent years. We kept away from or were quiet about them in the early movement years, because there was an attitude out there that sex toys were "P.I." (politically incorrect). I am a woman who enjoys penetration and have always liked the idea of a lover being directly on top of me and being able to penetrate me. And I have had the good fortune in the last decade to find women who could strap on a dildo and do just that. I am most definitely, in this respect, a "bottom." I also use vibrators for various autoerotic practices but rarely with lovers. For the most part I prefer my own body parts and also can't imagine that any vibrator can compete with my tongue.

When I do use a vibrator, I use it sparingly, because it tends to "numb me out." If I used a vibrator, say, and found myself later that day in a sexual situation, I would not be as intensely aroused as I might be, and I might not even experience an orgasm.

I have always enjoyed making love in places outside a bed or bedroom: in the woods, on a beach, in a car—but my favorite has been making love in a body of water, like a pond. I have made love in the water a number of times. Outside of the constant loss of lubrication, I can think of no other drawback to making love in the water, except perhaps this: Unless you are a trained Japanese pearl diver, it is quite difficult to go down on someone. If you can hold your breath for three minutes or she can come in ten seconds, you might want to try it.

I am now in my fifties and there have been some physical and mental changes, and also accommodations in lovemaking. I run across more and more partners who have also experienced change, some of it in the form of limited mobility or disability. The walls of my vagina are more sensitive than they once were, which means I don't enjoy being penetrated as hard as I once did. I don't have the agility I once had, which may be due to age and weight. Once I wanted to get all the sex I could, but now notice there are times when I'm not in the mood. (Of course, if I am "in love," I am almost always in the mood.)

I recommend both JoAnn Loulan's *Lesbian Sex* and *Ourselves, Growing Older,* which contain some good material on sex and aging and/or disabilities. The latter deals mostly with heterosexual women, but there is also lesbian content, and there are illustrations helpful to those who are of, or have partners with, limited mobility and/or a disease or illness. These things can happen to us—at any age.

In recent years I had an affair with a woman who had lost a breast to cancer. While that in no way limits mobility, it can be scary for someone who has a serious, life-threatening illness to have to confront each new partner with the news of her situation. My friend said it can trigger a partner's fears—and we all have fears around illness and body image. My friend feels that music festivals have made it all much easier, because women see each other nude and know what a mastectomy looks like.

Two former lovers of mine had genital herpes, and I was in a fairly long-term relationship with one. My partners were conscientious, safe sex was practiced on those occasions when needed, and I've never gotten herpes.

I've been lovers with a woman who had limited mobility and, let me say, imagination, desire, and intense passion can go a long way! "I can't move around the way I'd like," my lover said, and then added, smiling, "but you can always bring it to me!" We certainly invented some new positions for ourselves!

One thing I employ in my lovemaking is massage, sensual and sexual. I give back rubs before and/or after sex. If I am rubbing her back I may begin to not only rub, but kiss and stroke it, too. I like to take my tongue and, starting at the base of the spine, very lightly brush the tongue over the fine, small hairs along the backbone and run up the entire length to the neck. One of my ex-lovers said, "Hey, I like this better than sex!" Unfortunately for me, she did! Massage and back rubs are good ways to start foreplay and make nice afterplay, too. It's a fine way to help someone come down and go to sleep.

Most anything a woman wants me to do, I will do it. I love the way women look when I am making love to them: the way their faces look, the way they tense up before orgasm, the way they move their bodies, the noises they make. Goddess, they're beautiful.

(Author's Note: For reading suggestions, see bibliography on pages 293–95. Especially recommended are books by Wendy Caster, Pat Califia, and JoAnn Loulan.)

Lesbian Sexual Techniques

Wendy Caster

(Excerpts from The Lesbian Sex Book, *by Wendy Caster, copyright © 1993 by Wendy Caster. Reprinted by permission of Alyson Publications, Inc., Boston, Mass.)*

There are no rules in lesbian lovemaking, only preferences. People who claim that a woman *must* love doing A, or hate doing B, to be a genuine authentic lesbian are wrong. Similarly, there's no set vocabulary for lesbian lovemaking. Some women prefer euphemistic words while others go with blunt Anglo-Saxon terms. It's a matter of personal preference.

The topic of lesbian sex is so rich and exciting that entire books have been written on the subject. This excerpt focuses on two mainstays of lesbian sexuality: oral sex and penetration.

Oral sex is licking or sucking the clitoris, labia, or vagina, often to orgasm; it's also known as "going down on someone."

One typical approach to oral sex includes kissing her pubic hair, with special attention paid to the seam of labia right down the middle. On some women, the labia will be prominent and accessible; on others, they will be buried under tangled pubic hair. To gain access to her more hidden parts, you can lick along that seam of labia until she opens up, separate her labia with your fingers, or ask her to open her lips for you. Each way offers its own erotic thrill.

Once her lips have opened, you may see glistening pink, red, brown, or purplish flesh, with a shape resembling a flower. At the top of her vulva, where her inner lips meet, is her clitoris. Depending on her personal architecture, it might be readily visible or somewhat hidden. A simple way to find it is to lick up the length of her vulva; when you reach a little knob, which can be as small as a grain of rice or as large as a fingertip, you're there. Her moans of pleasure will affirm that you are at the right place. And if you're not sure, ask!

Of course, you're not required to go directly to her clit. There are all sorts of things you might want to try first. For instance, gently blow (or puff) air onto her whole vulval area. A focused stream will feel different than a more diffuse one, but both are likely to feel good.

Lick or suck her labia, or nibble them tenderly. Some women like stronger labial stimulation; make sure she is one of them before getting too energetic. Build the stimulation gradually.

Many women find it thrilling to be penetrated by their lover's tongue. This may not be easy to do, depending on the length and flexibility of your tongue and the size and shape of her vulva. Sometimes changing angles helps; if she's lying on her back, put a pillow under her hips so that her vagina is more accessible, then thrust your tongue in and out, or lick around the vaginal opening.

Try licking her slowly from her vagina to her clit. A more rapid version of the same stroke also works. Use the point of your tongue, or try wide flat strokes. The pressure can be hard, medium, or teasingly soft. Occasionally, soft strokes will tickle her unpleasantly; in that case, be more firm. Little by little, work your way to her clit—or else visit it occasionally, lick elsewhere, and go back, again and again.

Once you're ready to focus on her clit, try various approaches at various speeds and pressures, and note how she responds. Lick circles around her clit. Suck it gently or harder, as seems appropriate. Lick it directly or through her labia. Kiss it with soft wet lips. (Be careful to keep your teeth out of the way unless you *know* that's something she likes.) Try humming while she's in your mouth, to add a sort of vibrator effect.

One lovely stroke involves putting your entire tongue flat against her vulva, inside her labia, and slowly, almost imperceptibly, dragging it up along her clit. It may take many seconds for this stroke to be completed, during which her sensation builds subtly and steadily.

Whatever strokes you try, don't jump around too much from one to the other. Try subtle segues; finesse and grace count. But don't drive yourself crazy with performance anxiety; it takes time to learn what a woman likes sexually, and there's no reason you should be able to read her mind.

If she doesn't make sex noises or move much, that doesn't necessarily mean she's not enjoying herself. Some women are just quiet. Pay attention to the movement of her hips and the tension in her thighs, which can be revealing. And if you feel totally lost, ask what she likes.

As she grows more and more excited and seems to near orgasm, stick to one or two strokes that clearly please her. The closer she gets, the more she will desire steady and reliable stimulation. Once she seems very near, stick to whatever stroke you're using until she comes. (You can tell she's getting closer to orgasm through various cues: She may moan more, or more loudly, or more deeply. She may clench her hands or tense her pelvic area. Her breath will come more rapidly. She may thrash around a bit. Generally, she will exhibit a buildup of physical tension.)

Some women take longer to come than others. If you start to get tired, which you might, think of ways to keep up the stimulation without exhausting yourself. For instance, if you are licking her in circles around her clit, you can switch between making the circles with your tongue and making them by moving your head with your tongue loosely pointed; this gives some muscles a rest while others work. Interspersing wet, wet clit kisses with licking will also help.

If necessary, switch to touching her with your fingers. Do this as subtly as possible. You can slip your finger into your mouth and touch her with a very wet finger while your mouth is still against her.

A nice dessert offering, as she's coming, is to merge your licking into sucking, then hold a soft steady suck with your tongue motionless against her clit. This can make her orgasm feel longer and more intense. Stay still for a while, then either move your tongue away, or start working on *Orgasm II: The Sequel.*

While it's useful to have experience and technical knowledge when doing oral sex, the most important factor is to enjoy yourself. Because of past training that female genitalia are ugly (or smell like fish!), it may take a while to relax and savor going down on a woman. Some women never do get into it, but many find it one of the best ways to spend time on earth.

Take your time; discover what you really enjoy. You can learn as you go. Luxuriate in her taste and smell. Enjoy giving her pleasure. And feel your own pleasure as well! If you truly, wholeheartedly love licking her, she'll find that the biggest turn-on of all.

Despite the heterosexual model on which we were

all raised, penetration is not a required part of sex, and some women practice it rarely, if at all. When penetration does occur in lesbian sex, it generally (though not always) follows a fair amount of foreplay, including stroking, kissing, rubbing, touching, and oral sex (though some women prefer oral sex *after* penetration and others skip oral sex entirely).

The following discussion focuses on vaginal penetration with fingers from the point of view of the penetrator. For your partner's safety, make sure your nails are short and well filed before starting.

You and your partner have been messing around, and you're both turned on. You reach between her legs and stroke her. After a few caresses, her vulva unfolds and you discover that she is swollen, hot, and wet. (If she is not, you can always use a lubricant.) You resist swooning and continue stroking her. At the base of her vulva, toward her anus, you slip one finger into her vagina. (If you cannot find it, if you are nervous, or if you are shy, ask her to guide you in.) If she says she is uncomfortable with penetration, gently remove your finger and ask what she likes. She may want to continue the penetration, but at her own speed, or she may ask to switch to something else.

Assume all systems are go and you've got one finger inside her now. It may fit snugly or it may be lost in a relatively large space. If so, add another finger or two; some women will want your whole hand inside. In later lovemaking sessions you might *start* penetration with three or four fingers, but early on, take the time to learn her preferences. Also, since capacities can change with different levels of arousal and at different points in the menstrual cycle, she may want you to use more or fewer fingers at other times. (If she is wildly bucking up against your hand, go for it! The information a woman's body gives you always supercedes the information a book gives you.)

Once you are inside, start exploring. You can move your fingers gently in and out just the slightest bit or use long slow strokes—or vary quick short strokes with occasional long ones. Twisting your fingers will give her one sensation and bending them will give her another. Some women prefer that you not move your fingers at all.

Angles are important in penetration. If she is on her back and you're penetrating her palm up, try moving your fingers in and out in a straight line toward the back of her vagina. Then switch to a long stroke with fingers bent and tilted so that you are hitting the top wall of her vagina (imagine you're aiming at the middle of her pubic hair). You may find that her excitement takes a quantum leap with this angle. Vary which part of the vaginal wall you stimulate; some women are more sensitive toward the opening, while others are more sensitive toward their uterus. Be careful of bumping into her cervix: some women find that sexy, but for others, it's painful.

When you find the part of her vaginal wall that is most sensitive, chances are that you are at her G-spot, but don't worry about its name. Just keep trying different ways of stimulating her there; rub, drag, tap, stroke, and hit it with your fingertips. (The word *hit* may sound harsh, but many women adore the sensation.)

The timing of penetration can be tricky. Some women prefer a gradual buildup of intensity and speed, while others adore flurries of serious fucking separated by periods of quiet internal stroking. Follow her body's instructions, and, if you're not sure, ask. Under these circumstances, a gasped "Faster?" or "Harder?" or "Softer?" is plenty of communication.

While penetrating her, try rubbing or massaging her uterus, ovaries, belly, or pubic area with your other hand. This doesn't work for everyone, but it sends some women to another planet.

What happens if you get tired? You're human. But there are ways of going longer. Alternately rely on different muscle groups; for instance, move your fingers alone for a while, and then switch to moving your hand and lower arm together. Or keep your arm and fingers loose and move the whole unit from your shoulders. Occasionally adjust your body's position to vary the pressures on it.

The crème de la crème of sex for many women is penetration *plus*. The "plus" may be anal sex, or oral sex, or oral sex with belly rubbing, or oral sex with breast kneading, or anal sex *and* oral sex, or whatever wondrous combo you can invent and perform.

These combinations take skill, coordination, and confidence; don't expect to pull them off the first time you make love to a woman. (However, if you do, more power to you!) Gain experience in oral sex and in penetration before you combine the two, otherwise you may feel like you're rubbing your belly and patting the top of your head at the same time.

A fiercely fun threesome includes oral sex, vaginal penetration, and anal penetration. In one possible scenario, you start by licking her. As she grows more aroused, you add vaginal penetration and, then, a finger or two in her anus. (Or you can penetrate her anally first; the order doesn't much matter.) Once your finger is in her anus, you can pretty much ignore it, as the movement of you penetrating her vagina plus her hips rocking will be enough to stimulate her anally. Concentrate on the vaginal penetration and oral sex, which are plenty to keep your attention!

Just as there are no hard and fast rules about lesbian sex itself, there are also no rules about orgasms. Some "experts" claim that women do not, and cannot, have vaginal orgasms—yet plenty of women have them. For some women, reaching orgasm, whether vaginally or clitorally, is the point of having sex; for others, it is the icing on the cake. Some women are easily multiorgasmic; other women struggle to have just one. Some uniorgasmic women develop the ability to achieve multiple orgasms, just as some nonorgasmic women become orgasmic.

If you're happy with your orgasms as they are, that's what counts. If, however, you're not happy with your orgasms, or don't have orgasms, or have clitoral orgasms only and want to experience vaginal orgasms, there are ways for you to achieve more sexual satisfaction. First, start practicing. Try a vibrator with a special G-spot attachment; vibrators provide strong, consistent, and reliable stimulation. Do daily Kegel exercises to strengthen the muscles that spasm during orgasm. Try new angles, more foreplay, and erotica. Rather than focusing on the potential orgasm, enjoy whatever feelings you experience as they happen. With patience and practice, you can improve your sexual response radically.

Similarly, if you desire more orgasms, you can practice by yourself or with a partner. Experiment with maintaining a light motionless touch on the clitoris after the first orgasm, then gradually adding movement. Or try leaving the clit alone for a minute or two, then stimulating it gently. Switching the type of arousal may help: Use a vibrator for the first orgasm and a tongue for the second; or tongue for the first, fingers for the second; or vaginal for the first, clitoral for the second. If your level of arousal lessens after the first orgasm, add erotica or more foreplay for the second. Listen to your body; she will tell you what to do. (However, it is possible that her message will be "one is enough.")

And remember: There are no rules in lesbian sex. Enjoy!

Gender Jail

JoAnn Loulan

The title of this article comes from an old friend. We have known each other forty years, ever since first grade. She wrote me that she was looking for my books, "I'd like to say because I know you, but really the books are for me—I feel like I am in gender jail." The words jumped out as a concise way to explain what the concept of gender does to us. I want to show you the laws, the judge and jury, the sentence, and the rehabilitation of the prisoner of gender. I have worked from an essentialist's (one who believes in the true or essential nature of people) point of view to deconstruct anything in my path that relates to gender as we have known it. This article is the short version of that investigation. The longer version is my book in progress, *Gender Jail*.

It is crucial to question all assumptions about gender, especially for lesbians, because in many ways, being a lesbian requires breaking out of gender jail. But because we have been socialized within the dominant culture, we are still profoundly influenced by what we know to be its rules governing gender. We have been brought up to be heterosexual women, but, because we are not, we question whether we belong in our gender. As a result, our sense of self, the way others see us, and the way we relate to each other is compromised by this socially imposed vision of gender that does not apply to us, or perhaps to anyone. The impact of gender identity is all-pervasive and expressed in behaviors as wide-ranging as dress, demeanor, occupation, and relationships.

Within the lesbian community, there are many gender identifications, although we lack the vocabulary to communicate them. As a result, we fall into the trap of describing ourselves as feminine or masculine. This always sends me reeling. I do not think of women as masculine. The current masculine/feminine paradigm literally stops us from being able to explain who we are.

Lesbians' self-perception is also influenced by the dominant culture. Lesbianism is perceived as a threat to mainstream society and it is because we break gender rules. Therefore, the mainstream scrambles to explain lesbian existence, most often by projecting stereotypical heterosexual male and female behavior and attitudes onto lesbians, insisting on characterizing lesbians as either passive (as heterosexual males fancy heterosexual females) or as aggressive (as heterosexual males fancy themselves).

In this fantasy world, lesbians are divided into women who cannot get men and women who try to act like men. While this view is unrecognizable to, or even denied by most lesbians on an individual basis, the lesbian community does recognize and react to the existence of that stereotypical, fantasy world. As a result of this, lesbians waste a lot of their energy fighting the taunt that we are trying to be men. We are sentenced to defend why it is that we have broken out of gender jail. Our love relationships are constantly being compared to heterosexual models. We sometimes argue even among ourselves about what makes us lesbians. We demand that our partnerships be recognized in the same ways as heterosexual relationships. Queers could take that energy and spark an uprising and challenge the explicit and implicit gender laws on which society is based.

My own vision is that instead of two genders there are thousands, maybe millions. I ask you to suspend the belief that there are only two genders and to continue reading this with the belief that there are endless ways of being female and that all lesbian expressions of gender are represented within that set.

Over the years, many lesbians have told me that they identified as boys when they were growing up. They wanted to do what the boys did, dress as the boys dressed, and did not want to do what the girls did. In about the fifth or sixth grade, these girls were thrown out of or plucked from the boys' group by the boys, by other girls, by grown-ups, or by the girl herself out of shame, confusion, and humiliation.

I don't believe these girls actually identified themselves as boys. But faced with only two rigidly defined alternatives, they might have said to themselves, "If I don't feel like a girl, then I must be or feel like a boy." They wanted to kiss the girls and to throw a basketball, so by mainstream society's definition, they could not really have been girls.

Then there are the lesbian girls who appear to be good heterosexual girls. They dress according to proper gender rules, and they seem to like what straight girls are supposed to like. They may even go through the motions of dating boys. But if they end up being lesbians, they too have broken the gender laws because they want to kiss the girls and to watch the other lesbians on and off the court at the basketball game. Another gender heard from.

Other girls float back and forth between the two mainstream genders. They are able to dress in either gender camp as the situation dictates. They are able to play at the games of boys or girls. They may cause others some consternation about their gender affiliation, but they can conform in either situation and foil the naysayers. These girls are not part of the traditional female gender either. As lesbians, these girls/women are left to figure out yet another gender identification, once again, without the language to express it.

Many self-identified lesbians grew up not feeling that we were girls in the traditional sense. Whenever I ask in a lecture to lesbians, "Who here did not identify as a girl growing up?" about 70 percent of the audience raises their hands. The question in itself is provocative. What is a girl? Who is perceived by others to be a girl? How does a girl see herself? Does not identifying as a girl automatically make you a tomboy? Does this mean you are unable to do what other girls do? Does it mean that you hate being a girl/woman? Or hate girls/women? Not necessarily. Not identifying with your gender simply means not seeing yourself performing the gender role prescribed by society.

Growing up in a culture that did not even allow the idea of lesbianism as a sexual identity cut off many avenues of expression for young lesbians. We were either sexually experimenting with boys because we thought we had to, or were totally celibate because the alternative would have been unbearable. Some of the bravest of us were actually experimenting sexually with girls, but, for those of us born before 1965, this was extremely risky business. It is not necessarily easier for girls to have sex together now, but the taboo of breaking gender laws is weakening in modern times. However, this is truer in the areas of dress, occupation, and reproductive choice than in the area of sexuality. It is still quite taboo for girls to kiss girls.

Exploring the role of gender is critical to the lesbian community. Since we have been set up to defend ourselves against the accusation that we are men, or at least not "real" women, we often miss the opportunity to claim our true gender identities in our scramble to dismantle society's misconceptions. There are few words to describe this spectrum of gender. To be clear, this is not a discussion of transgendered people, although I am concerned that the word "transgender" itself implies having a foot in both genders. I believe that our brothers and sisters in the transgender culture actually have their own genders. They are not "men" or "women" by our culture's definition, but have their own powerful and unique gender identities.

A weapon the dominant culture and the lesbian culture have used against various lesbian expressions of gender is to describe some lesbian experience as a "role." This is especially true in reference to butch/femme. None of true gender identity is a role; there are simply different realities of gender identification. The lack of language to explain it doesn't mean that it isn't real.

It is important to note here that the current trend in psychology is away from believing in an essential (fundamental, inherent) nature, and toward believing in a socially constructed one (that is, one that is shaped by the interpretation of the dominant culture). Deconstructionism, a method of systematically dismantling societal preconceptions, has been used to examine the social construction of gender. Alternatively, the concept of essentialism has been combined with the concept of social construction to conclude that we have an essential gender nature that is shaped by social construction. I believe that the aim of both theories is toward returning us to our essential or true selves, in addition to ridding ourselves of the construction of our cultural mandates. In an objective effort to free ourselves, I hope we can create a new way of looking at gender.

We could go through thousands of examples to explore the variations lesbians create to identify with the female gender. The three categorizations of butch, femme, and androgynous, however, are the three most commonly used words in the lesbian community to classify the erotic nature of lesbians. I believe these three have gender differences between each of them and all three are different from heterosexual female gender.

I have written specifically about these categorizations in *The Lesbian Erotic Dance* (Spinster's Ink, Minneapolis, 1990). The problem with using these words is that they evoke tremendous reactions in lesbians. I believe that with the coming of age of feminism in the 1970s, the eroticism of the lesbian culture was diminished in an effort to fit into what I feel was an image of feminism defined by heterosexual women. The lesbian movement, in an effort to clean up its image, became sterile and political, creating a backlash against lesbian sexuality. Thus our sexual revolution was halted after the Stonewall Uprising in 1969. The butch and femme lesbians who had fought the good fight were made to feel unwelcome in the movement when they came out of the bars and into the streets. This was partly because they were working class, and middle-class intellectuals had taken over the movement. One cannot ignore the biggest component; those butch and femme women displayed a sexual aura. It was obvious that they were more than friends.

In an effort to transform and protect ourselves, the androgynous imperative emerged. Androgyny was a great relief for many women. Especially for women from before the 1970s who, although they did not identify as either butch or femme, felt compelled to choose one or the other in order to fit into the lesbian world. Unfortunately, androgyny has been promoted as the only way to be a good lesbian. The lesbian androgyne has lopped off the two extremes—she is neither too male or too female and thus the darling of post-1970s lesbians. The androgynous lesbian will bring no shame; she will appear strong and soft, able and vulnerable all at the same time.

The androgynous lesbian is not the problem. The problem is that the social construction of lesbian identity continually puts us in the position of needing to defend who we are. We spend too much time trying to convince society that we are not straight women who have had to settle for second best. Dealing with this prattle has taken our attention away from the real task at hand, which is to talk about our own expression of gender. If we are not actually women (in the traditional heterosexual sense) and we are not men, then who are we, after all? And how do we create a language to describe what we are?

The impact of ambiguous gender identification on sexual dynamics between lesbians is extreme. We often resort to vague and foggy descriptions of our complex relational connections. We make statements like "I'm attracted to all lesbians." Or, "I really have no preferences about who I relate to sexually." I do not believe that we have no preference regarding our sexual partners. I know how rigid we are about putting glasses away in the cupboard. Even entertaining the idea that we are not rigid about sex is unbelievable.

We are socialized to relate sexually through our gender. When we break gender boundaries, then how can we talk about sexuality in a way that makes sense? Expression of sexual attraction is one of the ways we have learned to express our gender. Sexual activity is also divided along cultural gender lines. This duality is often sidestepped in lesbian sex by eschewing any activity seen as too male, such as penetration, aggression, passivity, strapping on dildoes, and the like. Asking the question, "What percentage of the time while you are having sex do you make love to your partner and what percentage does she make love to you?" evokes bias. We want so to have our lesbianism pure from heterosexual tainting. This makes other questions about sex equally unnerving. Who is dominant? Who is submissive? Do you switch back and forth? Who does who first? How do you initiate sex, in a passive or an active way? How do you flirt? Do you use dildoes? Vibrators? Do you use fantasies? If so, do they include one partner being a man? Do you enjoy being sexually objectified? Do you enjoy objectifying your partner?

These questions can feel dangerous if you have no true gender identification. How do you explain that you like to aggressively initiate and then have your partner do you first and that you want to do her second but not for the same amount of time? But then, who is doing whom in lesbian sex? Is she doing you or are you doing her? When you allow someone to touch your body in a sexual way, is not all of it making love? As lesbians we have total freedom (should we choose to accept it) to make a new way of relating sexually, and we can choose the language to describe this process. Instead, we often get vague, do not even think about it, certainly do not talk about it, and are often too scared even to do it.

In the survey reported in *The Lesbian Erotic Dance,* femmes were the most likely group (of butch, femme, androgynous, none of the above, and self-defined groups) to penetrate their lovers in the vagina with a dildo. This number was not actually statistically significant, but did show a trend. The group least likely to penetrate their partners with dildoes were butches. Do butches not use dildoes out of the fear of appearing too male? Do femmes use more dildoes in an effort to prove they are not conventional girls? I suspect this simply means that lesbians cannot be defined by current gender jargon.

The lack of available words does not mean that there are no codes for lesbian gender behavior. One friend of mine who identifies as butch bemoans not having a butch summer camp when she was growing up. I asked her what butches would do at camp and she said, "You know, shove each other around." I know there are many butches who do not relate to this. There are perhaps femmes who want to shove, androgynous women who want to shove. We can always find the exceptions. I am trying to find the rules.

What does it mean when butches want to shove each other around? What does it mean if femmes like to feel protected by a butch woman? What does it mean if androgynous lesbians want to strap on a dildo? The same butches who want to penetrate their lovers could also be concerned with their lovers' feelings and needs (not something men are taught). The same femmes who want to be protected by their butch lovers most often can and do take care of themselves (not something women are taught). The androgynous women can take off the dildo when they are done (certainly not something that heterosexual males can do).

We are confronted by the social construction of heterosexual culture every day, but we have yet to discover the subtleties of the construction of lesbian gender culture. Even though the three most common gender identities in the lesbian world are discussed here, there are many more. We need to create more categories that lesbians would be proud to identify with. As lesbians we cannot wait for it to be safe to have our own gender categories. We need to claim them and then present them to the dominant culture. We need to move out of the discussion of male/female altogether. There is no such paradigm in the lesbian world. How do we break out of gender jail and claim that truth?

What imprisons us is our silence. What makes us feel shame is becoming accomplices with our jailers. We plea-bargain and point fingers at the bull dykes and fairy faggots as the ones who make it bad for the rest of us. What hurts us is becoming judge and jury and punishing other lesbians. We are kept in maximum security so that we will not alert the other inmates that the laws are the problem, not the people.

We must bust loose of gender jail. Alert everyone to the change. Allow each of us to find our own way to our own center. Create endless opportunity to tell the truth. No longer accuse each other but encourage one another to be alive.

III

Health

Lesbian Health Issues

H. Joan Waitkevicz, M.D.

Since *Our Right to Love* was first published in 1978, the feminist and lesbian health movements have caused a tremendous increase in the number of activist lesbian health care providers and educators in the United States. More has been learned, or is now being studied, about our health needs than can fit into one short article. I would like to list our most important concerns as I see them. By using the resource list at the end, the interested reader can go on to meet some of these remarkable women and their work.

What are lesbians' health concerns today?

1. We don't all have access to care. Thanks to the activism mentioned above, we now have two generations of lesbians who know what our health needs are, and are able to speak up and demand appropriate care even if our doctor or health care provider is less knowledgeable than we are.

Most mainstream health surveys, taken in lesbian organizations and gathering places, reflect this. They are likely to portray us as predominantly over twenty-five, white, upper-income, monogamous, and generally healthier than heterosexuals.

However, when surveys of less privileged women—teenagers, urban clinic patients, women in prison, women in shelters, or injecting drug users—ask, "Do you ever have sex with women?" 3 percent to 33 percent answer "Yes." These surveys go on to show that in these lesbian and bisexual women, the risk of serious illness, including HIV, is equal to, and sometimes greater than, comparable heterosexual women. And they and their partners are receiving no lesbian-directed health care. Indeed, they and their health care providers are unaware that it is needed.

2. We conceive and bear children. For lesbians seeking pregnancy, donor insemination should be facilitated by a good sperm bank or health professional, to reduce the risk of hepatitis B, HIV, and genetic or inherited illness. In many U.S. cities, these services are available to lesbians.

Studies have long shown that children raised in lesbian or gay households are as well adjusted as those with heterosexual parents. Sadly, in some states the right-wing legal establishment has disregarded this and taken custody away from lesbian mothers.

In situations where a lesbian couple separates, or the biological mother dies, the child's continuing relationship with the comother is important and may also not be protected by law.

3. We may have experienced rape, incest, or battering. Violence against women is being recognized, in the nineties, as the important health issue it is. Health care providers must also be sensitive to the fact that lesbians can abuse or batter their partners.

4. We may have a higher proportion of alcoholism than heterosexual women, because in some places bars are still the only lesbian social center. Gay and lesbian twelve-step recovery programs are abundant now, and there is a growing number of all gay/lesbian inpatient rehab facilities.

5. We may abuse drugs. It has been shown that lesbians who inject drugs are more likely to share needles, in the mistaken belief that lesbians can't get HIV. Access to nonhomophobic drug rehab programs, hepatitis B immunization, needle exchange, and risk reduction teaching will save lesbian lives.

6. Our sexual practices are diverse. In the 1970s, it seemed that health care providers assumed all women were straight. I fear that, in the 1990s, health care providers assume all lesbians have only oral-genital sex, with one partner, witnessed only by the cat, and less and less frequently as the years go on.

In fact we may be totally celibate (and may be embarrassed to declare it); be serially monogamous; have many partners; enjoy dildoes and other sex toys, voyeurism, fetishes, or sadomasochism. And, whether or not we identify as bisexual, 25 percent to 46 percent of us may have had sex with a man in the past three years; are more likely to choose a gay or bisexual man because he is a friend; and are less likely to use a condom because we really didn't plan to do it.

Good lesbian health care requires that every

woman, regardless of her appearance, age, or background, be asked her sexual history in a nonjudgmental way: "Do you have sex with women only, men only, or both, or no one at this time? One partner or more than one? Do you have any other concerns related to sex?"

7. We can catch, and pass on, sexually transmitted diseases. It is still true that lesbians have fewer sexually transmitted illnesses than any other group. However, trichomonas, bacterial vaginosis, chlamydia, ureaplasma, herpes, hepatitis B, intestinal parasites, and HIV can be passed from one woman to another just through oral-genital sex and mutual masturbation, as well as through the sharing of sex toys that enter the vagina or anus. If a lesbian is diagnosed with one of these infections, her health care provider must give appropriate advice for the protection or screening or treatment of her lover, depending on the condition.

Most lesbians I know seem more concerned with protecting their partner than with self-protection. If given life-saving information, we will usually act upon it. Unlike the other diseases listed above, hepatitis B and HIV are not curable with medical intervention, and are potentially fatal.

We must spread the word that if you have injected drugs, had sex with a man without using a condom, had a needle stick or blood exposure injury since 1981, had a blood transfusion in the United States from 1981 to July 1985 or in another country since 1981; or if you are not sure your past women partners are not at risk in any of these ways, you should practice safer sex.

There is disagreement among health care providers as to what constitutes "safe." The basis of this disagreement is that woman-to-woman oral-genital sex is extremely low risk (if neither partner has bleeding gums, mouth sores, genital sores, a vaginal discharge, or her menstrual period), but not completely without risk. Several woman-to-woman HIV cases are reported by lesbian clinics in the United States each year. Millions of lesbians have unprotected oral sex. The health authorities declare it is safe but have done no research. Lesbian health providers do agree that you should not touch blood; should cover with a condom any sex toys you intend to share; and should not pierce the skin with anything someone else has used. Many also advise you to cover your lover's vulva with a latex square or name-brand plastic wrap during oral sex

to avoid contact with vaginal fluids. A water-based lubricant on her side will give you, though dry, a sensation of moisture and add to her pleasure.

You can cut a latex glove to make a barrier that is larger, thinner, and easier to purchase than the old-fashioned dental dam. This is done by cutting off the fingers of the glove, then cutting along the back end nearest the pinky finger hole. When you open it up, it will be a square with a thumb in the middle, to insert into the vagina.

For women developing a monogamous relationship, and who have no recent risk factors, taking an HIV test together is an act of loving commitment. If both women are negative, they no longer need to use latex with each other.

Lesbian and bisexual women who have multiple partners should work on (or play with) eroticizing safe sex and making it a part of life, and should also consider taking the hepatitis B vaccine. Hot, sex-positive educational materials have been developed specifically for us.

8. As we get older, we face cancer and coronary disease, quite possibly to a greater degree than heterosexual women. As no large-scale studies have been done on lesbians in the past twenty years (indeed, few have been done on women), this statement is based on known risk factors, not on observed statistics.

More lesbians may be smokers, and smokers are more prone to lung, head and neck, and cervical cancer, emphysema and heart attack. Smoking cessation programs will save lesbian lives.

The alarming rise in breast cancer is the most urgent health concern of women in the United States today. Women who were never pregnant or had the first pregnancy over the age of thirty; who eat a high fat diet; who drink excessive amounts of alcohol; or who are very much over ideal body weight, are at higher risk of breast cancer. Clearly, this "profile" fits many lesbians.

Again, due to lack of research, lifestyle changes have not been proven to reduce breast cancer risk. Many lesbians with a family history of breast cancer are eating a diet low in fat and known food carcinogens, and avoiding toxic chemicals in the home. Breast self-examination and, at menopause or age fifty, yearly mammograms save lives through early diagnosis. Women with a family history, or who are over forty with difficult-to-examine breasts or other risk factors, may want to see a breast specialist yearly, and mammography after forty may be recommended.

The women's breast cancer movement, in which lesbians are playing a leading role, is also looking at the larger environment, with the strong suspicion that chemical and nuclear wastes and industrial pollution may play a part. Political, as well as individual, action may be what is needed.

Resources

Community Health Project, 208 W. 13th St., New York, NY 10011, 212-675-3559. New York's lesbigay clinic. Published *Lesbian Health Fair* manual in 1993.

Dr. Susan Love's Breast Book, by Susan Love, M.D.

Gay and Lesbian Medical Association, 273 Church St., San Francisco, CA 94114, 415-255-4547. Lesbian and gay physicians' organization. Its Lesbian Health Foundation funds research on lesbians.

Lavender Lamps, 208 W. 13th St., New York, NY 10011, 212-933-1158. National lesbigay nurses' organization.

Lesbian AIDS Project at Gay Men's Health Crisis, 129 W. 20th St., New York, NY 10011, 212-337-3532. AIDS advocacy organization. Published "Rites of Passion," a sexually explicit lesbian safe sex brochure.

Lesbian, Gay and Bisexual People in Medicine, c/o AMSA, 1890 Preston White Drive, Reston, VA 22091, 703-620-6600. Medical students' organization.

Lyon Martin Women's Health Services, 1748 Market St. #201, San Francisco, CA 94102, 415-565-7667. Lesbian clinic, research and educational organization. Published *Lesbian Health Care Information, Research, and Reports, 1993.*

Mautner Project for Lesbians with Cancer, 1633 Q St. N.W. #220, Washington, DC 20009, 202-667-2336. Mission includes advocacy, education, and direct service.

National Association of Lesbian and Gay Alcoholism Professionals, 1147 S. Alvarado St., Los Angeles, CA 90006, 213-381-8524.

National Breast Cancer Coalition, P.O. Box 98114, Washington, DC 20077-7347, 202-296-7477. A lobbying and educational group that publishes a newsletter.

National Center for Lesbian Rights, 462 Broadway #500A, New York, NY 10013, 212-343-9589. Lobbies on a national level for lesbian inclusion in medical research. Published *Lesbian Health Bibliography,* 1994.

National Lesbian and Gay Health Association, Box 65472, Washington, DC 20035, 202-939-7880. Sponsors an annual lesbigay health conference in which all health care professions are represented, and publishes a directory of lesbigay HCPs.

National Lesbian and Gay Task Force, 1734 14th St. N.W., Washington, DC 20009, 202-332-6483. Published *Lesbian Health Issues and Recommendations,* a lobbying tool, 1993.

National Women's Health Network, 1325 G St. N.W., Washington, DC 20005, 202-347-1140. Lobbying and education. Publishes the most up-to-date newsletter on controversies in women's health.

Pride Institute, 2445 Park Ave., Minneapolis, MN. 612-870-0833. An all-lesbigay alcohol and drug rehab program.

Safe is Desire, a lesbian safer sex theater piece on video.

Whitman Walker Clinic Lesbian Services, 1407 S St. N.W., Washington, DC 20009, 202-797-3500. Lesbian clinic with educational outreach.

Breast and Cervical Cancer Among Lesbians

Liza Rankow PA-C, MHS

Breast Cancer

It has been estimated that 182,000 new cases of breast cancer will be reported in the United States in 1994, and 46,000 women will die of the disease. Approximately one in eight women will develop breast cancer during her lifetime. It is unknown how many of these women will be lesbians. The exact causes of breast cancer are poorly defined. While there is some understanding of the conditions that may place women at increased risk of developing the disease, in the majority of diagnoses none of these identified risk factors are present. Risk factors for breast cancer can be divided into three groups: genetic, hormonal, and those related to external factors.

A woman is at increased risk if she has had breast cancer herself or has a family history of breast cancer in a first-degree relative—mother, sister, or daughter (or, far less commonly, a father, brother, or son). The genetic risk is greatest if the cancer occurred before menopause or was present in both breasts. Women who have their first menstrual period (menarche) at a young age, often described as before age twelve, or go through menopause after the age of fifty-five may be at increased risk. Women who have never had a child, or do not have children before their early thirties, also appear to have an elevated risk of developing breast cancer. There are several theories why this may be so. First, women who never have children go through more menstrual periods than women whose cycling is interrupted by pregnancy. As with early menarche and late menopause, the more years of menstrual cycling a woman experiences without interruption, the greater her risk. Another theory suggests that pregnancy and childbearing act to somehow mature the breast and make it less susceptible to changes that can lead to cancer. The years between the onset of menstrual periods and a woman's

first childbirth may represent a window of time during which dietary and environmental exposures can increase the risk of later developing breast cancer. Last, it has been suggested that under certain conditions the female hormone estrogen may have a role in breast cancer risk, especially at puberty and at menopause, times when the body's hormonal balance is in flux. While still somewhat controversial as risk factors, long-term estrogen exposure through oral contraceptives and estrogen replacement therapy, and high body weight (some estrogen is manufactured in the fatty tissue) may also relate to the amount of unopposed estrogen that is present in a woman's body over time.

Other factors that may increase the risk of breast cancer include alcohol consumption, particularly during the "window" of vulnerability described above, and possibly a diet high in fats. Finally, there is an increase in breast cancer among women who have received significant exposure to radiation. This has been noted specifically in women who received fluoroscopy treatments for tuberculosis, breast irradiation for mastitis (an inflammation of the breast, most common after childbirth), or radiation therapy for cancers such as Hodgkin's disease. There has not been an increased risk demonstrated by routine diagnostic chest X rays or screening mammograms.

The incidence of breast cancer increases with age, with three-quarters of cases occurring in women over fifty. The majority of women diagnosed with breast cancer have no risk factors present other than age. Given this fact, monthly breast self-exam, annual breast examination by a health care practitioner, and regular screening mammography are our best defense in the face of this epidemic. New advances in therapy have improved the chances for survival among women who are fortunate enough to receive timely diagnosis and have access to quality medical care.

Breast Cancer in Lesbians. The overall risk of breast cancer among lesbians is not known. There is evidence to suggest that some lesbians may be less likely to have children, and may have higher alcohol consumption and possibly higher body weight than heterosexual women. Lesbians who are estranged from their families because of their sexual orientation may not have access to accurate information about their families' medical histories.

Unfortunately, the research available has not

represented the full diversity of lesbians and other women who partner with women. Primarily younger (that is, twenty-five- to forty-five-year-old) white, well-educated, "out of the closet" lesbians have been sampled. Lesbians at perhaps greater risk of mortality due to limited access to cancer screening and appropriate medical care remain inadequately studied. These include, among others, older lesbians, lesbians of color, lesbians with disabilities, rural lesbians, and poor and working-class lesbians. Still, even among the comparatively "privileged" lesbians surveyed, dramatic barriers to cancer screening and medical services are evident.

Among those studied, lesbians received fewer mammogram and clinical breast exams, and were significantly less likely to perform regular breast self-examination than recommended by current standards of care. Lesbians share many of the same barriers to care experienced by all women. We are affected by lack of financial resources, inadequate insurance coverage, lack of transportation or child care, clinic hours of operation that conflict with work schedules, and language or literacy barriers. Self-care is often a lower priority compared to caring for others, and health *screening* is seen as an unnecessary "luxury" or "looking for trouble." Additional obstacles may be fear of painful, unknown, or embarrassing procedures, fear of test results (that is, finding cancer), and failure of health care providers to recommend screening. We are deterred by the racism, ageism, ableism, sexism, and class bias inherent in the medical system in this country.

Many lesbians avoid seeking health care because of negative experiences with homophobic practitioners. We may not know where to go to obtain affordable, competent, and sensitive care. Even sympathetic or supportive health care providers may be misinformed about the health needs of women who partner with women. For all of these reasons, lesbians may not receive medical care when it is needed. This delay in diagnosis and treatment can increase the severity and complexity of our disease by the time it is discovered, and therefore may increase our risk of dying.

On the Horizon. It is hoped that recently funded research initiatives that include lesbians will shed some light on the risk of breast cancer in our communities. Lesbian breast cancer projects around the country provide education and advocacy as well as direct services to lesbians with cancer and their loved ones. Cancer activists are working to increase state and federal funding of research and services to women who partner with women, as well as demanding exploration of possible links to environmental toxins, exposure to radioactive waste, and drugs and hormones in food that may relate to breast cancer incidence.

Cervical Cancer

While much remains unknown about the causes of breast cancer, the factors involved in the incidence of cervical cancer are better understood. Risk factors for cervical cancer include young age at onset of sexual activity, multiple past or present sexual partners (of either sex), history of sexually transmitted disease (STD), infection with certain strains of human papilloma virus (HPV—the virus that causes genital warts), exposure to DES in utero (DES is a drug that was given to pregnant women during the 1940s through the 1960s to help prevent miscarriage), cigarette smoking, and a history of abnormal Pap smears. Additionally, women who are HIV-positive appear to be at higher risk of developing cervical cancer.

Cervical cancer is a preventable disease. With regular Pap smears, cervical dysplasia (precancerous abnormal cell growth) can be found early and treated before cancer develops. Women die from cervical cancer when early changes in the cervix go undetected and untreated. *All* women should receive regular cervical cancer screening. The frequency of screening remains controversial, but should be based on an evaluation of each individual's risk and specific medical history. Many women assume that they are being screened for cervical cancer every time they have a pelvic exam or receive testing for an STD. This is often not the case, and it is important to clarify exactly what procedures are being done at each medical encounter.

Lesbians and Cervical Cancer

Research shows that lesbians are less likely than heterosexual women to receive routine Pap smear screening for cervical cancer. This is true even among lesbians with a past or current history of heterosexual intercourse, multiple sexual partners, and/or sexually transmitted diseases. Reasons for this include misinformation among both lesbians and health professionals about lesbian health care needs, and the false assumption that lesbians do not engage in behaviors that place us at risk. Health care providers often don't recommend screening for women who partner with women, and we ourselves may be unaware of our need for regular Pap smears. Lesbians less frequently require birth control or prenatal care than do heterosexual women, and are therefore less likely to receive routine preventive health care services. Some butch-identified lesbians may avoid cervical screening because of their discomfort with the vulnerability of an examination that requires vaginal penetration, particularly when performed by a male provider. Women who are survivors of sexual or other types of abuse may likewise have greater barriers to receiving pelvic examinations than women without that history. In addition, all of the barriers to care described in the discussion of breast cancer can affect cervical cancer screening as well.

While there has been increasing awareness of the importance of breast cancer research and services that address the needs of lesbians, the issue of cervical cancer among lesbians has remained largely invisible. This may be due in part to the stigma and silence surrounding a cancer associated with possible sexual transmission. Human papilloma virus (HPV), the causative factor in many cases of cervical cancer, can be spread through woman-to-woman sexual contact. Lesbians must be encouraged to adopt safer sex practices when needed to prevent the transmission of HPV and HIV (human immunodeficiency virus), thereby decreasing our cervical cancer risk.

What Is Needed?

Culturally competent outreach to *all* communities of women who partner with women is crucial, whether they self-identify as lesbians or not. Grassroots involvement of women from those communities is required to develop appropriate strategies for education, screening, and intervention. Regular screening for both breast and cervical cancer must be made accessible and sensitive to the needs of all women who partner with women.

Dedicated studies are needed to examine possible risks for cancer among lesbians. Specifically, these studies should accurately measure past and present alcohol and cigarette use, body mass (height and weight, as well as significant gains or losses), dietary fats, radiation and environmental exposures, use of oral contraceptives or hormone replacement therapy, menstrual and reproductive history, sexual history, and history of sexually transmitted diseases, including HIV. Clinically based research is needed on the transmission of STDs between female partners. Recruitment and inclusion of lesbians and women who partner with women should be mandatory in all women's health research, with questions regarding both sexual identity *and* behavior. Finally, education of the medical community must accurately address the health care needs and risks of lesbians and women who partner with women. Training is needed in conducting a sensitive, comprehensive, and culturally competent medical, social, and sexual history. Practitioners must understand the importance of appropriate screening and treatment guidelines tailored to each individual.

Resources

Lesbian Community Cancer Project, P.O. Box 138202, Chicago, IL 60613-1012, 312-561-4662.

The Mary Helen Mautner Project for Lesbians with Cancer, 1707 L St. N.W., Suite 1060, Washington, DC 20036, 202-332-5536 (Voice/TTY). Contact for the National Coalition of Feminist and Lesbian Cancer Projects.

Seattle Lesbian Cancer Project, 2732 NE 4th St., Seattle, WA 98015, 206-522-0199.

State Breast and Cervical Cancer Control Programs (funded by the Centers for Disease Control).

Women's Cancer Resource Center, 3023 Shattuck Ave., Berkeley, CA 94705, 510-548-9279.

Women's Community Cancer Project, 34 Day St., Somerville, MA 02144, 617-661-9313.

References

American Cancer Society. *Cancer Facts & Figures, 1994.* Atlanta, Ga., 1994.

American College of Obstetricians and Gynecologists. "Human Papillomavirus." Technical Bulletin #193, 1994.

Bradford, J., and C. Ryan. *The National Lesbian Health Care Survey.* Washington, D.C.: National Lesbian and Gay Health Foundation, 1987.

Butler, S., and B. Rosenblum. *Cancer in Two Voices.* San Francisco: Spinsters Books, 1991.

Denenberg, R. *Gynecological Care Manual for HIV-positive Women.* Durant, Okla.: Essential Medical Information Systems, 1993.

Denenberg, R. "I'm Gay, So Why Do I Need a Pap Smear." Lesbian AIDS Project Notes #2 (Spring 1994), 8 [Lesbian AIDS Project at GMHC, 129 W. 20th St., NY, NY 10011, 212-337-3532].

Henderson, I. C. "Risk Factors for Breast Cancer Development." *Cancer* 71, no. 6 (1993): 2,127–40.

Horton, J. A., ed. *The Women's Health Data Book: A Profile of Women's Health in the United States.* Washington, D.C.: Jacobs Institute of Women's Health, 1992.

Love, S. *Dr. Susan Love's Breast Book.* New York: Addison-Wesley, 1990.

Rankow, E. J. "Breast and Cervical Cancer Among Lesbians." *Women's Health Issues* 5, no. 3 (1995).

Rankow, E. J. "Lesbian Health Issues for the Primary Care Provider." *Journal of Family Practice* 40, no. 5 (1995): 486–93.

Stefanek, M. E. "Counseling Women at High Risk for Breast Cancer." *Oncology* 4, no. 1 (1990): 27–38.

Stevens, P. E., and J. M. Hall. "Stigma, Health Beliefs, and Experiences with Health Care in Lesbian Women." *Journal of Nursing Scholarship* 20, no. 3 (1988): 69–73.

(Note: The author wishes to thank Laura J. Ramos MPH, DrPH candidate, for her editorial comments in the preparation of this article.)

Getting Pregnant Through Donor Insemination

Barbara Raboy

The small but cheerful room is crowded with women, some in couples, others seated alone. Some of the women are in business suits, having arrived directly from work; others are more casually dressed. Two more women arrive but there are no more seats, so the leader of this group leaves to get a few more chairs. The extra chairs arrive and now the session begins. The leader, a health worker, welcomes everyone to the orientation session of the Donor Insemination Program at The Sperm Bank. These women are planning to join the increasing numbers of lesbians who choose to become parents, a phenomenon that some call "the lesbian baby boom."

Historically, donor insemination has occurred primarily through the medical establishment for the benefit of childless heterosexual couples. Even today, one need only peruse the medical literature specializing in fertility and infertility to experience the plethora of interest directed at infertile heterosexual couples. Lesbians and single women, however, have been largely denied access to medical establishment insemination services as well as infertility services. Discrimination against lesbians continues to be common practice. However, with the increased visibility of reproductive technology and a concomitant cultural change in the definition of the family, there has been a significant increase in the frequency of requests from lesbians and single women to be inseminated.

Donor insemination for lesbians is not new; it has been practiced within the lesbian community for decades. In the sixties and seventies, lesbians desiring pregnancy often asked a friend to locate a gay man who would be willing to donate sperm. It was common to see ads in local gay newspapers soliciting sperm donors. Semen samples from different donors were often mixed to minimize the donor's interest in the insemination outcome and to diminish his ability to claim paternity. These types of private arrangements remained, in a sense, "underground." Attorneys were usually not consulted. Contracts between the donor and recipient were only occasionally drawn up. Doctors and other health professionals were rarely consulted. If a woman were fortunate enough to live near a women's health center, or to know of a women's self-help group, she could probably get hold of a plastic speculum and learn how to study her cervix and cervical mucus, thereby determining her most fertile time. In a few areas, lay midwives offered assistance. Another alternative was to attend a natural family planning class, where women were instructed when not to have intercourse, "or else." Thus they learned when to inseminate. A few pamphlets addressing the mechanics of insemination were scattered about in some women's bookstores. When books were not available, women learned about insemination through word of mouth. Women learned how to inseminate with a syringe, eye dropper, or turkey baster. Many children were conceived by late-night drop-offs of semen in glass jars.

More recently we have been seeing a movement away from the grassroots, underground experience I've described above to one based in health care delivery. This shift is being driven by health and legal issues. The Acquired Immune Deficiency Syndrome (AIDS) epidemic has reduced the number of gay men who are eligible to donate semen. The AIDS epidemic has also contributed to an increase in the use of frozen semen while the use of fresh semen is decreasing. It is estimated that 50 percent of all gay men currently living in San Francisco are infected with the human immunodeficiency virus (HIV), the virus that causes AIDS. Currently, all sperm banks in the United States are required to quarantine donor semen for a minimum of six months. The sperm banks are required to obtain a negative HIV antibody test on the donor prior to releasing the semen.

The AIDS epidemic is helping to reshape the practice of donor insemination. Deciding to inseminate through a medical or health facility or sperm bank entails completing a comprehensive informed consent form in which it is explained that AIDS and other sexually transmitted diseases can be transmitted through semen. Many donor insemination practices require both the recipient and partner to be tested for HIV antibodies, which was unheard of five years ago.

In the legal arena, battles continue to be fought involving paternity and custody rights and the enforceability of contracts between a donor and recipient. Just a few years ago a sperm donor, known to a recipient, was awarded part custody of a child conceived from his sperm donation. In this particular case, the recipient and donor had known each other as friends and had not drawn up a contract. The judge ruled that the donor did have an interest in the child from an early time in the child's life, and that since a physician had not been involved in the insemination process, the donor was considered the legal father. Experiences like these have contributed to an increased request for donor insemination through sperm banks and other medical facilities. There has never been a legal contest between a sperm donor and recipient in California if a physician or sperm bank has acted as an intermediary.

Donor insemination is an effective method, providing a woman is fertile and the insemination is timed close to ovulation (release of an egg from an ovary). For most women, ovulation occurs about twelve to sixteen days before the first day of the menstrual period.

Many women opt to have an evaluation of their fertility before beginning the insemination process. The three most common fertility signs to check and chart are: (1) basal body temperature, which is body temperature after at least three hours of uninterrupted sleep; (2) changes in the amount, color, and texture of cervical mucus; and (3) changes in the diameter and position of the cervical opening, the os. Women can teach themselves the skills of checking and charting their fertility signs in a variety of ways: reading books; taking fertility awareness classes; or for women who find it difficult to predict ovulation, purchasing over-the-counter ovulation predictor kits, which are available at most drug stores and range from twenty-five dollars to sixty dollars per kit.

Insemination techniques themselves also vary. A vaginal-pool insemination is the simplest. Commonly done at home, it requires a sterile syringe, which is inserted into the vagina and directed towards the top part of the cervix. With this technique, the sperm is allowed to move through the cervical canal, the uterus, and into the fallopian tube to fertilize the egg.

An intrauterine insemination (I.U.I.) is often performed when a woman is experiencing a problem with her vaginal or cervical mucus that would make the vaginal-pool technique difficult to implement. As intrauterine insemination must be done using sterile technique, this type of insemination is considered a medical procedure and is therefore performed in a physician's office by a licensed medical professional. Typically, the practitioner places about 0.3 cc of semen into the uterus by using an intracervical catheter. The client is usually able to get up in a few minutes after this procedure.

How often a woman would need or want to inseminate depends on the length and variation of the fertile time and the availability of semen samples. Most women inseminate two times per cycle and become pregnant within one year or twelve cycle attempts. Overall pregnancy rates for donor insemination are between 60 and 80 percent. The miscarriage rate experienced with donor insemination is similar to that occurring throughout the population, averaging 20–25 percent.

Since 1982 the Sperm Bank of California has been serving women and couples throughout the United States and Canada. Its programs include donor insemination, private sperm storage, directed donor screening, screened semen for physician practices, semen analysis, fertility awareness classes, confidential HIV antibody screening, and health education. It currently distributes semen samples throughout the United States, Canada, South America, and Europe. The Sperm Bank is staffed with health educators, lab technicians, a licensed physician, and legal counsel. The Sperm Bank is a nonprofit, community-based health care facility. It became the first sperm bank to publicly open its doors to lesbians.

Since its inception, roughly one-third of the insemination clients are lesbian, one-third are single heterosexual women, and one-third are married heterosexual couples. In 1992 it reported a cumulative pregnancy rate of 68 percent (based on a one-year experience of timed inseminations).

The Donor Insemination Program (DIP) has a strong basis in self-help, health awareness and promotion, and self-insemination. The DIP includes an orientation fertility awareness class, comprehensive medical evaluation, and inseminations.

The recipient selects the sperm donor by studying the medical chart on each donor. Donors are given the option as to whether or not The Sperm Bank can release the donor's identity to resulting offspring when he or she reaches the age of eighteen. This option, known as "identity release," is a popular option for the majority of lesbians using

The Sperm Bank. The Sperm Bank also sponsors anonymous donors. All recipients and donors enter into formal legal agreements with The Sperm Bank for mutual protection.

The current practice of The Sperm Bank is to screen each donor applicant for a variety of health and fertility factors. All semen samples are held in the frozen state for a minimum of six months, at which time the donor is retested for antibodies to HIV. All sperm donors, once approved, are required to donate for a minimum of one year. During that year they are periodically retested. The Sperm Bank's policy is to permit no more than ten offspring per donor. Women who have their own donors can have The Sperm Bank perform screening on their donors as described above.

The Sperm Bank acknowledges issues about which some lesbian mothers have expressed concern. The staff is currently conducting research on the psycho-social aspects of raising donor-inseminated children in the context of a lesbian relationship. Some of the questions being raised today are:

1. How long do the adult relationships last?

2. What role does the nonbiological mother play and how secure is she in the family?

3. What would happen to the nonbiological mother's relationship with the child if the couple breaks up?

4. What type of legal documents are being drawn up for lesbian relationships and how are they affecting both the adult relationship and the child's life?

5. What are the dynamics of raising more than one child?

6. Which coping skills do lesbian mothers need to develop?

7. What issues do children who are raised in lesbian homes confront when making and keeping friends and in attending school? How well are these children integrated in the community?

There are many issues for lesbians considering parenthood. For some women the primary issue is deciding on a type of donor to select. For others, the issue is legal protection for the future child and whether to work with an anonymous donor or a known donor. If you would like to begin researching this complex decision, receive literature, or if you have questions or just want someone to talk to, the staff of The Sperm Bank would like to hear from you. They can be reached at 415-444-2014. Their address is Telegraph Hill Medical Plaza, 3007 Telegraph Avenue, Suite 2, Oakland, CA 94609.

Further Reading

Benkov, L. *Reinventing the Family*. New York: Crown, 1994.

Hammond, K. F., and B. K. Annesse. *Fertility Awareness Manual: An Instructional Guide for Clients*. San Francisco: James Bowman Associates, 1989.

Hitchono, D. *Donor Insemination: A Legal Summary*. New York: Lambda Legal Defense and Education Fund, 1984.

Martin, A. *The Lesbian and Gay Parenting Handbook*. New York: HarperCollins, 1993.

Noble, E. *Having Your Baby by Donor Insemination*. Boston: Houghton Mifflin, 1987.

Office of Technology Assessment. *Artificial Insemination Practice in the United States*. Background Paper. U.S. Congress, Washington, D.C. 20510-8025, August 1988.

Pies, C. *Considering Parenthood*. San Francisco: Spinsters Ink, 1985.

Wolf, M. "Checking Out the Sperm Bank." *Gaybook* (Winter 1990): 8–13.

Chemical Dependency:

The Journey Home

R. Elaine Noble

The field of chemical abuse research is about twenty-five years old. It is only in the last decade that women were included in this research. Sadly, lesbians have been the focus of studies only within the last few years, and most of these studies were not conducted within a rigorous scientific framework. One can think of several reasons for this, but regardless of competing hypotheses, it is almost surely the case that examining the lesbian and her addiction problem is not valued by society.

This is not surprising. A little girl is born into this culture with expectations of becoming a wife or a mother. Women now have a professional life, but the societal values that still pervade our attitudes can easily become internalized and guilt soon follows, producing a lesbian who hates herself and despises other lesbians.

My purpose in writing this article, however, is not to examine the meager literature on lesbians and their addictions, but rather to shed some light on lesbians and gay men within a treatment context. Most successful treatment programs are based in a strong foundation of research. Without such a foundation, treatment programs are suspect.

I am currently developing a sixty-bed treatment program for lesbians and gay men to be situated in Lynn, Massachusetts, called The Journey Home. Since I helped create the first treatment center for gay women and men in Minnesota a few years ago, as well as helping other treatment centers create an atmosphere in which gay people could be treated properly, I have a reasonably well-informed idea of what treatment is like for us as gay people. All of these treatment programs strive for a "gay sensitive" environment in which gay men and lesbians can be treated equally with heterosexuals.

What I have come to believe deeply, however, is that combining gay and straight populations within a treatment center typically does not work for a gay person. In this setting, lesbians and gay men do not feel safe and often do not disclose their lifestyles. Their treatment plans then are often not successful because they go through a twenty-one or twenty-eight day program not participating fully but instead enacting a charade.

There is also an unusual philosophy that pervades many treatment centers. Alcoholics and drug addicts are not acceptable for treatment if they show an inability to control their drinking or drugging. That is, alcoholics are not acceptable there if they show evidence of the problems that bring them to the treatment center in the first place. Ludwig, in his book, *Understanding the Alcoholic Mind,* also refers to this practice: "The catch-22 is that they must remain sober to receive help.... Alcoholics are regarded as sick—at least for purposes of hospitalization or treatment, but society tends to hold them responsible for their transgressions or crimes."

Often, a person who is unable to exhibit a certain type of behavior within a treatment center is discharged for "setting a bad example" for other participants," or "not cooperating in a group" and other such vagaries. It is no wonder that about 70 percent of alcoholics relapse within the first three months after discharge and 90 percent relapse by eighteen months after discharge (Ludwig, p. 51). If this rate is so high among the heterosexual population, one can understand why insurance companies, employers, and family members are questioning the validity of in-treatment programs.

One question comes to mind: If this model is not working effectively for the straight population, can it be working for lesbians and gay men? These questions are very personal to me. Nine years ago, I had a new relationship and there were fewer pressures to drink than ever before. Yet I allowed a therapist to convince me that "a stay" in an inpatient center would be of great help to me. I am not suggesting that I did not learn about my chemical addiction problem. However, as I look back on this experience in this "gay sensitive" treatment program, I now know I could have been treated much more humanely and cost-effectively on an outpatient level at a good lesbian counseling center. I was six months sober when I entered the treatment center.

What I learned from my own experience is that gay men and women do not fare very well in such programs. I was told to be honest about my lesbianism within a group context, and when I disclosed who and what I was, I faced hostility and shock from other group members and a group leader who said my lesbianism "is not important here." I did not participate in this group again.

I noticed that the 12 gay men and women within the 120-patient population were "staffed" more frequently than the other patients and more severely. Staffing is a form of emotional gang rape in which all the therapists surround a patient, taunting, asking rapid-firing questions, circling, yelling until the patient "breaks." It is commonly felt that only after a patient "breaks" that effective treatment can begin.

As Ludwig has pointed out, this form of treatment contributes to alcoholics leading shriveled lives and eliminates all risk-taking behavior. In fact, many others like myself find this treatment as abhorrent as the once widely used technique of electric shock, applied to an alcoholic when she or he tasted or smelled of alcohol.

After consulting a dozen major inpatient centers in the United States, I have come to believe that there is a world of difference between a "gay sensitive" treatment program and a "lesbian and gay affirmative" program. I believe it is almost impossible to train staff, administration, community, and heterosexual patients to a level of "sensitivity" toward lesbians and gay men that would enable successful recovery, especially now, in the midst of the AIDS crisis.

The addition of a gay or lesbian into a heterosexual therapy group sends emotional shock waves that greatly change the dynamics of therapy. It takes a very sophisticated therapist to keep the group from abusing the lesbian or gay group member. In the family program within a heterosexually oriented center, often the gay couple becomes the focus of the family group, making the gay family members inappropriately uncomfortable and permitting the heterosexual family members to "defocus" on their own serious issues. Once again, it takes a highly skilled therapist to handle these situations. My observations lead me to believe that as many as three out of four situations involving lesbian or gay clients are not handled well within a heterosexual treatment center. The concept of a "gay sensitive" program may be a myth existing only for marketing purposes.

The concept of a treatment center for a homogeneous population is not a new idea. Treatment centers for the black population and Native American population have shown a great deal of success. It is in this context that I began exploring the concept of a treatment center for lesbians and gay men that is *created, owned, and operated* by lesbians and gay men. A gay affirmative program can actually exist.

My experience has been that heterosexuals who own failing treatment centers want us to fill their beds, but do not wish to "share the corporate chair." It is important that we create, own, and operate our own health structures because no one else can better take our interests to heart. If I learned anything during my years in government service, it is this. If an issue does not affect your life, you do not take it seriously. Several treatment facilities guided by these ideas need to be developed. I am currently developing such a program myself. I encourage others to do so as well.

The environment in which we help each other probably should not be a hospital or dormitory setting, but rather a homelike setting that says to each person who stays there, "You are part of an accepting group, you are special, and you are unique." Each lesbian and gay man should be called a "client," not a patient. No one need wear uniforms and the staff need not be readily distinguished from clients. Each aspect of the physical environment, the staff, and the therapy should be designed to promote a feeling of self-efficacy in each client. In my facility, The Journey Home, program and staff training is based on twenty years' worth of research done by Dr. Ellen Langer of Harvard University. Dr. Langer's latest book, *Mindfulness,* states our objective in treatment.

Mindfulness is learning how to be situated in the present. It is drawing new distinctions. It is being sensitive to context. Mindlessness, on the other hand, is the reliance on categories and distinctions that were drawn in the past and an insensitivity to context. When mindful, the individual is aware and flexible; when mindless, the individual is rigid by default rather than by design. The mindful individual is creative and comes to understand that "risk-taking" is not as risky as previously thought.

Langer maintains that mindlessness is much more pervasive than most people assume. In a sense, people are "just not there." They do not know how the context determines their behavior. Hence, as long as they are mindless, they are powerless to change when the contexts they find themselves in are leading them to destructive, maladaptive behavior.

When discussing health issues in her book, Langer explores her ideas and research on addiction. Her work has shown that changing a person's context concerning his or her drinking or drug problem offers new optimism for treatment of chemical addictions that are often viewed as intractable. Her book is well worth reading for any lesbian or gay man with or without chemical dependence, because mindfulness shows us how to give new meaning to old stereotypes.

As for me, if my life holds any value it is in taking what society views as "bad" and trying to make it into something that is meaningful and a "good" part of the process Langer would call "mindful." My coming out in the late sixties led me to create the first gay radio program, called "Gay Way," and later, to run and get elected as a Massachusetts State representative, as the first openly gay person elected in the United States. It is my hope that by giving positive meaning to my life, someone else may be helped. And, so it is in dealing with chemical addiction, by creating this facility, by examining what has been so successful to me that I hope to help other lesbians and gay men. We are all on the same journey, the journey back to a more mindful and healthful self. As some point, we all embark on this journey . . . the journey home.

Recovering Alcoholics:

Alice and Sally

Edited by Eleanor F. Wedge

What has Alcoholics Anonymous meant to you?

Sally: I think that AA saved my life, and the principles of the program probably always will be the foundation of my life. AA teaches you skills in daily living. Perhaps most fundamentally it's a spiritual program, not in any organized or formal sense. That spiritual element, of believing there is something greater than yourself (whatever you want to call that), I think is crucial to one's recovery, and has been to mine.

But also, if it weren't for the gay movement, I don't think I ever would have stopped drinking. One night in 1970 I was listening to "Lesbian Nation" on WBAI, and they announced that there was this new gay community center in Greenwich Village. So I went down there—it was the Gay Liberation Front—and I met this woman who told me about AA, about alcoholism, and confronted me about my drinking. Shortly afterward she took me to my first AA meeting, in the Village.

The fact that this was predominantly a gay meeting meant a great deal to me, because all throughout the sixties I had struggled terrifically with my sexuality, like a lot of people, and my drinking was very much wrapped up with coming to terms with myself as a sexual being. Now I'm sure that I would have been an alcoholic no matter what. Anyway, I went back to some meetings although I continued to drink. And then one evening after work I met this woman again and she asked, "Have you had a drink today?" I answered, "Not yet." And she said, "Ah, you have your first day."

I had really done something incredible by not having a drink, because for years I had been waking up swearing I was never going to drink again, but usually by late afternoon I had already started. For the first two or three years I was in AA I wanted desperately to drink, but I'd heard enough about the progressiveness of the disease of alcoholism to know that I couldn't drink safely. Another reason I never drank again was that it was so hard getting sober the first time.

After I was sober maybe two years the first gay AA meeting started. I went a few times, but it was mostly men and did not fill my needs as a lesbian. So in 1973 I got together with a couple of other women and we started the first lesbian meeting. That was a very important group for all of us, and especially for women who were still actively drinking and then found there was a lesbian AA meeting they could come to.

In addition to staying sober I established friendships with many people in the program and came out of my isolation. Because drinking is a very isolating disease, whether you're in a bar or at home alone. Part of being in AA is that it is a fellowship, and you develop a sense of community with other people. And that is still true for me. Also, AA is, as they say, a bridge back to life. As the years have gone by I've become active in other areas. But I still go to maybe one meeting a week, and the contacts I have outside the meetings with other AA people are crucial to me.

What was so bad about your problem with alcohol that you were motivated to participate in AA?

Sally: I come from a family of very religious Protestants, teetotalers. My mother's father had been an alcoholic, and she was convinced that if I drank I would become one. So when I was young one of my greatest ambitions was to leave home and learn how to drink. Also, as a youngster, I think I had an unusual physical response to alcohol. My mother once gave me some Terpin Hydrate for a cold. It was absolutely terrible-tasting stuff, loaded with alcohol and codeine, but when it hit my stomach this warm, relaxing glow spread throughout my body. My mother kept the bottle on the kitchen window sill, and I remember sneaking in and taking swigs out of it.

When I left for college I started to drink. Not a lot, but every couple of weekends. And once I had a drink I spent the rest of the evening thinking about whether I would be able to continue to drink, and whether other people would notice how much I was drinking. So from the very beginning my drinking wasn't social, normal, having one or two drinks to relax.

And then when I was a senior in college I fell in love with a classmate. But it only lasted a couple of months. I was in such a state of grief and depression over losing this woman, and also coming out and graduating—it all sort of hit at the same time—that I just jumped into a bottle of Scotch and began to drink as much and as often as I could.

After a few months of this I said to myself, "Sally, if you don't get some help you're going to succeed in drinking yourself to death." And I went into therapy at that point. About six years went by, and even though I was better emotionally my drinking was getting worse—just because time was passing. The addiction always gets worse.

Did it interfere with your functioning, with your work?

Sally: You know, huge, dramatic things did not happen to me because of my drinking. It was much more of a quiet desperation. And I think that is real common with alcoholics or any kind of substance abusers. Most of the people around me didn't realize I had a drinking problem. I functioned relatively well on the outside. I was able to get to work almost every day even though I was hung over. And I didn't usually drink during the day. So, no, I didn't get fired. The drinking didn't interfere with my health in any permanent way, but I had terrible, vicious hangovers. I'd wake up in the morning and be sick as a dog until about two in the afternoon. I remember some mornings walking down the street holding onto the sides of buildings. But in some ways that pain was preferable to the inner, emotional pain. It's funny, but it sort of helped me survive. I could deal with it; it was a manageable, tangible thing. But the drinking was ruining me.

Alice, how did you become involved in AA?

Alice: Unlike Sally, I *had* lost jobs over drinking. There were times I wouldn't get to sleep until six in the morning, and there was no way I could wake up and get to work. But I was never a daily drinker. I would go on binges, drink for ten or twelve hours at a time and often wake up in my car somewhere, and it was daylight. I thought for many years that I was drinking over my sexuality. Although I loved being a lesbian I hated being a lesbian in this world.

By 1967 or so I was not getting through a week without getting drunk. I could never predict what the outcome of my drinking would be. I gave up the notion that I could control myself. And I would have mood changes. I would cry; I would get hostile; I would fight with people.

Anyhow, one day I was in bed and I heard on the TV: "If you have a problem with drinking, call this number." And it was AA. I got up; I couldn't stand upright—I had a terrible hangover—so I crawled across to the telephone and called, and they told me where there was a meeting. I don't remember a whole lot about the meeting except they said to keep coming back. Somehow I grabbed onto that, and I went for a few weeks. During that time I learned that in fact I was an alcoholic, and that if I didn't pick up the *first* drink I wouldn't get drunk. Anyway, I cleared up a little bit and I decided that although there was no way I was about to tell this group I was a lesbian (this was Queens, in 1967), this was a place to come to if the drinking ever got to be too bad. Meanwhile, I was going to try to get sober by myself. So for six years I became this person who could go for months without a drink. But then a feeling would come over me and I'd have a three- or four-day bash; I'd spend all my money, raise all sorts of havoc.

Meantime, I had joined the lesbian movement. One day I was in a bar after a Lesbian Feminist Liberation meeting, and it struck me that I wasn't really feeling bad about being gay, yet here I was getting drunk again the same old way. It wasn't learning to accept myself or waiting for the world to accept me that was going to cure me. I really just had to stop drinking and then work on what was left.

In any event, I went to this LFL demonstration in 1973 and someone there said, "There's this great thing starting, a lesbian AA meeting." I knew I had to go to it. I had no further excuse. It wasn't like I couldn't tell these lesbians that I was a lesbian!

So the day of the meeting I had what I knew was going to be my last beer. I didn't stand back like I did the first time I went to AA, but I didn't really want to socialize. I was so closed and really afraid of people; you couldn't get anywhere near me. I went once a week for a while; then, because I was afraid it was just a matter of time before I would be drinking again, I started to go more frequently.

It bothered me in the beginning, a lot of things they said—like, "It's one day at a time." I knew they meant, "You're not supposed to drink forever." Or that drinking was a disease. I was sure it was just a matter of will power. But people were so open and giving of themselves that after a while I believed them.

I had all this conflict, and then one day I was sitting at a meeting and I began to cry; and then I knew it wasn't just them and me anymore, but I was part of it, and it was us. I became more receptive and I had a year of very hard work on myself. Not that I haven't worked hard since, but that first year of sobriety was the hardest and most painful.

A couple of things were difficult for me in my recovery. One, I didn't think I was worth anything. I never remember having had any self-esteem. Going to AA meetings and working the program gave me the opportunity to collect some. I found people were interested in what I had to say. The other area that I had to work on was how I felt about myself as a woman—dealing with those so-called womanly qualities I didn't like: passivity, the need to be protected.

But the biggest single thing AA has taught me is that what I used to believe to be absolutely true might not be true. It's given me a sense of humor about myself. Things just don't matter the way they did. And that's a relief.

How has AA added to or help in your relationship?

Sally: It's been essential to know that there's something for each of us more important even than our relationship, and beyond it. It helps put things into perspective. The other thing is that it's given us guidelines on how to treat ourselves—so that I try not to be abusive or hurtful to myself because that certainly is not part of any healing program. And we try to do that with each other.

Alice: I remember seeing Sally at the first meetings I went to and thinking, "She's my type, but I'm going to stay away from her." I knew that I would get so interested in her that I would not be able to do what I was there to do. I had a crush on her, but

I knew that if I pressed anything it might push her away, and I didn't want to lose her as a friend. And they say in AA not to make major changes for at least a year—not to get involved. When I was sober one year and two days we became lovers.

Sally: That's the other thing that's been so important in our relationship, that we were close friends before we became lovers.

How did you finally get together?

Sally: I'd had a lot of affairs based on lust or fantasy, and these lasted only a few weeks or months. It seemed too scary to combine good friendship and affection with sex. But then a few months later I was ready. I still have a lot of fears, though, about commitment—being committed without being suffocated.

Alice: I have the opposite problem. When Sally feels claustrophobic she pulls away. When I feel her pull away I move forward and cling. But I learned that if I did that to Sally she'd leave. And, in fact, now I know I'm a whole person and Sally's a whole person, but it's still a marriage. The program has taught me that even if she left me there's nothing I can do to stop it. It would be real painful, but I have the resources now to survive.

Sally: Applying the principles of AA to our relationship includes living a day at a time—not projecting that we'll be together forever, but concentrating on the fact that we're together now. And if we have conflicts we try to work together to come up with solutions—it's not a matter of who's winning or losing.

Did AA affect your professional lives?

Alice: Oh, yeah. I was a barmaid most of my years, and I knew I couldn't do that anymore so I became an assistant bookkeeper. Not drinking, I had a lot more time and energy, so I went to night school, took accounting courses. After a year I got a job as a full-charge bookkeeper. Eventually I took another job with the understanding that I would succeed the vice president when he retired. But I didn't get the promotion—strictly because I was a woman. I felt devastated and humiliated, but within three months I made a decision to go into business for myself as an accountant.

Sally: My recovery has had a profound influence on who I am and how I work. I was in the social work field and then left it, doing odd jobs for a while. After I was sober a couple of years I went back into social work via alcoholism counseling. I finished my master's degree after I was sober four years. That was one thing drinking had interfered with; I'd had to drop out after completing one year of the master's program. Eventually, after I got my MSW and CSW degrees, I decided I would go into private practice and do the kind of work I like within the gay community. I work with a lot of people who have substance-abuse problems or who are in the AA program. Most of my clients are lesbians.

Well, the AA program has transformed both of your lives.

Resources

Alcoholics Anonymous, AA World Services, P.O. Box 459, Grand Central Station, New York, NY 10017.

Gay and Lesbian Alcoholics: A.A.'s Message of Hope, Hazelden Educational Materials, Pleasant Valley Road, P.O. Box 176, Center City, MN 55012-0176.

Renee Gosselin and Suzanne Nice, *Lesbian and Gay Issues in Early Recovery,* Hazelden Educational Materials, Pleasant Valley Road, P.O. Box 176, Center City, MN 55012-0176.

Sheppard B. Kominars, *Accepting Ourselves: The 12-Step Journey of Recovery from Addiction for Gay Men and Lesbians,* Harper and Row: New York, 1989.

The Invisibility of Lesbians with AIDS

Anne Harris

(Editor's Note: There is very little medical documentation of woman-to-woman sexual transmission of AIDS. But a significant number of women who identify primarily as lesbians have contracted AIDS through intravenous drug use or heterosexual sex. Anne Harris interviewed Amber Hollibaugh, director of the Lesbian AIDS Project at the Gay Men's Health Crisis, based in New York City. An earlier version of this article appeared in Network *magazine, July 1994, pp. 23–26.)*

In April 1992, more than ten years into the AIDS epidemic, and nine months before the Centers for Disease Control expanded its definition of AIDS widely enough to include *any* of the opportunistic diseases that affect HIV-positive women, Amber Hollibaugh helped form the Lesbian AIDS Project (LAP) at Gay Men's Health Crisis, and began a new chapter in the fight against HIV/AIDS.

The program is one of a kind. "There are other lesbian health programs that have an HIV component," says Hollibaugh, "and a lot of tired lesbians running around doing the work, but there is no other fully staffed and running program, as far as we know, in the world."

Despite disproportionately increasing numbers of women with AIDS in this country, researchers and health care workers have been slow to respond. AIDS cases among women in the United Sates rose 9.8 percent in 1992, while cases among men rose 2.5 percent. Nevertheless, apart from staff at centers such as Gay Men's Health Crisis, few people were noticing, and those who did notice didn't recognize what they were seeing.

"The Lesbian AIDS Project was supported by lesbians at GMHC for a year before the project started. A lot of us were doing regular AIDS work in the community, in every diverse community you can find, and we kept running across dykes who were HIV-positive. Nobody seemed to notice. Everybody kept saying, 'Lesbians don't get AIDS,' and we'd look at the stacks of files on our desks and say, 'I know the agency says lesbians don't get AIDS, but how come I've got seven cases?' "

By November 1993, 40 percent of AIDS cases worldwide were among women, and three out of four women in this country with AIDS were women of color. The few available statistics offer cryptic clues about the persistent invisibility of the lesbian AIDS population: By and large, HIV-positive women comprise preexisting minorities of gender, race, class, and sexuality.

While HIV-positive women do get many of the same infections that their male counterparts experience, hormonal differences in women create different absorption rates of medicine. And as almost all AIDS research has been conducted with white male subjects, much of what is known about AIDS and immunodeficiency disease in general is not specific to women's bodies.

To complicate matters, many lesbians are not comfortable coming out to their doctors and nurses. For many women who are closeted for economic reasons, who are bisexually active because they cannot afford to leave their husbands or families to live permanently with female lovers, who risk losing their children and extended families for an admission of homosexuality and/or HIV, or who have sex with men for money or drugs, the reality of being an "out lesbian" is remote. For these women, coming out to doctors and health care workers can be a dangerous—if not impossible—task. As economics, race, and drug addiction blur the lines of sexual identity, the invisibility of HIV and lesbianism in these women's communities becomes more and more entrenched. For many, the silence and isolation is unbearable.

Amber Hollibaugh has been working with HIV-positive men and women for more than ten years. Her recently completed film, *The Heart of the Matter,* about lesbians and AIDS, won the Freedom of Expression Award at the prestigious Sundance Film Festival. For Hollibaugh, there is no simple definition of *lesbian,* or of *a lesbian-with-HIV/ AIDS.* Her work centers on the immediate needs of "women-identified-women," she says, and encompasses "whatever that needs to mean." Depending on which community one is addressing, it can mean very different things indeed.

"The variety of ways that women—either for preference or survival—figure out who they sleep with or what they do (sexually) is often different from how they identify. It's the confusion of those two things that is really unhelpful. All communities have opinions that everybody learns quickly as part of the survival of being in that community. If you know in your community that there's a lot of attitude about whether you're really a dyke if you say you sleep with men, or you know that there's a lot of class stigma associated with drug use, and you have a history at some point in your life of shooting up, you don't talk about it. You drop it out of your history; you leave it alone. What we remember to tell each other is what we can bear, and we balance that against our need for a community. And it's not The Truth, in some simple way." This seems to indicate that, despite appearances, there is a politically active movement of HIV-positive lesbians. Hollibaugh is passionate about this fact.

"Absolutely," she says. "But they don't come out of communities where the more controversial lesbian feminists have drawn their political energy from. Their activism is a different kind of activism, and they come out of a different history. It's not that these women don't have agenda," stresses Hollibaugh. They simply have no voice.

"A lot of the work that is being done has been focused around prevention for white middle-class women who are worried about the possibility of HIV transmission, and it hasn't primarily been focused where lesbians are most at risk. The numbers [of lesbians living with HIV] are already substantial, and in any project where you have few resources, you have to make a pretty clear decision about where you're going to focus your work. My focus has been to say we're going to go into those communities that may not be identified as lesbian communities, where women partner with women, and where there are substantial numbers of lesbians who are never addressed as lesbians around HIV. They're targeted as women who use drugs, or women who have sex with men, or any number of other things, but they're never talked to as women who partner with other women. Because of that, there is never any information, resource, knowledge, support, or respect for them as dykes."

The numbers are disproportionately higher still

at drug rehabilitation centers and programs—up to 30 percent who identify as lesbian, and more than that if you include those women who partner with other women but don't identify as lesbian. Clearly, the issue of HIV and lesbians is complicated not only by our lives as mothers and users and wives and employees and welfare recipients, but by the sweeping definitions that the government agencies that supply survival money seem to need to impose. Surviving with AIDS or HIV, then—particularly for women—is not simply a matter of health. It is pure politics.

For such a diverse client community, marginalized for reasons of class, race, and gender, concerns vie for priority on the roster of services offered by the Lesbian AIDS Project. While Hollibaugh and her staff may be able to address issues of isolation, health care services, and safer sex with the women who find their way to Manhattan, what about those women who don't even make it to GMHC? Is it hard to sustain successful outreach programs when many don't reach back?

"I think the success of the project has been that the number of lesbians already affected by HIV is really profound. They need resources and support and services that are directed to them specifically. The problem has never been finding them, the problem has been trying to figure out how to make sure the project serves those very specific needs that these women have.

"This is clearly like every other susceptible population, and there's been much misconception because people have thought it hinged on transmission, and it doesn't hinge on transmission. For example, outreach to gay men isn't about how you got HIV, it's about the fact that you're gay. And if they're gay men who use needles, you need to reach gay men who use needles; if they're gay men who also have sex with women, you need to talk to them about that. But it's not that they're less gay, regardless of the transmission route. And lesbians are the same." But with few statistics, and a correspondent paucity of financial resources, there was little being done, even within the gay community. "People here [at GMHC] recognized that, and they acted. It was a big leap, because there were no statistics. They took a chance, and I think it's really a proud thing."

In January 1993, the CDC broadened the official definition of AIDS to include infections involving the cervix, uterus, and ovaries. It was the first government agency to identify opportunistic infections afflicting women only as a result of the AIDS virus. As a gesture, it was nice. But now, a year and a half later, at the time of this writing, a spokesman at the CDC National AIDS Hotline says that there is still no statistical breakdown for lesbians. "Categorization is by types of exposure, and because reports of woman-to-woman oral contact remain unconfirmed," he explained, the CDC has conducted no tests on lesbians and AIDS as of October 1994. But do lesbians transmit HIV? "Call Amber Hollibaugh at GMHC in New York," the spokesman advised.

The broadened definition certainly made possible health services for a segment of the female PWA population who were previously denied services completely, but in terms of acknowledging lesbians, things have not changed substantially since 1992.

"It was a wedge, but not in any way completely what we needed," responded Hollibaugh. "Sixty-five percent of HIV-positive women who died before January 1993 died without an AIDS diagnosis, which means they died without access to services. Thirty percent of those women were dykes. The cross-over [result] is that there are a lot of issues of sexually transmitted diseases, of what [lesbians] do with each other, that we really need to be looking at seriously. That's a very uncomfortable conversation in the lesbian community.

"We're not comfortable talking about anything sexual. Why would HIV be any different? Whether we need to practice safer sex, or in what context, or how to get what we want, the truth is, we're not comfortable with our own bodies. And as a result, we have very little information that is helpful."

The correlation Hollibaugh draws between traditionally stilted sex talk within the lesbian community and a pervasive lack of AIDS awareness is grim. As we now know, the most effective tool in fighting the disease is education and communication, and if lesbians are still afraid to talk about sex, we'll never talk about AIDS. The result is high-risk behavior.

Apart from questions of sexual freedom, the politics of AIDS can carry with it the rhetoric of the women's movement of the 1970s. Many women in the lesbian community feel that the epidemic is not directly affecting them, and that they have filled the role of caretaker long enough. Hollibaugh, who has been a leading figure in both AIDS outreach work and the "sex wars" debates of the late seventies, believes that the epidemic has neither galvanized the community nor created an irreparable fissure. HIV/AIDS simply requires a response.

"Some of us have a primary identification of being queer, while some lesbians primarily identify with other women. I don't feel like I've been taking care of gay men. I feel like a part of my community was devastated, and all the forces we've been working against politically used it [AIDS] to marginalize *all* parts of the community: women and men, people of color, young people, you name it. The new conservative right loved it, and makes no distinction between lesbians and gay men.

"For me, it was a direct attack. The attitudes people had when I was walking with a friend who had lesions wasn't like I was one removed. I felt that they were talking about me. HIV is devastating to the building of a broad lesbian and gay movement. It has devastated the agenda that we would have created together, or apart, because everything's had to be focused [on the epidemic].

"Had it been lesbians, they would have been equally prepared to let *us* die. That gay people should die for being gay is unacceptable to me. And I don't care whether the gender is male or female. It is unacceptable to me that gay people's lives are expendable. And that isn't about liking men. I just find it completely unacceptable that gay people can be treated as less than human parts of the culture. You know, I'll fight with gay men, be separate or together with them in the ways that I choose, but it's *my* choice. It is not the choice of the straight world to make a decision about the value of our lives."

(For more information about The Lesbian AIDS Project, or for a very sexy Safer Sex Handbook (with pictures!) for Lesbians, call GMHC 212-337-3532.)

New Age Lesbians:

Women of Substance and Spirit

Jan Crawford

Open any women's newspaper. Study the bulletin board at any women's bookstore. You will find women, many of them lesbians, eagerly and earnestly willing to offer you the moon and the stars (the astrologers), to comfort your body and soul (the massage therapists), introduce you to the realm of crystals and healing energies (the psychics and healers), and offer you safe conduct through the emotional drama of your life and beyond (the transpersonal therapists).

There may also be ecofeminists who speak to you about the relationship between man's treatment of you as woman and man's treatment of the earth. Vegetarians and animal rights women will ask you to remember our relationship to nonhuman beings. Herbalists and acupuncturists will urge you to consider alternative medicine. Political women will ask you to join them in helping oppressed women worldwide. You will be invited to join the peace movement or the Green party, a group that practices global village consciousness and acknowledges feminism as an important element in their philosophy.

Witches, Goddess worshipers, feminist Christians, Jews, and students of Buddhism will invite you to join them in their exploration of the spirit. Native Americans, African Americans, and other women of color will speak about their lives and spiritual paths.

Although many of these women would not define themselves as such, all this and more can be viewed as part of the New Age. Later in this article we will look more critically at the "New Age." These two words can, at their best, suggest an era that offers the possibility of expansion into the widest dimension of one's being. At its best the New Age is about balance and about questioning our relationship to mystery.

Balance describes the movement from a profoundly male-determined world to a world in which there is a growing knowledge of what is true, unleashed, unoppressed femaleness. The next step will then be to allow a blending of both femaleness and maleness in a new way that creates deep harmony and creative caretaking of the earth and space. Balance, then, is the melting of dualities into new paradigms that feel truer because they are based on sounder reality. Some of the major challenged dualities are those of God and "man," body and mind, heart and mind, humans and nature, thinking and feeling.

Experiencing *mystery* is for some the act of acknowledging that we cannot wrap numbers and "objective" intellect around everything we see and feel. Learning the limitations and inappropriateness of the intellect can become a freedom rather than a frustration. The return of wonder and what Buddhists call "don't know mind" can become a source of excitement and relief rather than simply fear of what we do not "know."

And, of course, there is the greatest mystery: Who are we? Are we our minds? Are we our bodies or our emotions? Many of the paths within the New Age spectrum of beliefs imply we are these elements of self in a much more fully explored way than we have heretofore imagined or experienced. At the same time, paradoxically, the separate self can also be seen as an illusion. Some believe the idea of a separate autonomous self is simply a social construct. The individual, bounded, communally isolated self is a modern Western phenomenon, not necessarily the only way of defining experience.

Lesbians are embracing many different paths leading each to her own way of questioning limiting ideas and conditions of the past. Women who work in world peace movements question the belief that there will always be wars, that wars are an inevitable part of human nature. Women who work with astrology question the idea that there is no fathomable pattern behind our experiences and lives. Many women question the belief that the only effective healing system is allopathic medicine.

Women who work with crystals and healing question our limited concepts of energy and suggest that with loving intent, the power of crystals or the hands themselves can interact with energy systems in the body that bring about a healing balance in the body and psyche of the receiver. And others believe direct physical work on the body, nutrition, and exercise can have profound influence on health and spiritual growth.

The reemergence of the Goddess is perhaps one of the most profound phenomena for our culture and communities. In a conversation, sculptor Nancy Azara, who teaches a class, "The Search for the Mythical Goddess," described three approaches to meeting with the Goddess: "Some women worship the Goddess as a living being outside themselves. Others internalize the Goddess and feel her within themselves." And others, like herself, relate to the Goddess as inspiration to "reclaim our own inner power and our own inner selves and as seeing ourselves somewhere deep inside as the ultimate and infinite strength and wisdom ... all the things that our society attributes to God."

And as ecofeminist Charlene Spretnak points out, the Goddess for many is not simply "Yahweh with a skirt."[1] Prepatriarchal religions very much recognized the Goddess immanent in nature and in loving relationship to all other beings of nature, a view in opposition to a powerful God separating himself from and dominating nature—and woman.

Wicca or witchcraft is one form of Goddess wor-

Chrystos, Native American activist, artist, and writer.

ship and perhaps the oldest form of worship. Starhawk, a witch and leader in women's spirituality, explains that in witchcraft "the image of the Goddess inspires women to see ourselves as divine, our bodies as sacred, and changing phases of our lives as holy, our aggression as healthy, our anger as purifying, and our power to nurture and create but also to limit and destroy when necessary, as the very force that sustains all life. . . . In witchcraft flesh and spirit are one."[2] Starhawk and other recognized witches such as Zee Budapest also frequently stress action as a part of worship—that outer work best accompanies inner work and that reidentifying with witches is a reaffirmation of "our right to be powerful."

And perhaps because they also focus on the interrelatedness and interdependency of all forms of nature, Native American religions and traditions are increasingly being studied and practiced by lesbians. Sweat lodges, smudging (a rite of purification and blessing), chanting, and dancing may touch ancient longings to dissolve completely into the Great Spirit. Dyani Ywahoo, of Sunray Meditation Center, and Brooke Medicine Eagle are among a number of popular women teachers. Luisah Teish is one of the teachers who introduces us to African spiritual practice.

One increasingly finds significant numbers of lesbians seriously involved in Middle Eastern and Eastern forms of spiritual practice. For example, lesbian singer/songwriter Meg Christian has been a devotee of Gurumayi for several years and now travels with her frequently. And at the 1988 Celebration of Women in Buddhist Practice in San Francisco, many of the conference planners and attendees were lesbians. Author Sandy Boucher suggests that "it may be that lesbians are drawn to Buddhist practice because as homosexuals in a heterosexual homophobic culture, we have learned to take nothing for granted, to question everything, and to create a path for ourselves. Buddhism, a method of investigating absolutely everything, is thus familiar and compatible with our position in the world."[3]

Buddhism and other Oriental philosophies particularly question the idea of a separate self. Ecofeminist Susan Griffin refers to the paradox of self/no self and women when she says:

Moving beyond the "self" doesn't mean effacing the "self" in the way women and oppressed people are often asked to do. . . . Moving beyond the self happens in meditation when you're really present—when you couldn't be more deeply seated in the "self," that's when suddenly your heart opens. Everything that separates you from connecting with all of life feels so petty and without importance.[4]

Some lesbians have brought many of the foregoing perspectives back into Judeo-Christian traditions. It is not unusual now to find seriously involved women rabbis, ministers, and laypeople who include or adapt Goddess worship, Native American, or Buddhist principles into their Christian or Jewish practices.

The very act of committing to women has helped many women acquire the safety to begin to explore and develop their spiritual selves. In itself, loving a woman is boundary-breaking, pioneering, inventing life beyond habitual and traditional structures.

Episcopal priest and feminist liberation theologist Carter Heyward proposes that lesbians' erotic power is our most creative liberating power, our sacred power and "that which many of us call our God or Goddess." She boldly suggests that lesbians are "icons of erotic power," living gladly on the margins.[5]

And many lesbians feel that another woman can mirror one more exquisitely, reflecting back one's truth in one's own language. This mirroring may allow a deep relief and acceptance of one's value in a way that then allows a release of fear and an expansion into undreamed possibilities of being.

Many today are suggesting that if this age is about experiencing relatedness more deeply, "unmitigated femaleness"[6] can bring two intuitive people together in ways that accentuate relationship rather than separateness. We may be more inclined toward the partnership model (versus the domination model) that Riane Eisler describes in her book, The Chalice and the Blade.

Mainstream psychological theory has tended to pathologize lesbians by suggesting that we are regressed to an infantile position of fusion with the mother. However, Julie Mencher of The Stone Center at Wellesley College points to the fact that recent infancy research suggests there is no original symbiosis or fusion with the mother. Therefore, fusion, or what I prefer to call the capacity to merge, is not regressive. In fact, it may represent in many circumstances an evolved capacity to live fearlessly in the reality of oneness.

As lesbians, we know, too, that we can play with androgyny, exploring and dissolving roles and seeing gender-determined stereotypes as merely a belief system, not the only reality.

As members of Virginia Woolf's "Outsider's Society," we have a perspective, a critical distance. Erica Jong suggests that lesbians "owe no allegiance to man . . . and are freer to disclose the hypocrisies of the patriarchal system."[7]

Last, we all know it takes courage to choose to expand beyond tradition, and courage is something lesbians, as society's outsiders, get many opportunities to develop and exercise.

There are some challenges, however, that the lesbian life presents to spiritual work. Because of enforced isolation some of us may tend to become overly dependent on our relationships rather than feeling or creating spaciousness with our loved ones. Because of oppression, some of us are confused about issues of gender and tend to be caught in rigid male role emulation. And worse, internalized oppression as well as sexism and homophobia sometimes unconsciously cause us to devalue ourselves and our partners, creating the fall into abusive behaviors. In a lighter vein, the New Age also provides new opportunities for competition among women, some of them amusing: Two friends were recently quarreling over which was the queen in a past life.

And because in couples we may be both be "emotional" (rather than "rational"), we can sometimes overprocess life, drown in emotion. Also, because of oppression, claiming and developing a lesbian identity is for most so painful, it is often difficult to then let go of that identity on that level where any grasped-to identity is an encumbrance to spiritual fulfillment.

There are also some real challenges and dangers to participation in the New Age, lesbian or heterosexual. Involvement can be a sign of trying to buy the magic bullet, the quick fix. It may provide an excuse for militant narcissism. Our egos may simply be trying to buy glamour, excitement, and a new place to exploit human needs. And as has previously happened in other social/political movements, homophobia and feminism can again be subsumed to "larger issues."

At the 1988 Transpersonal Psychology Conference in Monterey, California, one of the popular female leaders within that field suggested in her workshop that the feminist movement would have been better named the "animus movement"—in other words, the movement in which women simply sought male power, sought to become male. Another young woman leader implied that, of course, everyone knew the women's movement had been a mistake.

These examples illustrate that the New Age movement can diminish or even attack feminism. For some it will be a choice to fully develop lesbian feminism itself as a transcendent path. For those women, lesbian feminism will have as much or more ability than any other path to answer the questions and needs of the soul.

Whichever path we choose, for the first time in Western patriarchal history, we may have an opportunity to imagine a world where power, male or female, is less the issue than clarity, connectedness, and creative communication, where the development of separate "autonomous" self may not be the last step (or even a desirable step) in personal evolution. We may begin to ask ourselves questions like, "What is the source of this immense inner silence?" "How can I learn to touch that place in myself and others more?" "How much safety and spaciousness do I create for those around me?" "How do I remember we share one heart?"

Notes

1. Charlene Spretnak, "Ecofeminism: Our Roots and Flowering," *Women of Power* 9, 7.
2. Starhawk, *The Spiral Dance* (New York: Harper & Row, 1979), 9.
3. Sandy Boucher, *Turning the Wheel: American Women Creating a New Buddhism* (New York: Harper & Row, 1988), 26.
4. Barbara Gates, "Made from the Earth," *Inquiring Mind* (Summer 1987).
5. Carter Heyward, *Coming Out and Relational Empowerment: A Lesbian Theological Perspective* (work in progress), Paper No. 38, The Stone Center, Wellesley College, 1989.
6. Dr. Margaret Nichols, "Doing Sex Therapy with Lesbians: Bending a Heterosexual Paradigm to Fit a Gay Lifestyle," in *Lesbian Psychologies*, (Urbana: University of Illinois Press, 1987), 244.
7. Erica Jong, "Changing My Mind About Andrea Dworkin," *Ms.* (June 1988), 64.

Further Reading

Boucher, Sandy. *Turning the Wheel: American Women Creating the New Buddhism.* San Francisco: Harper & Row, 1988.

Budapest, Z. Suzsanna. *The Grandmother of Time.* San Francisco: Harper & Row, 1989.

Friedman, Lenore. *Meetings with Remarkable Women: Buddhist Teachers in America.* Boston: Shambala, 1987.

Griffin, Susan. *Woman and Nature.* San Francisco: Harper & Row, 1978.

Heyward, Carter. *Touching Our Strength: The Erotic Power and the Love of God.* San Francisco: Harper & Row, 1989.

Plaskow, Judith. *Standing Again at Sinai.* San Francisco: Harper & Row, 1990.

Starhawk. *The Spiral Dance.* San Francisco: Harper & Row, 1979.

Stone, Merlin. *Ancient Mirrors of Womanhood.* Boston: Beacon Press, 1979.

Teish, Luisah. *Jambalaya.* San Francisco: Harper & Row, 1985.

Women of Power (a magazine), Box 827, Cambridge, MA 02238.

Leslie Gohlke

Hannah Lamitie

Lesbian as Healer:

Nancy Johnson

Interviewed by Jan Crawford

What was the personal crisis in your life that motivated you to explore healing?

I was born and raised in a small town south of Salt Lake City, and in the 1950s my family and I were exposed to the fallout from the nuclear bomb testing that the U.S. government conducted in Nevada. It spread through the skies, in the air, in the rain, and dumped on everyone hundreds and hundreds of miles in every direction. The radiation poisoned the soil, the water, the food, and even the cows' milk.

As Mormons we were raised to believe that the government would protect us. With our trusting attitudes we were a setup. The government knew that those clouds were poisonous. (They had opened a hospital in Nagasaki to study cancer patients and radiation victims. Therefore, they knew!) But not once did they warn the people in those areas of Nevada and Utah of the danger to our health. We were told to stay inside after the tests, but that was all.

In my young adult years I was sick: nausea, headache, hives and rashes, narcolepsy; then I developed cancer of the thyroid. My thyroid was surgically removed, and I thought it was over. But a year later I had a spread of cancer through the lymph system in my neck. My jugular vein and a shoulder muscle were also diseased. At that time I had radical neck surgery; ninety-eight lymph nodes and hundreds of lymph veins were removed from my neck, my shoulder, and up into my head. The surgery was very maiming. And the healing process was long, painful, difficult. Later I had a small tumor removed from my hand. And a year later I had more tumors on the left side of my neck, making me a candidate for more surgery.

At this particular time I was seeking alternatives. I needed to find another way to heal myself, because I felt that my body would be so sick from another surgery that I wouldn't survive another six hours of anesthesia. So when my therapist suggested that I try psychic healing, I said yes, not knowing what is was, but I trusted her—and I was desperate. She explained to me that a colleague of hers had taken some healing classes where she learned how to use white light, entering by visualization into your body, and that it had been known to remove tumors from people's bodies. So I went to my surgeon and said, "I really have to try this." And he said, "Come on, Nancy. You can't wait. You don't have time for this." And I said, "I've got to try." And he said, "How much time do you want?" And I said, "Two weeks." I could have said two hours or two years, because I had no concept of what I was talking about at all.

So my therapist and I arranged for this healing to take place, which was done by distance—we were in different sections of the city. My therapist was a channel between the healer and me. She visualized me and the white light was transferred to me in that way. And two weeks later, the three tumors that I had on the left side of my neck were gone. And I thought, "I've found it! Now I have the answer!"

© 1991 Ann Meredith

Laura and Connolli.

Today a number of people come to see you for healing, and you also teach people to heal. What form does healing take now?

It has taken a number of different forms now. My healing work has taken the form of hands-on healing, which is basically placing one's hands in and around the aura of a person—that is, the person's energy field. Some time ago I found that in the process of visualizing white light, I could see things that were not of my mind—images, faces. And sometimes I would get feelings that had nothing to do with my own feelings. Gradually, as time passed, I began to trust more in these images, and in working in and around those energies—the energy field, and feeling where there is dis-ease and discomfort. And working around changing that dis-ease and making it easy, calm, comfortable.

I'm not really conscious of using my own energies in this. I simply feel that my hands can calm down the space—can, if it's turbulent, ease the turbulence; if it's hot, cool it down; if it's cold, warm it up. Anyone can do this. It's a technique called therapeutic touch. It's used in hospitals to eliminate pain and discomfort and dis-ease without medicines, so it's the kind of thing people can do for each other, one-on-one. It's very natural. For example, if someone has a bellyache or a headache, it's very easy to fix it by simply touching the aura around the stomach or head and feel that area calm down and become comfortable.

But many of us, while we can be healing, haven't developed the visualization techniques, and that's the difference between healing and being a healer.

Yes.

What is the source of this healing power?

People call it many things. I think of it as ancient memory. People call it God, or Jesus, or angels, or a distinct higher power. I feel it as a very strong field of energy that flows around us all the time. If I'm sensitive to it I can put my hands out and touch the energy field that belongs to us.

We have become so uncomfortable by stress, by pain, by heartache, by unmet physical and emotional needs that the "air" begins to vibrate around us, and that prevents the natural flow of energy from settling easily on the body. The energy itself is a healer; it sometimes needs to be channeled to come into the aura. Sometimes the problem starts with the aura and enters the body; it goes both ways.

Do you see healing as always curing a person of her illness?

It's so obvious that we can't cure everyone. There would be no death if we could cure every illness. It's against divine law for there to be a healing of immortality. Our bodies can only function for seventy, eighty, ninety years. But I feel there are some people who fall into discomfort and dis-ease who are not meant to succumb to death at that time, and those people who have a willingness, a design, an intent to live, who have a focus and meaning in their lives, are able to use the healing energies that are offered to them, and live.

The other side of it is that often the healing process must extend into a death and dying process. And the healer must be ready to accept the inevitability of someone's time to pass, and to try to help that passage be as comfortable and easy as possible, with the least amount of trauma and inner and exterior conflicts possible. If that passage to death can be done easily, we enter into a new spiritual kingdom with joy, with acceptance—not grieving and feeling that we've missed life, that we're leaving behind unfinished business, but we just move into the new space, and that in itself, I feel, is a healing act.

Is there any way in which being a lesbian is related to being a healer?

A lot of healers aren't lesbians, but I feel my lesbianism is related in that living out of the social norm prepared me to investigate an internal strength that if I had not been a lesbian I may not have sought. I knew, growing up as a lesbian, that my lesbianism was not going to make people happy with me. So I didn't look to make people happy. I didn't mind committing social misdemeanors, and so I had the strength eighteen years ago to try this new alternative, psychic healing, when it was not as well known as it is now.

I would like people to stop being so frightened about psychic healing and stop feeling that it's a magical, mystical, unfathomable realm. It's mystery, but it's not magic. It's an inner wisdom we can all benefit from. Let it be resumed in our lives as a God-given right rather than as meddling in God's world or the devil's world. One knows it's good work from the healing and health and the general opening of one's heart that happens from that work. It's fear and ignorance that keep us from it. Our patriarchal system over the past three thousand years has made us women ashamed of our intuitive, deeper insight. I think that we are capable of literally healing the world, if we remembered how.

IV

Lesbian Activism

Reminiscences of Two Female Homophiles:

Part II

Del Martin and Phyllis Lyon

The Stonewall riots of 1969 in New York City are memorialized every year by lesbian and gay pride celebrations throughout the country and are often credited with the birth of gay liberation. From our perspective, however, Stonewall was a turning point in the existing lesbian and gay movement which began in 1950. Without the national organizing and visibility preceding it, Stonewall could not have happened.

The Mattachine Foundation, which began in 1950 in Los Angeles, was composed of very secret small meetings in individual homes. Outside of the organizers, members of one group did not know members of other groups. Eventually, in 1952 some people broke away from the Mattachine Foundation to publish ONE magazine. In 1953 the Mattachine Society was formalized as a nonprofit organization and moved to San Francisco. And in 1955 the Daughters of Bilitis (pronounced Bileetis) came into existence in San Francisco independently, without any knowledge of the other organizations.

The times dictated the need to band together as a matter of survival. Senator Joseph McCarthy's campaign to rid the federal government of Communists and their sympathizers was extended to include homosexuals. Those suspected of being homosexual were purged from the State Department, other federal departments, and from the armed services. Of those who were dishonorably discharged from the latter, some were let go because they were believed to have "homosexual tendencies," and some were heterosexuals found guilty by association.

The homophobic hysteria spread to the private sector. Gay bars were subject to periodic raids by police. Names and addresses of those arrested were printed in the newspaper. Police often phoned employers to inform them of employee arrests. Some police officers beat up suspected homosexuals and warned them to get out of town.

Careers were ruined. Teachers lost their credentials. Others lost professional licenses. Many lesbians and gay men were disowned by their parents. Some were excommunicated by religious institutions to which they had belonged. They lost friends and other means of support. Teenagers, if their parents found out about them, were sent to a shrink or institutionalized. Some lesbians and gay men, of whatever age, were so devastated they saw suicide as the only way out.

We had moved in together in 1953 in an apartment on Castro Street in San Francisco, a Catholic working-class neighborhood that twenty years later became the hub of gay and lesbian activity. Even though Del was a native of San Francisco, we didn't know any lesbians and felt very isolated. We went to lesbian bars, but the women we saw there seemed to be in cliques. We were shy and didn't know how to mix in; we felt like tourists. Through a gay male couple who lived around the corner from us we finally met a lesbian couple. One of them called us one day in 1955 to ask if we would like to join in the formation of a lesbian club. We said, "Of course!" Little did we know what was going to happen to our lives.

Eight of us got together to form a secret lesbian social club as an alternative to the bars. We would meet in homes where we could have some privacy, we could dance and also be able to meet other lesbians. The idea came from a Filipina who loved to dance. She told us that in the Philippines homosexuals were much more accepted than in the United States. Another member suggested the name Daughters of Bilitis. It came from "Songs of Bilitis," by Pierre Louÿs, a narrative lesbian poem in which Bilitis was purported to have lived on the isle of Lesbos at the same time as Sappho. If asked, we could always say that DOB was a society interested in Greek poetry or a women's lodge such as the DAR and Daughters of the Nile. Unfortunately, in later days the media thought it sounded like a women's auxiliary.

We learned later that the makeup of our original membership was "politically correct." There were four couples: two women of color (the second one was Chicana), two lesbian mothers, four blue-collar workers, and four white-collar office types.

After the first year DOB only had about a dozen members. We decided to go all out. We rented a post

Lesbian Herstory Archives, DOB Collection

office box and shared a tiny office with the Mattachine Society. We published *The Ladder* as a local newsletter, but the response was so overwhelming it soon became a national magazine.

We also sponsored public discussion meetings in a small downtown auditorium. The "public" was comprised of lesbians and gay men, giving them the freedom to come and hear about the organization and learn about their rights without giving themselves away. Our choice of speakers—attorneys, psychiatrists, psychologists, marriage counselors, and other professionals—was designed to allay our fears, validate us, build self-confidence and self-esteem. Up to then everything we read or heard about homosexuality indicated that we were "illegal, immoral, and sick."

By 1958 DOB had grown enough to warrant getting our own office. Del found a place in an ideal downtown location. The manager asked, "What kind of an organization is it?" Del replied, "It's an organization dealing with the sociological problems of single women." And the manager said, "Oh, great! I have a friend who would be interested." After we moved in, it didn't take long for her to find out what kind of an organization DOB was. We never heard from her friend.

In 1959 both the Daughters of Bilitis and the Mattachine Society became a focus in San Francisco's mayoralty race. The incumbent mayor was accused of "harboring homosexuals" because both organizations had their national headquarters in the city. The story broke in a weekly newspaper and on the radio. Mayor George Christopher was outraged that the topic came up on the radio during the dinner hour when children could hear it. Throughout the campaign he never once mentioned the "H" word. We learned later that the police had checked out DOB with the office building manager who vouched for us as good tenants. What a threat we were! DOB and Mattachine combined probably had fewer than a hundred members at the time. Christopher won the election, but nine thousand voters went to the polls and "passed" on the mayor's race.

By 1960 the Daughters had gone national, with chapters in Los Angeles, New York, Chicago, and Rhode Island. The organization held the first National Lesbian Convention in the penthouse of a San Francisco hotel. It was, in a sense, DOB's "coming out," and most of the members wore "appropriate" attire (skirts, heels, earrings) for its first *real* public event, which was also the largest such gathering of homosexuals up to that time, with two hundred in attendance. The "homosexual detail" of the police department showed up to check us out. The first and foremost concern of the police was, "Does your organization advocate wearing the clothes of the opposite sex?" Del, as the national president and spokeswoman, could comfortably say, "Look around. Does it look like it?"

DOB membership waxed and waned over the years. Chapters began, faded, started up again. Although *The Ladder* was mailed in "a plain brown wrapper" and we assured our members "Your name is safe," the number of subscribers was nominal. We tried putting *The Ladder* on the newsstands (there were no women's bookstores then) but there was no place for it. It didn't fit in with *Ladies Home Journal* and it didn't fit in with the "porn" or news magazines. Besides, lesbians wouldn't buy it anyway because for identification purposes we had added the words "A Lesbian Review" on the cover. When our book *Lesbian/Woman* came out in 1972, we ran into the same problem. Closeted lesbians would invite us over to meet their friends and add, "Bring books."

Until 1962, *ONE,* Mattachine, and DOB were the only homophile organizations, sometimes referred to as the Big Three. It was a lot easier to keep track of what was going on in the movement then. In San Francisco during the early sixties, gay bars banded together in the Tavern Guild to act jointly to protect themselves and their patrons against harassment by police and beverage control agents. Other grassroots groups sprang up across the country. In 1966 representatives of fifteen homophile organizations and publications met in Kansas City to plan communication, cooperation, and strategy on a national scale for the growing American homophile movement. The idea was to meet each other and share, not form another organization. However, a sort of umbrella organization did develop—NACHO—North American Conference of Homophile Organizations. It had a short but busy life.

The turning point of the movement, however, particularly in the West, was the formation of the Council on Religion and the Homosexual (CRH) in 1964. The Reverend Ted McIlvenna of the Young Adult Project at Glide Urban Center, San Francisco, arranged a three-day retreat in Mill Valley, California, involving fifteen clergymen from across the country and ten gay men and five lesbians (DOB) from the Bay Area. What resulted was the breakdown of stereotypes on both sides, recognition of a common humanity, and the suggestion that San Francisco be the "test city" in which to organize and promote a continuing dialogue between the church and the homosexual.

The Council on Religion and the Homosexual was the first organization to use the "H" word in its name. (It was also the first to obtain a 501(c)3 tax deductible status from the IRS.) That was bad enough. Associating religion with the homosexual stirred immediate conflict with many congregations, church authorities, and the police. The archbishop of the Roman Catholic church in San Francisco forbade priests from having anything to do with CRH. The Board of Rabbis kept silent except for Rabbi Eliot Grafman, who did address one meeting of CRH under a heavy veil of secrecy. Protestant churches (Methodist, Episcopal, Presbyterian, United Church of Christ, Lutheran) were represented by ministers on the CRH board of directors, however.

The fireworks began in earnest when DOB and five other homophile organizations decided to sponsor a drag ball as a fundraiser for the newly born, and incorporated, CRH. Two of the ministers talked to the police about necessary permits and found themselves embroiled in theological debate. One officer exploded, "If you won't enforce God's law—we will!"

The ball was to be held on the evening of New Year's Day 1965, at California Hall in an area busy by day but relatively quiet by night. The cops insisted they could not be sure there would be no disturbance on the street, even if guests in "drag" were driven to, and picked up at, the curb in front of the entrance. The clergy thought they had settled the matter. On the night of the ball some fifty police officers, in uniform and plainclothes, with a patrol wagon and numerous police cars well in sight, had floodlighted the entrance and were taking photos (both still and movie) of everyone entering or leaving the building. It was like the grand entrance made by movie stars to the Academy Awards in Hollywood—only the implications were far more grim.

More than five hundred lesbians and gay men (some of them teachers, others in "sensitive" jobs) crossed the picket line of cops to gain entrance to the hall where the CRH clergymen and their wives awaited them. Three attorneys and a heterosexual woman were arrested for "interfering with the police in line of duty." One of the attorneys, Herbert Donaldson, thought his legal career was at an end as he was hauled off to the police station. But eighteen years later almost to the day, he was appointed a municipal court judge by Governor Jerry Brown. The American Civil Liberties Union volunteered to defend them. When the prosecution rested its case, the judge, without hearing a word from the defense, directed the jury to bring in a verdict of not guilty—not on a point of law as we had hoped, but on a technicality. In writing up the police report, officers had said they had been denied entry to the building. In actuality they had come inside, at least as far as the foyer.

The CRH Ball was San Francisco's Stonewall. It had a tremendous impact on the religious community, the police, and the political scene. The day after the ball, seven very angry clergymen called a press conference at Glide Methodist Church to express their outrage and dismay at the way the police had "broken faith" with CRH and for all the "deliberate harassment" and intimidation of those attending the ball.

The story made the front page of the *San Francisco Chronicle* and was picked up by the wire services. Letters came from all over the world. Lesbians and gay men who had never before heard anything positive about homosexuals from their priests, pastors, or rabbis rejoiced. Letters of support came from the liberal North and hate letters of condemnation from the conservative South. The United Church of Christ, which ordained the country's first openly gay minister, Bill Johnson, lost some parishioners but did not back down from the national nondiscrimination policy it adopted after many sessions between CRH members and the church leadership. The Episcopal Diocese of California adopted a similar policy but did not implement it after Bishop James Pike retired, although his successor, Kim Myers, had attended the CRH retreat and was the one who suggested San Francisco as the test city. Today there are lesbian and gay groups like Dignity or Af-

firmation or Integrity within most religious denominations to remind them that "practicing heterosexuals" do not have a corner on God.

During the trial it was revealed that the police were prepared to make wholesale arrests at the CRH Ball. They had fifty arrest cards with them. Inspectors Rudy Nieto and Dick Castro, who engineered the fiasco, were demoted to the car boosting detail. Most importantly, Elliot Blackstone, of the Police Community Relations unit, was assigned as liaison to the gay community. This meant that finally the city "fathers" had been forced to recognize our existence and were now ready to deal with us as a bona fide minority.

The Council on Religion and the Homosexual was an activist organization. For example, it played a role in the formation of NACHO and participated in its first national demonstration on Armed Services Day in May 1966, to protest the treatment of lesbians and gay men in the armed services. The clergy were very much in evidence during the "Ten Days in August" that year when the Daughters of Bilitis held its fourth national convention and involved every branch of San Francisco government in dialogue with the lesbian/gay community. They were also involved when the Society for Individual Rights (SIR) held public discussions on an variety of subjects and produced a statement signed by researcher Evelyn Hooker, Ph.D., and Joel Fort, M.D., director of a San Francisco mental health agency, that homosexuality per se was not an illness, when NACHO met to plan strategy for future action. In September The Reverend Clay Colwell challenged the California State Fair authorities in court for denying CRH a display booth. We lost the case but won more public exposure by handing out leaflets at the gate than we would have had in a booth.

In the aftermath of the CRH Ball police estimated there were seventy thousand homosexuals in San Francisco. To which we replied, "And we all vote." CRH held the first gay-sponsored Candidates Night in Glide Church. Candidates who were used to speaking before groups of twenty-five to fifty found an audience of two hundred.

In February 1972, the Alice B. Toklas Memorial Democratic Club was formed in San Francisco. In July, Jim Foster, its founder, and Madeline Davis, of Buffalo, New York, addressed the Democratic party's national convention, on television, presenting the platform committee's minority report on the need for a gay rights plank.

When the women's movement resurfaced in 1966–67, it made a great deal of difference to lesbians, especially to members of DOB. In retrospect we found that DOB was a feminist organization without knowing it. We didn't know the word *feminist*. We called each other "girls," and we'd never heard of sexism, but we knew what it was like. We didn't get equal pay for equal work. We didn't have the same opportunities men had in education and employment. Many lesbians joined the National Organization for Women because they understood that women's issues were lesbian issues and hoped that discrimination against lesbians would become a women's issue.

We first heard about NOW on the radio. Inka O'Hanrahan, who was then national treasurer, said they were starting a Northern California chapter in San Francisco. We thought it was great that straight women were finally getting it together. When we received a membership blank we discovered that NOW had a reduced rate for couples. We decided we were not about to go back into the closet and joined as a couple. O'Hanrahan honored our couples membership and said, "There must be more of you. Bring them around." Betty Friedan, who was national president, did not agree. The couples membership was soon abolished.

We did not experience the antilesbian discrimination our sisters did in New York City. When Friedan ordered local chapters to sponsor women's coalition conferences, many lesbian groups solidified their position in the movement. In New York they were excluded, and the Lavender Menace disrupted the meeting. Rita Mae Brown and others quit NOW in protest, and the lesbian question continued to be a source of friction at national board meetings. After Aileen Hernandez succeeded Friedan as national president, she asked us to convene a lesbian rights workshop at the 1971 conference in Los Angeles. In preconference interviews Friedan predicted lesbians would break up the organization. We expected to be referees in a heated discussion. A resolution acknowledging that discrimination against lesbians is a feminist issue was passed by an overwhelming vote.

The lesbian/gay movement has undergone many changes. The homophile movement of the fifties and sixties became the more militant gay liberation in the early seventies. Many lesbians, fed up with the sexism of gay men, became more involved with the women's movement. The crisis created by Anita Bryant in Dade County, Florida, in the late seventies spread across the country and brought us together again. Evidence of a new partnership appeared when organizations changed their names from simply "Gay" to "Lesbian and Gay" (to the media and the public, "gay" means "male"). The AIDS epidemic of the eighties has sparked more physical violence and political attacks. With each crisis, however, our movement has become more effective and ever stronger. The March on Washington of 1987, which drew 400,000 lesbian, gay, bisexual, and heterosexual activists from all over the country, showed that we will not be deterred until our full rights as citizens have been secured.

Despite the religious crusades of the radical right, we continue to make gains. Half the states allow consenting adult lesbians and gay men to have sex in private. Many cities, labor unions, businesses, and other institutions extend benefits to domestic partners of lesbian and gay employees. More than a hundred local government ordinances and nine state statutes outlaw discrimination on the basis of sexual orientation. The Hate Crimes Act, passed by Congress in 1990, includes penalties for violence against lesbians and gay men, and representatives of our community were invited to the White House for the ceremonial signing of the bill by President George Bush.

Although headlines in the daily papers shouted "Lesbian Lawyer Challenges Incumbent Judge," Donna Hitchens was elected to the superior court in San Francisco on June 5, 1990. The number of "out" lesbian and gay elected and appointed officials in all levels of government keeps growing. All of those who ran as incumbents in 1994 were reelected. Many school districts have adopted Project 10 programs to provide counseling and correct information to self-identified lesbian and gay students, and general education about homophobia and homosexuality to students, teachers, and administrators.

The greatest setback has been the AIDS epidemic and the slow, reluctant response of the federal government to what was originally dubbed a "gay" disease. Lesbians and gays have been leaders in educating the public that AIDS does not discriminate on the basis of gender or sexual orientation.

Another setback was the Congressional defeat of President Bill Clinton's attempt to lift the ban against lesbians and gays in the military. To Clinton's credit are two presidential firsts: an executive order to lift the ban on security clearances and public support for the Employment Non-Discrimination Act of 1995. In the same year the fourth White House Conference on Aging and the fourth United Nations Conference on Women, held in China, put sexual orientation on the agenda for the first time.

A great deal of progress has been made in the four decades since we became involved in what was then called the homophile movement. The lesbian/gay/bisexual/transgender movement is now worldwide. There is still much to be done, but the foundation is there. We have no doubt that indeed we are in the Gay Nineties and that gains will continue into the next century.

Visibility as Power for Lesbians

Jean O'Leary

(Editor's Note: This article is based on a keynote speech delivered by Jean O'Leary at a NOW Lesbian Conference in San Diego.)

Today I want to talk about power. I want to talk about visibility. For us, I believe, visibility *is* our power!

The first sign of major visible power for the gay rights movement was the Stonewall riot in 1969, when gays fought back for the first time during a police raid on a bar in Greenwich Village. Lesbians can certainly relate to what happened at Stonewall, and we celebrated its twenty-fifth anniversary with as much pride and passion as anyone. But I think we have to admit that the lesbian community, on its own, and apart from the women's and gay communities, hasn't had its Stonewall yet. We haven't had that symbolic confrontation between the power of our dreams and the brutality of the billy clubs that want to break them apart. That may explain why we're in this room attending a conference where we are "Searching for the Lesbian Agenda."

Now some would say, and rightly so, that we do not need a public Stonewall—that every woman who dares to assert herself as a lesbian, as a woman independent from men, faces her own private Stonewall. But something very different happens when a woman finally discovers and then *acknowledges* to others in our community that she is a lesbian. It is the beginning of visibility, and of power. When we seek each other out, when we band together, prepared to battle for our freedom, our right to love, for our children, our homes, our jobs, and our lives—that is the beginning of political power.

I truly believe that visibility *is* the lesbian agenda. We must begin mapping out that agenda, choosing the priorities where we will channel our power. We must do this for ourselves and for the women who

Mary Wickline

Jean O'Leary, keynote speaker, NOW National Lesbian Conference, San Diego.

would not, dared not, or could not join us at this conference.

There is a large gap between the immediate needs of the corporate lesbian and the lesbian separatist. Because of this, we must not only tolerate but celebrate the differences among us. Unity, much as we'd all like to experience it, is not the crucial issue we face today. It is survival!

And the question of the day is: What will attract our enormous numbers to join an effort that will ensure our survival? Clearly, we must first be visible. Invisibility and the fear of public disapproval have kept millions of lesbian women in unhappy marriages or languishing in heterosexual relationships.

This is one important group of lesbians we must reach. It's funny. Somehow the men who run our society have made some women believe they are better off being discriminated against—or, as it's sometimes referred to, "being put on a pedestal"! A suffragist once said: "Men want to put women on a pedestal and then leave them there to dust it." A lot of women feel that they are getting preferential treatment when in reality they are only one man away from poverty.

Too long women have been pouring their love energies into men, who in turn, full of vitality and creativity, go out to become our presidents, our congressmen, our doctors, our lawyers, and our corporation men, shaping the oppressive institutions that keep women "in their place." It's time for *us* to fill these roles, to break the chains of second-class status—at the link that will be most effective. It is time to encourage women to turn to women at all levels and start working for ourselves . . . to start loving ourselves.

And that effort begins here today, this weekend, with those of us who are willing to be recognized, to be counted. There are hundreds of us here today. But there are millions of lesbians—and potential lesbians—around the country. It is our job to reach them.

But before we start designing our public relations campaign, we have to look at visibility in our own backyards. The first thing we must examine is our role in the feminist and gay movements. In many ways we have been the backbone of these movements, yet we've been relegated to the background of both. Without an agenda of our own, we've been benchwarmers in someone else's ball game—given a few symbolic turns at bat, but never a place in the starting lineup.

It is only recently that we have seen marked progress in the understanding of lesbianism as a feminist issue, and the welcoming of our visible participation in women's shared struggle. In the past we have often been forced to remain closeted and in the background by our own heterosexual sisters who were afraid of negative public opinion and sensational media coverage.

We have worked tirelessly for the feminist agenda, demanding free abortion when we cannot even have legal sex, equal pay for equal work when we cannot even keep our jobs, child care centers when we cannot even keep our children, and equal sharing of household chores when we cannot even live together openly.

Feminists, above all, should recognize and acknowledge the connection between lesbianism and feminism. If any woman is successful outside the home, she is called aggressive, overbearing, castrating. Worse yet, she is labeled a lesbian. Feminists must take a political stand in partnership with lesbians and strip the opposition of their strongest verbal weapon . . . the lesbian label. If we don't confront this issue every time it is raised by those who would try to separate and divide us, we are all in danger of being picked off, one by one. Hiding lesbianism encourages us to remain afraid of ourselves and to inflict injustice on one another because of our fears, and isn't that what sexism is all about?

And we can't just focus on educating heterosexual women to support us. Again, we must claim our very real and powerful identities. As lesbians we can't hide behind feminism because we're afraid to come out.

Sometimes women won't come out because they are afraid of losing approval, of losing influence. They must understand that to be out *is* to be influential. Some women are not used to power. And we've got to learn fast. Men attack the weakest within their ranks, and this is unacceptable. But what is worse is that women attack the strongest within our ranks, and this must stop!

Each of us, whether we choose to take overt power or not, must understand that it is not a limited commodity. With an understanding of power, and through our visibility, and in partnership with the feminist movement, we will create a framework of power and a political environment that will touch the lives of women everywhere—in our households, at our workplace, in our boardrooms, in our courtrooms, and in legislative chambers throughout this nation.

And what about the gay movement? This movement at least supports our lesbian identity and speaks to the happiness, fulfillment, and pride in loving someone of our own sex. But we know that gay politics will never cut deeply enough to eliminate the sexism in a sexist society, and that to be freed as gay people would still leave us oppressed as women.

Having said that, I think we must examine the political context in which we are operating and acknowledge that if we don't take some serious steps soon, our very survival will be at stake. In this age of AIDS, lesbian issues and women's presence in the gay movement have all but disappeared from the public eye. It is up to us to resurface.

As our brothers succumb to this deadly disease, we will be called upon to take more upfront leadership roles. We can't come to these positions with our skills alone. We must come with a vision. And that vision begins with the understanding that this plague, which is devastating our movement, our community, has a tremendous impact on lesbians as well as our gay brothers. We are already seeing a right-wing backlash against our community characterized by sharp increases in physical assaults on lesbians as well as gay men—and renewed attacks on our civil rights.

Aside from this, what does AIDS mean for us? It means devastating personal loss, to be sure—and also a threat to our movement's financial support. Gay men now provide 80 percent of the funding that keeps our shared movement alive. And I'm not just talking about our organizations and our political battles—I'm talking about our institutions: our restaurants, our newspapers, our shops, our places where we congregate, find each other, and where new people are able to come out safely. I don't want to wake up five years from now and find out they have disappeared.

Men provide most of this funding now, but we must also start giving like we have never given before. It must become a habit, an obligation, a duty, and yes, a privilege. I understand the economic disparity that we face, and I am still saying the same thing: We must give. We are only as strong as we collectively make up our minds to be. And we must attract to this movement women of means who will underwrite and create new institutions.

But personal loss and the financial impact of AIDS are not our only reasons for concern. Politically, we are in this just as deeply as our gay brothers. The Ethels and Freds sitting home watching *The Loveboat* in Kansas believe lesbians are linked to AIDS just as surely as gay men are. And when Jesse Helms gets up on the floor of the Senate to stop AIDS education funding and says, "It's time to call a pervert a pervert," you and I know he's talking about us, too. And when local sheriffs say that gay bars ought to be closed because they contribute to the spread of AIDS, you can bet they don't say, ". . . except for the lesbian bars." It's just a matter of time. And when a landlord kicks a person with AIDS out of his apartment, or an employer refuses to allow a man personal leave from his job to attend his lover's funeral, that slap ought to be felt just as hard on the face of every lesbian in America.

So should we be concerned about AIDS? You bet! Discrimination isn't confined to gay men; instead, it has a snowball effect. Lesbians must be prominent in this struggle because the enemies we face in government, in the courts, and in the media when we're fighting for AIDS issues are the same enemies we face when we are fighting for our rights as women and as lesbians. And so often these issues are just old-fashioned hatred, bigotry, and homophobia—repackaged by the right wing as "health concerns about AIDS."

For nearly two decades our community has built a political movement that would result in true freedom for lesbians and gay men. Now so many thousands of those men who have devoted their time and energy and dedication and love and commitment are dying. An entire generation of gay men. Our allies and friends. Dying or dead. I feel as though we're the lucky ones. We have been spared. But with our good fortune comes a responsibility to generations of lesbian and gay people to come. And most important of all, a responsibility to ourselves.

There's an old Chinese proverb that says, "If we don't change our direction we will surely end up where we are headed." We must be aware of where we want to go and what we want to accomplish.

We have tremendous potential as lesbians. The gay and feminist movements have tremendous potential for us. But only if we are visible, only if we use the power that we have—only if we *come out*.

I'd like to talk about coming out on a personal level for just a minute. The thought of revealing yourself as a total and whole human being (that is, as a lesbian) can be very frightening. Economic security—the prospect of losing a job or risking a promotion—is a real concern for most of us. But what is the cost of staying in the closet? You need to choose—and some of you already have chosen—what price you will pay for the lie you live. It's harder to be self-loving when you are constantly guarded, when you have to remind yourself that it's too terrible to let people know who you really are. Real pride and self-love are not permitted in the closet. We *pass,* and life passes us by.

How will your life change? Well, there's a possibility you may lose that job. But there's also a very good chance you *won't* lose it—and what a waste of worry and energy in the meantime keeping up a false impression. There was a time when coming out on the job nearly always meant you would lose it, or that your career would be ruined. But today, many employers don't care anymore what their employees' sexual orientation is. Maybe it's time to look for one of *those* jobs. In any case, there is no security in life, so why do we try to play it so safe? Instead, let's take all that energy we use to defend and protect ourselves, and turn it into a strength to be more powerful, more loving, more creative—to be whole.

Some of you are probably thinking, "Hey, listen. I'm fine just the way I am. Just leave me alone." And I say that you are *not* fine, that you are just settling. As long as we continue to believe what society has taught us—that our sexuality, our lifestyle is a personal, private matter—society as we know it will not change. They don't have to deal with us. And we can go on living a half-life in the confines of the closet, living in fear that we may be found out.

The person who has nothing to hide has the greatest power of all. As much as we are capable we have to come from an honest and integrated place. We must be acutely aware of who we are and be willing to live that way . . . and why? Because we are the product of our dreams and our desires. We actually create our own destiny.

Now there are limitations; we live in a dangerous world. And those who would tell you they are fearless are lying to themselves. There are good reasons to be afraid in this world, but being whole means having the courage to live out our choices in the face of difficult situations or confrontations.

I—the real me—the intrinsic self is not up for grabs. You can fail in a lot of things, but you can never fail at being yourself. Hang on to that strength, hang on to that core. Even if you are not in the closet, we all have special closet doors. Some of these doors are closed to family, some to friends, some are locked tightly at our jobs. But remember, those doors are locked from the inside. Now, more than ever, it is our duty to ourselves and our community to open them whenever we safely can. That safety is each person's own personal decision. No one—not I, not your family, not your friends, not the Supreme Court or right-wing fundamentalists—no one but you holds that key, and I urge you to turn it whenever you feel strong enough.

Finally, I want to talk about what we as a political force are capable of . . . a vision that we have not yet dared to grasp. We have to put ourselves out there and take our lumps, and proudly claim our victories. In order to win true freedom in our private lives, we must fight public battles.

Government affects every minute of our lives. It affects the air we breathe, the streets we drive on, what our paycheck is really worth, and most important, our freedom. When we are identified by our numbers, the power is awesome, because our numbers are awesome. And that is the basis upon which politicians make their decisions. They acknowledge and respond to the power of a constituency group that can be identified by impressive numbers, by financial contributions, by large numbers of votes. A community is only as politically powerful as its ability to affect an election.

If there were no other reason for you to come out, just your raw political power would be enough. You have the ability to change the way people live—specifically, the way *you* live. And we are not one-dimensional people; we are one of the most sensitive, caring communities in this country because we know what it's like to be oppressed. So our power will help others.

And you have the power, you know. Each of you is a part of a power so awesome that it's hard to acknowledge—because acknowledging that power means you are responsible for it. Unused power is a waste. However insignificant you may think your lives are—and they are not insignificant—know that you are being called on to create a difference.

The time has come. We are the future of feminism, and we are the future of gay rights. And we could be the future of this country. We are ready to be seen and heard. And we must not scale down our ambitions and settle for less. We cannot retreat to the closets. Never again. Our cause is just, our mission is clear, and our means are moral. Let's change this world—together!

Karen Clark:

Minnesota State Representative

Interviewed by Ginny Vida

(Editor's Note: Since this interview, Representative Clark was reelected in 1992 and 1994, and has been particularly active in the areas of economic conversion, child care, Native American issues, lead abatement, and housing. She has been chair of the Housing Committee since 1990, and was instrumental in bringing about the long-awaited passage

Karen Clark, Minnesota State Representative.

of the Minnesota Gay and Lesbian Rights Bill in 1993.)

When was it you first decided to run for office and what inspired you to do that?

I was invited to run in 1979 by a progressive caucus within the local Democratic party here. In Minnesota the Democratic party is called the Democratic Farmer Labor party, or DFL. There was a caucus formed within the state DFL party here called the Farmer-Labor Association (FLA), and I had joined it a year or two earlier. The FLA was one of the first mixed organizations I had worked in for awhile. A lot of my organizing activity in the three or four years before that had been pretty much devoted to community organizing within the lesbian community.

I guess the seeds for the decision to run for political office were sown many years prior. One significant event was in 1975 when I went to Sagaris, a six-week feminist theory institute in Vermont, and I had the opportunity to study there with a number of folks, including Charlotte Bunch, Rita Mae Brown, and others. One of the people who spoke to one of my classes was Elaine Noble, the assemblywoman from Boston. She was the first lesbian who had run for office in a state legislature, and she was very inspiring. I guess I didn't think of myself in that role, but I'm sure that her example planted a little seed, and later when I was asked to run by the FLA caucus, which was really a coalition of people who represented a lot of different interests that I'd been working on for years, I remembered Elaine as a role model, and thought, "Well, I guess I can do that."

The reason I was asked to run, I believe, was that I had such a broad base of interests and organizing experience for the thirteen years prior to that. I had been very active in the antiwar movement, civil rights movement, antinuclear issues, affordable housing, lesbian and gay issues, in my union [the American Federation of State, County, and Municipal Employees—AFSCME], and in neighborhood health care—women's health and reproductive rights issues. I was involved in organizing to try to provide women with options for birth control and abortion. It was illegal in Minnesota then, so we had to try to find the resources to help people get abortions outside the state or the country. At any rate, I had been involved in a whole array of is-

Dale McCormick, State Senator, Maine.

sues, so when they were looking for someone to challenge an incumbent who had really lost touch with the neighborhood, they asked me to think about running. And I was shocked, I must say. Public office was not something I had ever thought about for myself. I really saw myself as a more of an organizer. I was good at it—I think that's actually why I won—why we all won. A lot of us were organizers. We organized to take over the local Democratic Farmer Labor party machinery in my district, did it, and moved on down the road with that. A lot of people who had never been involved with electoral politics decided that year that they would work within the process to run me for election and see if there was a place where we could get some voice.

Could you explain why this particular incumbent was vulnerable?

Well, actually he was a majority whip in the Senate. So he wasn't considered a weak candidate, but he was very out of touch on women's issues. He had been warned at the DFL endorsing convention four years earlier that he should be voting prochoice, and he wasn't; he was antichoice in a district that supported the right to choose abortion. That was one issue. The main issue was that people just felt out of touch with him. So he was vulnerable; lots of people didn't know who he was. Eventually I started running for the state senate. Because we were successful in organizing within our local precinct caucuses and a great majority of the party delegates had decided not to endorse him but me instead, about a month before our endorsing convention he decided not to run for reelection; he decided to retire. So his spot became open.

So then the woman who had been the state representative for the previous eight years decided that she should run for that open senate seat, too. So she and I kind of went to it for awhile over the endorsement, and eventually I made a tactical decision to run for the house of representatives instead of the senate, because we were quite confident we could win that. And I had so many feminists calling me and saying, "Don't you two women run against each other. You're both good—don't make us choose." So even though my supporters were so determined, they went along with me in a decision that we made at a huge community meeting. We felt it was most important to have a victory for a progressive candidate, and we could win if we went for the house.

So it was the right decision. It was a little unusual to run the first time and win, but we were so well organized. We had all these organizers from all these different movements that got involved in the campaign, including many people who felt pretty alienated from the electoral process at that time.

What has happened from there is that we were able to go on to elect a number of other progressive candidates to the city council. And I'm really pleased to say that I had some role in helping to establish our first progressive legislators' caucus. There are just a few state legislatures around the country that have these. We don't call it a caucus; we call it a "study group." It's made up of a cross-section of people, a number of whom were also pretty involved in their communities on a real grassroots basis before they got elected. That's a long answer to your question.

You were openly identified as a lesbian, weren't you?

Oh, sure. As I mentioned, I had spent a number of years prior to that working in the lesbian community before I became involved in the Farmer Labor Association. It was a real conscious decision to get involved in that organization and to get involved in broader-based politics. We decided that we wanted to work on a number of fronts.

Was your lesbianism an issue in the campaign?

Oh yes, it's been an issue in every campaign. Sometimes it's been a more extreme issue than in others. In the first campaign it was a very big issue, although I was endorsed by the Democratic party because we took it over in our district. And I was endorsed by my local union, whose support was very crucial as it turned out. We were trying to get nurses unionized at the county hospital where I worked as a nurse practitioner. I was a representative to the Minneapolis Labor Union Central Council for our local AFSCME union and was very active in trade union politics. That helped me very much when I decided to run for office, because I not only got my political party's nomination, but labor's endorsement as well, although that wasn't easy, either. Lesbianism was an issue in the labor's endorsement, too. The guys didn't know what to think of it, but did come around with support because of my union work.

Anyway, although I had the Democratic Farmer Labor party's endorsement, I did have a DFL opponent in the primary election who called himself a progressive Democrat, who went door-to-door talking to people about the "lesbian issue." My Republican opponent wasn't quite so strident on this issue; in fact, I think he courted the gay community at the time, too. He is probably the only liberal Republican who ran against me. In every race since then, it's been very conservative, right-wing Republicans who have opposed me. But I'm pleased that the people I represent never bought it. I've always adopted the strategy of "Yes I'm a lesbian—and what are the other issues you're interested in? These are the issues I'm committed to and here's what I want to do to represent you." We also did some training to help people volunteering in my campaign figure out how to handle the lesbian baiting. For example, my district has a lot of senior citizens in it. I represent twenty-two high-rises that house mostly low-income elderly and disabled people. Some of my elderly supporters got lesbian-baited just for supporting me. They were challenged by some of their neighbors about my being a lesbian. We had to teach these wonderful elderly women about how to answer an antilesbian challenge. I mean first they learned to say the word—it was just incredible. And over the years for some campaign workers, it has been quite a challenge.

When the FLA first asked me to run, I said, "Do you know what you're going to say about this issue?" Some of the campaign workers were skittish about dealing with this issue and didn't want me to run as an openly gay candidate. But the majority just said, "We'll handle it. This is part of our coalition. We're just going to figure out how to do it." And we all worked so hard, we were able to overcome whatever disadvantage that might have given us. And that's happened every year since. Despite the continued lesbian baiting, nearly each election I've won by a higher percentage. Last year I won by almost 75 percent. It doesn't seem to be an issue that my constituents have enough trouble with that it stops them from voting for me.

What was your percentage the first time you ran?

I think it was 66 percent.

So that was very good, too.

Yes, it's never been real low.

That's really something to be proud of.

Yes, I'm real proud of the people who put the campaigns together for me, and I'm proud of the people in my district. One thing is that this is a very needy district, and people are not easily distracted by bigotry in a campaign; in fact, they have very high standards. When that tactic has been used, I've just talked about the issues that people are very concerned about in their daily lives.

Could you talk about what you're trying to do for your district? What are your priorities?

My agenda that I first ran on and that I continue to run on each year is an agenda of economic and social justice issues, and it deals with the necessities—you know, of affordable housing, jobs, affordable health care—especially for senior citizens and low-income people, and civil rights. I represent a lot of minority folks. I have one of the highest concentrations of urban American Indians in the country, growing African American and Southeast Asian communities, and a very high concentration of elderly and disabled folks, too. And, of course, I have my 10 percent lesbian-gay population. So civil rights issues have always been important.

There are also a lot of single parents in my district, the majority of whom are women. It's the lowest income district in the state. It does have a strong working class as part of it. It doesn't have much middle-class population.

A lot of the seniors are living in subsidized housing. I don't the know the percentage on AFDC, but it's higher than average, I suppose. It's a typical inner city district. Low income and working poor, working class—people struggling from paycheck to paycheck. Ninety percent are renters, so affordable housing has been a real big issue, and the rights of renters has been an ongoing issue. Affordable health care and child care have also been something I've worked on a lot and received some awards for. Job creation, workers' rights, women's rights, civil rights, issues of the elderly in general—basically I would say some of those real survival issues. And utility regulation, issues like that. Recently the increase in crime, particularly drug-related crime, has risen to the top of the list of issues that I'm concerned with. There has been a dramatic increase in crime in my district.

Minnesota has been known for its clean living. So it's a shock in some ways to go to the legislature and describe what's going on in our inner city neighborhoods. In fact this year we have an initiative that's called The Year of the City or the Year of the Neighborhoods. We're trying to get our legislature to focus on the three major cities, targeting housing and economic development in Minneapolis, St. Paul, and Duluth, which each have a lot of problems—unemployment, drug addiction, crime, as well as the deterioration of housing. We're trying to prevent some of the problems they are experiencing in Detroit or Los Angeles, and I think we have a good shot at it, because it's a state where people expect a lot of themselves. We have many very strong grassroots organizations. I represent five neighborhoods, and each of them has a very active neighborhood organization that I work with, respond to, am accountable to. And they are all in a "fight-back" mode right now, trying to deal with issues like boarded-up housing, which is proliferating all over, and disinvestment caused by federal tax laws. The Reagan administration's so-called tax reform took away a lot of incentives to landlords to keep up their buildings because of a loss of certain tax advantages. I'm hoping we can reclaim more home ownership for the people who live in those houses.

What do you feel especially that you've been able to accomplish for your constituents?

Well, one general thing, which is access to the system, to government. My office has always been a place where a lot people have come to understand what government can do for them, and for a lot of low-income and minority folks this has been an access point. And then there are some precedent-setting specifics—like a job creation bill and the worker right-to-know bills that passed in 1983, the Indian Family Preservation Act that passed in 1985, the Economic Conversion and Child Care Task Forces I've chaired but have yet to pass fully all their recommendations into law. One of the bills I'm really happy that we passed was the bias-related "hate" crimes bill.

The gay issue is holding up passage of this bill in New York State.

It had always held ours up, too. We first tried to pass a bill increasing penalties for hate crimes in 1983. Last year I tried a different strategy. I worked very hard on the legislation—then I turned it over to another individual to be the chief author. I

learned some things—that sometimes you have to step back in order to go forward. I went back to my organizer role, more behind the scenes on this one for awhile. One of the things we did was to have the governor create a state task force that went all over the state holding hearings on all bias-related crimes. From that we were able to build a movement, a coalition, and so after doing that for a while, we had the statewide base for passing the bill, and I spoke to one of my very good friends in the legislature who happened to be Jewish, and he was able to finish the job and pass the bill. And we now have a state law for the first time that includes the phrase "sexual orientation."

I worked a lot with the disabled community, helping to establish many community-based resources for the mentally retarded. I'm proud of the some of the empowerment bills I've been able to pass for them—self-respecting legislation.

Those are certainly things to be proud of. What advice would you have for other lesbians who are considering running for office? What do you think you've learned about getting elected and how to succeed in this area?

First of all, I would never advise anyone to run for office just because they are gay or lesbian. I wouldn't advise people to vote for someone just because they are gay or lesbian either. I think we deserve to have well-rounded, broad-issued progressive candidates representing us, and from what I can tell, every one of the gay and lesbian officials from around the country who have won elective office have been people who have had a broad-based agenda, and they happen to be lesbian or gay and are open about that, proud of it and work hard in office to represent gay and lesbian people, but it's just one part of a whole social and economic justice agenda that we have. So the first point is the person needs to be multi-issued, committed to justice on many levels, and willing to work in coalition. In order to get elected you have to do that. Most single-issue candidates don't get elected. The other point is that gay and lesbian people need to be twice as good, work twice as hard, be twice as committed, and I sure know that's particularly true for women candidates and officeholders. The standard to which elected women and people of color are held is much higher than that for white men. I hope in the future it may be easier. I really struggle to find balance so I can enjoy the fruits that I'm trying to create for others.

Has the national media taken note of your being elected? Have you had much exposure?

Yes, over the years, from the majority media, the progressive media to the right-wing media. I get called to speak to national groups occasionally about legislation that has to do more often with other progressive issues than gay or lesbian concerns.

One other thing, when you were first elected to the legislature, what was the reaction of other legislators toward you? Did they feel comfortable with you as a woman, as a lesbian? Has there been any change in their reaction to you over the years?

Oh yes, I would say people didn't know what to expect. In fact, a very good illustration of that discomfort was the first week that I was here, a friend of a friend who worked over here—one of the staff people—at the end of my first week in office, came in and closed the door, and said excitedly, "I just have to tell you—you'll never guess what people are saying about you." So I said, "What's going on?" And he said, "Well, they're saying that Karen Clark is a really *nice* person." I can't imagine quite what people expected.

Over the years, I think the major issues my colleagues have discomfort with now is more often around progressive political issues. My lesbianism is still an issue for a very few. But there's so much more that we're working on—and legislators are basically extremely polite. So it doesn't come up much very directly.

Have your politics changed since you've been in office, or are you still pretty much the same

progressive that you were when you were first elected? And have you found the need to compromise more than you thought you'd have to?

Well, I would have to say that my progressive instincts are still in very good shape. But I have certainly learned to work in a system which does involve negotiation. It's like being involved in the labor movement—you push for as much as you can, and settle for less than what you'd like, but you live to fight another day. So the kinds of compromises are similar to what you experience in other walks of life. I think I have a longer term view now. When I first came here I think I thought I had to pass everything at once. I guess I've had enough victories to know that over the long term they are possible, and also I have seniority now. This is my ninth session. I've been elected five times; I have to run every two years. Most of it's been fun. I wish the terms were longer, because every two years I have to go out and ask people to contribute and spend time getting reelected, but on the other hand, every two years I get treated to knocking on the doors of many of the people in my district, and that's very enjoyable. If I need to decide whether I want to continue doing this job, I go back and spend more time with the people I represent. They're like most of the people in this country—they expect the best of themselves and want the best of life. And there is so much goodness, and even though the problems are so severe, there is still a lot of hope there. I think what Jesse Jackson said, "Keep hope alive," is very applicable.

Anything else you'd like to say?

I do take it as a special responsibility to encourage other gay and lesbian people to run for elective office. There's nothing like having our own people at the table. We can have very good representatives, but there's nothing like having our own voice. We have an educational role to fulfill.

This year for the first time I'm the chair of a major committee, so for the first time I have my own administrative assistant—I've always shared a secretary and had no full-time staff. This year I have both of those. And I need that seniority to move my agenda forward in the house.

So it isn't just important to get elected, but it's important to stay in there and increase your base and your influence.

Yes.

Karen, you're really such an inspiration to lesbians around the country—to women around the country. Thank you.

An Interview with Martina Navratilova

Michele Kort

RuPaul, in star-spangled supermodel drag, is a hard act to follow. Maybe that's one of the reasons tennis superstar Martina Navratilova, in forearm-revealing T-shirt chic, took such a deep gulp of air before striding to the podium and addressing the marching minions in Washington in the spring of 1993.

"I am not going to cry, don't even try . . ." she warned, like a schoolmarm, as the throng gave her a

Martina Navratilova.

© Natt Nevins

swelling ovation. Maybe she was referring to her emotional courtside past, like the time she boo-hooed at the U.S. Open in 1981 after losing a hard-fought match to Tracy Austin—but winning the formerly hard hearts of the New York crowd.

This crowd had loved Navratilova for years, swooning over her butch athleticism and femme vulnerability and her ever-more-open sexual preference. They'd stuck with her through the "bisexual" years, through the bitter galimony lawsuit filed by her ex-lover, and now this appearance was a reward of sorts: No longer just a famous "known" lesbian, Martina Navratilova was finally a member of the *community*.

"What our movement for equality needs most," she began, numbering herself with the Washington million, "is to come out of the closet. . . . Let's come out and let all the people—read heterosexual—see what for the most part straight and square and boring lives we lead. . . .

"My sexuality is a very important part of my life, . . ." she continued, "but still is a very small part of my makeup. In any case, being a lesbian is not an accomplishment, it is not something I had to study for, or learn, or graduate in. It is what I am, nothing more, nothing less."

The applause for that line was probably heard at the White House, if not all the way back in the former Czechoslovakia, from whence Navratilova defected in 1975 at the tender age of eighteen. She left to compete at the highest levels of tennis without government control, but now she tells us there may have been other reasons as well (read on).

At first she was pudgy, inconsistent, and temperamental, but eventually she molded herself into a cool, sleek hitting machine, overpowering opponents with her mighty serve, deadly net game, and slithery backhand slices. Archrival Chris Evert had to start lifting unladylike weights to keep up with her. Indeed, every woman tennis player post-Navratilova realized that the little skirts they wore belied the sweaty work they'd have to do to compete in the game the expatriate had restyled in her own image.

Besides her legendary on-court exploits—18 Grand Slam singles titles (plus 38 in doubles and mixed doubles), including 9 Wimbledons and 4 U.S. Opens; an unbeaten streak of 74 matches in 1984 (the year she earned more than any other athlete except three boxers); 167 singles titles overall, more than any woman or man in tennis history; 332 weeks ranked number one; and almost $20 million in lifetime "official" tennis earnings (not counting appearance fees,

endorsements, and such)—Navratilova drew attention for her love and a mouthiness as well. The revelation of her affair with novelist Rita Mae Brown nearly threatened her quest for U.S. citizenship, and she seemed to backpedal in describing her next "friendship" with basketball star Nancy Lieberman, who became her trainer as well as (it's no longer an open secret) her lover. Then came the seven seemingly blissful years ensconced in Dallas and Aspen with former Maid of Cotton/mother-of-two Judy Nelson, who upon their Martina-initiated breakup sued Navratilova for half her earnings (and revealed a videotaped agreement backing up the claim).

Meanwhile, Navratilova became a gadfly of sorts, speaking out about everything from recycling to AIDS. When Magic Johnson announced his heterosexual exploits along with his HIV status, Navratilova decried the double standard that allows male athletes to sleep around with impunity while females would be tarred as sluts. She also didn't want anyone to forget that if Johnson had been gay, the public would have been far less forgiving.

"I've been doing benefits for AIDS since before it was politically correct," she said on a sunny 1993 August afternoon in Manhattan Beach, squeezing out her words between healthy bites of fruit, pasta, and green salad in the players' lunch tent. She's just come from a practice session for the annual Virginia Slims tournament, which, in lesbian terms, is the hard-court version of the legendary annual Dinah Shore golf tournament.

By week's end, Navratilova will have beaten Arantxa Sanchez Vicario in a come-from-behind match to take her eighth title in Manhattan Beach, and Sanchez Vicario, fifteen years her junior, will have lauded Navratilova in her Spanish-is-my-native-tongue syntax: "She is the best volley in all history. You are the one who has to make all the run and the passing shots." Two years later, the torch will have been passed: Sanchez Vicario will be number one in the world, and Navratilova will have retired from singles play after an emotional farewell tour.

But back then, Navratilova, her neck weighted down with crystals and a chain full of pride rings, was already anticipating what life would be like away from tennis. This interviewer had spoken with her at length twice before and found her cool and guarded; this time, she was warm, charming, and remarkably open. As she said herself at the march, "By coming out . . . we make ourselves personal, touchable, real. We become human beings."

I heard you had a great time at the March on Washington.

It was unbelievable. I would have paid to have been there. I was a wreck doing the speech, but I wanted to be a part of it.

You were nervous?

Wouldn't you be, talking to a million people? And I was reading something I wrote myself—the ego it took to think they would want to listen to what I had to say. But I figured if they booed me in the middle of the speech I'd say, "Hey, don't blame me, I'm just a tennis player!" Apparently they did listen, because people told me they came out because of the speech. That whole weekend would make you want to come out, because you felt part of the bigger group. You didn't feel so alone.

Did the march feel like a sort of debutante ball for you, being so publicly out?

Almost, I guess. It was nice to be able to be public and not feel like an outcast, an outsider, embarrassed about who you are. Which I've felt—not in the sense that I'm ashamed of being gay, but I've gotten the feeling in public that people are staring at me and my date, or whoever I'm with, thinking—"Oh, that's Martina's latest." I may not even be with that person, but people assume we're together if it's a woman. There a sexual undercurrent, or undertone, or judgment. And it was just so nonjudgmental to be a part of that weekend in Washington. There we were, and we had something in common, but we're beyond the sexuality. It's the straights who really concentrate on the sex part, and gays don't pay attention to it. It's not the most important thing in our lives.

How did you feel being the brunt of Liz Smith's rumor about you and k. d. lang?

Oh, it was ridiculous. If it had just ended ... but then they pick it up in Europe, they pick it up in magazines, and because she wrote it, it's *fact* now. Paparazzi took pictures of me and my sister in Rome, and wrote that it was me and k. d. lang. And then two weeks later they said it was me and Cindy Nelson—and it was still my sister. It snowballs and you can't get rid of it. Then Liz Smith writes a retraction, but by then the magazines have picked it up, and they don't print a retraction. It's just annoying. I think it was Lea Delaria who made a joke that people were happy these two lesbian women found each other—as if there are only two in the whole country. You have to laugh at it—we were the only gay people in that place; therefore, we must be together. And I wasn't even with k. d., either going or leaving. Liz Smith had all the facts wrong. k. d. was with her mother. I did see her at a post-bash party.

But you are friends with her.

Absolutely. I adore her, I love her. I want to be a groupie and see her perform. I want to be a groupie for Melissa [Etheridge] and Indigo Girls as well. I'm a good groupie, period.

Athletes always want to be rock stars.

And vice versa, rock stars want to be athletes. I want to learn to play an instrument. But not to be in a band—just to play.

You also recently appeared at a Gay Games fundraiser in New York where they raffled one of your rackets for eighteen thousand dollars, and then you offered a tennis lesson that went for thirty thousand dollars. How was that experience?

Unbelievable. A woman at the same table with me bought the lesson. She's from Atlanta, and that's where I've been for a month, playing Team Tennis. But I said she had to come to Aspen for the lesson. I said I'd throw in a dinner. I didn't know who was going to win it, but I figured I'd have fun.

Could you have appeared so publicly at gay events a year ago?

I've been out, but I haven't sort of been waving the flag. I was always told to lay low so I wouldn't throw off potential sponsors. Not pretend to be someone else, but just keep quiet. I finally realized I wasn't getting any deals anyway, and I was tired of laying low. I speak out on all the other issues, and this one is as important as any of them to me.

I sort of got thrown into the spotlight as well with Amendment 2 happening in Colorado, because I live there. All of sudden everyone wanted to talk to me; all of a sudden I'm this expert on gay rights.

You say you aren't going to worry about speaking out in terms of sponsors, but have you continued to pursue sponsorships without success?

I just don't get any answers. Things are always happening, but when push comes to shove they go sign Chris [Evert] or . . . somebody noncontroversial. I think it's even beyond the gay issue—it's just that I'm controversial. Have you ever heard Michael Jordan speak an opinion on anything he feels strongly about?

But do you think the climate will change for gays in sports? Will someone coming out after you have an easier time getting endorsements?

At a lot of companies it would be a nonissue now. Look at Banana Republic, or the Gap. They don't give a shit. It would depend on the company, really. People just don't want the stigma attached to them, and it may not have anything to do with endorsements. Someone may not be endorsable anyway; they may not have that big a name.

You said before in *The Advocate* that there were maybe five lesbian players among the top three hundred on the tour.

In the top one hundred. Probably it's a little higher. It's not that sports makes you gay, but you're more exposed to those feelings because you're around women more. You have a choice. One year there may be five lesbians, one year there may be ten.

But no one's coming out.

No. And there are some gay men tennis players, no one's come out. It will be interesting to see when another athlete comes out, because I'm sort of the Lone Ranger out there. At least in the entertainment industry there are more, men and women. That's why it was so great at k. d.'s concert in New York. If someone wants to take a picture of us, I don't have to hide about it. She's out, and it felt so relaxing to just be out and not pretending.

It's hard to ask somebody to [come out]. You're exposing yourself not just to your friends and family, but to the whole world. There are gay football players out there, but they're not going to come out for all the tea in China, because of the public and peer pressure they'd feel. It's much different for someone in the public eye, because you always have to do interviews. Even if you say you won't talk about it, you're going to have to expend the energy, and then it's going to be "the gay football player." That's what my speech was about in Washington. You don't read about "the heterosexual tennis player." I'm just speaking as a human being, not as a gay human being. . . . But it just overtakes all the other tags, and it's disconcerting. Like Barbra Streisand said at the Oscars, it will be great when they don't say, "the first female director," but just "director." Hopefully one day those tags won't be there.

You've been increasingly outspoken about political issues—do you see yourself pursuing politics or activism in the post-tennis future?

Not politics; activism, yes. I think I can make more difference as an activist than a politician. Besides, I can't run for president anyway, so why bother?

And you don't mind being a lesbian spokeswoman?

It's not something I've strived for, but I'm not going to run away from it either. If I can make a difference, then I accept that responsibility with great pride. I'm just astonished I can make a difference. I always try to right wrongs, and if I can right this wrong, it's important to me.

When your autobiography *Martina* **came out, Rita Mae Brown wrote that all the energy you put into being number one in tennis took away from the energy you put into yourself as a person. Do you think that was fair?**

It's fair. You have to sacrifice, and athletes, generally speaking, are very immature human beings. At thirty they're not where normal thirty-year-olds are, because all their effort goes into the sport and they don't work on . . . personal growth.

But I've been working on that a lot the last couple of years. After Judy, I went to a therapist. I've done major personal growth the last two and a half years, especially this year, because I've been single for the first time and I've really spent time on my own, by myself. I had a blast! Wish I had done it sooner.

Still single, eh?

Yeah. Well, I'm seeing somebody, but I'm taking things slowly. In the past it was "Let's get married tomorrow." I've learned.

We've all watched your public coming out now, but what about the private side of coming out? You were a little coy about it in your autobiography. Did you start coming out when you were still in Czechoslovakia?

I left Czechoslovakia about three months after I realized I was gay. . . . I knew I was going to be gay for the rest of my life. Looking back now, I realized that may have had something to do with my decision to leave, because I knew I couldn't be gay in Czechoslovakia, because that country is so repressive—was so repressive. They used to put gay people in institutions there.

So when you came here, was it hard for you dealing with your personal coming out?

I realized that morning [after first being with a woman] that my life would just be a whole lot more difficult, but I knew that that's where my heart was. I thought, "Okay, so that's what I've been feeling all these years."

How do you envision your life when you hang up the rackets?

First, I'll have unscheduled time. Because I've never had that. Even a month off. I'm sure I'll be doing political stuff. There are so many good causes out there—recycling, environmental stuff, animals, kids, old people, AIDS, gay rights, women's rights.

Were you always so concerned about issues?

I always had this great urge for fair play. Unfairness drove me *nuts*. If I saw a bigger kid beating up on a little kid, I would go help out. That was just inborn in me. I would help old people across the street, carry their bags. And I still do. Or give up my seat for an old woman or man, without thinking. I couldn't believe when other people didn't do it. I guess I'm just doing it on a bigger level, but I always had that sense in me. If I cut up an orange, I'd give my friend the bigger half. I'd feel guilty if I took the bigger half.

These days that would be called codependence.

If that's what it is, I don't care.

Copyright © 1995 by Michele Kort

Lesbians in the Media:

Myth and Reality

Victoria A. Brownworth

Lesbian chic.

This is the new media buzz phrase of the nineties, coined when lesbians suddenly began appearing everywhere in the media in the summer of 1993. Lesbians had been as unknown to the media prior to May 1993 as they had been to Queen Victoria: They simply didn't exist. When an article appeared in a newspaper or magazine or when a news story hit television and the issue was "homosexuality," lesbians were not part of the equation. The focus was always on gay men. Lesbians were the invisible women. But in the hot summer of lesbian chic, it seemed that lesbians had *arrived*. First there was a cover story in *New York* magazine that discussed lesbians and style. Recently "out" lesbian pop icon k. d. lang was on the cover. That piece was followed by stories in other mainstream magazines that had never mentioned lesbians before, let alone feature them as an issue of "chic." *Mademoiselle* did its first-ever story on lesbians. *Vogue* featured lesbian fashion. And the *coup de grace* was lesbians—not gay men—on the cover of *Newsweek*. By midsummer, *Vanity Fair* had interviewed k. d. lang and featured her on its cover as well.

Lesbians were as hot as the heat waves that blistered most of the country. Movies with lesbians, what lesbians were wearing, lesbian authors, and lesbian pop stars like lang and Melissa Etheridge were the E ticket items (best seats in the house) in the summer of 1993. Lesbian activists applauded the media attention, though some, like former executive director of the National Gay and Lesbian Task Force (NGLTF), Urvashi Vaid, were bemused by it. Noted Vaid, "We've always been here. Why is everyone just noticing us *now?*"

Why indeed? What caused the sudden shift in focus?

The phenomenon of lesbian chic has its roots in the years of invisibility that came before the media blitz. An invisibility that activists like Vaid, or the cofounder of the Lesbian Avengers activist group, writer Sarah Schulman, say has not been eradicated with a few magazine covers and a flurry of sound bites. Said Schulman, "I won't say I'm not pleased to see lesbians getting media attention. My question is, is it the right attention, is it the kind of attention we want and need. Or is it just more lip service?"

Linda Villarosa, senior editor at *Essence* magazine and one of the country's most visible lesbians of color, believes the shift in media representation of lesbians is lip service at its worst. "I refused to be associated with the whole lesbian chic thing," said Villarosa, who had declined interviews with several magazines featuring lesbian stories. "I felt that the whole thing was to make the media feel good for discovering us. And did you notice how many women of color were mentioned in all these references to lesbians in America? There were two quotes—one from Urvashi and one from [African American writer] Jackie Woodson. I was not about to be another token." Villarosa added passionately, "If you are going to write about lesbian visibility, you have to write about more than a handful of famous, out white women."

Villarosa's response is reflective of the reality of media representation of lesbians in the United States—representation of lesbian lives has yet to be mainstreamed. Pop icons and New York fashion trends are not the sum total of lesbian life in the United States. And in the months that followed the big blitz in which some lesbians believed the media had finally taken notice of 10 percent of America's women, lesbians receded into the media gray areas once again. Several serious issues regarding lesbians hit the news in the ensuing months. A study was released that posited lesbians were at higher risk for breast cancer than other women—nearly three times the risk factor—but media coverage was relegated to the queer press. Antilesbian violence overtook violence against gay men in several major cities in the statistics; then two lesbians in Ovett, Mississippi, were targeted for violence by the entire town when they turned their ranch into a spiritual retreat for lesbians. This news did not qualify for mainstream attention either. In fact, NGLTF had to force the FBI and the Justice Department to investigate. Even after an investigation was launched, the media continued to ignore the story.

Media treatment of the situation in Ovett, Mississippi, typifies the focus—or lack of—on les-

© Kathryn Kirk

Lesbian float, Lesbian and Gay Pride March, 1989.

bians in the print and electronic media. While the summer of 1993 may have brought lesbians into the public eye in what appeared to be a dramatic wave of attention, the type of attention lesbians received was actually little different from what it had been in previous years.

A close examination of the heightened visibility revealed the same perception of lesbianism that has prevailed in the United States for the last fifty years. Each of these stories portrayed lesbians as hypererotic figures. In the *Newsweek* article, which was by far the most diversified, a glossary of essential lesbian terms was appended. There were five: lipstick lesbian, butch, femme, vanilla, and sex-positive. This glossary is the litmus of how evolved media (and by extension, mainstream America's) perception of lesbians has become. Rather than a focus on the civil rights struggles of lesbians, rather than an examination—cursory though it might have been—of lesbian lives in the United States and the

diversity of those lives, the one actual news story on lesbians portrayed women identified by their sexual behavior and their dress.

Had this been a story on any other minority—or even an article on heterosexual women—with sexuality and dress as the locus, there would have been widespread outrage over what would have been perceived as racial, ethnic, or even gender stereotyping.

"It's indicative of how little attention we've received in the media that any of us are excited by these articles," noted Ruthann Robson, professor of law at City University of New York and one of the country's leading experts on lesbians and the law. "The reality of lesbianism in the United States comes down to exclusion in almost every area, whether it is legal, social, or cultural. So in a way it is not at all surprising that lesbians would find the sudden attention evidence of inclusion—even if that is not really the case."

Schulman, whose Lesbian Avengers group was incorporated specifically to draw attention to lesbian issues, says that getting the media to address lesbians in an ongoing fashion is paramount. "What we need is recognition of lesbians as a minority group with the same value as other groups, the same value as straight America."

But that kind of recognition is slow in coming. In 1994 there were an estimated 15.5 million lesbians in the United States—10 percent of the women in the country. Lesbians represent one of the largest minority groups in the United States, but are represented least in the media. This underrepresentation, or in some cases, lack of any representation, is not just a matter of reportage. In addition to newspapers and magazines, lesbians are also absent from television, movies, and books, except when those media are produced by lesbians for lesbians.

Television and film are two areas in which the standard for lesbian visibility has not changed in over thirty years. By 1994 there had not been a film made by a lesbian director in Hollywood since 1933 when Dorothy Arzner made her last film. Films about lesbians, whether produced in Hollywood or as independent productions, have overwhelmingly been visions of lesbians as sex-driven, out-of-control maniacs. Frequently these women are actually killers, as in *Windows* (1983), *The Hunger* (1987), or *Basic Instinct* (1992). Lesbianism on the big screen has almost always revolved around death: The women are either murderers or suicides (as in *The Fox* [1968] or *The Children's Hour* [1963]). Lesbianism, as portrayed in nonpornographic films, is a terrible fate; women are driven to either kill or be killed. Only a handful of films have any kind of healthy perspective on lesbian relationships. *Desert Hearts* (1985) remains the only feature film in which lesbians are the central characters and are both alive and together at the end of the film. But it took the director, Donna Dietch, over ten years to raise the money to make the film and another two years to find a distributor for it. And in the nine years following the film's release, she has not been able to get funding for another lesbian feature film. Tim Hunter, an award-winning director (and a straight man) optioned the film rights for lesbian novelist Katherine Forrest's detective thriller, *Murder at the Nightwood Bar*. Hunter plans to shoot his film, but he has experienced several years of delays in securing sufficient funding to produce it.

Other films made from original lesbian source material have suffered from delesbianization. Alice Walker's Pulitzer Prize–winning novel, *The Color Purple,* when brought to the screen, had none of its lesbian character intact. *Fried Green Tomatoes* (1991) also became the story of female friendship only when it was realized as a film.

Television has had more success with bringing lesbians to the screen, but also more controversy. Between 1989 and 1994, no fewer than forty lesbian characters had appeared on drama series, sitcoms, soap operas, and movies made for television. But few of these characters were different from their film counterparts. In Donna Dietch's miniseries of Gloria Naylor's novel, *The Women of Brewster Place,* two of the main characters are a black lesbian couple. But one is dead at the end of the movie. And when the movie was made into a drama series for television, the lesbians were left on the cutting-room floor.

The long-running series *L.A. Law* introduced a lesbian character in 1991, an attorney who becomes romantically interested in another woman at her law firm. But one kiss and one suggestive evening later, the other woman had left the show, citing creative differences, and the lesbian character rediscovered her bisexual nature.

Bisexuality was the sentence for another lesbian character, played by bisexual comedian Sandra Bernhard on the top-ranked sitcom *Roseanne.* Bernhard's character spent one season romancing Morgan Fairchild and the next involved with Tim Curry. As the character explained things to Roseanne, "It's not about labels." However, an episode scheduled to air in early 1994, in which Bernhard and Roseanne spend the evening in a lesbian bar, finds Roseanne being kissed by Mariel Hemingway. Affiliate stations around the country refused to air the episode because of the kiss. But in fact, the kiss on *L.A. Law* was far more provocative. On *Roseanne,* no actual kissing was seen by viewers, only the back of Hemingway's head. The most interesting aspect of the *Roseanne* episode came at the end of the show, when Roseanne's husband became sexually aroused by his wife's description of her lesbian encounter. *This* was the groundbreaking scene: Lesbianism has always been an area of titillation for heterosexual men; the sitcom may have been the first TV program to address that issue. But sexual explicitness remains a heterosexual area on television. Lesbian characters who are not portrayed as murderers, potential suicides, bisexuals, or women otherwise unhappy with their status as lesbians have not yet found a place on the small screen, just as their film counterparts have not found a place on the big screen.

"Legally and socially, lesbian sexuality is very threatening, historically," explains Robson. "Lesbianism is often *perceived* as a crime, even if there is no *actual* criminal statute covering it. There is a definite threat attached to women who are lesbian. As a consequence, lesbians either suffer invisibility or cultural backlash."

That backlash can take many forms. When deconstructed, the heightened perception of lesbian visibility in the nineties is actually just a subtle reworking of earlier attitudes toward lesbians. Perhaps the most obvious example of this was the k. d. lang cover story in *Vanity Fair*. Backlash iconography was implicit in the cover photo: lang was posed in a barber's chair, dressed in a man's suit. Her face was covered in shaving cream and she was being shaved by supermodel Cindy Crawford. Crawford was dressed in a bathing suit and short, stiletto-heeled laced boots. This cover states emphatically that lesbians dress like men, act like men and are after what men want—luscious babes half-naked in fetish attire. Inside photos show lang and Crawford licking each other, and the one pull-quote in the story refers to lang's desire to have a penis.

The clarity of this stereotype is definitive in a straight magazine. And this clarification of just *who* mainstream American media thinks lesbians are is reinforced on television and in films, as well as in newspapers and magazines. There is no subtle nuance here: This is not a message that lesbians have arrived, are accepted, and are being reconsidered in mainstream terms. Rather the so-called lesbianizing of the media epitomizes the pornographic and medical stereotyping of lesbians since Freud: Lesbians are either women who want to be men and have "male" desires, or lesbians are women who are deranged, unhappy, or at best, really aren't sure they *are* lesbians or don't really *want* to be lesbians. Lesbians may have become more visible to the mainstream via the media, but that visibility is, as Schulman and Villarosa suggest, questionable.

The efforts by groups like Lesbian Avengers to bring the totality of lesbian life into the mainstream, however, *is* working. Militant actions to create interest in lesbians as media subjects have helped to force attention where none has previously existed. And as other civil rights movements can attest, media inclusion of any sort is the first step toward visibility. Thirty years ago, in the heyday of the black civil rights movement, Bill Cosby (in *I, Spy*) was the only black on television. Today, over 29 percent of network programming includes African Americans or is solely directed toward African Americans, who represent 12 percent of the total U.S. population. And it has only been in the last few years that African Americans have been portrayed in their diversity on television, in film, and in other media. The early representations were, as Villarosa attests, "about stereotypes. Certainly one of the reasons *Essence* was created was to meet the needs of black women who were not being addressed by other women's magazines. That is why the lesbian and gay press has been so important to building visibility for lesbian and gay Americans. We need to see ourselves in the media in positive and affirming ways."

Most lesbian activists harbor reservations about the current focus on lesbian "chic," unsure if it is either positive *or* affirming. "My life is not a *trend*," notes Robson, "and I think that many of us resent being characterized as a fashion statement for hip heterosexuals. I worry when words like 'tolerance' are used, when our lives are so minimized and so reduced. This is just another way of putting lesbians in their place. I think it's dangerous to overlook that reality."

Yet other activists believe that any media attention for lesbians is a step toward greater visibility, and by extension, toward achievement of a civil rights agenda. But visibility without consciousness, typified by the *Vanity Fair* cover, creates other problems, reinforcing old stereotypes and creating new ones without ever defining *who* lesbians really are, exploring the range of their lives beyond the confines of sexuality and fashion. For although lesbians are finally out of the media closet, they remain one-dimensional figures, objectified as well as vilified. Twenty-five years after Stonewall, lesbians are still struggling for visibility in the media—visibility of a diverse and comprehensive nature. Visibility remains the most vital issue for lesbians in the nineties, an issue that goes far beyond the limitations of lesbian chic.

Bearing Witness in the Age of AIDS

Virginia M. Apuzzo

(Editor's Note: The following article is based on a speech presented by Virginia M. Apuzzo at the Summit on HIV Prevention for Gay Men, Bisexuals, and Lesbians at Risk, July 1994, in Dallas. As a prominent national leader of the lesbian and gay movement, Ms. Apuzzo has vigorously promoted increased funding for AIDS-related research and services and has called upon lesbians and gay men to join forces in responding to the AIDS crisis.)

Nikki Giovanni, an African American woman, writes in her poem "Dirty Windows" about what exists outside of those windows—the hostile, probing, peering judgmental and oppressive world—and suggests that the inside is safe and secure. Through dirty windows, she says, they can't see inside . . . but then . . . I can't see outside either.

So often over this weekend I have heard and felt that some individuals' worlds have become smaller, more closed, more constricted in an effort to feel safer, to avoid the pain of contact, to deal with grief. I understand and share that. And I respect that. But I believe that if we as a community are to thrive, and if we as whole persons are to enhance our ability to live fully, then we must come out again.

© JEB (Joan E. Biren)

The AIDS Quilt, Washington, D.C., 1987.

There are many forms of closets, and our pain, fear, and grief must not become our emotional closet. We have a *movement* that seems to have sought refuge from AIDS in a new closet. Our movement will suffocate unless we throw open the doors of that closet, too!

We need that movement back in the AIDS effort. Consider some of what it was able to accomplish when it was engaged in this effort—*in the Reagan-Bush era*. It spoke to matters related to the insurance industry, to the health care industry, and it raised questions related to the role of schools in the face of the most critical health crisis of our time.

It spoke out with an insistence that the intransigence of religious institutions not be permitted to cost the lives of their members. It raised for public repudiation the posture of a renegade Justice Department that would have conspired in the discrimination of those disabled by AIDS. Our position on the question of the HIV test, insurance, and employment, framed in the context of predictive tests, touched millions who would be at risk for conditions ranging from Alzheimer's to Huntington chorea, diabetes and hepatitis B.

Ours was a call aimed at the very posture of government towards its citizens. And we recognized that our ability to make the essential linkages to other groups in our society—on whom these issues also impinged—would determine the extent to which we would complete the long political transformation of our community from an issue to be dodged to a constituency to be reckoned with.

Additionally, if community development is indeed an essential strategy for AIDS prevention, then those organizations that purport to represent us must step up to the plate, commit the resources, and do the job. Without the kind of community development that lesbian and gay movement organizations can help to provide, our AIDS prevention programs will not be sufficient to sustain the comprehensive support our people need to prevail over the long haul.

Our second order of business is to come to grips with the question of whether or not we want this movement of ours to really be a movement for social change. Unless and until that question is squarely faced, we will bicker about strategy, we will be divided by differing objectives, we will be cut off from other significant alliances.

Unless and until we address this question we will be high on the rhetoric of our diversity and low on coming to grips with how it does, in fact, separate us—male and female, rich and poor, people of color and whites. Unless and until we confront the implications of this question, we will see our movement as a series of events and not a process; we will read these events as signposts with no agreement on where we are going—or how to get there. And while we bicker about whose job it is to take the initiative here, our people are dying.

Once there is consensus regarding our commitment to social change, the agenda will not require a five-year plan to formulate. And, it will be abundantly clear why HIV *must* have a place on that agenda—HIV/AIDS looms so large precisely because it brings with it so many of the crucial problems our society has left unresolved:

> *The face of AIDS is poverty unaddressed.*
> *The face of AIDS is racism unchallenged.*
> *The face of AIDS is sexuality unresolved.*
> *AIDS is a worldwide war on drugs fought with a slingshot.*
> *It's four million street kids worldwide.*
> *It's homelessness in every city in this country.*

Each of those issues involves our community. Each requires a commitment to fundamental change in society.

My last point is the most difficult for me to address. As I listened to my brothers speak of unprotected sex and the rise of drug use, I asked myself what my response would be if they were straight men speaking of unprotected sex with women.

I know I would be enraged.

I want to understand all of the driving elements of complexity here, I want to work to build all of the supports necessary to help my brothers through the lifetime of assaults that have diminished their sense of selves—but most of all I want them to live.

I have renewed appreciation of the courage and integrity it took for Jesse Jackson to stand up and talk about the tragedy of black-on-black violence. He knew how complex the issues were, how long the oppression had been perpetuated, how absent the institutional support for self-esteem.

While I hear the pain that has given rise to acts which ignore the danger to self and others by unprotected sex, I must say to you: We cannot afford to ignore the issue of taking responsibility. Self-determination and responsibility must stand side by side or we have anarchy. And we have more death.

Consider the logical limits of failing to take responsibility in this regard. Consider it in the cost of lives and resources. Look at the environment of unsafe sex and increased drug use and remember that silence equals death.

This crisis must bring us, as other crises have brought other communities, back to the glaring realization that we share this time, this space—this life—together. That for all that distinguishes us, one from the other, be it language, culture, race, class—what we do share is what must be most cherished, and that is life.

For the AIDS community, this conference represents a significant step. It remains for our movement to take the next step. I believe a local and regional process that culminates in a lesbian/gay/bisexual summit has great potential. In the context of such a summit the movement should outline its AIDS agenda clearly, articulate its values boldly, and move ahead fearlessly.

Whatever else we do in this movement of ours, we must come together around something which speaks to more than the agenda I have seen to date. We must create in this world of ours an environment that will enable us to bear witness to the truth of our lives . . . we must bear witness to the love in our lives.

And critical to our role as humans on this planet, we must bear witness to the lives that tie us inextricably to other lives. In short, we must say "Yes" to our lives—a yes that talks back to every institution resolved to silence us. A yes that acknowledges that the life of the soul cannot flourish or thrive amid brutality and terror, bigotry, violence, and disease.

Our future will have a history that will mark this moment. Let it say of us that we were the freedom fighters in the ultimate liberation movement. That we left no one behind as we struggled to fashion something new and healthy and just.

Let it say of us that we loved one another fully, fiercely, and deeply and that we fought to save each of our lives, and we treasured those lives. Let it say of us that we built a community and institutions in that community that would live on after us to care for and teach and learn from our young people. Let it say of us that we cherished our time together and that our work was a hymn to life. Let us aspire to have them say of us what we would say of the heroes and heroines not here today.

A few lines from the poet Stephen Spender:

I think continually of those who were truly great
Who, from the womb, remembered the soul's history
Through corridors of light where the hours are suns
Endless and singing. . . .

The names of those who in their lives fought for life,
Who wore at their hearts the fire's centre.
Born of the sun they travelled a short while towards
*   the sun,*
And left the vivid air signed with their honour.[1]

Brothers and Sisters—breathe deeply.

Notes

1. From "I think continually of those," *Selected Poems* by Stephen Spender. Copyright © 1934 and copyright renewed 1962 by Stephen Spender. Reprinted by permission of Random House.

V

Education

Over the Rainbow:

The Struggle for Curricular

Change

Elise Harris

(Editor's Note: An earlier version of this article appeared in the September/October 1993 issue of Out *magazine.)*

One early morning, October 1992, in Brooklyn, several hundred New Yorkers trundled off chartered buses from nearby Queens and the Bronx. They made their way to Chancellor Joseph Fernandez's board of education office at 110 Livingston Street, toting placards with such slogans as GAYS FIREBOMB CARS? Someone would later explain that they thought this was the case, but they weren't sure, so they added the question mark. They may not have had all their facts down that morning, but one thing was certain: If a domineering chancellor of the board of education was trying to teach sodomy and show gay pornography to their first-grade children, it was worth getting up at 6 A.M. to protest in front of his office.

A few months earlier, on June 23, a similar group of picketers gathered in L.A. outside the board of ed offices to protest the observation of June as Gay Pride Month in the Los Angeles Unified School District. A San Fernando Valley representative of Parents and Students United—which organized the demonstration with the Christian Coalition—lamented that her kids would have to take "Bedroom 101" as drafted and approved by "the special-interest board of indoctrination." One parent's poster addressed the only openly gay member of the board: JEFF HORTON: GET BACK INTO THE CLOSET!

These tense skirmishes are just the tip of the iceberg. "We've had some very bloody battles over the curriculum," muses Barbara Huberman of the North Carolina Coalition on Adolescent Pregnancy.

Huberman was instrumental in getting a comprehensive sexuality education curriculum implemented in the New Hanover County school system. "Down here, there's a lot of Jesse Helms mentality—they have the same opposition to any critical thinking," she says. "There was one really young, vibrant principal, Joe something, in the Gaston public schools, who was really gung ho to start a progressive school called The Odyssey School. The odyssey—like education as a lifelong journey. But he was found dead one day in his garage. There were rumors about whether he was murdered, or was it suicide? Most of us like to think it was an accident. The police never closed it out.

"So there's a lot of self-censorship across the board down here," she continues. "I mean, it's not so much what happens as what they think will happen."

Next to the harsh political realities of these adult games, the infamous "Children of the Rainbow" curriculum, a 443-page teachers' guide to conducting lessons in New York first-grade classrooms, seems like child's play. The guide was written during the tenure of Chancellor Fernandez and under the direction of multicultural education director Evelyn Kalibala. It contained three pages on families and family structure, a universal first-grade topic, except that this curriculum included gay- and lesbian-headed families. Another brief section, written primarily by Bronx first-grade teacher Elissa Weindling, was called "Fostering Positive Attitudes Toward Sexuality" and explained that queer teens were more likely to drop out of school, commit suicide, and abuse drugs than their peers, and urged educators to lend a hand. The curriculum's bibliography listed three children's titles from the gay imprint Alyson Wonderland: *Gloria Goes to Gay Pride*, *Daddy's Roommate*, and the notorious *Heather Has Two Mommies*, which has become a symbol for the entire fiasco, held up in school board meetings coast-to-coast as "proof positive" of a massive gay-recruitment conspiracy targeting the nation's schoolchildren.

Heather was written by the Northampton-based Lesléa Newman in 1989, when "Children of the Rainbow" was a mere twinkle in Fernandez's eye. But 1989 was the beginning of this story in another way as well. During the hot summer that year, several heinous hate crimes were perpetrated in New York neighborhoods. Yusuf Hawkins was killed by

Joyce Hunter, cofounder, Harvey Milk High School, New York City.

© JEB (Joan E. Biren)

a white mob in Bensonhurst, Brooklyn, and Julio Rivera, a gay Latino, was murdered in a parking lot in Jackson Heights, Queens.

In response, on November 15, 1989, the central board of education adopted the multicultural education resolution submitted by the late Chancellor Green. The resolution stated that programs would "take appropriate steps to bring about the elimination of practices which foster attitudes and/or actions leading to discrimination against students, parents, or school personnel on the basis of race, color, religion, national origin, gender, age, sexual orientation, and/or handicapping condition." That is, the hope was that this document would help stem the rising tide of hate-motivated crime in the city.

"If a six-year-old first grader is learning to hate, at sixteen, they're old enough to beat up a gay person," says Francine Marchese, a member of the direct-action group the Lesbian Avengers and a preschool teacher in Manhattan. Matt Foreman of the New York City Gay and Lesbian Antiviolence Project notes that in 1992, 31 percent of perpetrators of gay-bashings were under age eighteen. "People aren't born to hate," he adds, "they're taught to hate. [A multicultural curriculum] is not a panacea, but it's the only way we can have any hope of heading off this violence." (While both left and right swear that what Johnny reads in kindergarten will shape his beliefs and behaviors for years to come, there has been very little academic inquiry or public discussion investigating these assumptions.)

There were, therefore, two major reasons to fight for gay and lesbian inclusion in public school curricula. One was accuracy, to represent the full spectrum of human family life and kinship structures. Gay and lesbian parents wanted their children to see their lives included and represented, and to prevent ostracism at the hands of other children. And the body of queer activists, nonparent and parent alike, felt that curriculum inclusion helped prevent violence against gay men and lesbians. Unfortunately, the usual assertions were made that those pederastic, devious queers had something entirely else in mind.

If the heart of the curriculum conundrum is the

bugaboo about old men in trenchcoats and predatory female gym teachers, its "professional" expression is found in the war over "age-appropriateness"—the freeze-dried educational buzzword for determining what a child can understand and at what age. Among education experts, there was little debate: Most agreed the "Children of the Rainbow" was a good first-grade curriculum. One of the few who questioned the age-appropriateness was Sandra Feldman, the president of the United Federation of Teachers, who now insists she was "the first and strongest supporter of the curriculum," although at the time she told *The New York Times* that the Rainbow was "a mistake."

"Of course first grade is age-appropriate," says gay parent Doug Robinson, who has two sons, ages four and seven, and is cochair of New York's Center Kids. "By the first grade, kids know all the defamatory words. You hear them in the playground." Nor does he think that the introduction of gay families would prompt uniquely uncomfortable questions for educators to answer. "The curriculum doesn't explain gay parents' sexuality or how a child is conceived, it identifies who are the parents of that child." In 1991, *Newsweek* determined that there were 7 million children for whom "the parents of that child" were gay or lesbian.

The pro and anti extremes of the Rainbow battle spoke such different languages that the debacle could hardly be characterized as a debate. On the anti side were parents, some who felt their rights were violated by Fernandez's top-down administrative style. "We send our children here," says Queens parent Cathy Laffin. "We have the right to say what they learn." Other parents were inspired by the rhetoric of Christian evangelicals—many saw a video by conservative activist Dolores Ayling, in which she read a passage from a 1987 "Speaking Out" op-ed piece in Boston's *Gay Community News*:

We shall sodomize your sons, emblems of your feeble masculinity. We shall seduce them in your schools, in your gymnasiums, in your locker rooms, in your youth groups . . . wherever men gather together. They will be recast in our image and come to crave and adore us . . . all churches who condemn us will be closed. Our only gods are handsome young men.

The article was intended as "a Swiftian satire of right-wing paranoia," says *GCN* editor Michael

Bronski. "To take it literally is like believing *Spy* magazine when they say that Donald Trump and the Dalai Lama were separated at birth." But literally it was taken—in New York, in Birmingham, Michigan, and in the *Congressional Record*—and it has since gone wherever organizations associated with the "New Right" or the religious Right have seen fit to go.

Mary Cummins, the president of the rebel School Board 24 in Queens that rejected the Rainbow, also put the "dis" in disinformation, alleging that the curriculum was "dangerously misleading homosexual/lesbian propaganda . . . to promote acceptance of sodomy and cover up its dangers." Her appeal was targeted at the majority of parents who, it would later be apparent, had never read the curriculum (it contained no references to sexuality). At a UFT meeting attended by six hundred riled-up teachers, Sandra Feldman found that only five of them had actually read the curriculum they were protesting.

Advocates of the curriculum naturally saw things differently. "The mission of a public school system run democratically is to accept fundamental differences and conflict," says pro-Rainbow activist NTanya Lee, a member of Black AIDS Mobilization (BAM). Schools, she says, need to "educate young people to think for themselves."

It is important to recognize that multicultural curricula aren't necessarily "politically correct" and usually don't champion queers. Most matter-of-factly acknowledge "diversity," but they don't sweep controversy under the rug. They take divorce, single parenting, adoption, and the existence of gay men and lesbians for granted. In early grades, schools may teach that name-calling and gay-bashing are wrong. But homosexuality is usually only included in high school health and AIDS curricula, with the parental "opt out" provision typical of sex education programs. In the eleventh and twelfth grades, for example, Seattle's Family Life and Sexual Health (FLASH) curriculum explains the Kinsey scale, the difference between homosexual acts and gay identity, and the history of antigay discrimination and cites various studies that attempt to explain the origins of sexual orientation or determine what percentage of the population is gay. But FLASH also advises teachers, "Some people here may believe that homosexual behavior is wrong. Others may consider it as acceptable/right as heterosexual behavior. Respecting one another's differing opinions will be important." The curriculum's resource list mentions gay organizations like the Metropolitan Community church and Parents and Friends of Lesbians and Gays as well as Metanoia Ministries, an organization "that provides counseling from a Christian perspective for people who want to change their gender organizations."

"Multicultural education will always make some of us uncomfortable," says Lee. "Parents don't want kids to think for themselves; they're scared of difference and conflict. But otherwise, there's only indoctrination."

New York City's battle was not the first or the last curriculum conflict. California has been a center of controversy since the notorious Briggs Initiative to outlaw gay teachers in 1978. But as a case study, New York brings together many of the most common elements of battles across the nation.

The cornerstone of religious Right organizing in New York was the involvement of religious communities of color, such as Reverend Ruben Diaz's Bronx evangelical ministry. "These are places where racial lines can be crossed if you speak the same language in terms of religious faith," says Lee. "The reason the Right were so successful was because they took the common knowledge that schools are failing and gave people a credible explanation. Gay and lesbian organizations didn't give a credible explanation, they just said, 'Include us!'" When Cummins played the race card, it went over brilliantly in New York's tabloid press: In an atmosphere where "gay was used as a code for white" and affluent, according to lesbian parent and first-grade teacher Lisa North, gays and lesbians were set up as were fighting the "real minorities," blacks and Latinos.

The high-profile duels between the white gay men and lesbians and socially conservative members of racial minorities only contributed to the frustration of gay men and lesbians of color. When members of Gay Men of African Descent (GMAD) approached an organization called People About Changing Education (PACE), they hoped to get openly gay African Americans to go to their local school board hearings to counter religious Right testimony, but "there was resistance," recalls Lee. Said one black gay man, "I want to fight both racism and homophobia, but our kids are so desperate for some curriculum that teaches them about

who they are. Maybe we should concede on the lesbian- and gay-headed families for the moment, so kids can at least start learning basic black history in public schools."

When analogies between gay experience and racial minority experience were asserted by white gay men and lesbians, they not only fell on deaf ears among people of color, but also backfired, creating not solidarity but resentment. "The white middle-class folks would make an analogy between gays and the situation of blacks in the segregated South to try to win the people of color," says one white school board member. "But it made the people of color absolutely furious! And the whites just didn't get why." Not only were the differences between the two prejudices unarticulated, but many of the queer activists had no history of antiracist organizing, which made their appeal to the civil rights movement seem disingenuous.

On the other side, Cummins was no champion of people of color herself. Until 1993, her all-white school board did not reflect the predominantly Asian, Latino, and black Queens district it represented. In late 1993, a recently elected Asian American woman on School Board 24 went public with the accusation that Cummins had called her "slant eyes." Cummins denied it in the press, but insisted that it would have been her First Amendment right to say it if she wanted. She apparently felt no sense of hypocrisy when, at the Christian Coalition's 1993 Road to Victory conference, she said that the historical figure she most identified with was Rosa Parks.

As is often the case with Christian Right organizing, what appeared to be a grassroots movement of parents was in fact supported by larger conservative organizations. The school board's lawyer, for example, was John P. Hale, the long-standing attorney for New York City's Catholic archdiocese, who also represented conservative central school board member Irene Impellizzeri when she sued the UPA for calling her a "racist." (She had remarked at the Cathedral Club in Flatbush, Brooklyn, that "in the inner city a high proportion of poor children have to carry out their escape without having before them . . . any moral models except their teachers.") Cummins is a board member of the Family Defense Council (a right-wing group affiliated with the Oregon Citizens Alliance), whose founder—and Cummins's close friend—Howard Hurwitz repeatedly hailed her in print. But in most media, she continues to be praised as one-grandmother-against-the-system and an icon to conservatives everywhere.

The New York scandal has had lasting effects. Most school districts have voted to postpone educating students about gay families until the sixth grade, the age advocated by board of education vice president Impellizzeri. Fernandez's contract was not renewed, and the subsequent schools chancellor, Ramon Cortines, retained a highly abridged version of the curriculum. The repercussions of the fiasco have reached at least as far as Pennsylvania, where in April 1993 Governor Casey caved in to pressure from the right-wing Citizens for Excellence in Education (a.k.a. the National Association of Christian Educators) and asked the state board of education to remove the curriculum diversity mandate "Appreciating and Understanding Others" from its new guidelines.

The ground has shaken even in predominantly liberal Massachusetts. Republican Governor William Weld, frequently lauded as a "hetero hero," responded to a campaign of intense educational activism by gay and lesbian teachers by creating the groundbreaking Commission on Gay and Lesbian Youth and instituting a nondiscrimination policy to help queer kids in the state's schools. But in May 1993, Weld, a potential presidential candidate, implemented every youth commission recommendation except gay and lesbian curriculum inclusion.

Newton, a suburb of Boston, would seem to be an odd target for a Christian Right backlash: "It's largely professional and close to half Jewish," says Newton history teacher Bob Parlin. In 1992, the ten-thousand-student school system developed a "somewhat gay-positive" sex education curriculum for its secondary schools and circulated a resource pamphlet listing famous lesbians and gay men throughout history, while gay/straight alliances popped up in the schools, sometimes bringing in gay and lesbian speakers.

In response, a small right-wing protest group of about thirty people formed, calling itself Newton Citizens for Public Education (NCPE). One element that distanced the group's spokespersons, Brian Camenker and Marsha Ciccolo, from Christian Right associations was their Judaism. "How can you call me a Christian fundamentalist?" Camenker asked the media. "I'm Jewish." Camenker admitted, however, having attended organizing meetings at a local evangelical church, Grace Chapel. Equally

strange bedfellows had cropped up in New York, where orthodox Jewish rabbi Yehuda Levin, Roy Innis of the Congress of Racial Equality, and John Cardinal O'Connor's Catholic archdiocese all distributed Christian Coalition voter guides for the May 1993 school board elections, which nonetheless saw elected three openly gay school board members and saw defeated some of the "stealth" candidates running—right-wing candidates who don't acknowledge their views on several key issues and who deny their ties to religious Right organizations.

Despite setbacks in the Northeast, gay-inclusive education has enjoyed limited success in other areas of the country. In Virginia, a 1987 health mandate requires that each school district develop age-appropriate curricula for topics including "human sexuality" and "respect for others." In conservative Fairfax County, controversial topics including homosexuality are introduced at the ninth-grade level. According to educator Gerald Newberry, Fairfax County was also the site of religious curriculum backlash. But gay organizers got mainstream groups like the League of Women Voters, the American Association of University Women, the PTA, and religious leaders to testify in favor of the curriculum, heading off the attempt to imply a division of gays against nongays. The late introduction of gay-themed lessons and the "opt out" provision—less than 2 percent of parents have opted out in the past two years—made the battle more winnable. "And lots and lots of education," adds Newberry. "If education is not done upfront, there's going to be a backlash."

Frequently, it is students themselves who bring gay people in to speak to a class. In Meridian, Idaho, a suburb of Boise, three teachers were suspended after they permitted one female student to invite three lesbian parents to speak to a student group. The battle in the rural town got Citizens for Excellence in Education (CEE) involved, and their involvement divided parents into two factions and produced teacher self-censorship. "Another teacher was going to discuss events in Somalia," says Meridian Education Association president Cindy Betz, "but was afraid about the multiculturalism, because CEE is opposed." The school board of Spencer, Wisconsin, killed a student-initiated set of three to five lessons on gay issues, including gays in the military.

But the success of gay-inclusive curricula in the state of California suggests that perseverance pays off.

In San Francisco, the Bay Area Network of Gay and Lesbian Educators (BANGLE)—formed in 1975 as the Gay Teachers Coalition—has been working on gay-inclusive curricula for more than fifteen years. In Los Angeles in 1984, Virginia Uribe founded the maverick dropout prevention program for gay and lesbian youth, Project 10. The program has led conservative state legislators to try to cut off funding to the entire L.A. school district. Some schools in the San Francisco Unified School District informally introduce the topic of gay and lesbian families in kindergarten.

The most challenging battle in California was the successful one for a statewide mandate to include gay men, lesbians, and bisexuals in health education. California's health textbooks are especially important, since as one of the largest markets for textbooks in the country, it strongly influences what publishers include. The Gay and Lesbian Alliance Against Defamation (GLAAD) was up against right-wing opposition and responded by deluging the board with information and by mobilizing youth. "We spent five thousand dollars sending each member of the curriculum committee a copy of the [1989 Department of Health and Human Services] youth suicide report. We sent them so much stuff, one member of the board of ed asked us if we had our own printing press," reports GLAAD's Jessea Greenman.

Many in New York are increasingly tired of the time and attention given to the Rainbow at the expense of other crucial issues such as teen pregnancy, drug abuse, school overcrowding, and funding inequities. New York school board president H. Carl McCall once remarked to a roomful of television cameras and reporters that they were never around for educational issues, "but put sex on the agenda, it's something everyone will pay attention to. We will do our best to entertain you. We want to move up in the ratings."

But the religious Right groups that oppose gay-inclusive curricula have more than just sex on their minds. In Pennsylvania, for example, Citizens for Excellence in Education has formed alliances with taxpayer groups that do not want to fund school building programs. Many candidates endorsed by the religious Right also support voucher systems that would use tax money to subsidize private or religious schools. Although the silent majority that relies on public education is clearly the enemy of our enemy, it remains unclear whether they are friends of the lesbian and gay community. And as

Lee reminds us, "Gay and lesbian people aren't going to make it by themselves."

Curricula

Listed below are the top titles from the curriculum wars:

Birmingham, Michigan's health curriculum—three hours of class time are on sexual orientation—is available through Frank Colasonti, Jr., P.O. Box 893, Birmingham, MI 48012 ($5).

You can get a copy of Seattle's state-of-the-art sex education curriculum, FLASH, through Elizabeth Reis, Seattle-King County Department of Public Health, 110 Prefontaine Place South, Seattle, WA 98104 ($25–$50 per unit).

Cropping up throughout the country are conservative "abstinence only" sex ed curricula such as *Free Teens; Families, Decision-Making, and Human Development; Teen Aid; Sex Respect;* and *Facing Reality.*

Arthur Lipkin has written a thoughtful eight-to-ten lesson unit on the Stonewall riots, good for high school sociology or U.S. history classes that include the civil rights movement. It's available through Lipkin at the Harvard Graduate School of Education, 210 Longfellow Hall, Cambridge, MA 02138 ($10).

Resources

The Project 10 resource directory—*Project 10 Handbook: Addressing Lesbian and Gay Issues in Our Schools*—is available through Friends of Project 10 Inc., 7850 Melrose Avenue, Los Angeles, CA 90046 ($22.50).

The Hetrick-Martin Institute, an organization for New York City's lesbian, gay, and bisexual youth, publishes *You Are Not Alone,* a youth organization directory available through the institute at 401 West Street, New York, NY 10014 ($5).

Videos

The Report, a company headed by the pastor of the Antelope Valley Springs of Life Ministries brought us *The Gay Agenda* and has now released *Part Deux: The Gay Agenda in Public*

Schools, alleging that gay and lesbian teachers are recruiting kids in public schools.

Gay Youth, a video for high school audiences, can be ordered from Pam Walton, BANGLE, Wolfe Video, P.O. Box 64, New Almaden, CA 95042 ($66).

Children's Books

Author of *Heather Has Two Mommies* and *Gloria Goes to Gay Pride*—both from Alyson Wonderland—Lesléa Newman also offers *Saturday Is Pattyday,* about a boy whose lesbian parents separate. Alyson also publishes *Belinda's Bouquet,* a story about a girl who is taunted about her weight. Her friend's lesbian mom reassures her, "Your body belongs to you." Ask at your local bookstores.

Project 10:

An Outreach to Lesbian

and Gay Youth

Dr. Virginia Uribe

Can a counseling program that addresses the special problems of lesbian and gay youth be developed on the high school level? Can the issue of homosexuality be brought "out of the closet" without antagonism and controversy? Nearly ten years ago, as a veteran teacher and counselor on the campus of Fairfax High School in the Los Angeles Unified School District, I said "yes," and Project 10 was born. Named for the statistical portion of the general population (10 percent) believed to be primarily homosexual, Project 10 began as a response to the unmet needs of this silent minority in the educational system.

Spurred by a singularly nasty incident involving a young man who was ridiculed and harassed for being gay, my personal and professional life began to fuse for the first time in a career that began over thirty-five years ago. I invited a small, informal group of self-identified lesbian and gay youngsters to meet once a week at lunchtime, and before long the group had grown to twenty-five or more "regulars." We spent these early meetings in rather unstructured "rap" sessions, talking about the problems they were encountering in the school setting. Although none of this was measured quantitatively, it was obvious to me that most of these students reflected societal attitudes of discrimination against them. Low self-esteem and feelings of isolation and alienation were common. Mostly, there was an overwhelming feeling that they were not okay. Although the majority of these young people were very intelligent, very few were performing at a level consistent with their native capacity. Many were involved in self-destructive behavior, including substance abuse and attempted suicides, and were on the verge of dropping out of school. The most significant thing to me as an educator was their feeling that they existed in a box, with no adults to talk to, no traditional support systems to lean on for help in sorting out their problems, and no young people like themselves with whom they could socialize. In effect, adolescent lesbians and gays are stranded in an environment that shuns their very existence.

At that point, the principal of Fairfax High School, members of the Los Angeles Board of Education, and I began to make plans to formalize Project 10 and develop a model that could be used for other schools and other school districts. Since there was no precedent for any program dealing with lesbian and gay youth, we formed an advisory board and set about attempting to identify the needs of this target group. First, we felt we had to break through the walls of silence surrounding the subject of homosexuality so that young people struggling with issues of sexual orientation could be reached. Second, we had to provide a safe and supportive atmosphere so that they could talk about their sexuality in a nonthreatening way. Third, we had to train adults to examine their homophobia and to develop a nonjudgmental posture that would serve as a guideline in dealing with lesbian and gay youth.

In essence, we were trying to develop a model at Fairfax High School that could be replicated in other schools and in other school districts. Staff members attended workshops, Project 10 signs were put up in various offices throughout the school, and we began to let it be known that a confidential support group targeting lesbian and gay youth would be facilitated by a counselor. As word of this program began to spread, the phone began to ring off the hook. Counselors, school nurses, school psychologists, and others called Fairfax High School seeking information and expressing the need for such a program.

On a personal note, there were some interesting ramifications about the emerging program. A newspaper article had come out in which I was identified as a lesbian. Although I was prepared for this to be public knowledge, I did find it amusing that the *Los Angeles Times* was so afraid to print that piece of information that they referred to me as an "avowed lesbian." This disclosure about myself caused a slight shift in focus toward me rather than the program for a while, but by and large it was a nonissue to all but the fundamentalist bigots.

The Los Angeles Unified School District now allows one half-time position for the coordination of the Project 10 program throughout the district. Services of Project 10 include workshops and training sessions for administrators and staff personnel, informal drop-in school site counseling, outreach to parents and significant others, liaison with peer counseling, substance abuse, and suicide prevention programs, and coordination with health education programs that encourage personal responsibility and risk-reduction behavior among lesbian, gay, and bisexual youth.

Since its inception in 1984, Project 10 has affected the lives of thousands of lesbian and gay adolescents. The Project 10 model has been duplicated in approximately thirty-five of our fifty senior high schools, and we work closely with both middle and elementary school teachers. As the program has become known through the media, inquiries pour in from large and small school districts. To handle the large volume of requests for written information, a tax-exempt support group, Friends of Project 10, Inc., was formed in 1986. Friends of Project 10 produces educational materials that are distributed to any school district upon request. Educators are provided with information on different issues that contribute to the understanding of lesbian and gay youth, and it is our goal to see that they return to their students with greater effectiveness and sensitivity.

In 1988 the National Education Association, the largest teachers organization in America, passed a resolution calling for counseling on issues of sexual orientation in every high school in the country.

Project 10 is not without its critics. Most vocal is the Reverend Lou Sheldon of the Traditional Values Coalition in Anaheim, California. He characterizes the program as a "recruitment program" and has constantly lobbied politicians to pass legislation to stop Project 10. A courageous school board stands firm against his ilk, and continues its commitment to serve all children, especially those that have been traditionally excluded by hate and bigotry.

Not a day passes that we do not receive heartbreaking letters—stories of broken lives, wasted years, lost potential. Letters like the one from Mary Griffith whose teenage son committed suicide because he couldn't face life being gay; or the letter from "Jane," raped by her uncle and kicked out of her house because she was a lesbian; or the sixteen-year-old lesbian who felt her life would have no meaning until she was old enough to go to the bars.

In all these cases, couldn't the schools have helped? What if there had been a sympathetic adult to talk to? What if there had been someone to tell them they were okay—that they didn't have to make their journey for self-acceptance alone?

Perhaps we could have offset the mindless, vicious, insensitive attacks upon their spirit made by right-wing politicians and religious figures who preach hate instead of love. In my mind, Project 10 should not be controversial. We are talking about life and death issues. If we lose these children, we lose them to death or to the streets. We can no longer allow unchallenged discrimination and crippling self-hate to be the legacy of our gay and lesbian youth.

I ask all readers of this article to examine their own commitment to champion unpopular causes and provide leadership in the battleground of equality within our educational system.

For further information, write Dr. Virginia Uribe, Fairfax High School, 7850 Melrose Avenue, Los Angeles, California 90046.

Further Reading

Blumenfeld, Warren J., and Diane Raymond. *Looking at Gay and Lesbian Life.* Boston: Beacon Press, 1988; rev. ed., 1993.

Boston Lesbian Psychologies Collective. *Lesbian Psychologies.* Urbana: University of Illinois Press, 1987.

Cavin, Susan. *Lesbian Origins.* San Francisco: Ism Press, 1985.

Crooks, Robert, and Karla Barr. *Our Sexuality.* 3rd ed. Menlo Park, Calif.: Benjamin and Cummings, 1987.

Gay and Lesbian Alliance Against Defamation. *Media Guide to the Lesbian and Gay Community.* 80 Varick St., #3E, New York, NY 10013.

Harbeck, Karen M., Ed.D. *Coming Out of the Classroom Closet.* Binghamton, N.Y.: Harrington Park Press, 1992.

Project 10 Handbook. A resource directory for teachers, guidance counselors, parents, and school-based adolescent care providers. Available through Friends of Project 10, Inc., 7850 Melrose Ave., Los Angeles, CA 90046. $22.50.

Rafkin, Louise. *Different Daughters.* Pittsburgh, Penn.: Cleis Press, 1987.

Rench, Janice E. *Understanding Sexual Identity.* Minneapolis: Lerner Publications, 1990.

Video

Gay Youth: An Educational Video for the Nineties, produced by Bay Area Network of Gay and Lesbian Educators, c/o Wolfe Video, P.O. Box 64, New Almaden, CA 95042.

Who's Afraid of Project 10? Two-minute video, produced by Scott Greene, available for educational purposes only from Friends of Project 10, Inc., 7850 Melrose Ave., Los Angeles, CA 90046.

Virginia Uribe, Director of Project 10, Los Angeles.

Lesbians in the Academic World

Margaret Cruikshank

In the essay titled "Lesbians in the Academic World" in the first edition of *Our Right to Love,* I discussed the invisibility of lesbians and predicted that the field of women's studies, then relatively new, would help to correct this situation. Twelve years later, many more lesbians are "out" on campus, students as well as teachers and administrators; the field of lesbian studies has established itself; a few notable lesbians have won big tenure battles; professional organizations have added gay/lesbian caucuses; and lesbian issues can be raised in a wide variety of courses. In general, lesbians are not as stigmatized as they were in the 1970s, and this change can be felt in the college and university world, especially at the large universities.

As the gay and lesbian liberation movement has grown in numbers and power over the last decade, its presence is more obvious on campus through campus gay/lesbian organizations, and thus lesbians are more openly a part of campus life than they were before. UCLA has a lesbian sorority, for example, a change that would have been unthinkable when I wrote my original article. Lesbians are less isolated; they can find each other. Today a student who is just coming out is far more likely to know someone on campus to talk to about her feelings, perhaps even a lesbian or gay counselor, than her older sister would have been in the 1970s.

Students on campuses where gay liberation has made no visible impact are still beneficiaries of it, to the extent that they know it exists and feel a part of it. On such campuses, women's studies is often the only "safe space" for lesbians. Through these growing programs, lesbian students and teachers have become more aware of each other, both in classes and in informal social gatherings.

Hundreds of lesbians take part in the yearly conference of the National Women's Studies Association. The publishers' exhibit at this event is a dramatic sign of the growth of women's studies and the concomitant growth in women's publishing. This has had a major impact on lesbians in the academic world. The sheer number of books by and about lesbians on display at these conferences would have been inconceivable ten years ago. The phrase "lesbian studies" was not in existence when I wrote for the original *Our Right To Love.* At that time, a professor, a graduate student, or an undergraduate who wanted to write on a lesbian topic worked on her own or with leads from a few friends. Today she has a shelf full of resources and she can call or write to a number of women for guides to future research. She can learn about femmes in the fifties, about the lives of famous writers such as Willa Cather and Emily Dickinson, whose lesbianism could not be acknowledged by

Karen Schmiege on graduation day, Pratt Institute, New York City.

© 1984 Wilma Jane Weichselbaum

the literary establishment, and about the experiences of lesbians of color. Articles on lesbian subjects have appeared in professional journals in many fields, including psychology, sociology, education, social work, literature, history, anthropology, and gerontology. Consequently, lesbian scholars have more outlets for publishing than they had ten years ago.

In the beginning, literature and history seemed to dominate lesbian studies, but this is no longer true. Much work has been published in the social sciences, and even fields such as nursing and physical education are being examined from a lesbian perspective. As a result of this unfolding of lesbian studies, there are now young women scholars who have grown up knowing that lesbian studies is a significant branch of women's studies. They can take lesbian studies for granted, using it as a lens through which to view the rest of the university.

Although lesbian studies has its base in women's studies, it has benefited from the gradual expansion of gay studies. The Multicultural Lesbian and Gay Studies Program at the University of California at Berkeley, for example, now publishes a journal called *Out in Academia*. A graduation requirement of an ethnic studies class at City College of San Francisco can now be satisfied by a class in gay literature or gays in film; CCSF is the first college or university to count a lesbian/gay course for graduation and to have a department of gay and lesbian studies. The Center for Lesbian and Gay Studies, CUNY Graduate Center, New York City, sponsors conferences and serves as a clearing house for ongoing projects across the country. Yale and Harvard have hosted national gay studies conferences. Lesbian scholars' work is well documented in the *Gay Studies Newsletter* published by the gay caucus of the Modern Language Association. No one can keep track of this burgeoning scholarly activity except with computers. I did a bibliography for the anthology *Lesbian Studies* (1982) by poking around in bookstores, skimming bookshelves at friends' houses, and looking through my files. The editor of the revised edition of *Lesbian Studies* (in progress), Linda Garber, has used computers to prepare a book-length bibliography of lesbian studies. In 1979, I personally knew most of the "out" lesbian scholars in the United States who were part of the women's studies network; now there are probably over four hundred in the United States. And re-

search on lesbian topics is being conducted in many other countries as well.

Equally significant is the number of graduate students who have chosen lesbian subjects in the last decade. From corresponding with some of them I see that, unlike most graduate students, they have the chance to do truly original work. Have most undergraduates who are lesbians been influenced by lesbian studies? I don't know. It depends on their school. In the rural South or at a Catholic college, probably not. At a large university in a metropolitan area, the chances are better, especially if the lesbian students can attach themselves to a women's studies program or a women's center, or if they have access to a women's bookstore. Because lesbian studies is fairly new, a well-read undergraduate with a sense of grassroots lesbian feminism with access to a good library can make an original contribution to the field. Even a modest project like taping interviews with middle-aged lesbians and old lesbians can be very valuable. Hundreds of small towns and villages in America have a lesbian past, retrievable if someone finds the lesbians who collected, wrote down, and took pictures at parties.

There is another side to the current story of lesbians in the academic world, unfortunately, the disheartening side. Most professors who are lesbians are still in the closet. Those few who have published on lesbian topics often need two resumes, one giving the true titles of their works and others substituting "women" for "lesbians" or omitting the lesbian work entirely. Very few college or university lesbians in America can feel completely comfortable crossing the campus while holding hands with another woman. "Kill All Dykes and Faggots" graffiti is common enough to remind lesbian students and teachers that even though people on campus may be more open-minded than people in general, campus tolerance can be temporary or illusory.

Increasing lesbian visibility has been met by a backlash that takes various forms: physical attacks on lesbians, attacks on property, attacks on women's studies departments for "promoting" lesbianism, and more subtle signals that "you've gone too far" to lesbians and heterosexual feminists who align with lesbians. For example, reports from distressed faculty members at one college indicated that a dynamic women's studies program had been shut down, apparently because too many women came out as a result of their participation. The program had to be killed in order to be saved from the leaping lesbians. Lesbian baiting has occurred at schools where women's studies per se or a particular course or instructor has become controversial, for example at Cal State Long Beach, where fundamentalist Christians infiltrated classes, and at the University of Washington. The stamina and psychic energy needed to fight back diverts attention from solidifying women's studies, and the demoralizing experience of seeing gains lost can divide victims of homophobic attacks. In addition, hardly any university or foundation money goes to lesbian research projects. Lesbians often must wait until they are tenured to come out and/or to choose research topics relevant to their own experience. Perceptions of their "difference" may well prevent them from getting tenure. The university is like a club: Those who belong want to add others who think, dress, and teach the way they do. On all three counts, lesbians may be threatening. Worst of all, lesbian academics have few, if any, colleagues.

The sense of being an outsider that results from this situation has both potential strengths and dangers. Outsiders often see more clearly than those on the inside. But it is psychologically draining and undermining for a lesbian academic perpetually to feel that she does not belong in the tight little circles of academia. Here differences of temperament enter in: Some lesbians flourish in the academy and find it a haven; others find it oppressive and constraining.

The number of women faculty and administrators has increased in the past ten years, a change which has certainly benefited those who are lesbians. But there is no affirmative action for lesbians, and such a reform will not come from within the male-dominated university. The ideal situation would be this: Lesbian students and teachers would be *recruited* in order to improve universities, to make them more diverse, more representative of the female population, and more reflective of the social change created by feminism since the late 1960s.

While it seems thoroughly unlikely that in our lifetimes lesbians will actually be *valued* in the academic world, it is also unlikely that they will drop out of sight or fall silent, or that scholarly investigation of lesbian topics will cease. Not so many years ago, if a bold woman in freshman English had waved a well-worn copy of *Rubyfruit Jungle* and asked, "Why isn't *this book* on the reading list?" she would have been ostracized. On many campuses today, nothing has changed—such a woman

would still pay a high price for her daring. On the other hand, what has changed is that in some classrooms on some campuses, an assertive lesbian speaks not only for herself but for many others, and she knows it.

Because I've had the privilege of teaching lesbian and gay literature several semesters, I have seen how the study of literature is transformed by lesbian consciousness. Many other disciplines can be seen in a new light when gay and lesbian issues are raised. While our numbers are small, this work of re-vision will go forward slowly. But the powerful ideas of gay liberation and lesbian feminism are beginning to be influential in the academy, and their impact will no doubt be greater in the future. Even a powerful phrase such as "compulsory heterosexuality" (Adrienne Rich) can change the way people think.

Listed below are a few of the important books by feminists published since the first edition of *Our Right To Love*. I also recommend essays on gerontology coauthored by Mina Meyer and Sharon Raphel, for example, in the text *Women-Identified Women*, edited by Potter and Darty; and essays on lesbian politics and ethics by Julia Penelope and by Sarah Hoaglund in *Trivia* and *Lesbian Ethics*.

Further Reading

Adelman, March. *Long Time Passing: Lives of Older Lesbians.* Boston: Alyson, 1986.

Allen, Paula Gunn. *The Sacred Hoop: Recovering the Feminine in American Indian Traditions.* Boston: Beacon, 1986.

Anzaldúa, Gloria, and Cherríe Moraga, eds. *This Bridge Called My Back: Writings by Radical Women of Color.* Watertown, Mass.: Persephone Press, 1981.

Beck, Evelyn. *Nice Jewish Girls: A Lesbian Anthology.* Trumansburg, N.Y.: The Crossing Press, 1984.

Blackwood, Evelyn, ed. *The Many Faces of Homosexuality: Anthropological Approaches to Homosexual Behavior.* New York: Harrington Park Press, 1986.

Bulkin, Elly, ed. *Lesbian Fiction.* Watertown, Mass.: Persephone Press, 1981.

Bulkin, Elly, ed. *Lesbian Poetry.* Watertown, Mass.: Persephone Press, 1982.

Cruikshank, Margaret, ed. *Lesbian Studies.* New

York: The Feminist Press, 1982; rev. ed. in progress, Linda Garber, ed.

Curb, Rosemary, and Nancy Manahan, eds. *Lesbian Nuns: Breaking Silence.* Tallahassee, Fla.: Naiad Press, 1985.

Faderman, Lillian. *Surpassing the Love of Men: Romantic Love and Friendship Between Women from the Renaissance to the Present.* New York: William Morrow, 1981.

Faderman, Lillian. *Odd Girls and Twilight Lovers: A History of Lesbians in Twentieth Century America.* New York: Columbia University Press, 1991.

Freedman, Estelle, and John D'Emilio. *Intimate Matters: A History of Sexuality in America.* New York: Harper and Row, 1988.

Frye, Marilyn. *The Politics of Reality: Essays in Feminist Theory.* Trumansburg, N.Y.: The Crossing Press, 1988.

Jay, Karla, and Joanne Glasgow. *Lesbian Texts and Contexts.* New York: New York University Press, 1990.

Kitzinger, Celia. *The Social Construction of Lesbianism.* London: Sage Publications, 1987.

Krieger, Susan. *The Mirror Dance: Identity in a Women's Community.* Philadelphia: Temple University Press, 1983.

Lorde, Audre. *Sister Outsider: Essays and Speeches.* Trumansburg, N.Y.: The Crossing Press, 1984.

McNaron, Toni, ed. *The Sister Bond: A Feminist View of a Timeless Connection.* New York: Pergammon, 1985.

O'Brien, Sharon. *Willa Cather, The Emerging Voice.* New York: Oxford University Press, 1987.

Potter, Clare. *The Index to Lesbian Periodicals.* Tallahassee, Fla.: Naiad Press, 1986.

Rich, Adrienne. *Lies, Secrets, Silences: Selected Prose 1966–1978.* New York: Norton, 1979.

Smith, Barbara, Gloria T. Hull, and Patricia Bell Scott, eds. *All the Women are White, All the Blacks are Men, But Some of Us are Brave: Black Women's Studies.* New York: The Feminist Press, 1981.

Vicinus, Martha, Martin Duberman, and George Chauncey, Jr., eds. *Hidden from History: Reclaiming the Gay and Lesbian Past.* New York: New American Library, 1989.

Zimmerman, Bonnie. *A Safe Sea of Women* (lesbian fiction). Boston: Beacon Press, 1990.

The Lesbian Experience in Sport:

The Good, the Bad, and the Ugly

Pat Griffin

Picture a women's locker room. Imagine this locker room filled with women talking and laughing as they change into their team uniforms. See women bending to lace up their athletic shoes and pulling on warm-up jackets. Hear the showers dripping in the background and locker doors slamming. Watch the trainer applying the last strip of tape to a tender ankle.

Now, look more closely. Right there in the middle of the locker room sleeping on the floor is a huge lavender elephant! This incredible animal is taking up so much space that the women have to squeeze around the edges of the room to get by. Everyone wordlessly tiptoes carefully past the pastel pachyderm on her way out the locker room door. But no one seems to notice. No, wait. They know the elephant is there; it's just that no one acknowledges its presence. All the women move quietly around the elephant, careful not to awaken the creature slumbering in their midst.

How odd, you say! Welcome to the lesbian experience in sport. Like women ignoring a giant lavender elephant sleeping in the women's locker room, the world of women's sport has chosen to tiptoe silently around the issue of a lesbian presence. This is not easy because there are lots of us there: coaching, competing, officiating, and more rarely, administrating.

A lot is happening in the silence while the lavender elephant sleeps. In the silence, the whispered accusation "Dyke!" is enough to send many women in sport scrambling for cover behind boyfriends, dresses, makeup, long flowing hair, or other conspicuously displayed elements of heterosexual drag. As long as the "L" word can be used to intimidate, no woman in sport—lesbian, bisexual, or heterosexual—can claim control over her athletic experience.

Ann Bancroft, first woman to reach the north pole traveling by dogsled expedition, 1986.

To borrow a phrase from Whoopi Goldberg, lesbians have been in sport since air. Our stories are woven into the fabric of women's sport. But like a quilt with missing patches, the silence about the lesbian experience in sport weakens the whole quilt. It is high time that our stories were told and our voices heard. The lesbian experience in sport is varied, extensive, and rich. Some of our experience is good, some is bad, and some is downright ugly. All of it needs to be told.

The Good

For many of us, sport has been a home. For those of us who discovered early in our lives the joy of softballs thwacking into leather gloves, basketballs swishing through hoops, or muscles singing with fatigue at the end of a long run, sport has been a place to be a different kind of woman. Through our sport experiences many lesbians find our first community of women. Many of us also find our first loves. The intensity of training, winning and losing, and laughing and crying together as teammates creates enduring emotional bonds among women athletes. For many of us our lesbian teammates become our family, accepting who we are in ways our biological families do not. We have developed an extensive underground social network that provides support on and off the field of competition. In a world that offers little acceptance and few visible role models for lesbians, sport has provided a space to be with women and images of strong women who have broken free of the femininity game and who cherish and nurture their strength. From our seventh-grade crushes on the big tough women who were our gym teachers to our first sexual experiences with a beloved teammate, sport has provided a context to discover who we are.

Despite a well-founded fear of being accused of recruiting young and innocent girls, many of our coaches, gym teachers, and older teammates have recognized us "baby dykes" as we grope our way through the silence. They have extended a welcoming hand and shown us a way to be who we are when the rest of the world refused to acknowledge our existence. That these older lesbians in sport have managed to do this largely from the closet makes the accomplishment all the more amazing. Many of us cherish long-standing relationships with these lesbian mentors: a favorite gym teacher, our first high school coach, or the college coach we worked our buns off for. We enjoy reconnecting with these women again and again through the years as we have become teachers and coaches with our own special group of younger lesbian athletes who surprise us from time to time with unexpected visits or letters from afar.

Before it was chic to go to the gym and work out in sleek, brightly colored Lycra tights, before women were assured by men that women who work out are sexy, we were already in the gym pumping iron, running, and throwing ourselves into sport with a passion and commitment unappreciated by the outside world. We weren't there to make ourselves more attractive to men. We didn't really care what men thought. We were there because it felt good, because the challenge of sport burned in us, because being an athlete is part of who we were, and yes, because we wanted to look good to other women, too.

Some of us have made good friends of heterosexual teammates and coaches. We have come out to these friends and found that they care about us and they have become allies. Some of them stand by us when things are difficult and help us celebrate the good times, too.

Martina Navratilova has broken the silence as our first self-affirming and publicly out lesbian professional or Olympic athlete. Her grace and courage on and off the tennis court inspires us. We celebrated her final victories as she wound down a stellar career and we applauded her political activism in supporting Gay Games IV and helping to defeat an antigay civil rights law in Colorado.

Another good part of the lesbian experience in sport are the openly lesbian sport leagues and activity clubs flourishing all over North America. Lesbians who love sport can join local and national groups sponsoring competition and recreational activities in just about any sport from softball (our national pastime) to rock climbing, from scuba diving to sea kayaking, from tennis to mountain biking. Some of these groups operate from a commitment to feminist principles; exploring alternative competitive forms that change the structure of sport to accommodate the feminist values of the women who participate. In addition, the Gay Games, an international celebration of lesbian and gay athletics and arts, will convene its fifth quadrennial event in Amsterdam in 1998. In the summer of 1994 Gay Games IV attracted over ten thousand athletes from over forty countries to New York City for a week of competition and celebration. Gay Games is one of the largest international sporting events in the world and a source of pride and freedom for lesbian and gay athletes and coaches used to competing in the homphobic and hostile environment characteristic of most mainstream athletic experiences.

Over the last few years, the words *lesbian, gay,* and *homophobia* have come out of the closet in the physical education and athletic world. The annual convention of the American Alliance for Health, Physical Education, Recreation, and Dance includes academic and awareness programs on homophobia in sport and physical education. All of these programs attract capacity audiences. Additionally, feminist sport sociologists and other sport academicians are publishing scholarly articles exploring connections among sexism, heterosexism, and sport.

Finally, some women's sport organizations and college athletic and physical education departments are beginning to provide homophobia education for their memberships. All of these educational efforts are healthy signs of a willingness to begin treating homophobia in sport as a serious professional concern.

Young women athletes are growing up in a world where attention to the needs and concerns of young lesbian, gay, and bisexual people in school is becoming a more integral focus of LGB organizations and mainstream educational organizations. Teachers, coaches, and other professional educators are learning more about their responsibilities to make schools safe for lesbian, gay, and bisexual young people. We can hope that these changes will help young lesbian athletes to bring a greater sense of self love, hope, and entitlement to their athletic experiences. And that their young heterosexual teammates will bring fewer prejudices and fears about lesbian teammates and coaches.

This is some of what is good about the lesbian experience in sport. It will be important to remember these experiences because the rest of this piece is about the bad and the ugly side of the lesbian experience in sport.

The Bad

All of the good in the lesbian experience in sport must be viewed in the context of a culture that denigrates women in general and vilifies lesbians in particular. For a woman to take herself seriously as an athlete, she must challenge everything she has learned about being a woman in a male-dominated society. Lesbians in sport are a lightning rod for this society's fear of powerful women. It is our name that is used to intimidate and divide women in sport. It is our fear of being named that has kept us silent, denying our own presence. And it is the use of our name against us that breaks our spirit, deadens our sense of outrage, and keeps us tiptoeing around, grateful for the silence. This is the bad part of our experience in sport.

When Billie Jean King's lesbian relationship with Marilyn Barnett became public, the women's sports world held its collective breath in white-knuckled silence until the headlines faded and we could breathe a sigh of relief and return to our camouflaged protection. Often, the best a lesbian in sport can hope for from her colleagues is that they will help to keep her secret. Because Billie Jean broke the silence, even against her will, she was on her own, at least in public.

Another bad part of the lesbian experience in sport is how the concept of femininity is used to make women athletes fearful of stepping out of "appropriate" gender role boundaries. Femininity in women's sport is a code word for heterosexuality. Women coaches and athletes are encouraged to dress more femininely and are offered makeup application workshops and hairstyle seminars to improve their appearance and marketability. A college women's team actually posed for their team brochure as seductive Playboy bunnies complete with tails and ears, apparently in hopes of attracting more fans to their games: women's athletic contest as girlie show.

Sometimes concern about lesbians in sport is not veiled at all. For instance, it is not unusual for parents of prospective college women athletes to ask if there are lesbians on the college team or if a woman coach is married. An information packet from one university team assures parents that only "wholesome friendships" among women athletes are encouraged. Having a husband or other conspicuous indications of heterosexuality are often unspoken qualifications for women seeking coaching positions or professional women athletes seeking commercial endorsements. This heterosexualizing of women athletes and censoring of lesbians in sport takes a psychological toll on lesbians and teaches heterosexual athletes and coaches to fear and resent their lesbian teammates and colleagues.

Another bad aspect of the lesbian experience in sport is our image among lesbian feminists outside the sports world. We are often seen as insular and cliquey. We are frequently criticized for our lack of involvement in political struggles beyond improving sport opportunities for girls and women. We are looked down on by some lesbian activists for how deeply closeted we are and for letting them fight our battles for us. Our enjoyment of competition and other feminist taboos, like doing our best to defeat "sisters" on the other team, have earned us Neanderthal ratings in the evolution of feminist consciousness.

Some of this criticism is earned. We can do better in making connections with other women's issues as well as with other lesbians who are not into sport. We need to start coming out and speaking for ourselves rather than hiding on the fringe, letting others do the scary work for us.

Many lesbian feminists who are not athletic, however, have too quickly discounted the small acts of courage that lesbians in sport have taken because we have taken them from the closet. It is important to remember that simply being a woman athlete is an act of defiance in a male-dominated society where sport has an almost sacred meaning for men and the development of masculinity. A lesbian athlete is the embodiment of much that is antithetical to the maintenance of a male-dominated society: a strong, independent woman. Being a visible, activist, lesbian feminist athlete is nothing less than an act of gender terrorism in a male-dominated society. We await the leader of this movement . . . and she will come.

The Ugly

The ugly part of the lesbian experience in sport includes incidents of blatant discrimination, crude harassment, open lesbian baiting, subtle intimidation, cowardly innuendo, and outright lies. Examples of these antilesbian actions are common knowledge in the lesbian underground in sport. Ask any woman who has any consciousness of her lesbianism and who has been in sport as an athlete, coach, or administrator for a few years. She will have her own collection of horror stories to tell. Here are a few I know.

Male newspaper reporters and sportswriters have snooped around trying to find someone who will reveal the sexual orientation of suspected lesbian professional tennis players, golfers, and top-ten college basketball coaches. There is a list of college women basketball coaches coded by sexual orientation. This list is circulated to parents of prospective college basketball players. There are legions of lesbian coaches and athletes who have been fired or dropped from teams, not because of any inappropriate behavior or ethical violation, but solely because of their sexual orientation. Some were told so directly, counting on the lesbian's fear of public disclosure to keep her quiet. A lesbian college coach told me that after she accepted a coaching job, her women's athletic director, a lesbian herself, told the coach that she would be fired if she was seen at the women's bar in town or anywhere in the company of known lesbians.

Other lesbians believe they have lost their jobs or slots on the team roster because they were lesbians, but circumstances are often more ambiguous, and they could never prove anything even if they chose to fight their dismissal. For example, a lesbian professional basketball player told me how she was cut from the team not long after her coach saw her participating in a gay rights march. Such is the slipperiness of discrimination. Some coaches are open about their antilesbian policies, however, publicly stating to players and parents that they will not allow lesbians on their teams.

Some lesbian athletes and coaches are subjected to harassment or intimidation. A softball coach told me of a game in which her team was dyke-baited by the opposing team while they were in the field. Her players were called "lezzies" and "dykes" while the opposing coach sat in the dugout with her team, apparently unwilling to stop her athletes' behavior. Homophobic slurs are scrawled on locker room walls and anonymous notes are stuck in lockers or under office doors. In one case a lesbian coach came home one night to find "Dyke" spray-painted on her garage door. A lesbian high school coach told me of being called a dyke from a passing car full of male students while she was walking down the street. Another lesbian physical education teacher was called "queer" from a school window while she was outside teaching a class on the athletic field. Still another lesbian high school coach and her partner were followed by a school administrator to see if they lived together and whom they socialized with.

A lesbian college volleyball coach told me how a rival male coach used innuendo about her lesbianism to persuade recruits to attend his school rather than hers. She found out about this from one of her athletes who, as a high school prospect, had ignored his sleazy ploy. Another lesbian college coach, who was assumed to be heterosexual by her male coach colleagues, told of being present around the Mr. Coffee machine when the men idly speculated about which women coaches were "queer" and who slept with whom.

Some lesbian athletes are "mistakenly" left out of plans for team social gatherings. One soccer player told me how she and her lover, a teammate, were intentionally told to meet the team in the wrong place so that they would miss a ride to a party with the rest of the team. Another teammate confessed this to her afterward. Both lesbians eventually left the team after several similar incidents occurred during the rest of the season.

The stereotypes that some so-called "leaders" in women's sport have about lesbians are appalling. I would have expected women who have been in sport all their lives to have learned more about their lesbian teammates and colleagues. That they haven't is a testament to the silence and ignorance surrounding lesbians in sport. A prominent women's sports advocate once told me that she thought lesbianism was "abnormal and characteristic of lonely women who preyed on impressionable young girls who are vulnerable to peer pressure and coercion." Another woman during the same depressing conversation shared a story she had heard from "a friend of a friend" about a team on which a small, powerful clique of lesbians "forced" all the younger athletes to have sex with them as a kind a team initiation ritual. I was horrified to realize that she seemed to accept this as fairly typical of teams that include lesbian athletes.

For lesbian athletes who also are black, Latina, Asian, Native American, or poor, these ugly experiences are compounded and made more painful by the racism and classism they encounter in sport. These lesbian athletes often feel like outsiders, not only among white, middle-class heterosexual teammates, but among white lesbian teammates as well. We must learn to listen to and appreciate the diversity among lesbian athletes. We need to be sure all of our voices are present in the chorus, not just a few.

These stories represent some of the good, the bad, and the ugly in the lesbian experience in sport. It is time to open the closet door and let fresh air sweep in to awaken the lavender elephant. We have suffered gross cruelties in silence. We have been grateful for small bits of private understanding and silent tolerance when we are entitled to nothing less than our full public acknowledgement in women's sport. We have created a strong and thriving network of lesbian friends and lovers despite the pressure to deny our own existence. Once the lavender elephant awakens, anything is possible. We are powerful, but we must believe it first. The alternative is another generation of lesbian athletes who believe their only option is suffocation in a tightly locked closet.

Picture a women's locker room. Imagine the room full of women athletes of all colors. If you close your eyes you can hear laughter and comfortable talk as different voices join the ebb and flow of conversation. These women are really listening to and hearing each other. Someone over by the water fountain is excitedly talking about a new woman lover. There is laughter and teasing, hugs and pats on the back. Someone else down at the end of the row of lockers is upset because she and her male lover are ending their relationship. A lesbian friend comforts her. Plans are made to have dinner together as a team after practice. Suddenly, the locker room door opens and bangs against the wall. Conversation stops. An anonymous male voice shouts angrily into the locker room, "Dykes!" The women stop and look at each other in surprise. Then, as one, they turn to the door and shout back, "That's *Ms.* Dyke to you, buster!" They laugh. They finish dressing for practice. As they leave the locker room, some are arm-in-arm. The name-calling incident is forgotten as they anticipate a good workout together. You see, they own the word now. These women athletes, lesbian, bisexual, and heterosexual, have taken back its power and it cannot hurt them anymore.

Further Reading

Alguire, J. *All Out.* Norwich, Vt.: New Victoria Press, 1988 (Fiction).

Boutilier, Mary, and Lucinda SanGiovanni. *The Sporting Woman.* Champaign, Ill.: Human Kinetics, 1983.

Burton-Nelson, M. "A Silence So Loud It Screams." In *Are We Willing Yet? How Women Are Changing Sport and Sport Is Changing Women.* New York: Random House, 1991.

Burton-Nelson, M. *The Stronger Women Get, The More Men Love Football: Sexism and the American Culture of Sports.* New York: Harcourt Brace, 1994.

Cahn, S., *Coming On Strong: Gender and Sexuality in Twentieth-century Women's Sport.* New York: Free Press, 1994.

Coe, Roy. *A Sense of Pride: The Story of Gay Games II.* San Francisco: Pride Publications, 1986.

Garrett, K. *Lady Lobo.* Norwich, Vt.: New Victoria Publishers, 1993.

Griffin, P. "Silence Encourages Fear, Discrimination." *USA Today* (September 18, 1992), 10C.

Griffin, P. "Changing the Game: Homophobia, Sexism, and Lesbians in Sport." *Quest 44* (1992), 251–65.

Griffin, P. "Homophobia in Women's Sport: The Fear That Divides Us." In *Women in Sport: Issues and Controversies,* edited by G. Cohen, pp. 193–203. Newbury Park, Calif.: Sage, 1993.

Griffin, P. "Homophobia in Sport: Addressing the Needs of Lesbian and Gay High School Athletes." *The High School Journal 77,* no. 1/2 (Oct–Nov, 1993/Dec-Jan, 1994), 80-87.

Lenskyj, Helen. *Out of Bounds: Women, Sport, and Sexuality.* Toronto: Women's Press, 1986.

Levin, Jenifer. *Water Dancer.* New York: Pocket Books, 1982 (Fiction).

Levin, Jenifer. *The Sea of Light.* New York: Dutton, 1993 (Fiction).

Lopiano, D. "How Should We Handle the Lesbian 'Problem' in Women's Sports?" *The Advocate* (September 8, 1992), 96.

Navratilova, Martina (with George Vecsey). *Martina.* New York: Knopf, 1985.

Patton, C. "Gay Games III." Z 3, no. 11 (November 1990), 98–102.

Rogers, S., ed. *Sportdykes: Stories from On and Off the Field.* New York: St. Martin's, 1994.

Rounds, K. "Why Men Fear Women's Teams." *Ms.* 1, no. 4 (1991), 43–45.

Solomon, A. "Passing Game: How Lesbians Are Being Purged from Women's College Hoops." *Village Voice* (March 20, 1991), 142.

The Spirit Captured: The Official Photojournal of Celebration 90—Gay Games III. (P.O. Box 3848, Vancouver, B.C. Canada V6B 3Z3).

"Sportsview: Homophobia in Sports." *USA Today* (September 18, 1992), 10C.

Zipter, Y. *Diamonds Are a Girl's Best Friend.* New York: Firebrand, 1988.

VI

Religion and Spirituality

Lesbian Women in Protestant Churches

Virginia Ramey Mollenkott, Ph.D.

From my earliest childhood, long before I was given a name to call it, I knew that I was attracted to girls rather than boys. And from my earliest childhood, I also knew that I loved God and wanted my whole life to be centered on serving God. Instinctively, I knew to hide the first reality and speak only of the second. But now that I am sixty-two and publicly identified as a lesbian Christian, the world feels more comfortable to me than it did for the many years when my sexual orientation seemed to clash with my Protestant Christian commitment.

At some deep level I have always known that the love of God cannot be taken away from any of Her children, as witness the apostle Paul: "I am sure that neither death, nor life, nor angels, nor principalities, nor things present, nor things to come, nor powers, nor height, nor depth, nor anything else in all creation, will be able to separate us from the love of God in Christ Jesus" (Romans 8:38, RSV). That surely would include the ignorant attitudes and policies of various churches! I have written several books concerning the apparent conflicts between lesbianism and Christianity to show that the interpretations causing the conflicts are not essential and in fact contradict basic overarching Christian doctrines. Although I very much respect lesbian women who have moved out of Christianity, Judaism, or Islam into Wicca or other feminist spiritualities, I consider it vital to freedom of choice that women realize that, should it feel right for them, they can stay within organized religion in order to call each tradition toward implementing its own liberating insights.

In Protestantism, we have a long way to go to overcome heterosexism. What makes the world more comfortable for this lesbian Christian in 1994 is the fact that in every denomination, there is a sizeable and growing minority church-within-the-church that is devoted to justice for all people, female or male, rich or poor, handicapped or fully abled, "first world" or "two-thirds world," of any and every color, age, shape, and sexual orientation. Admittedly, there is a deadly repressive, Bible-thumping, heavily funded right wing in every Protestant denomination. But there is also a quieter, poorly funded, yet equally determined group devoted to human justice.

Take, for example, the Evangelical and Ecumenical Women's Caucus (before 1990, the Evangelical Women's Caucus International). Founded in 1973 and drawing its membership from the tiny minority of feminists in conservative churches, the EEWC devotes itself to achieving full and equal justice for women in the home, the church, and the world at large. Members are convinced that when it is contextually interpreted, the Bible supports human equality-through-mutuality.

In 1986 at its seventh international conference, the EEWC membership voted to support civil rights protection for lesbian women and gay men. As a result, almost half of the membership pulled out in order to found a different organization that identifies heterosexual marriage as the only proper expression of human sexuality. But those who remained in EEWC had caught a vision of genuine inclusiveness and were no longer willing to deny recognition to the many lesbian women who had faithfully given their energies to the organization from its inception.

At the eighth EEWC conference during the summer of 1988, lesbian Christians shared their stories in plenary sessions along with heterosexual church women. Participants were strongly supportive of one lesbian woman who explained that because her church offered no ceremony for a life-covenant between two women, she and her partner "got down on our knees in the middle of the living room and married ourselves to each other in God's presence." One heterosexually married woman who had previously believed her church leaders' statements that it is "impossible to be both lesbian and Christian" said that although she had been lonely as a feminist in a fundamentalist congregation, she now realized that lesbians in the church must feel "not only lonely, but desolate." She pledged herself to do everything she could to end that desolation.

I had been a keynote or plenary speaker at four of the eight conferences of EEWC and a workshop leader at two others, but 1988 was the first year I ever felt fully at home among my evangelical feminist sisters. Knowing that their inclusiveness embraced my sexuality as well as my intellect and religious commitment, I could at long last feel comfortable. The 1994 conference was planned and organized by two lesbian women from Chicago.

But EEWC is a very special group of people. During that same summer of 1988, when EEWC was affirming its lesbian minority, delegates to the General Conference of the United Methodist Church voted overwhelmingly to retain their earlier prohibition on the ordination of "self-avowed, practicing homosexuals," and by an even bigger vote continued to condemn "the practice of homosexuality" as "incompatible with Christian teaching." Thus a mainline Protestant denomination with over 9 million members continues to repudiate first-class citizenship for its gay minority.

I know many lesbian women who lead lives of quiet desperation as ministers in the United Methodist Church. The 1988 decision has nailed their closet doors shut with a claustrophobic vengeance. Why do they stay? Because they feel genuinely called to the Methodist ministry. The price they pay is any integration of their public and personal lives, and the toll on them is tremendous. The same thing is true for gay clergy in most other Protestant denominations.

At the 1988 General Conference, the United Methodists founded a task force to "study homosexuality as a subject for theological and ethical analysis." Yet they also prohibited the use of any church funds "to promote the acceptance of homosexuality." The negative slant of the funding decision gave a clear directive to the task force even before it met, and in 1991 its majority finding was simply that the church should no longer be "unequivocal" about calling homosexuality "incompatible with Christian teaching." Even that was too much for the General Council on Ministries, which voted to "receive and refer" rather than to "adopt and commend" the report on homosexuality.

Within the United Methodist Church, however, there are some individual congregations that welcome lesbian women and gay men and support the ordination of qualified gay people; appropriately, they call themselves "Reconciling Congregations." But the United Methodist General Conferences repeatedly send them strongly repressive signals.

Meanwhile, the largest denomination in American Protestantism, the 15-million-member Southern Baptist Convention, has passed an even more repressive resolution. It states that homosexuality—

the orientation as well as the behavior—is "a manifestation of a depraved nature," a "perversion of divine standards," and an example of today's "moral decline." In this manner, the church that supported slavery in the nineteenth century and opposed racial integration in the twentieth century continues its history of oppressiveness. Yet even within the Southern Baptist Convention, I know individuals who are appalled at the stand their church has taken and who are doing their best to bring about change. In 1992 several Baptist churches in North Carolina took a stand against the convention's refusal to ordain lesbigay people and bless their unions. Everywhere it's the same: Even when the official stance denies first-class citizenship to gay women and men, there is a group of people determined to share the good basics of life with everyone everywhere. They embody hope.

The Episcopal church leaves ordination decisions up to the local bishops. Several bishops have indeed, with full awareness, ordained qualified lesbian women and gay men to the priesthood. But Episcopalians are divided in their response, and they are currently embroiled in controversy over whether or not to recognize lesbian and gay relationships by providing a ceremony of holy union. The novelty here is that the inclusive movement is spearheaded by two bishops: Paul Moore and John Spong.

The new coalition of Lutheran churches will ordain lesbian women and gay men, but only if they promise to live celibate. Thus the followers of Martin Luther (that sixteenth-century champion of justification by faith alone) are enacting the paradox of requiring their gay/lesbian clergy to *earn* their ministries by the sacrifice of either their sexual fulfillment or their integrity. The situation is similar in the Presbyterian Church, where gay women and men are welcome as members but are ineligible for ordination. Presbyterian congregations that differ from the national stance by supporting the ordination of qualified gay people call themselves "More Light" congregations. One of them, the Downtown Presbyterian Church of Rochester, New York, called an "out" lesbian woman to be one of their pastors, and received the support of their synod and presbytery, but was forbidden by the national church to install her. In 1993 they made her their evangelist-at-large, to help educate Presbyterians on lesbian and gay issues.

The climate for gay women and men is usually acceptable in Quaker meetings. It was the Quakers who several decades ago compared gayness to left-handedness, a very helpful analogy; but even the Society of Friends has recently been assailed by a repressive and vocal right wing.

To my knowledge, apart from the Metropolitan Community Church (a church I love but which is the subject of a different essay) the only Protestant churches that have a policy of ordaining qualified uncloseted gay women and men are the Unitarian Universalist, the United Church of Christ, and the United Church of Canada. Unitarian churches have been most gracious about welcoming lesbigay congregations to use their facilities and also to join in Unitarian services and leadership. But in the United Church of Christ, even though ordination is available, local congregations tend to avoid calling an openly lesbian, gay, or bisexual person to be their minister. Here again, although a righteous minority would welcome lesbigay people as pastors, heterosexism and sheer ignorance retain their stranglehold on the majority.

I think often about a nineteenth-century poem by Arthur Hugh Clough called "Say Not the Struggle Naught Availeth." The final stanzas read:

For while the tired waves, vainly breaking,
Seem here no painful inch to gain,
Far back, through creeks and inlets making,
Comes silent, flooding in, the main.

And not by eastern windows only,
When daylight comes, comes in the light.
In front, the sun climbs slow, how slowly,
But westward, look, the land is bright.

Although it would be easy enough for lesbian women to say that patience with Protestant churches is useless because they will never change, I propose that we empower ourselves with Clough's metaphors. In the votes of national church conventions, indeed, sexual justice may seem to be a "tired wave" that gets nowhere; but away back in the "creeks and inlets" of those church members who love justice and are determined to see it done, the tide is quietly swelling.

Every Protestant denomination has its lesbian/ gay support group: Integrity (Episcopal), Lutherans Concerned, Brethren/Mennonites Concerned, Evangelicals Concerned, Presbyterians for Lesbian and Gay Concerns, Affirmation (United Methodist), American Baptists Concerned, Affirm (United Church of Canada), National Gay Pentecostal Alliance, Friends for Lesbian and Gay Concerns (Quaker), the United Church Coalition for Lesbian and Gay Concerns, Honesty (Southern Baptist Convention), Gay, Lesbian, and Affirming Disciples Alliance (Disciples of Christ), Reformed Church in America Gay Caucus, Seventh-Day Adventist Kinship International, Axios (Eastern Orthodox), and Emergence International (Christian Scientist).

Every June for the past seventeen years, the interdenominational Kirkridge Retreat Center in Bangor, Pennsylvania, has held an event called Gay, Lesbian, and Christian where Catholic and Protestant people come together to celebrate the integration of their sexuality and spirituality. And every fall, a group of women gather there for Sisterly Conversations: Current Concerns Among Lesbians of Faith. A few other Christian retreat centers are also beginning to develop programs to bring gay people of faith together. And as an "out" lesbian, I continue to receive many invitations to present the cause of justice at seminaries, colleges, and church conferences all over the country, as do other "out" lesbians I know.

In 1990, CLOUT was formed: Christian Lesbians Out Together. This lively group has provided a warm presence at major Christian conferences since its inception. Lesbian women who would like the churches to feel their clout are welcome to write to CLOUT, P.O. Box 460808, San Francisco, California 94146-0808.

When I was a girl, no religious book or journal spoke of lesbianism except as either sickness or sin. Now, however, supportive religious books are available, and Christian feminist publications like *Daughters of Sarah* (Chicago) have printed positive depictions of lesbian lives. A justice-oriented journal, *The Other Side* (Philadelphia), has devoted several issues to positive discussions of female and male gayness. Mainline religious journals like *The Christian Century* welcome relevant input from lesbian women and gay men. And when the United Methodist Church put the Reverend Rose Mary Denman on trial for heresy because she became an uncloseted lesbian, a liberal journal named *Christianity and Crisis* devoted an issue to that trial, printing the full testimony of Ms. Denman's witnesses.

Wrote the editors of *Christianity and Crisis*,

We present the testimony here because we believe the issues raised by Denman's case are important, and not only in the United Methodist Church. If a person is qualified for ordination, we fail to see why loving a member of the same sex disqualifies. Denman had been ordained and serving churches for four years before she fell in love with Wini Weir. Why does entrance into a committed relationship decrease one's ability to pastor? . . . It is not practicing lesbians and gays who threaten the church, but the acts against them, their exclusion from fellowship and ministry that endanger the church which was called to be an inclusive community of love.

When I was a young lesbian Christian, if I had ever seen or heard any pronouncement as affirming as that, I might have been able to avoid some of the mistakes I made. It is up to each woman to decide what her own priorities are; but I hope that lesbian women from Protestant churches will not allow themselves to be robbed of their spiritual self-esteem and their capacity for joyous worship. And I hope that many of us will be called to challenge the churches to become in reality what they are supposed to be: communities that embody in the world the inclusive love, justice, and mercy of God Herself. Times really *are* changing; social justice really *is* making some headway. "In front, the sun climbs slow, how slowly, / But westward, look, the land is bright."

Further Readings

Christians and Homosexuality: Biblical and Ethical Issues. Includes descriptions and addresses of supportive religious organizations. Available for $5.00 from The Other Side, 300 W. Apsley, Philadelphia, PA 19144.

Denman, Rose Mary. *Let My People In: A Lesbian Minister Tells of Her Struggles to Live Openly and Maintain Her Ministry.* New York: William Morrow, 1990.

Scanzoni, Letha Dawson, and Virginia Ramey Mollenkott. *Is the Homosexual My Neighbor? A Positive Christian Response.* Rev. ed. San Francisco: Harper, 1994.

Scroggs, Robin. *The New Testament and Homosexuality.* Philadelphia: Fortress Press, 1983.

Catholic Lesbians

Beth Gorman

Catholic lesbians are visible and active in Catholic circles and the gay and lesbian movement all across the country. We are found in all major cities and we are in remote rural areas. We are in religious communities and we are in the pews of many of our local Catholic parishes. Some of us are silent, but more and more of us are coming out in numbers through the support of such organizations as Dignity/USA, the Conference for Catholic Lesbians, New Ways Ministry and through the affirmation of writings contributed by Catholic lesbian women.

Growing up in the cultural environment of the Catholic tradition leaves a lifelong impact on an individual's values and religious outlook. These values often make it difficult to integrate one's homosexual orientation within the context of the patriarchal and homophobic Roman Catholic Church.

Catholic lesbians and gays who wish to express their Catholicism in the community life of their parish have suffered enormous oppression. We have felt isolated and even alienated in the pews and confessionals in our Catholic churches. Most of us either opt to remain silent about our sexuality, or just leave.

Dignity's Emergence

In the late sixties and early seventies the silence of our lives as Catholics became intolerable for many. In homes in major cities across the United States and Canada, small groups of Catholic gays and lesbians came together as marginalized Catholics to celebrate mass. As these small groups became larger and more visible in the gay and lesbian community, they began organizing politically. These Catholic gay and lesbian people eventually began to call their groups Dignity. Through the network of gay periodicals these Catholics were encouraged to send representatives to Los Angeles and officially form Dignity/USA as a national organization in 1973.

The founder of Dignity's New York chapter, John McNeill, published his book, *The Church and the Homosexual*, in July 1976. His writings focused on a positive approach to the moral and theological aspects of ministry to gay and lesbian people in the Roman Catholic tradition. This publication brought new hope and a better understanding for Catholic gays and lesbians of their rightful role in the Christian community.

Dignity organizers were hopeful in the fall of 1976 when the National Conference of Catholic Bishops made a statement in their pastoral letter, "To Live in Christ Jesus," that "homosexuals, like everyone else, should not suffer from prejudice against their basic human rights. They have a right to respect, friendship, and justice. They should have an active role in the Christian community." This statement allowed many parishes and Catholic facilities who supported the need for ministries to gay and lesbian Catholics to open their doors to Dignity chapters. On the other hand, the bishops' statement went on to include the church's teaching that homosexual activity is morally wrong. Therefore, many parishes and dioceses upheld this teaching and used it as a basis to keep other Dignity chapters from ever having access to meeting space on Catholic church property.

During the period between 1976 and 1986, Dignity/USA grew to over a hundred chapters across the United States with more than five thousand individual members. Then in the fall of 1986, a major crisis arose when the Vatican's Congregation for the Doctrine of the Faith sent out the "Letter to the Bishops of the Catholic Church on the Pastoral Care of Homosexual Persons." The document referred to gay and lesbian people as "disordered" and labeled their sexual expressions morally evil. It also called on the Catholic bishops to deny use of Catholic church property to any groups that did not adhere to the church teaching regarding homosexuality. This communication has come to be known as the Ratzinger letter.

Slowly, Dignity chapters from various parts of the country were asked to move their gatherings off Catholic-owned property. By Dignity's seventh Biennial Dignity Convention in the summer of 1987, over 10 percent of the chapters had been expelled from Catholic church facilities. Dignity's re-

sponse was to take a formal stand rejecting the Ratzinger letter and reiterating its own statement of position and purpose by affirming that gay and lesbian people can express their sexuality physically in a manner that is loving, life-giving, and life-affirming.

Since this statement was issued, about 25 percent of the Dignity chapters have been expelled. But the Dignity chapters are no longer leaving silently. Many have received media attention by holding demonstrations such as exodus liturgies, in which strong statements are delivered about the church's injustice and inhospitality.

The Vatican sent another letter to the United States in 1992 reaffirming the Church's opposition to homosexuality. This letter also encouraged bishops to oppose all laws banning discrimination against gays and lesbians. Dignity USA responded when its national president, Kevin Caligari, went to Rome and tacked a copy of the document onto the office door of the Church's Congregation for the Doctrine of the Faith and stamped it "Return to Sender."

New Ways Ministry

Dignity has not been the only movement that has given support to gay and lesbian Catholics. In 1977, New Ways Ministry was born. This group was founded by a priest, Bob Nugent, and a Catholic nun, Jeannine Gramick. They sought to promote the education and consciousness raising of ministers, educators, religious and the nongay church community of the needs of gays and lesbians both in society and in the Catholic community. Headquartered in the Washington, D.C., area, this organization continues to issue publications and provide workshops all over the country focusing on awareness of gay and lesbian issues and concerns.

Conference for Catholic Lesbians

In the early 1980s New Ways Ministry sponsored a retreat for Catholic lesbians. Many who attended expressed concern over the lack of lesbian spirituality in Dignity chapters and local parishes. The time was long overdue for Catholic lesbians to come together with our power and talents to plan and organize and to create. The conference for Catholic lesbians was held in the Pocono Mountains in the fall of 1982. Over one hundred lesbians came to hear well-known Catholic/Christian feminist speakers such as Jeannine Gramick, Mary Hunt, Mary Mendola, Theresa Kane, and Virginia Mollenkott.

The need for a new organization was quite obvious when lesbians gathered from not just the United States but Canada and South America as well. We were all moved by the feminist rituals, the sisterhood of Catholic lesbians, and the wonderful feeling of a "discipleship of equals" evident in this gathering. We insisted on continuing this movement. A collective of leaders from this group started the wheels moving and the Conference for Catholic Lesbians (CCL) became a national organization in 1983.

Today there are CCL groups in most major cities across the United States. The national collective is based in New York City. Typical CCL meetings are potluck dinners with feminist rituals in the homes of members. The national collective also continues to sponsor the national conference every two years to renew and affirm the Catholic lesbian movement.

CCL's participation in a Catholic feminist movement, called Women's Church Convergence, has been very beneficial to the active visibility of lesbians in feminist Catholic circles. Many CCL members hold seminars and are invited to be guest speakers at Women's Church Convergence biennial conferences.

Catholic Lesbians' Testimonies

Two noteworthy books depict the lives of Catholic lesbians in well-developed anthologies. *Lesbian Nuns: Breaking the Silence*, edited by Rosemary Curb and Nancy Manahan and published in 1985, gave people an opportunity to hear stories about lesbianism in the lives of women religious. It also brought a new respect to Catholic lesbians in CCL organizations, Dignity chapters, and Catholic communities.

In 1982, Barbara Zanotti edited a collection of essays by lesbians sharing their Catholic experiences and the effects of Catholicism on their lives. The book, *A Faith of One's Own*, shares a diversity of ways lesbians express their Catholic background in the feminist lesbian lifestyle.

We have been very gifted with the opportunities to hold hands with many good men and women on our journeys as lesbian Catholics. Dignity, Conference for Catholic Lesbians, and New Ways Ministry have provided the environments to help us choose our paths. We look forward to the future that awaits us.

Resource List

Conference for Catholic Lesbians (CCL), P.O. Box 436, Planetarium Station, New York, NY 10024; 212-663-2963 or 718-680-6107. A national organization of women who recognize the importance of the Catholic tradition in shaping lives and seek to develop and nurture a spiritual life that enhances and affirms lesbian identity, and who proclaim their existence as Catholic lesbians. There are twenty CCL groups around the country.

Dignity, USA, 1500 Massachusetts Ave., N.W., Ste. 11, Washington, DC 20005, 202-861-0017; Fax: 202-429-9808. An organization of lesbian, gay, and bisexual Catholics working toward development of a sexual theology for acceptance of gays and lesbians in the Catholic Church. It has one hundred chapters throughout the United States. It also publishes *Dignity Newsletter* monthly, price included with membership.

Lesbians and the Universal Fellowship of Metropolitan Community Churches

The Reverend

Sandra Lynn Robinson

The Reverend Sandra Robinson and La Paula Turner, UFMCC.

Bernadette Gibson

The year 1968 was a historic marker for the lesbian and gay community. The events leading up to the Stonewall riot began a new era of political unity for gays and lesbians in a society that had just witnessed the assassinations of two of history's most celebrated and charismatic leaders, Dr. Martin Luther King, Jr., and Attorney General Robert Kennedy. During the fall of that devastating year, the Reverend Troy D. Perry, a Pentecostal clergy who was ousted from the Church of God because of his homosexuality, began to have worship gatherings at his home in Los Angeles. Twenty years later, the original gathering of twelve has grown into an international Christian denomination of over twenty-four thousand members, friends, and adherents who worship in over three hundred churches around the world.

Although this young denomination was founded by a gay man, feminist consciousness was quickly recognized as the salt that flavored the stew. The Universal Fellowship of Metropolitan Community Churches (UFMCC) is a unique Christian denomination, not only because of its special ministry to lesbians and gays, but also because of the significant leadership roles of lesbians in the church from the beginning. Today, there are seventeen thousand lesbians worshiping in Metropolitan Community Churches (MCCs). UFMCC has nearly four hundred licensed and ordained clergy, and half of them are women.

Lesbian consciousness radically changed the original assumption that lesbian and gay Christians in this new church would eventually return to the traditional Christian denominations who would "someday" accept us. Instead, lesbians brought the awareness that our spiritual struggle was against oppression in all of its forms, based on Matthew 11:28, "Come unto me, all you who labor and are overburdened and I will give you rest." Unlike traditional Christianity at the time, Christian lesbians saw the essential function of the church as a struggle for justice. They believed that this justice must be acted out, not only in outreach ministry, but in the liturgy of worship. They addressed racism, sexism, classism, and the shutting out of differently abled and physically challenged people as vigorously as homophobia.

It was not easy for the denomination to accept the radical ways that lesbians proposed to implement a spiritual justice agenda for the church. Many formative battles were fought over inclusive language, female leadership roles, scriptural interpretation of God imagery, and inclusion of people of color into denominational leadership.

Lesbian leadership in UFMCC includes rigid fundamentalists and lesbians for whom God is "Goddess" and lesbians who are feminist fundamentalist. These women challenge patriarchal assumptions of traditional church, and find in scripture words that bring justice rather than condemnation.

Most openly lesbian women of color who are clergy are members of the UFMCC. While Anglo-feminist lesbians brought the demand for a truly inclusive church, lesbians of color pushed aside the shades of denial that would trivialize racism within the denomination. Renee McCoy, an African American lesbian, led this struggle for eight years until Third World Ministry became an integral part of UFMCC structure. Now Third World Ministry (renamed Department of Peoples of Color) has conferences that address leadership and education, AIDS in the minority communities, and building multiethnic/multicolored congregations. There is also an active White People Healing Racism network, which is committed to identifying racism as an evil of society and finding ways of neutralizing its effects on people.

Creative African American lesbian clergy and lay leaders are now prominent in roles that affect UFMCC structures and systems. Evangelist the Reverend Delores Berry was the first African American lesbian ordained in UFMCC, and sat on the committee which set the standard for ordination of UFMCC. The Reverend La Paula Turner was the first black lesbian elected to the governing body of UFMCC—the General Council. The Reverend Sandra Robinson became the first African American president of Samaritan College, UFMCC's professional school, which trains clergy and lay leadership. These women and a number of others are role models for increasing numbers of lesbians of color interested in pursuing the ministry and lay leadership through UFMCC.

The UFMCC has an effective outreach ministry to other denominations and religious groups. Through the Department of Ecumenical Witness and Ministry, currently staffed by the Reverend Kittredge Cherry, the fellowship continues an eleven-year dialogue with the National Council of Churches in the United States and with the World Council of Churches. In 1981 the UFMCC became a center of controversy when its application for membership to the National Council of Churches (NCC) was tabled despite their membership committee's determination that UFMCC is eligible for membership. The NCC was not ready to accept a denomination with a special outreach to the lesbian and gay community. In 1987, Elder Nancy Wilson, coauthor of the NCC application, accompanied Elder Troy Perry to an audience with Pope Paul II and other denominational leaders, because of the continued process of dialogue and conversations with the NCC.

UFMCC was formed in order to provide a safe place for lesbian and gay people to worship God without pretense or harassment. Men and women discovered new kinds of relationships where they could be friends with each other without having to meet any particular kind of social codes or sexual expectations. Lesbians began to create safe space for sharing their stories of pain and rage, and found a supportive and healing lesbian community.

The UFMCC community has put much time and energy into studying how scripture speaks to lesbians and gays and how God is evident in our lives. To meet this challenge the Faith, Fellowship, and Order Commission was developed and chaired by the Reverend Jennie Boyd-Bull, a feminist theologian who brought her particular skills of biblical interpretation to the task. As a member of the NCC's Faith and Order Commission, she influenced the document, "Experiment in Understanding," which is the study of the UFMCC published by the NCC.

The inclusive movement that prescribed nonsexist attitudes in UFMCC was begun by Elder Freda Smith, a former Salvation Army officer who came into the fellowship and became the first woman elder and vice moderator of the Board of Elders. Through her efforts, the sexist language of the denominational bylaws was changed.

UFMCC owes a significant part of its expansion to these lesbians and many others who pioneer new theology and establish new paradigms for a whole and healthy spiritual life.

Lesbians looking for a Metropolitan Community church in their cities or who want more information about the women mentioned should call or write to: UFMCC, 5300 Santa Monica Boulevard, Suite 304, Los Angeles, California 90029, 213-464-5100.

Lesbians and Judaism

Rabbi Nancy Wiener

I am a Reform rabbi and I am a lesbian. I was ordained by the Reform movement, whose lay and rabbinic governing bodies have explicitly stated that these two things are not mutually exclusive. These words, while encouraging, are also disappointing. They do not affirm lesbians who are rabbis; they simply disregard as irrelevant that very important part of our lives. I find that offensive and painful as a Reform Jew and as a lesbian.

Judaism taught me many things that I hope to bring to and teach through my rabbinate. I was taught that the world is perfectible, that human efforts can radically alter the world, and that it is our obligation, as Jews and as human beings, to work actively to eradicate injustice. As I studied Jewish history, learned about anti-Semitism, and followed current events, I was taught to ask one key question: How can we make our world more equitable and just?

When I studied the Holocaust my teachers and rabbis expressed their outrage at a dictator who could persecute and murder people for just being who they were, and at a world that could stand by and allow mass extermination to take place. When I learned about charity, I was taught that the Hebrew root for the word is *right.* Hence, charity is not inspired by pity; it is inspired by a sense of fairness—a desire to make things right. As a member of a small minority in American culture, I was taught to be proud of who I was, comfortable with what made me "different," and centered enough in my identity as a Jew not to be shaken by external pressures to act to the contrary or change.

While growing up I was proud of my family and community because of their willingness to stand up for what they felt was right and fair. I saw them working long and hard for the changes they believed necessary to improve the lives of minorities: Jews, blacks, women, the poor. They invoked rabbinic teachings that were applicable and unabashedly dismissed those they felt violated their fundamental moral and ethical beliefs.

I have come to realize that, because I am a lesbian, most Jews will not apply these values of fairness to me. The more traditional Jews (Chasidim, Orthodox, and the official voice of Conservative Jews) are guided by laws contained in the Torah and

Rabbi Linda Holtzman, Philadelphia.

© 1991 JEB (Joan E. Biren)

strictly interpreted by generations of rabbis: *Halakhah.* They see lesbians as sinners who are breaking long-held religious prohibitions. Even many non-Halakhic Jews, members of the Reform and Reconstructionist movements, have strong objections to lesbians and gay men.

As a lesbian, I find greatest acceptance in the Reform and Reconstructionist movements. By the mid-1970s, congregations identified as "gay and lesbian outreach congregations" (a euphemism for congregations with predominantly lesbian and gay members) were allowed to become members of these movements. Their representative bodies consistently vote in support of legislation designed to protect civil rights for lesbians and gays and prevent antigay violence. In the 1980s, in response to the AIDS crisis, they initiated campaigns to educate teenagers and adults about homosexuality and safe sex. A growing number of mainstream synagogues in large metropolitan areas have begun to make concerted efforts to encourage gay and lesbian Jews to become members.

These are not small changes, but they still fall short of the ideals and teachings that I understand to be the backbone of liberal Judaism. In practice, the acceptance of lesbians and gays is limited. By and large, we do not feel comfortable at most synagogues. We are told we are welcome as long as we don't overtly display or "flaunt" our relationships. These phrases, restricting self-expression and natural interaction, still are spoken by those who identify themselves as accepting. A significant amount of education and sensitization is still necessary; fortunately, an increasing number of congregations are sponsoring workshops and other programs with these specific goals.

In *theory,* the Reform and Reconstructionist movements have opened the doors for lesbians and gay men to become rabbis. Neither movements' seminaries consider homosexuality to be grounds for immediate rejection any longer.

Since the late 1980s, life at these seminaries has become increasingly more comfortable. Lesbian and gay students have found it possible to be "out" to most classmates, some faculty members, and even some administrators. Discussions about homosexuality and homophobia have become commonplace. Now, classes on life-cycle rituals even include discussions on commitment ceremonies. In 1988 lesbian and gay students at Hebrew Union College in

New York, one of the Reform movement's North American seminary campuses, even formed an organization that achieved equal status with all student organizations. Nevertheless, there are still many members of the seminary communities who are opposed to these attitudinal changes. To date there are no openly lesbian or gay students at the Conservative seminary.

Life at the two seminaries with open admissions is not, however, reflective of life beyond the seminary walls. Lesbian and gay students quickly learn that sexual orientation cannot be openly discussed with their student congregations. Lovers do not enjoy the same privileges as heterosexual spouses: invitations to seminary-sponsored and congregational events, paid transportation to and from the congregations, and accommodations for overnights. The schools' policies are far ahead of the congregations their graduates serve.

When in June 1990, newspapers around the United States sported headlines announcing "a landmark decision": the Central Conference of American Rabbis (the professional organization for Reform rabbis) would recognize openly gay and lesbian rabbis as members, I received many phone calls from friends and family congratulating me on this great advance. To their dismay, I responded with heightened anxiety. The committee members who issued the decision stated that they were "acutely aware that the inability of most gay and lesbian rabbis to live openly as homosexuals is deeply painful." Yet, they concluded that "in light of the limited ability of the Placement Commission or the CCAR to guarantee the tenure of the gay or lesbian rabbi who 'come out of the closet' the committee does not want to encourage colleagues to put their careers at risk."

This professional organization took a position that encouraged the gay and lesbian rabbis utilizing its job placement and job security services to live a duplicitous existence. The gay and lesbian rabbis were told that they would be better Jewish leaders and models as self-acknowledged liars, living secretive lives implying self-shame and loathing, than as honest forthright Jewish lesbians and gay men. Institutionalized Reform Judaism counseled us to act in ways that many of us find personally offensive and antithetical to being an effective spiritual and communal leader.

Most lesbians approach the job search as I did,

with great fear and trepidation. We resent, yet respect the warning that coming out to a prospective congregation can lead to professional suicide. (Applying to a "lesbian and gay outreach synagogue" is the only exception to this rule.) We search our souls to establish our own professional and personal priorities. We enter the rabbinate because of our love of and commitment to Judaism and our desire to perpetuate it. We also value our own integrity. Those of us with lovers want to find a position that will put as little strain on the relationship as possible. Those without lovers want to find employment in areas where there will be possibilities of meeting someone.

The vast majority of lesbian rabbis who are serving congregations are closeted. In recent years, a number of lesbian rabbis have come out to their congregations, congregational leaders, Jewish institutional superiors, and co-workers without losing their jobs. Most avoid raising the issue. No "out" lesbian rabbi has yet arrived at a new congregation with her lover. Unattached lesbian rabbis "pass" (by default) at congregations. Many more lesbian rabbis would love to serve as congregational rabbis, but are not willing to compromise their integrity by denying or limiting their personal lives. Many of us therefore seek out noncongregational positions as administrators, chaplains, and teachers.

It never ceases to amaze me that a group that knows the pain of being a minority in a culture stressing homogeneity, that has lived through historical periods in which there were forced conversions, that was threatened with complete extermination during the Holocaust just because they were Jews cannot understand that they are now the oppressors inflicting pain through their prejudice toward and rejection of actively Jewish lesbians and lesbian rabbis. We are being told by liberal Jewish groups that we are welcome to participate *but*—they still aren't sure we aren't subversive, they still aren't sure we can promote Judaism and Jewish values, they still aren't sure they want lesbians to be leaders in their home congregations (although, of course, "in theory" we should be allowed to exist!).

The liberal Jewish movements have made changes that were unimaginable only a few years ago. But they still have a long way to go to create an environment in which lesbians and gay men can freely and openly participate in all aspects of Jewish life, including the rabbinate. I now sign my name to this article, something I feared doing just two years ago. I now do so with pride. May the day come soon when such freedom will exist for all of us.

Further Reading

Artson, Bradley Shavit. "Judaism and Homosexuality." *Tikkun* 3, no. 2 (March/April 1988), 52–58.

Balka, Christie, and Andy Rose, eds. *Twice Blessed: On Being Lesbian, Gay, and Jewish.* Boston: Beacon Press, 1989.

"Can a Homosexual Rabbi Serve As a Role Model?" *Reform Judaism* (Winter 1990).

Kahn, Yoel. "Judaism and Homosexuality." *Journal of Homosexuality* 18, no. 1–2 (Winter 1989).

Kirschner, Robert. "Halakhah and Homosexuality: A Reappraisal." *Judaism* (Fall 1988), 450–58.

Wicca:

A Spiritual Journey

Cory Baca, Interviewed by

Karol D. Lightner

My name is Cory Baca. I am forty-five years old and was raised by a Mexican father and Scotch-Irish mother. I attended a Catholic school attached to the convent, and after seventh grade, boys and girls were segregated in the classroom. We wore uniforms and went to mass on holy days of obligation.

As a kid I loved the liturgy and ritual, and the concept of Mary. My favorite ritual was making an altar to Mary every day. I had a very dysfunctional family, and church structure did a lot during my late childhood and early adolescence to hold me together. But as I got older, I realized I didn't have what they called Faith. When I started to become sexual (at that point I was dating men), the church dictates on chastity until marriage didn't make any sense to me.

Also, I could not accept the second-class position of women in the church. All women who did not go into the convent were expected to marry, and then give up their jobs and their entire existence to stay at home and have kids. I couldn't buy that.

I went through a long period in which I did not define myself as a spiritual person. When I first became a feminist, in the early seventies, the first literature about the goddess appeared. Reading Merlin Stone and Elizabeth Gould Davis, I began to see the focus of a god figure as *female* instead of male. It made a tremendous amount of sense to me. After I became a feminist, the transition from feminism to lesbianism was just another step in the right direction. Wicca was another step on the same path; it all flowed together.

Around 1981 I began to go to *Califia* community and women's music festivals, where I suddenly found myself in a community of women who were also discovering women's and lesbian spirituality.

That was when I began to go to circles with other women. I met women who had also just begun to read Z. Budapest's *The Holy Book of Women's Mysteries* and Starhawk's *The Spiral Dance,* and we began to do rituals and keep the sabbats. We did not know what we were doing when we started; we just went to each quarter of the ritual space and read out of books to call the elements. We didn't really have a sense of what it all meant, but we knew we had to cast a circle to contain power. It was like being in kindergarten, starting at the beginning, learning and recovering the spirituality that we had lost for so many generations.

At that point, like many other women, I did a lot of studying. The groups we had started got more and more proficient at conducting rituals as we acquired knowledge and abilities.

Wicca (also called Witchcraft, the Old Religion, or Paganism) is a spiritual system for organizing your beliefs much in the way that people organize their beliefs around Christianity or Buddhism. The roots of Wicca can be traced back into prehistory, to the Stone Age, when goddess figures were carved in stone and goddess images were painted on the walls of caves in southern France and other parts of Europe and the Mediterranean.

It is an ecologically oriented spirituality, with great respect for the earth and with the belief that there is spirit in everything. Animals, plants, rocks—all have power, all have meaning and a place on the earth. Wicca is focused on female energy and on being a part of nature rather than attempting to subdue it.

About three years ago I started studying the Celtic form of the craft and was recently initiated in a ceremony, including a ritual at which I swore not to betray the confidentiality of the order and to uphold the Wiccan Rede "An'it harm none, do what ye will." I had originally come out into feminist Wiccanism through the lesbian community.

There are differences between feminist Wicca and other forms of the craft. For a time I thought that going back to the craft that had been invented by lesbians in the late seventies! Several years later I realized there were other people, men and women, who were Wiccans and Pagans. Some Wiccans believe that their traditions survived in Europe and the Americas, passed along from parent to child, centuries before the Burning Times in the Middle Ages.

I met some women who define themselves as traditional witches. They learned their craft from their parents, and their childhood and adolescent social circles were largely defined in terms of an extended family—friends who practiced the tradition and kept it totally secret from the rest of society. They were appalled at the explosion around them in terms of the newfound popularity of the craft.

I have also met a considerable number of people, male and female, who practice some of the more modern forms of the craft, such as the Gardnerian and the Celtic. Although these traditions harken back to the Middle Ages and before, their revival began in Britain and only began to be publicized in the 1950s. How much of modern practice is taken from the older traditions and how much has been created recently, nobody will ever know.

The form of the craft most associated with the lesbian community is the Dianic form—for Diana, the moon goddess, also called Artemis. The Dianics were lesbian goddesses who roamed the woods with hordes of female followers; they were huntresses and also the protectors of the wild and of women, especially women in childbirth. Diana is also the name of one of the great mother goddesses. The Dianic form of the craft, unlike other forms, is specifically dedicated to women, focusing on the goddess in her many forms, and will very rarely bring in a male god or element. Their worship usually has a political or social aspect.

While I could not relate to the male as god, the female as god feels like a more intimate, personal relationship; you are the representative of your own spirituality. If you wish to create a circle and invoke the Goddess, you can do it yourself. You don't have to wait to find a priest or shaman. Of course, if you are apprenticed to someone, you may make a contract in which you do not do certain rituals until you have been trained, but there's nothing in the conception of Wicca that gets between you and the immediate practice of your own spirituality or religion.

Wicca is attuned to the earth and to the seasons, like Native American and other forms of shamanism. Life and the year are a circle in which death is considered a transformation, but still a part of the life cycle, which is connected to our belief in reincarnation. We die, we are reborn, we live out the path we have chosen; we die again, we go to the Summerlands, and we come back again, frequently with the same group of people to work out whichever path we chose.

Wiccan celebrations, particularly in terms of the yearly cycle, not only center around the changing of the seasons and our own individual changes, but also the cycle of life, death, and rebirth. In the larger ceremonies, which are called sabbats, women celebrate alone or in groups called circles. In my tradition the *Hallowmas,* which we know as Halloween, is the most sacred of holidays because it marks the time of death and rebirth. During this time, the veil between the physical and spiritual worlds becomes very thin; the two worlds touch, and individuals have access to both.

Hallowmas is followed by a solar festival called *Yule* (called Christmas in some religions), the time of rebirth and the reentry of light into the world. That's followed by *Candlemas,* the time of initiation and of childhood, which is followed by *Spring Equinox,* a time of balance that celebrates growth and adolescence. Then follows *Beltane,* or Mayday, the second most sacred time of year, the time of coming into the prime of life, of generation and sexuality. *Summer Solstice* celebrates the fullness of life and the apex of physical power and beauty. *Lammas,* in early August, celebrates the first harvest, the first sign of the arrival of the time of darkness in the midst of plenty. *Harvestime,* or Thanksgiving, is celebrated at the *Fall Equinox* when the light and the dark are again in balance. Then Hallowmas comes again. They are defined as opposites: Yule, or Winter Solstice, is the opposite of Summer Solstice. Yule is the darkest time, but the light is beginning to emerge; at Summer Solstice it is the lightest, but the light begins to wane.

Many of these traditions have been usurped by the Christian church. The Jewish, Islamic, Chinese, and Hindu calendars are also organized around these dates. Winter Solstice is extraordinary in that practically all the peoples of the world have celebrated it in some way. Wiccans also celebrate the moon, whose cycles echo the menstrual cycle and the cycle of life, death, and rebirth. This is a time for women alone or in groups to focus on their needs and wants, to work in concert with the moon's energy.

The Wiccan tradition I practice does not believe in the concept of sin or the devil, or of control by an outside hierarchy; there is more of an emphasis on the ability of the individual and the community toward self-determination. Wicca began as a matriarchal religion and only later encountered a patriarchal religion that tried to impose upon it a system of external control.

The concept of the devil actually came out of the Middle East and into Europe with the Romans. During the Middle Ages, the Christian church attempted to unify the entire world under its dominion. When the concept of the devil, and good and evil, came into Europe, it brought with it the notion that good was embodied by Christ and the church. It was the church's duty to eradicate evil, which was defined as anything *not* sanctioned by the church.

As it became politically powerful, the church ran into grassroots resistance from the peasantry and those who practiced the old religion of the earth. For a long time, the old and new religions existed side by side, but at some point the church decided to eliminate the old religion. The Inquisition was created to stamp out both the old religion and any other dissent.

At about the same time, medical science and doctors were trying to eliminate the herb women and midwives. Between 6 and 9 million people, mostly women, were killed during the Burning Times.

When you kill off significant numbers of people who pass down a tradition, such as herb and medicine women, and scare the remainder into being very careful about what they pass down to the next generation, that information will then be contaminated. After a couple of generations the devil created by the Inquisition became associated with the teachings of the old religion. The old religion had Cernunnos, god of the hunt, and in the Mediterranean, Pan, the goat-footed god. These images became fused with the church's concept of the devil—which is precisely why "Satan" looks the way he does!

The religion created by the Inquisition— Satanism—still exists and is seen as a rebellion against the order being imposed from above. It is *not* part of Wicca.

In the contemporary revival of Wicca, an attempt has been made to trace the roots of the old religion to define the practice of Wicca in order to recover what was lost in its persecution. One unifying concept that has been discovered within Wicca is the law of threefold return. What you send out, you will get back threefold. It's a part of karma. If you send out negativity, destruction, and death, it will come back to you threefold. If you send out positive energy, love, acceptance, and caring, that will come back threefold.

If you are interested in Wicca, I would advise that you search among your friends to find people who are involved with women's spirituality. You can also check the women's newspapers and magazines to find open circles that you can attend. Also, you can check the bulletin boards in magic or occult shops and look for classes that are being given and contact names and phone numbers. You can actively seek out people who are in the craft. Or you can start the way I did—get some friends and some books and begin on your own.

Women's spirituality in the Wiccan tradition has just sort of exploded on the scene in lesbian culture. I was at the Michigan music festival, and the number of workshops on women's spirituality and the emphasis on it was absolutely incredible. Several major people in New Age and women's spirituality and Native American spirituality were there. The Michigan Music Festival now begins with what amounts to an old religion invocation. At the West Coast festival there was at least one women's circle, and there was a Dianic convention in the Midwest. What I am seeing in the community is that Wicca is everywhere.

Further Reading

Adler, Margot. *Drawing Down the Moon.* Boston: Beacon Press, 1987—overview of recent developments within the craft.

Budapest, Z. *The Holy Book of Women's Mysteries.* Oakland, Calif.: Wingbow Press, 1989—an introduction to the Dianic Craft.

Jong, Erica. *Witches.* New York: Abrams, 1981.

Starhawk. *The Spiral Dance.* New York: HarperCollins, 1989.

Native American Spirituality

Beverly Little Thunder,

Interviewed by Karol D. Lightner

I am a Lakota Sioux, forty years old, and the mother of five children. Growing up, I was very closeted, because I knew no other Native American lesbians. So I got married at a very young age. My parents were alcoholics. I spent half of my time growing up in Los Angeles and half growing up in South and North Dakota with my relatives. This gave me an opportunity to be in touch with who I was as a Native American woman and to communicate in the Anglo world.

I spent many years being in marriages that didn't work out. After I had all of my children and was divorced from my children's father, I met a woman and came out to her. We had a beautiful relationship for a few months, and then my ex-husband found out about it and threatened to take the children away.

I panicked. So my lover moved back to San Francisco and I stayed in Los Angeles. A few weeks later I met an American Indian man and married him. I thought that if I went into court and had a husband, how could they say I was a lesbian?

I was also very active in the American Indian Movement (AIM). Women are treated as second-class citizens in our movement. Anytime I spoke up in a meeting it was as if they'd say, "Shut up—don't bother us; this is important business."

Sweat lodges were run primarily for the men; there'd be thirty or forty men there—and twenty women outside beading, talking, and cooking so we'd have food after the ceremony. After the men were finished it might be two in the morning before the women would get into the lodge, and we'd be told, "Take your children into the lodge; teach your children." But it is difficult to wake up five children at 2:00 A.M. and drag them into a sweat lodge.

When I suggested that maybe we needed to have both a women's and men's sweat lodge, I was yelled at and belittled in front of everyone. It was apparent to me that if I wanted to have any voice, I had to have a husband, so I had a number of reasons to stay with this man, even though he was abusive and an alcoholic.

I went to ceremonies, practiced the sweat lodge and prayer ceremonies with my children, and began to Sun Dance in Davis, California. Within a few years, a lot of women began to come to me to learn about the Sun Dance.

Sun Dance is one of the most powerful, important ceremonies of the Lakota people. The men usually pierce their chests and are tied to a tree with a fifty-foot rope. The tree is cut down and "conquered" by the men before the ceremony, then brought to the arbor circle in which the dance takes place. Our belief is that this is an umbilical cord to the center of our Mother Earth, represented by the tree, and by dancing until their flesh tears from the piercing, the men believe they are giving birth—as if they are breaking the umbilical cord. A woman can do that by giving birth to a child, but a man needs to give to his people in a different way. The women are told that they can support the men by dancing behind them, but basically the women are not the focus of the ceremony.

After my third year of dancing, I was asked to take care of the new women and non-Lakota women. And I was being listened to—but it was because sitting next to me was a man. I resented it; it was too high a price to pay. After five years of this marriage, I realized I needed to be living my life in a truer form, as an open lesbian.

About that time I began sneaking to the women's bookstores, and there I picked up the first edition of *Our Right To Love*. As I flipped through the pages, I saw a picture of a beautiful Indian woman and my heart just stopped. I very quickly read her story and thought for a moment, "Oh, no! Somebody read my journal and wrote it in here."

The woman pictured and interviewed, Barbara Cameron, was a Sioux, from Pine Ridge. After I had made an intense search to locate her, she finally called me one day and said, "Seven women have given me your phone number and said you wanted to talk to me." When I told her of my fear and my loneliness, she was very warm, receptive, and supportive.

Several Indian women who had come to Sun Dance had confided to me that they were lesbians. When I came out to them, they said, "Why haven't you spoken out?" And I said, "Because I'm afraid." I prayed hard about what it would mean to come out. I prayed that either things would be easier for me with my husband or that the Creator would send a woman into my life, someone who followed the pipe and cared about children, and it would be nice if she was Sioux!

I also began working with the Gay American Indians in San Francisco. I did the pipe ceremony with them. (The pipe ceremony is a prayer ceremony involving the use of the pipe, which is a part of the Lakota tradition and whose significance is similar to that of the cross in Christianity.) I realized that many of my gay sisters and brothers were not visible because they were usually in the bar, strung out on cocaine. I tried desperately to connect with some of them. To this day, I don't know if I was successful.

My greatest fear was that if I came out, someone would take the pipe away from me and I wouldn't be allowed to go to ceremonies. I couldn't imagine not being able to go to a Sun Dance or a sweat lodge, because these had become the very center of my life, my spirituality.

I've learned since that I can make a pipe; I can put up a sweat lodge. All this power was inside me. But I didn't know this at the time. Knowing these things inside your heart is the key to setting you free.

Eventually I left my husband and came out. I went with my friend to Sun Dance and she danced for two days. Then we came out to everyone we knew. During that year I was told I really ought to think about not coming to the ceremony, but we went anyway, in spite of the warnings, to a meeting of women I had danced and prayed with.

But my friend was told that the men didn't want her to dance. It was quite painful for her—they wouldn't let her in the lodge where the women, supposedly in the middle of a prayer ceremony, were yelling and calling her derogatory names. Six men came up to drag her away. But she knew that if she took her clothes off, put her towel on, and loaded her pipe, the Sioux men would hesitate to come near her.

Later that day, though, she danced on the side of a hill by herself. Three of the women kept coming by and calling her derogatory names. Later, some of the men informed her that they weren't the ones who didn't want her to dance; it was those three women. One man spoke with her alone and told her his brother was gay. He lived in San Francisco and didn't come home because he feared experiencing what was happening to her.

Some of the elder women came to talk to me and said that gay and lesbian people had been very sacred and honored at one time, but with the coming of the missionaries, that had changed. One told me, "If these people knew what they were doing, they would have had a tepee set up with food and clothing; all you'd have had to do is come, because they would have been so honored to have your presence here." At the end of the ceremony the woman brought us four paper plate holders, all she had to give. I thought a lot about her afterwards.

We were told by several women that we didn't need to be there with those people who were harassing us, that we could do our own ceremony. We went back to Arizona and prayed about it for a year and decided we needed to do a Sun Dance for ourselves—a lesbian Sun Dance.

After praying about it, we at first thought we'd go on a hill by ourselves, bring a tape recorder, tape the songs, and dance for four days. During those four days we have no food or water: We fast and we dance from sunrise to sunset. When we began planning what we would do, we were told that there were women who were willing to support us. We started off with about twenty women who said they would come the next year.

One woman offered us the use of her land, so we began putting out the word. We didn't have much money and could only send so many flyers to bookstores to put out a call to other Native American lesbians. We decided to open it up to all women, all colors, although we asked that only women of color who had been at a ceremony in previous years dance the four days. The other women could learn the songs and sing for us, drum, and tend the fires that need to be kept going throughout the ceremony, and cook for the drummer and the singers, who eat for the dancers. As long as the singers are well fed, it is believed that the dancers will have the strength to continue.

We held the ceremony in July and there were over one hundred women. Every color of the rainbow was represented and it was a powerful reclaiming of a ceremony that I think is going to become a women's ceremony. I don't know that it will always be called a Sun Dance; that may change.

But at this time we are reclaiming the ceremony to be ours. We did not kill a tree and bring it to the arbor—we planted a tree. We felt it was much more appropriate for women to be giving back to our Mother Earth than to be taking from her. We also didn't pierce ourselves, because we've all given birth, all had our monthly cycles, all suffered for our Mother Earth. We did take small flesh offerings—little nicks out of the arm.

Traditionally, women had been told they could not come to ceremony with men when they were in their moon time, because it is believed they are so powerful at that time that the good, positive spirits will stay away from the men if a woman is there on her moon. A woman carrying the pipe or feathers should put those things down and not touch them when she is on her moon. So we made a major integral change here; we reasoned that since we are women, another woman being on her moon is not going to threaten us. She's only going to share that energy. We threw that rule out the door, and I'm sure there are people in the Indian community who are really upset about that, but it has proven to be a powerful bond for all the women coming to our ceremonies.

The eagles came all four days of the ceremony. The eagle is a powerful symbol among most Native American tribes. The eagle's presence is considered a blessing because the eagle carries your prayers to the universe. The men usually blow on eagle bone whistles. I had an eagle bone whistle and I blew on it. I am sure there are Native Americans, especially men, who would say, "A woman blowing an eagle bone whistle? The world is going to fall apart!" But it didn't. The eagles heard the whistle—and blessed us with their presence.

It wasn't so hot that we couldn't dance throughout the day. The unity and healing that took place and the consciousness that was raised among women was beautiful. I had dreams of the ceremony before it happened, so I knew what needed to be done there, but none of my dreams prepared me, because the ceremony far surpassed anything I had envisioned.

I know there is growing movement towards Native American spirituality among women. We were told that the time for taking care of Mother Earth is now and that the women should be doing it. All the people of the earth—red, yellow, black, white—the colors of the four directions, were given a quarter of the earth to take care of. The Native American people, including everyone from the North to the South Pole, were given this quarter to take care of. At this time, to my knowledge, we are the only people still living on our quarter of the earth who are trying to take care of the earth; even though everyone should.

For a long time we were told by our elders, "Don't let the white people know our ways—they will exploit them." But the time has come for all those different colored people to learn how to take care of the earth; it's their home, too. We Native American people can't do it alone.

Our responsibility as Native American women, Native American people, is to teach those around us. Our prophesies have said that it is the women who are the backbone of the nation, and that's happening now with women of all colors. A vision was shared with me of each of the sacred hoops—red, yellow, black, and white—all being broken. But those hoops were beginning to mend, and the red would be the first to mend. As they all mended, they would touch.

If you put four circles together, you have a little star space in the center, and that is the coming-together space in which you create the ceremony that will help heal our Mother Earth. I think that the Sun Dance is beginning to do that.

For those women seeking to find their balance and to find out who they are, I would say look inside yourself, at the power inside of you. That connection with Mother Earth is inside of you. I don't want to advocate that everyone come running to the Sun Dance; for some people it is not going to be that way.

But respect yourself and respect the things that you have inside of you; believe in yourself. So many women keep looking for someone to say yes, you are a medicine person, yes you can be taught these things. You can be taught the dynamics of praying with the cedar and the sage, to go outside and offer water to our Mother Earth, but all you have to do is *remember* these things. You don't have to relearn them because you already know them.

VII

Lesbians and the Law

Lesbians and the Law:

Sex, Families, and Work

Paula L. Ettelbrick, Esq.

Representing lesbians in our pursuit of justice in the courts is a bit like stepping into a New York City taxicab—you trust that you'll reach your final destination, the question is what kind of terrifying moments will you face along the way. The law regarding lesbian rights has certainly been full of extraordinary accomplishments, particularly in the last ten years. But it has also been, at times, a terrifying ride.

Thousands of cases representing the interests and concerns of lesbians have been brought to the courts to establish our legal rights in the quarter century since the Stonewall Rebellion. Rights to housing and access to public accommodations. Rights to military service and law enforcement jobs. Rights of lesbian and gay student groups to recognition and funding. Immigration. Withdrawal of arts funding from lesbian performers. Policies against sex education and safe sex education in schools. Addressing antigay violence. Rights of Irish lesbians to march in the St. Patrick's Day Parade.

As important as these and many other cases are to lesbian equality and liberation, the core issues—issues that affect most of our lives on a day-to-day basis—can be clustered into three general areas: sex, families, and work. Do we have the right to have sex free of criminal prosecution and to claim our sexual identity free of social stigma? Will the families we create be recognized legally and socially? Can we work in our chosen jobs and earn our livelihood free of discrimination? The day we have fully succeeded in answering "yes" to all of these questions is the day that we can declare victory for lesbian equality. Certainly, there will still be battles. But rights to have sex, form families of our choice, and work as open lesbians will lead to genuine change in all other areas of our lives.

Decriminalizing Lesbian Sex

The right to have sex and to openly claim our sexual identity as lesbians, bisexual women, or just plain queer individuals is a central component of our fight for liberation. The denial of that right and the stigma attached to lesbian sexuality forms the cornerstone of discrimination against us in other areas of our lives. Thus, the challenge to laws criminalizing adult, consensual sex must lie at the heart of our movement.

The truth is that the United States Supreme Court has never explicitly recognized that *anyone*—lesbian or straight—has an inalienable right to have sex without government interference. Certainly, all women discover that their "right to have sex" is full of governmental interference once they get pregnant and seek an abortion. Our history is replete with criminal laws banning any sexual activity but that which is marital *and* reproductive. Criminal laws such as those that ban oral and anal sex between consenting adults in private, or other "crimes against nature," are intended to regulate human activity and enforce sexual conformity. The effect of not conforming, aside from possible criminal prosecution, is stigma, discrimination, and the denial of basic civil and social rights.

Lesbians, by our identity, desires, and conduct, are nonconformists to this social ideal and a threat to the moral order. As women who live in the world independent of men and who choose sex with women, whether exclusively or occasionally, we are the ultimate outlaws. We share with all women the retribution for daring to make our own sexual decisions without men's coercive influence or governmental interference. As a result, a necessary component to our legal and political movements toward equality must include challenges to the laws that define what is socially and legally allowable sex (reproductive, heterosexual, marital) and what is not (anything else that a woman might choose). Because the sex we have with women, whether considered illegal or simply immoral, forms the basis for discrimination against us, we cannot ignore the need to challenge these laws. Nor can we simply act as if conforming in other ways to society's demands will move us towards equality. First and foremost, we much challenge the view that our sex is bad, ugly, and immoral.

The most important legal case—and most trau-

© Tom Tyburski

Paula L. Ettelbrick.

matic loss—in our never ending battle for equal citizenship is *Bowers v. Hardwick,* a challenge to Georgia's sodomy law that was decided by the United States Supreme Court in 1986. The court, which earlier had never directly addressed the question of whether there is a constitutionally protected right for two adults to engage in sex, made it painfully clear in *Hardwick* that such a right certainly does not exist for lesbians and gay men.

The case involved a gay man named Michael Hardwick who was in the bedroom of his home having sex with another man when an Atlanta police officer walked in (he was let into the house by a guest) to serve him with an arrest warrant for an outstanding disorderly conduct charge (which was not sex-related). After seeing the two men together, the officer arrested them and charged them with vi-

olating the Georgia sodomy law, which bans oral and anal sex between two adults, straight or gay, even when performed in the privacy of their own home. Though the charges were dropped against Mr. Hardwick, the facts provided a unique opportunity to challenge the absurdity and intrusiveness of this law and to attempt to set a precedent in the United State Supreme Court so that all similar laws would be struck down.

Unfortunately, the court gave us a stinging repudiation of our assertion that the state has no business outlawing consensual sexual acts between two people, particularly when performed in private. In a sweeping and incredibly hostile decision, five of the nine justices on the court rejected our arguments that the same right to privacy that promises women the right to decide to have an abortion free of the government's interference should also be extended to cover the right to engage in sex with another adult of one's choosing. In an undignified display of judicial malice, these Supreme Court justices called our claims "at best, facetious," (in other words, a joke) and unleashed an unprecedented venomous attack on lesbians and gay men. While Justice Harry Blackmun (who wrote the seminal abortion case, *Roe v. Wade* in 1973) wrote a passionate dissent berating the other members of the court for their distortion of legal precedent and inability to consider the human dimension of sexual expression, the harm had been done.

From a legal perspective, the loss in *Hardwick* was nothing short of devastating. The highest court in the country turned us away with an opinion so nasty and cursory as to give the most powerful legal support to antigay bigots. The court repudiated the idea that sexuality is something central to human existence and identity. The decision supported the idea that lesbians and gay men are undeserving of basic constitutional rights and upheld traditional support for marital, reproductive sex as the only form worthy of legal protection. In so doing, the court approved the ultimate form of governmental intrusion by giving police officers the right to enter our bedrooms, observe our activities, and arrest us if those activities do not conform to the ideal of heterosexuality.

The decision left in place sodomy laws in twenty-five states as well as the District of Columbia. We had hung our hopes on the belief that we could prevail in the Supreme Court. (We nearly did win.

Justice Powell originally voted in our favor, which would have given us a 5–4 victory, but he switched his vote before the decision was released. After his retirement from the court, Justice Powell publicly admitted his regret over the position he took in *Hardwick*.) A victory in *Hardwick* would have invalidated all remaining sodomy laws. Most importantly, it would have established the legal—though not social—acceptance of our right to engage in sex with a same-sex partner. Instead of simply going down in flames, however, lesbian and gay legal advocates quickly shifted our strategy and embarked on a state-by-state campaign of challenging sodomy laws under state constitutions and/or seeking repeal of the laws in state legislatures. To date, courts in Kentucky and Michigan have struck down their sodomy laws, while legislatures in Nevada and the District of Columbia have repealed them. Legal challenges have been brought in Texas, Mississippi, Louisiana, and other states, but many have failed on technical grounds having nothing to do with the central question of the right to sex.

Hardwick has been used by courts and advocates across the country as the legal justification for denying rights to lesbians in other areas of our lives. The Missouri courts have used this decision as the justification for taking children away from lesbian mothers. In Kansas, a federal judge relied on *Hardwick* to justify upholding the firing of a man perceived to be gay. The City of New York used the *Hardwick* decision to argue in court against providing domestic partner benefits to lesbian and gay employees. The entity that has most taken advantage of the tragedy of *Hardwick* is the federal government, which has unabashedly used *Hardwick* to uphold its discriminatory policies in the areas of security clearances, the military, and employment in certain government agencies like the FBI.

Despite the legal devastation wrought by *Hardwick*, the loss actually helped to clarify for our allies the oppression and level of intrusion we face as lesbians. The decision deeply offended most fair-minded people who feel that at least our bedrooms should be off-limits to the state. But so long as the Supreme Court's decision in *Hardwick* stands, which it is bound to do for many years, it will stand for the proposition that our right to make intimate decisions about our sexual conduct in keeping with the nature of our identities as lesbians is "at best, facetious."

Legal Recognition of Lesbian Relationships

It is understandable why some lesbians would desire to marry if that option were available. Beyond the social recognition provided by the institution of marriage, married couples benefit from numerous legal and economic advantages, such as preferential tax treatment, social security, retirement, a right to sue in the event of the death or injury of a spouse, and the protection under laws governing property distribution.

However, if we were to focus solely or even primarily on legal marriage as a goal, we would be foolishly ignoring the protections that already exist as well as the opportunity to challenge the worldview that only married couples are deserving of protection and benefits. Furthermore, holding marriage out as the ideal relationship leads us to accept the idea that only sex within marriage is appropriate and worthy of legal protection. The history of marriage has clearly revealed that it is, at its core, an institution bent on regulating women's sexuality, decisions, and lives. Thus it is worthwhile for lesbians to continue our successful work of developing new avenues for recognition of our families that are equal to the treatment given to married couples.

Marriage. Marriage is strictly a matter of state law and, at the moment, no state in the country has ever given legal sanction to a marriage between two women or two men. Though some marriage laws are gender neutral (that is, they do not specify that only a man and woman may marry each other), most laws are quite explicit. In the 1970s, courts in three states (Minnesota, Kentucky, and Washington) ruled that marriage is defined as "a union of man and woman, uniquely involving procreation and rearing of children," thereby rejecting the claims of same-sex couples that they should be granted a marriage license. However, in 1993, significant legal ground was broken when the Hawaii Supreme Court responded to a challenge by lesbian and gay couples to the marriage exclusion by ruling that the state marriage law may be struck down as unconstitutional sex discrimination unless the state can convince the court that there are compelling reasons for denying same-sex couples the right to marry. But before we start plunking down cash for wedding bands studded with triangular pink stones or send off nonrefundable deposits for honeymoon cruises around the Hawaiian Islands, it is important to take a look at what this decision is and the many fights we will face around the country should the court ultimately decide that lesbian couples can marry in Hawaii.

Two constitutional arguments were presented to the state supreme court in the Hawaii marriage case. First, the couples wishing to marry asked the court to recognize that marriage is a fundamental constitutional right (as the U.S. Supreme Court has acknowledged) which should be extended to lesbian and gay couples. The Hawaii Supreme Court categorically refused to recognize such a right for lesbian and gay couples. The court acknowledged that such a right exists for straight couples, but said that the traditions and history of the state and the country have always rejected the notion that lesbian and gay couples should be able to legally marry.

Though it refused to recognize a fundamental constitutional right, the court did accept the couples' argument that the marriage law, which allows a woman to marry a man but denies her the right to marry a woman, discriminates on the basis of sex. The case, therefore, will go to trial in 1995 on the question of whether the state can show a compelling reason for denying a marriage license to same-sex couples. Given the court's rather schizophrenic decision, the outcome of this case is still very much a toss-up.

If the Hawaii court does ultimately require the state to give marriage licenses to same-sex couples, the question becomes whether lesbian couples from other states may go to Hawaii to get married. Assuming Hawaii's residency requirements for marriage are not so strict as to make it impractical, couples who married in Hawaii would need to have the marriage recognized by their own state of residence for the marriage to be meaningful. States may choose to recognize the marriage or, as many will likely do, may refuse to do so claiming that same-sex marriages violate the state's public policy, a decision that would spawn years of legal challenges across the country. In addition, we will likely face a political battle as the right wing strives to use its ballot initiative strategy to amend state constitutions to deny lesbian and gay couples the right to marry. One way or another, we are a very long way from the day when lesbian couples will be able to marry routinely. As a result, the movement for family equality must press forward on all fronts, and

Roberta Achtenberg, former member, San Francisco Board of Supervisors, and former Assistant Secretary for Fair Housing and Equal Opportunity, HUD.

Mary Wickline

not seek change in the marriage laws as the sole or perhaps even primary thrust of our agenda.

Partner Benefits. One of the most common ways in which the partnered relationships of lesbians are denigrated is through the provision of employment benefits coverage or other privileges to a married person and her family, but not to an unmarried couple. The indignities and outright discrimination are felt in hundreds of ways: the employer who denies paid bereavement leave for a lesbian whose partner has just died, though she could have taken the time if it was a more distant relative or certainly a spouse; the airline that refuses to allow a lesbian to use her frequent flyer benefits for her lover, even though the policy would allow her to take a cousin-in-law on a trip; or the sickness death insurance plan that pays a benefit to a surviving spouse of one who dies after a long illness (even if they had only been married one day), but not to a surviving partner (even if they had been together for a decade). Insurance laws, tax laws, social security benefits, workers compensation laws, housing laws, and business practices of all sorts irrationally extend privilege to families joined by marriage over those joined by love alone. Some of the inequalities between married and unmarried families are merely irritating and absurd, while others result in severe economic or emotional hardship. The right to marry would not fully remedy the inequity between unmarried employees and married employees, thus perpetuating discrimination against those who choose not to marry their lifelong companions.

Our movement has successfully convinced a number of employers to provide what we have come to call "domestic partner benefits," that is, employment benefits such as health insurance, family sick leave, bereavement leave, household moving expenses, tuition reimbursement, and the like that are routinely given to the spouses and families of married employees but denied to the partners and families of unmarried employees. Since a large portion of an employee's compensation is made up of these kinds of benefits, unmarried employees who cannot obtain these benefits are paid substantially less than their married co-workers. Through legal challenges, domestic partner ordinances mandating that municipal employers provide such benefits, and successful advocacy with hundreds of private employers, we have begun to see substantial shifts toward greater pay equity. Cities like Berkeley, New York, San Francisco, and Seattle provide domestic partner benefits to municipal employees. A growing number of companies, such as Levi Strauss and MCA Entertainment, as well as major universities, like Columbia University, New York University, Stanford, and the University of Iowa, also provide benefits. Unfortunately, many private employers and universities have met only part of their obligation by providing benefits only to lesbian and gay employees, thereby perpetuating discrimination against other unmarried employees.

In addition, legal challenges have been brought to expand the definition of the term "family" as used in state legislation, which grants privileges to traditional families over others. One notable victory was in New York, where the state's highest court ruled that a lesbian or gay couple must be included in the term "family" under the state's rent control laws. Thus, when one partner dies, the survivor is allowed to remain in the apartment, despite the fact that her name was not on the lease, just as any other family member is allowed. Challenges to expand family definitions have been brought in the context of unemployment insurance, crime victims compensation laws, and negligence law. Through wills, powers of attorney, and other documents, we have the power to make a number of very important decisions that will preserve our intentions and family relationships.

Legal Documents Available to Lesbians. It is a myth that lesbian families are completely without protection unless we marry. No lesbian has done more to raise the consciousness of our community about the need to legally protect our relationships than Karen Thompson. When her lover, Sharon Kowalski, suffered disabling injuries in a car accident, Karen fought for years in the Minnesota courts to win the right to be named as Sharon's guardian and to have Sharon come home with her. Because of Sharon's parents' abhorrence and denial of the fact that their daughter was a lesbian, and because the law allows an unmarried woman's parents to make decisions about her life if she takes no other action to delegate that authority, Sharon's parents were able, with the initial assistance of the courts, to cut Karen out of her life. While Karen and Sharon won their legal victory in the end, their story is a tragic reminder of the disrespect facing unmarried women, lesbians, and disabled women in the court system. It is also a lesson about the need to protect ourselves, to the extent possible, in the event of illness, incapacity, or death. The following extremely brief and incomplete discussion is no substitute for talking with a lawyer or consulting any number of books on the market that discuss these matters fully.

Nominating a Conservator or Guardian. Every woman fears that if she is in an accident or becomes seriously ill, she may be incapacitated to the point of being unable to care for herself. Each state has a legal mechanism for adults to choose or nominate someone to manage their finances and personal care should that occur. Usually, such an appointment must be made with court approval, though a few states allow a written nomination of guardian to take effect immediately upon incapacity for individuals suffering a terminal illness. Except in unusual circumstances, the court will generally appoint the person nominated. Without such a nomination, properly drafted, signed, and witnessed, it is probable that a blood relative, instead of the woman's lover or friend, will be appointed to take care of a woman's finances and to make her medical decisions regarding treatment and care. It is highly recommended that the appointment be drafted by a lawyer so that all the technical requirements are met to assure enforceability. Nomination must be made *before* a woman is faced with an emergency. Once a woman becomes ill, she may lack the requisite capacity to execute the nomination. Planning ahead is the requisite first step toward protecting ourselves.

Powers of Attorney. Depending on the state, there may be a number of different documents that can be executed to enable a person to delegate to another trusted person the ability to carry out financial transactions or make medical decisions on her behalf. These documents are generally called "powers of attorney." The persons assigned decision-making powers under such a document does not need to be an attorney. It can be anyone—lover, friend, blood relative—whom the person trusts and wishes to empower to take certain actions on her behalf if she is unable to do so.

In some states, powers of attorney include only the ability to perform financial transactions for the person giving the power, and then only if that person is mentally competent. For instance, if someone needs to be out of the country for an extended period of time, she can appoint her lover or friend to handle any financial transactions on her behalf until her return. This may include withdrawing money from accounts, selling her car, or signing checks. But should the person die or become mentally incompetent, the power ceases to have effect. As always in the law, there are exceptions: Some states do allow for a durable power of attorney that will remain in effect should the person become mentally incompetent (for example, in a coma), but will expire at death.

Finally, a number of states allow for a "medical power of attorney" which allows one to delegate to another person the power to make medical decisions in the event of incompetency. Recognizing that our relationships face very different challenges within health care settings, lesbian lawyers have creatively worded these documents (or created new documents) to entitle the lover or friend to have priority over anyone else, even blood family, to hospital visitation if for any reason visitation is restricted. Even in states where the medical power of attorney for health care is not recognized, lawyers are encouraged to add clauses to traditional powers of attorney or to execute "consents to medical treat-

ment" to encourage health care providers to respect the wishes of the patient to allow her lover or friend to visit and to make medical decisions if the patient cannot make them for herself. With such a document executed and on file with the doctor, the likelihood that blood relatives will be given priority in visiting or be allowed to make medical decisions is minimized. We constantly hear about lovers being denied access to intensive care when a blood relative (who may not have seen the patient in years) is allowed in. A medical power of attorney executed well in advance of need may be a way of avoiding such a tragedy.

For very practical reasons, it is recommended that the medical power and the financial transaction power be assigned to the same person. For example, let's say that Pam is a comatose patient who was brought to a religious hospital in a small town after a car accident. Pam thought ahead and gave her medical power of attorney to her lover, Beth, but gave her power of attorney for financial transactions to her sister. Beth believes that the hospital staff are not giving Pam appropriate treatment and are unduly hostile to her because they know she and Pam are lesbians. Beth decides that Pam would get better treatment (and the two of them more respect) if she were moved to the university hospital in the city 150 miles away. Because Beth cannot afford the expense of the ambulance transfer, she asks Pam's sister to withdraw money from Pam's bank account. Pam's sister is deeply religious and wants Pam in the religiously affiliated hospital. The sister refuses to use the financial power of attorney Pam gave her to withdraw the funds. This conflict could have been avoided if Pam had assigned both powers to Beth.

The powers given by these documents can be sweeping, so it is advisable to consult an attorney with any questions, not only to understand the extent of the powers, but to make sure the documents are properly drafted. These documents, like many mentioned here, are revocable should you wish to change the person who would have so much power over your life.

Drafting a Will. Every lesbian should have a will. If she dies without one, the law presumes that she wanted her property to go to and all decisions to be made by her parents, siblings, or grown children—in other words, blood family members. Even if there is not much property at issue, decisions about funeral and burial, providing for pets, naming a guardian for a minor child, or giving special mementos to certain people may be taken care of in a will.

Also, a will allows one to designate an executor whose job is to ensure that the provisions of the will are carried out according to the wishes of the deceased. The executor is also the person legally entitled to go through the deceased person's belongings in order to gather the property and disburse it. Naturally, many of us would rather have someone we trust performing this role. If the desire is to have special items of personal property go to people other than family members, or if the wish is to give property to some family members but not others, a valid will must be executed.

It is important to first note two common misconceptions. First, in no state in the United States can two women marry one another. While this might seem self-evident to many, surviving partners have tried to convince courts that they were "spouses" in all respects and that, therefore, a surviving lesbian partner should be treated as a spouse for inheritance purposes. "Spouse" is a legal term of art requiring a legal marriage, and courts have ruled that lesbian and gay couples, even those who were together for years and were "married" in a ceremony, are not spouses within the meaning of the law that governs the distribution of property when a person dies without a will. On the other hand, a properly drafted, signed, and witnessed will provides virtual assurance that a woman's property will go to whomever she has designated.

Which leads to the second point: Anyone may draft a will leaving her property to anyone she wishes (with some exceptions; for instance, one cannot fully disinherit a spouse). The fact that a lesbian has left all or most of her property to her lover or to the Lesbian Herstory Archives does not give family members a legal reason to challenge the will. As long as the will is properly executed and the woman was mentally competent to decide how she wanted her property distributed at the time she signed the will, that document will be considered valid. It is critical, however, that she not wait too long to have a will drafted, and that she update her will at times that significant changes occur in her life (such as a new lover, having children, a significant increase in property). If she is very ill by the time she gets around to making a will, it will be more difficult to prove she was competent at the time it was executed, leaving a greater possibility that family members may attempt to challenge the will or succeed in overturning it.

As mentioned, most states allow funeral plans and burial instructions to be spelled out in a will. If omitted, blood relatives may be able to thwart such plans by immediately removing the body to another jurisdiction. Family members may have removed the body, held a funeral in the deceased person's childhood hometown, and buried her before a lover or friends could protest that the person, in fact, wished to be cremated with a memorial service in the local women's center. This kind of tragedy can be avoided by careful planning.

One last word about wills. People often ask if they can use form wills bought at the stationery store, or if they can make a "holographic" will—one in their own handwriting. In some states, using one of these wills might be better than having no will at all. The validity of those wills, however, can very easily be contested, and blood relatives may be tempted to contest a will when the property is left to a nonrelative. Most people do not need to fear the wrath of their blood relatives the way lesbians have been forced to. In other states, form wills and holographic wills are never recognized as valid, and therefore all of the deceased woman's property would pass just as if she had no will. For both of those reasons, it is important to take all precautions and to assure that whatever protections the law does provide are utilized successfully. If at all possible, consult an attorney who is knowledgeable about lesbian family issues and have a will drafted for your protection.

Contracts, Life Insurance, Bank Accounts, and Trusts. Annuities, IRAs, and Keogh plans are all forms of contracts. The beneficiary a woman names on the contract gets the proceeds automatically when she dies. Title to these things passes outside the will. Thus, it is important to make sure that a woman keeps current with her named beneficiary. If her beneficiary dies or if they are lovers who break up, she must execute a new designation of beneficiary.

Life insurance policies are another method by which a woman can benefit a lover or friend. In the past, some life insurance companies have refused to allow a lesbian to name her lover as a beneficiary. Many companies no longer practice that form of discrimination. For those companies that do discriminate in this manner, one may either look into whether the discrimination is prohibited by state law or simply get around the problem by naming a blood relative as the beneficiary. After the policy is issued, file a change of beneficiary to name a lover or other person of choice. Oddly enough, companies have no restrictions on changes of beneficiaries. Of course, if the person dies in the interim period, the relative takes the money unless their benevolence leads them to give the money to the real person intended to receive it.

Bank accounts can be held in joint tenancy for convenience or because the contents are jointly owned. Accounts also can be held in trust for someone to whom title to the account will pass automatically upon the death of the account's owner. The advantage to creating such a "trust" is that the beneficiary has access to the money while the owner is still alive. But at her death the beneficiary takes title without the account having to go through probate or court-supervised distribution. Further, these assets cannot be part of a will contest by blood relatives.

Joint Tenancy or Joint Ownership of Property. Assets held in joint tenancy pass automatically to the surviving joint tenant. In fact, property held in joint tenancy *must* go to the surviving joint tenant after death and cannot be passed on to another person through the will. Many lesbian couples choose to own their homes as joint tenants. If one dies, the other has an automatic right to keep the home; blood relatives cannot take it away, even if there is no will.

There are many tax consequences to owning joint property, especially if each party did not contribute equal shares in buying the property. Also, property ownership may affect eligibility for Medicaid or other government-funded benefits programs.

Lesbians as Parents

Custody and Visitation. Conflict over child custody and visitation when a marriage involving a gay parent dissolves is the most commonly litigated conflict in the area of lesbian and gay rights. Courts have reflected society's aversion to children being raised by lesbians and gay men, even if they are the parents, whom the law generally prefers over all others. Traditionally, the mixture of lesbians and children has evoked the worst kind of prejudice and homophobia. Lesbians are characterized as selfish, sex-crazed deviants who are chronically unhappy, if not mentally unfit. Lesbians care more about their "lifestyle" than their children. Lesbians are bad role models for children because of their tendency to recruit children into homosexuality. Lesbians' hatred of men provokes them to refuse to provide children with healthy male role models, which, of course, *all* other children have. Lesbians are the source of stigma for their children. Lesbians are criminals. Even if a lesbian mother is a godly and unblemished creature, her children are still likely to turn out gay, a presumptively substandard outcome that must be prevented even at the cost of severing a loving relationship between mother and child.

Despite the sustained efforts of legal advocates who attempt in each lesbian mother custody case to bring judges around to a more rational—and realistic—view of who lesbians are, these are still the opinions of many of them. They are reinforced by the structure of family law that does not include our families and, in fact, is terribly out of date with the way most families live. Fortunately, after forty years of lesbian mother custody cases, the majority of courts have moved toward the conclusion that a mother's sexual orientation, in and of itself, is not grounds for depriving her of custody or visitation. Yet, in a handful of states, the fact that a parent is gay would be grounds for finding her unfit to raise her child.

The most notorious recent case is that of Sharon Bottoms, whose own mother successfully convinced a trial court that Sharon is immoral, engaged in illegal sexual acts in the Commonwealth of Virginia, and thereby unfit to raise her two-year-old son. The trial court's decision to take the child away from Sharon and put him in his grandmother's custody, as outrageous as it sounds, merely conformed with prior Virginia case law finding that a parent's homosexuality makes her unfit to parent as a matter of law. The Virginia Court of Appeals reversed the lower court's finding in 1994, and the case is now pending before the Virginia Supreme Court for a final ruling on the rights of lesbian parents.

Lesbian parents who live with their partners, take their children to gay pride parades or other gay events, or are very "out" as lesbians in their communities seem to be most vulnerable to challenges to their parental rights. Often, the children's biological father will seek custody after he has remarried, on the claim that he can provide the better family environment for the children. Despite nearly three decades of a lesbian/gay rights movement, and many more years of standing up for our rights as parents in courts around the country, we face our greatest legal difficulties when we are pitted against a more "traditional" looking family in child custody cases.

Adoption and Foster Parenting. Adoption and foster parenting have come out of the closet for lesbians in the last decade. While most lesbians may still adopt without fully revealing their sexual orientation unless asked to do so, many more have successfully adopted or become foster parents having fully revealed that they were lesbians. Only the states of Florida and New Hampshire outwardly ban lesbians from adopting or foster parenting. Through its notorious Dukakis-era regulation, Massachusetts effectively denies lesbians the option to become foster parents by listing us last on the list of desirable households for placing children. The Ohio Supreme Court ruled several years ago that a gay man be allowed to adopt so long as it is in the child's best interests. In so ruling, the court overturned a viciously homophobic decision by the court of appeals, indicating that sexual orientation should not be used as the basis for denying adoptions in the state of Ohio.

Most states neither allow nor outlaw adoption or foster parenting by lesbians, though radical right-wing efforts to deny general civil rights to lesbians have zeroed in on introducing legislation in some states to deny this parenting option. At this time, though, decisions are made very much on a case-by-case basis. In most states, if the adoption is recommended by the person who performs the home study (many of whom know they are dealing with a lesbian couple), and is not objected to by the guardian appointed for the child, the judge will grant it. The most difficult obstacles are often encountered not at the courts but the adoption agencies, which still prefer to place children with married couples rather than unmarried parents or lesbian couples. Most adoptions for lesbians go forward as single parent adoptions since joint adoptions have not been attempted except in a couple of instances. (Strategically, we have gone forward first with second parent adoptions to test the waters on how courts would react to lesbians parenting together. In those cases, no matter what the judge decides, the child will stay rightfully in the home since she or he is already the legal child of one of the

women.) Because of the difficulties with domestic adoption agencies, lesbians have turned increasingly to foreign adoptions, which often require a great degree of caution about going forward as "out" lesbians. The courts or government officials in the foreign country may refuse to allow the adoption if it is known that the prospective parent is gay.

Parenting with a Lesbian Partner. Despite slow but certain progress in the custody, visitation, and adoption areas, lesbians have become increasingly proactive during the past decade in establishing their rights to have children through adoption and donor insemination. The judicial response to these efforts has predictably ranged from dishearteningly negative to nearly unanimously positive.

Most lesbians who parent with a partner are concerned about the legal rights of the nonbiological mother should they break up or should something happen to the nonbiological mother. It is always best, where possible, to settle disputes over "post-divorce" child custody and visitation without resorting to the courts, a naturally hostile environment for most lesbian parents. Couples who have drafted a clear agreement outlining which of them is to have custody should they break up, the frequency of visitation that the other parent may have, and how they will share financial support for the child are usually better equipped to abide by their agreements.

Unfortunately, where the biological mother has refused to honor the agreement and the nonbiological mother has resorted to legal action to establish her rights as a parent, the courts have been overwhelmingly unreceptive to the notion that a nonbiological lesbian mother should be considered a full and equal parent. Nearly all of the cases involved lesbian couples who became parents through donor insemination or adoption with the explicit (though not usually written) agreement that the nonbiological or nonlegal parent has the same rights and responsibilities as the one who gave birth or adopted. These agreements contravene the workings of the law, which generally only recognizes biological or adoptive parents as legally recognized parents. In these cases, the biological/adoptive mothers have recanted on their promise to treat their partner equally, knowing that the law would prefer them over their former partners. In all but a couple of cases, the courts decided that the partners had no legal standing to claim any parental rights.

Where the biological mother has died, inducing her blood family to try to take custody away from the surviving partner, who is the child's other mother, courts have shown much more compassion in finding that it would be best for the child to remain with her other mother, particularly after having suffered the loss of her biological mother. In many of these cases, courts have relied on the documents drafted by the women, in particular the deceased parent's will naming her surviving partner as the child's guardian.

To further solidify their family relationships and protect themselves against the inconsistency of courts, lesbian advocates originated the idea of and procedures for second parent adoptions, most notably through the National Center for Lesbian Rights. In these adoptions, the "second parent" is the nonbiological parent who is nonetheless sharing parenting responsibilities with her partner, the biological (or in some instances, adoptive) mother. By successfully arguing that the child's interests would best be served by allowing the second parent to adopt without disturbing the legal rights of the biological mother, lesbians have broken new ground in securing family rights. If granted, a second parent adoption allows for the nonbiological mother to be treated in all legal respects equal to the biological mother.

It is estimated that more than two hundred second parent adoptions have been granted by judges in states as diverse as New York, Texas, California, Washington, New Jersey, District of Columbia, Minnesota, Pennsylvania, Rhode Island, and Oregon. The state supreme courts in Vermont and Massachusetts have interpreted state law to allow for second parent adoptions in all courts throughout those two states. The issue is on appeal in a few other states. Until a state's supreme court or legislature has allowed for second parent adoptions, however, judges are not required to rule with any uniformity and they can refuse to interpret adoption law to allow for these procedures. It is still best to proceed with caution.

Using a Known Sperm Donor. Many, if not most, lesbians have experienced wonderful success with known sperm donors. On the other hand, many lesbians have learned the hard way that using a known sperm donor can serve as a recurring threat to their parenting autonomy. The natural tension in these situations is caused less by the individuals and more by the system of family laws, which will declare a sperm donor to be a full parent, even if the parties decided he would play only a limited role in the child's life, and would ignore the lesbian coparent, even if the parties agreed she would be a full and equal parent. As a result, the sperm donor wields a great deal of power over the family relationship should he change his mind and seek rights as a full parent.

This was the situation in a particularly contentious case between a donor in San Francisco and the lesbian mothers in New York. The donor agreed to donate sperm with the stipulation that he would not be a "father" to the child. He was introduced to the daughter when she was about three years old, after which he visited with the family (which consisted of the lesbian mothers, the donor's genetic daughter, and another daughter who was the genetic offspring of another donor) anywhere from one to four times a year, depending on the year. When the child was about nine years old, the donor decided he wanted to introduce her to his genetic family. The mothers refused his request as being far outside their agreement that he would be known to the child as her genetic father but would have the role of a close family friend. Never was it intended that she develop a full father-daughter relationship. At their refusal, the donor filed a paternity action. The trial court denied his request. The appellate court reversed the lower court and declared him to be the father. Though the case is on further appeal, the effect of the current ruling is to allow him full rights as a parent. He has the right to seek custody and, should he die, his family, who has never met the daughter and her family, will now have the legal right to seek visitation.

For their own good reasons, many lesbians want to use known donors. But for those couples who are legitimately concerned about whether a court will uphold an agreement with a known donor, the best defense is to use an unknown donor.

Keeping Our Jobs: Nondiscrimination in the Workplace

Just as our sexual identities and relationships are an integral component of our identity, a job or profession to which we are dedicated is very much related to our self-esteem and sense of accomplishment.

When it is denied or taken away for a reason as irrelevant to our ability to do the job as our sexual orientation, we lose more than our livelihood; we lose our sense of value in society. Because the injustice of employment discrimination lies in its power to deny our very livelihood and self-worth, the struggle for civil rights, particularly in the employment area, is essential to our sense of equality in the world.

The basic rule of the American workplace is that of "employment at will"—that is, an employee may be fired or refused a job for any reason whatsoever. As with all laws there are exceptions, an important one being that set forth in civil rights laws: The decision to fire an employee may not be made on the basis of the employee's race, sex, age, religion, ethnic origin, disability, or any other factor prohibited by federal, state, or local law. The assumption of these laws is that characteristics such as sex or race simply are not relevant to one's qualifications for a job.

Sexual orientation, however, is not a protected classification in most civil rights laws. Federal laws that ban discrimination based on many of the criteria listed above do not ban discrimination against lesbians and gay men. Only eight states (Wisconsin, Massachusetts, Vermont, Connecticut, Hawaii, New Jersey, California, and Minnesota) and the District of Columbia have outlawed certain forms of discrimination against lesbians and gay men. Approximately one hundred cities and counties include sexual orientation in their civil rights laws. A number of state governors have issued executive orders barring such discrimination against state employees, though these orders are subject to withdrawal when a new governor comes into office. Thus, in most parts of the country, though a lesbian cannot be fired because she is a woman or because of her race, she can be fired or refused a job solely on the basis of her sexual orientation. In most regions of the country, discrimination against lesbians is fully legal.

In 1994, the Employment Nondiscrimination Act (ENDA) was introduced into the United States Congress. If passed, an unlikely event given the Republican sweep in that election year, it would provide uniformity to employment law by banning sexual-orientation-based discrimination in all corners of the country. All employers (with the notable exception of very small employers and religious employers), both private and public, would be required to treat lesbian employees equal to nonlesbian workers. Since it is clear that many state legislatures will never ensure that lesbians are protected in their jobs from irrational and bigoted supervisors, this federal bill is critical to ensuring equality and uniformity of treatment.

While federal statutory protections elude us, some strides have been made for public employees—those who work for federal, state, or local government. A most obvious example was the 1993 United States Senate's confirmation of Roberta Achtenberg, an out lesbian and former activist, to her position at the Department of Housing and Urban Development, making her the highest level out lesbian (or gay) appointee in federal government. Her confirmation was followed a year later by the confirmation of Deborah Batts to the federal bench, making her the first out gay person appointed and confirmed to the federal courts.

Government employers have at least minimal constitutional constraints on their treatment of employees. At the very least, courts have held that a public employer must show a relationship between the employee's sexual orientation and her/his ability to do the job. In recent years, federal employment policy has provided that a person may not be considered unsuitable for federal employment merely because the person is gay or lesbian, or engages in sexual activities with someone of the same sex. Some federal agencies, like the Departments of Justice and Health and Human Services, as well as the White House, have issued personnel directives that include sexual orientation in the list of characteristics that may not be used as a basis for making employment decisions.

For federal employees needing security clearances in order to qualify for certain jobs, the answers are much less clear. Courts have paid great deference to the claims of the military, FBI, CIA, and Defense Department contractors that lesbians pose a security risk and, in the case of the military, adversely affect order and morale. At the very least, a lesbian seeking a security clearance is likely to be subjected to an expanded investigation to satisfy the agency that she, herself, is not a security risk. Some are granted the clearance; some are still denied. The military saga, of course, continues, no thanks to the United States Congress, which responded to the president's desire to lift the ban against lesbians and gay men serving in the military by passing a federal law banning them from serving. (Before that point, the ban had been in the form of an administrative regulation of the Department of Defense.)

The situation for state and local governmental employees is somewhat less clear. Where there is no state or local civil rights law, the courts have been erratic in their willingness to extend constitutional protection to lesbian and gay employees. Historically, lesbian and gay school teachers have been the most vulnerable to legislative or electoral attempts to ban them from teaching. In the mid-1980s, the Oklahoma legislature passed a law that threatened to ban lesbians and gay men who were involved in public advocacy on behalf of gay rights from teaching in the schools. The court struck it down as an infringement on teachers' First Amendment rights, since even advocacy outside the classroom was banned. However, the Washington courts upheld the dismissal of a gay high school teacher on the grounds that his sexual orientation rendered him immoral. The dismissal of a bisexual teacher who came out to a colleague was also upheld by federal court in Ohio.

Unionized employees may be protected by legally enforceable collective bargaining agreements that ban sexual orientation discrimination. It is unclear whether private employment policies that promise equal opportunity to all employees, including lesbians and gay men, have any legal effect at all in the world of "at will" employment. While these policies might demonstrate a corporate consciousness about equal treatment of lesbians, they may not be worth the recyclable paper they are typed on in a court of law.

Conclusion

No article on legal rights in the 1990s would be complete without a cheery discussion of the maneu-verings of the right wing in this country. In every state, every locality, the right wing is organizing itself to cheat us out of the minuscule, but hard won, victories that we have gained. By claiming that we are asking for "special rights" and pointing their self-righteous fingers at us as precipitating the disintegration of the heterosexual family, they have embarked on a misguided campaign to subvert the democratic process. Lesbians and gay men have been the perfect vehicle for them. It is easy to whip God-fearing people, and others, into a frenzy about the threat that we pose to civilization. So much misinformation and stereotyping still exists about who we are. We've seen the success of this effort in Colorado, Cincinnati, and Florida, where citizens voted to prevent the passage of any laws that would treat lesbians and gay men equal to other citizens. Similar antigay ballot measures in Idaho and Oregon were narrowly defeated.

Fortunately, so far, courts have struck down these voter initiatives as violating the basic right of lesbian and gay citizens to have access to the political process. But we cannot count on the courts forever. If we are to preserve the progress we have made and if we expect to go forward with our struggle for equality, we must get down to basic organizing. Our right to sex, family recognition, and work are the precise areas most frequently targeted by the right wing. This must be the main focus of our organizing as well. Our visibility in the world has threatened those who would like to destroy us, but it has also contributed overwhelmingly to our success.

Serving Proudly, but in Secret:

Lesbians in the U.S. Armed Forces

Miriam Ben-Shalom

These are the times that try men's souls: The summer soldier and the sunshine patriot will, in this crisis, shrink from the service of his country; but he that stands it now, deserves the love and thanks of men and women. Tyranny, like hell, is not easily conquered; yet we have this consolation with us, that the harder the conflict the more glorious the triumph.

—Thomas Paine, "The Crisis," December 1776

Since the Stonewall riot of 1969, what previously had been unthinkable for lesbians and gays became a grudgingly granted reality: acceptance into American society, some measure of respectability, and even some civil rights legislation at local and state levels extending equal protection under the law to an oppressed minority. Increasingly, lesbians and gays demanded and won those simple basic rights that most American citizens take for granted.

Yet strong pockets of resistance remain. In spite of monumental efforts by organized lesbian and gay veterans everywhere from 1990 through 1993, the strongest of these bastions of bias, bigotry, and discrimination is an institution of our own federal government: the Armed Forces of the United States. The U.S. Armed Forces have a long and checkered history of discrimination against minorities. They resisted the integration of people of color into their ranks and still deny women the right to serve in equality, even after decades of more than ample proof that women can serve well in all military situations, including combat operations. During all these decades, they refused to lesbians and gays the same opportunities. Blacks certainly have broken through the barriers; women have challenged tired stereotypes and won some victories with the help of politically astute representatives. But lesbians and gays remain beyond the pale, considered unfit to serve and thus classified with convicted felons and other moral reprobates.

The reasons still cited by the military in denying the opportunity of service to lesbians and gays, in spite of five major studies commissioned by government and the Pentagon and a plethora of minor studies and polls, are curiously reminiscent of the reasons given for excluding blacks and women from integration into the armed forces. In 1941 a naval memorandum expressed the following views about black sailors:

The Presence of such soldiers adversely affects the ability of the service to—maintain discipline, good order, and morale; foster mutual trust and confidence among service members; ensure the integrity of the system of rank and command; facilitate assignment and worldwide deployment of service members who frequently must live and work under close conditions affording minimal privacy; retain members of military service; maintain the public acceptability of military service; prevent breaches of security.

A 1993 document about homosexuals in the armed forces used similar language:

The worldwide deployment of United States military forces, the international responsibilities of the United States, and the potential for involvement of the armed forces in actual combat, routinely make it necessary for members of the armed forces involuntarily to accept living conditions and working conditions that are often spartan, primitive, and characterized by forced intimacy with little or no privacy.

The prohibition against homosexual conduct is a longstanding element of military law that continues to be necessary in the unique circumstances of military service.

The armed forces must maintain personnel policies that exclude persons whose presence in the armed forces would create an unacceptable risk to the armed forces' high standards of morale, good order and discipline, and unit cohesion that are the essence of military capability.

The presence in the armed forces of persons who demonstrate a propensity or intent to engage in homosexual acts would create an unacceptable risk to the high standards of morale, good order and discipline and unit cohesion that are the essence of military capability."

Although time has shown amply that blacks and women serve well—beyond what might have been expected—lesbians and gays remain the "monsters in the dark." The armed forces still refuse to consider them to be responsible, capable, honorable human beings.

While lesbians and gays everywhere have rallied around the AIDS crisis (and rightly so), the lesbian or gay military veteran remains in no small measure something of a pariah in his/her own community, subject to profound disrespect and harassment. In addition to rejection by mainstream organizations for veterans and active duty personnel, gay and especially lesbian veterans face harassment from a part of the lesbian population that employs tactics of verbal abuse and confrontation, slash-and-burn character assassination, and even physical violence far more often than male gays. For whatever reasons, many lesbians seem to be overtly hostile to lesbian servicewomen or veterans. Perhaps most at fault are the self-styled lesbian separatists. While decrying discrimination and violence against women, with thoughtless abandon they regularly label military lesbians as "baby killers" and "patriarchal sellouts." They are quick to say that a lesbian who finds herself under investigation or who sees her military career ruined "got what she deserved." Military lesbians, turning to what should be their community, are met with coldness, silence, and rejection.

If there is any support at all, it comes from male gays and lesbigay veterans' organizations, with the fairly recent exception of Lambda Legal Defense and Education Fund. It remains the realm of non-lesbigay organizations to champion the cause of military lesbians and gays.

Yet lesbians keep entering the military. Using the Kinsey statistic that 10 percent of the population is homosexual, there are currently about thirty thousand lesbians in uniform. This estimate (which is low) is based on Department of Defense statistics, which say that there are about 300,000 women in all branches of the armed forces. These women are a proud lot. It is difficult to explain the pride that military lesbians and veterans carry inside themselves. They are exceedingly independent, bright, assertive women, used to responsibility; many have a "take charge" attitude so necessary to be a leader in the military. Many have dealt with the rigors of war (Vietnam, Desert Storm, Somalia). They have been and continue to be proud to serve a country that does not love them as much as they love it. In 1990–91, for example, of 450 lesbigay veterans who answered a call by the Gay, Lesbian, and Bisexual Veterans of America to volunteer and return to service for Desert Shield/Desert Storm, over 200 were lesbian veterans. They are an intensely patriotic group—not flag wavers, but people committed to serving America and doing their very best to preserve the ideals of the American dream. They are finding their way into the political arena and into local leadership positions, as well, due to their very visible involvement in challenging military discrimination. It is interesting to note that many of the current challenges in the federal court system belong to lesbians, although the hype of mainstream media seems to focus on white gay males, as a rule. They are very aware of their vulnerability to exposure, yet they persist in doing superior work under incredible stress. It is no coincidence at all that within the lesbigay veterans' movement, lesbians were and continue to be very well represented in leadership roles. (A compliment must be extended to the vast majority of male gay vets, who have welcomed them and reached out, encouraged, and supported them above and beyond the call of duty.) It is certainly safe to say that if by some miracle, all the lesbians in uniform decided to "come out" on the same day, the current discriminatory regulations restraining and excluding military service for homosexual Americans would be revoked immediately.

Yet, despite an excellent collective service record, the U.S. military establishment seems bent on eliminating some of the best from its ranks. In addition to unresolved issues surrounding sexual harassment and civilian mythology that the military services somehow are more inclined to "punish" male homosexuality and to "tolerate" it among military females, the facts show absolutely otherwise. It is very clear that military women are at least five to eight times more likely than their male counterparts to be harassed, threatened, discharged, or even imprisoned under military law.

The Department of Defense itself provides the startling proof of such selective actions against military women in a three-year study that concluded in 1987. The results of this study, reported in the February 20, 1988, issue of the *Army Times*, surprised even the Department of Defense. As of September 30, 1987, the total number of discharges for homosexuality for all the services averaged about two thousand per year. An average of five out of every ten thousand men in uniform were discharged annually for homosexuality; an average of sixteen out of every ten thousand women in uniform were discharged annually for the same reason.

The navy, to no one's great surprise, led the rate of discharges: 0.27 percent of female *enlisted* force was discharged as compared to 0.13 percent of male *enlisted* forces. For both male and female officers, the discharge rate was 0.02 percent. The marine corps discharged 0.33 percent of female *enlisted* as compared to 0.04 percent of male *enlisted*; officer rate was 0.01 percent for men and 0 percent for women.

Statistics for other branches of the service tell the same sad story: army discharged 0.17 percent of women to 0.05 percent of men. Only the air force seems to have had some semblance of sanity: Only 0.001 percent of women and 0.004 percent of men were discharged.

It is hard to come to a true reckoning for officer discharge rates, as an officer faced with separation from service for homosexuality may instead submit a request for resignation. In many such cases, the stated reason for resignation may not show that the underlying cause was homosexuality.

Although these figures are somewhat dated, the new sets of statistics coming from the Defense Department have not changed. It appears that as a result of Desert Storm alone, over nine hundred military gays and lesbians were discharged, some after serving in a combat theater under a perverse "stop-loss policy," which halted their discharges for war and reinstated proceedings once the war was over. Some seven hundred lesbians and gay men put their military careers on the line and came out, having believed that President Clinton would overturn the ban on homosexuals in service. These numbers do not include those who were discharged by reason of witch-hunt or other investigative measures, so it is safe to say that discharge numbers will show a rather substantial statistical increase for 1991, 1992, and 1993.

What do these figures mean for the lesbian still in uniform? They mean, quite bluntly, that in spite of the much touted "Don't Ask, Don't Tell, Don't Pursue" policy, difficult times are still ahead. Not only are the new regulations vague, confusing, and contradictory, but their very draconian nature seems to be encouraging the services to pursue convictions of lesbians under military regulations prohibiting sodomy. Sodomy remains a felony offense under the Uniform Code of Military Justice (UCMJ) and carries punishment ranging from fines to imprisonment. (It should be noted that Article 125 of the UCMJ is gender neutral; in other words, it does not discriminate between homo- and heterosexual acts of sodomy.) Defense Department statistics indicate, however, that heterosexual discharges under Article 125 are so very rare as to be statistically insignificant—less than 1 person per 100,000 military persons. And, charges of heterosexual sodomy are almost always linked with other felony charges, such as rape or child molestation, both of which are also proscribed by the UCMJ.

What then, can be said in the light of such bleak statistics? Amazingly, against all odds, federal courts have been ruling consistently against both the old policy and the new "Don't Ask" fiasco. Women are playing a major part in these challenges: Zoe Dunning, Dusty Pruitt, Heidi DeJesus, Nadine Flynn, Margarethe Cammermeyer, Elli Work, and others have pending actions in the courts. Only time can tell how these cases will turn; it must be hoped that the courts will see the same merit as they have in cases involving gay men. It is apparent that the Defense Department itself will change its policy concerning homosexuals *only* as a result of legislative action arising from legal challenges. It is certain that the military will *not* change of its own accord due to any sense of fairness or for any reasons of social consciousness.

Resources

Bay Area Military Freedom Project, 2744 Sacramento Street #206, San Francisco, CA 94115-2160, 415-673-1370.

Chicago GLBVA, 5445 S. Hyde Park Blvd., Chicago, IL 60615, 312-752-0058.

GLBVA National, 414 Stone Wood, San Antonio, TX 78216-1624, 210-545-2643.

Gold Coast GLBVA, 611 Halyard St., Port Hueneme, CA 93041-1215, 805-984-3259.

Alexander Hamilton Post #448, The American Legion, P.O. Box 31428, San Francisco, CA 94131-0428, 415-648-8488.

Indiana GLBVA, P.O. Box 26100, Indianapolis, IN 46226, 317-895-1038.

Lambda Legal Defense and Education Fund, 212-995-8585.

Military Law Task Force, 619-233-1701.

Minerva (a historical publication), 20 Granada St., Pasadena, MD 21122, 410-437-5379.

Monterey Bay GLBVA, 556 Cuesta Dr., Aptos, CA 95002, 408-688-8162.

Orange County GLBVA, P.O. Box 337, Irvine, CA 92650-0337, 714-651-8376.

Pacific Northwest Veterans, 114 NW 81st St., Seattle, WA 98117, 206-782-9080.

Pallas Athena (publication for women/lesbian vets), P.O. Box 1171, New Market, VA 22844.

Palm Springs GLBVA, P.O. Box 5012, Palm Springs, CA 92263, 619-778-4824.

San Diego Veterans Association, P.O. Box 89196, San Diego, CA 92138, 619-267-6664.

Service Members Legal Defense Network, P.O. Box 53013, Washington, DC 20009, 202-265-8305, Fax 202-328-0063.

Tribute Regiment For Equality, 5500 Alcott Dr., Sacramento, CA 95820, 916-383-0940.

Utah GLBVA, 33352 Van Cott, Salt Lake City, UT 84112, 801-585-4538.

Veterans C.A.R.E. Los Angeles, P.O. Box 292292, Los Angeles, CA 90029-8292, 213-662-4862.

Veterans C.A.R.E. Redwood Empire, P.O. Box 855, Nice, CA 95464, 707-274-1303.

Veterans for Human Rights, 208 SW Stark #306, Portland, OR 97204, 503-223-1373, Fax 503-241-0059.

A Lesbian Military Story:

Nathalie (Natt) Nevins

Interviewed by Ginny Vida

You showed me a picture of yourself with this award, a statuette that you were presented by President Eisenhower for entertaining the troops. It looks like a Hollywood "Oscar." How did that come about?

I won the award for winning first place as female vocalist in the worldwide talent contest sponsored by the air force, which was a great experience. I was in the U.S. Air Force from 1956 through January 5, 1959. Count Basie was one of the judges. The contest winners were organized into a permanent party show called "Tops in Blue," with a full orchestra. We went out on the road and entertained military and civilian audiences all over the United States and parts of Europe and the Far East, and also appeared on *The Ed Sullivan Show* on TV.

The statuette that you see in the photo was patterned after the "Oscar"—we called it the "Roger." When the tour ended I had served as airman first class in the air force for nineteen months.

Were you a lesbian at the time?

I was just coming out at this time. As a matter of fact, during the course of the show I was engaged to marry a very nice young man but realized by the end of the tour that I was a lesbian and broke off the engagement. Thank God I did not get married.

This period in my life was a very positive one until the end of the show. Then I had my first experience with the fact that it was not wise to let people know that you were gay. We had a young black man in our show, a dancer, who was caught in a compromising position with another black man. One

Natt Nevins and her mother with U. S. Air Force Roger Award.

minute he was part of our show and then he was gone. I found out that he was put out of the show for being homosexual. After that I came to grips with what I was, but realized I had to be very careful. I didn't realize to what extent until the show ended and I was transferred back to Lackland Air Force Base in San Antonio.

What happened there?

I was an airman first class in charge of entertaining services for an airmen's service club. They had many of those in the air force. That's when I was in the closet but there was no more straddling the fence dating men. I knew by that time I was a lesbian.

And they started a witch-hunt there?

You heard about the witch-hunts from Pat Bond in the film, *The Word Is Out.* It was a very serious time for a lot of people—a time for hiding, not having any legal rights. It was not like today, where women or men who are having a problem with the military can go to certain gay organizations for legal services. As I understand it, it was a fallout from the McCarthy era in "cleaning out" the homosexuals, the pinkos, the queers from the armed services.

We would go to certain gay clubs off the base, and from time to time the military police would raid the clubs and try to pick up whatever military personnel were there. When you went you wouldn't take any ID with you; certainly you wouldn't wear a uniform. And sometimes the MPs were paid off by the people they caught. One of the gay clubs that my gay friend George and I used to go to—we had set up a type of lighting system so that if the MPs came in the front door, the bar owner would step on something behind the bar and the light would go on in the back room and everyone would switch partners. Some of the funniest people would be dancing together.

But this friend of mine, Jay, who was nineteen

years old and from Arkansas, was going with an officer from the base and was to have met her at this gay club in San Antonio. I was also supposed to have gone that night, but could not make it. But the club was raided by the MPs and the air police, and Jay was taken into police headquarters at Lackland Air Force Base and raped, sodomized, and beaten by eleven men, and then thrown into the psychiatric ward of the hospital. They kept her there three or four months. They were probably planning to hold her there until she signed papers admitting that she was a homosexual, and then they would give her a dishonorable discharge.

My gay friend George and I heard about Jay's being in the psychiatric ward and both of us went to see her. She was a basket case. They were using shock treatments on her and had her all doped up—she was like a zombie. And she had no rights. I would say to her, "Look, just get out of the service. Get your discharge, because it's not going to be as heavy on you as it would be on a man." People were not going to ask a woman, "Were you in the service?"

I was warned by my friends not to even see Jay, because they could throw you out of the service through guilt by association. We were told by some of George's gay friends who were air police that both our names were "on the list" because we went to visit. So George and I decided to get married. And the minute we became engaged, our names were taken off the list. On our honeymoon night we each drove to be with our lovers—mine in Austin and his in San Antonio. The funny thing is it started a lot of marriages in the air force, because people thought, "Why not?" I knew a lot of career officers who married gay men to protect their time in the service.

But I was told after we came back from our wedding that Jay had committed suicide. They said she took an overdose. She was so traumatized by what

had happened to her and felt so desperately alone. And the sheer frustration of being called a queer, not having any recourse, no legal protection. Jay felt so degraded and had no support from her family. I wrote to her mother and father after her death and said we could identify the men who were responsible for her assault, and I got a very brief note back from her father saying that their daughter was dead and that she was queer, and we should just leave it at that.

Were the men who assaulted her ever prosecuted?

No. But George had a couple of air police friends who were big and tough, and one night they took a couple of these guys out and beat the hell out of them. And that was the only recourse that we could even feel good about.

But I felt so very frustrated by this whole experience that the only thing I knew to do was to get out of the service and tell my story whenever I could. I think back on the times when I would have liked to remain in the service. I received awards and did a lot of permanent party shows. And I think I could have stayed, but there was no staying there because it was insane.

So when I see people today fighting for their careers, I think our community should support them, because the military is the last foothold—the last stand for us. I think the armed forces lose a lot of good talent with their antigay policies. I am sometimes reminded of a statement by General Patton, who was supposed to have said, "You give me a bunch of homosexuals and I'll win the war for you."

I've talked to service people who liberated Dauchau or today are fighting hard for recognition as gay vets, or fighting to stay in the military. Let's support these people. That's where we need to put some of our efforts.

A Conversation with Colonel Margarethe Cammermeyer

Interviewed by Ginny Vida

(Editor's Note: Colonel Margarethe [Grethe] Cammermeyer has had a long and distinguished career in the United States Armed Forces ever since she joined the army as a nursing student in 1961. She was awarded the Bronze Star for her fourteen-month service as head nurse of a soldiers' medical and later neurosurgical ward in Vietnam. In 1985 she received the Veterans Administration Nurse of the Year Award, for which she was chosen from over thirty-four thousand candidates. At the time of her dismissal from the military, on June 11, 1992, she was the highest-ranking officer to have been separated by challenging the military's ban on homosexuals serving in the military.

On June 1, 1994, a federal district court judge in Seattle ordered the military to reinstate Colonel Cammermeyer to the position she held upon her dismissal. Judge Thomas S. Zilly ruled that "the Government has discriminated against Colonel Cammermeyer solely on the basis of her status as a homosexual and has failed to demonstrate a rational basis for doing so. . . . Mere negative attitudes, or fear are constitutionally impermissible bases for discriminatory governmental policies." Judge Zilly further ordered that any record of Colonel Cammermeyer's sexual orientation be expunged. Pentagon officials appealed the decision and requested a stay of the implementation of the decision. The request was denied by Judge Zilly and later by the Ninth Circuit Court of Appeals. Colonel Camermeyer returned to duty with her unit in the National Guard in July 1994.)

How long and where did you serve in the military?

I joined the military in the Army Student Nurse Program in 1961, finished my last two years of col-

lege and then went on active duty, and served as an officer of the Army Nurse Corps on active duty from 1963 to 1968. During this time I served in Texas; at Fort Benning, Georgia; Nuremberg, Germany; Ft. Lee, Virginia; Vietnam; and Fort Lewis, Washington. Then I was separated from the military because as a woman you couldn't have dependents. I had to leave the military because I was pregnant with our first child. Then in 1972 the regulations changed. I went back into the military in the Army Reserves and served there until 1988. I then transferred over to the Army National Guard and continued until my separation in June 1992.

What were your most satisfying accomplishments while you were in the military?

On active duty it was, I think, my tour in Vietnam. From the active duty perspective, that was the epitome of why I had joined—to be available and to care for the sick and wounded during war. In the Army Reserves there were some war game exercises that we participated in that really demonstrated that

Colonel Margarethe Cammermeyer.

Photo Credit: Firooz Zahedi/NBC

we were ready to be mobilized and could respond to a national emergency. The third was that as chief nurse in Washington with the National Guard, my role was to get a new hospital ready, to be prepared for the state emergency. There were a number of things that happened along the way.

There surely was much to be proud of. What were the circumstances that led to your dismissal?

As I mentioned earlier, I have some kids. My husband and I were married for fifteen years. I had four sons. I ended up getting divorced in 1980, and went through a whole process of coming to terms with why it was that I didn't want to be married. Over the next eight years I came to realize that I was a lesbian. That was a personal realization, having only to do with me and my identity. But by that time in my military career, I had an aspiration to be chief nurse of the National Guard. With my military experience and having almost completed my doctorate, I thought that I would be a good candidate. To finish my military preparation, I needed to go to the war college. And for that I needed a top-secret clearance. In the course of that investigation, when I was interviewed, there was a question having to do with homosexuality, and I said, "I am a lesbian." And that was the beginning of the end.

Did you know that they were going to ask you that question?

I did not know what the nature of the questions would be, nor did I know what the regulation was at that particular time. I had assumed that my mere statement would not cause my separation, but I was also not aware of the policy itself.

So you thought that if you were honest, you would not be separated.

Yes, and I certainly did not believe that honesty was the worst policy, but also by that time, in the course of my twenty-three years in the military, I had challenged the military's policy a number of times, on things that had happened to me. And the military had corrected them. I had won each of these separate cases. I had this track record of success.

You had a little faith in the system, then.

Absolutely. I thought that you fought the system within the system and they would see the error of their ways, and I believed that they would judge me by my actions, and not by my words.

Could you have stayed in the military if you had misrepresented yourself?

Yes, there is no question about it. And as Senator Nunn and others have said since, that with the policy the way it is today, I would not have been separated because I would never have been asked.

Looking back, if you had not acknowledged your lesbianism, would it have been worth it to stay in the military?

I don't think that anything is worth it if you compromise your personal integrity. But that is my own bias at this point. You know, the question might be asked a different way. Would I have put myself in that situation? I suppose that at the time I applied, I had made some decision that I would go forward regardless of the consequences. I have this belief that things happen because they are supposed to happen. So sometimes we may nudge them a little bit, but still in all, as I try to find meaning in all of this, that's how I internalize it and make things okay.

Your book, *Serving in Silence*, was published recently. How do you hope readers of the book will benefit from your experience?

People who know that they are gay or lesbian already know what the process is of coming to terms with it. I think what I'm hoping is that when someone who has not lived it reads the book and finds out that our lives are every bit as complex and as basic and as down to earth as anyone else's and that we deal with the same tribulations and same good things and bad things—they will see that our lives are no different. The only thing that may make us different is our sexual orientation; we are all existing on this planet, occupying equal space, and it's really no big thing; what's the big deal.

Did the experience of doing the book help you deal with or resolve the injustice that you were subjected to?

The book was not my therapy. It was never intended to be. I wrote the book because I was asked to write it, not because I needed it for my own therapy. I essentially had to be convinced that I ought to write it. What it helped me do probably more than anything else was get an understanding of how we become part of the culture of the time. In the fifties, when I was growing up, there were standards and societal norms for the role of women, and yet we didn't know enough at that time to question them. We fell into roles society had mapped out for us. But over the years with exposure through the media—with television, with movies, with so much bombardment from outside, we have also come to see the opportunities that we have, and come to understand that no one has to be discriminated against. No one has to meet other people's expectations within the social norm, just because of their gender. They should not have less opportunity just because of who they are. The women's movement and the civil rights movement have raised the social consciousness.

How do you feel about the military's "Don't ask, Don't tell" policy?

It's very important to clarify that that policy is no longer a policy; it's the law. This means that the military no longer has any say; only Congress can change the law. That in itself is an abomination— that personnel policies of the military have to be mandated by Congress, rather than for the military to have the opportunity to change policy as they see that the climate is changing. It's now only one of two personnel policies that are controlled by Congress. One has to do with the role of women in combat, and the other with gays in the military. It's horrible that the policy/law exists and we are chal-

lenging it in the courts. It does nothing to protect people who are not in a position of power. It does nothing to afford safety for women against sexual abuse and threats because they may not be open to invitations and solicitations and that sort of thing. At first glance, people may not think it's a bad policy, but when you have to live it, it is no different and no less threatening than previous policies.

I think that if it had been a personnel policy that could be adjusted as the military saw that things were changing, then it may have been a first step, because President Clinton never had an opportunity to implement the policy that he would have liked. He told me, among others, that he wanted [a true, non-discriminatory protective policy], but there was tremendous pressure from special interest groups, both within the military and without—again, male-oriented, male-dominated organizations that by themselves probably had no experience with gays and lesbians, so it's part of the patriarchy.

Barbra Streisand directed a movie about you. How did this come about?

Early after my separation I was contacted by a number of producers, but Tri-Star contacted me and said that they were working with Barbra Streisand, and were interested in exploring whether or not I might be interested in a movie. I went down from Seattle to Los Angeles and met with Barbra Streisand and Neil Meron and Tri-Star and a number of other people with my attorney, and we talked about whether or not this was a wise and prudent thing to do. And again, they felt that it was a social issue that needed to be addressed directly, and I was convinced that this was perhaps something that needed to be done. So I consented. Then over the next few months there was talk about it. Glenn Close agreed to play my part and later Judy Davis agreed to play my partner, Diane. Allison Cross, who wrote [the TV movie] *Roe v. Wade*, wrote the screenplay, and this summer the movie was shot on location in Vancouver. The movie aired on NBC in early 1995.

Colonel Cammermeyer, thank you.

Strategy and Stamina:

Passage of the Gay Rights Bill

in New York City

Lee Hudson

On January 6, 1971, two years after the Stonewall rebellion sparked the modern wave of the gay rights movement, New York City became the first municipality in the country to introduce civil rights legislation for gay people. In the beginning it would be educational, the leaders felt—a bill that was unlikely to pass. But the legislation represented a goal—some said a tactic or tool—for liberation. Echoing the black, feminist, and peace efforts, and announcing the beginning of an openness for larger numbers of gay people, the bill was an assault against the closet of guilt and shame.

But it was not until April 2, 1986, after a fifteen-year struggle, that the bill finally became law. Fifty-five other jurisdictions were to pass some form of protection before New York did. Yet few bills were as comprehensive and none contended with the size, geography, or diversity of its population. Because of these factors and the length of time that the legislation was publicly debated, the New York experience provides a model of social struggle and change—and perhaps some lessons for gay rights proponents elsewhere.

Generally considered a liberal bastion of celebrated differences, New York is comprised of five boroughs of 7½ million people: One in four is born abroad and eighty-five thousand immigrants settle annually in the city. These cultures bring together a complex mix of religious and sexual mores—few sympathetic to the homosexual. As those working on the legislation found, any "celebration of differences" did not include lesbians and gay men.

Opponents argued that the gay community was not a "legitimate" minority comparable to populations defined by race, religion, ethnicity, disability, or creed. Opponents also maintained that homosexuality was a choice, an option that could be re-fused—rather than part of a person's sense of self. Others argued that discrimination was not a problem, that the gay community was a privileged population, both wealthy and well-placed socially.

Over time, the challenges were voiced, examined, and met. Year after year, gay men and lesbian women, in increasing numbers, resisted society's efforts to keep them underground and deny their existence. No longer willing or able to pay society's price for safety, they would not ransom their identity for a social blink of acceptance. Power, they discovered, lay in visibility and self-respect.

A number of events, persons, and strategies converged to create the successful legislation and get it through the thirty-five-member city council. While its moral time had long since come, it was not until 1986 that the political pieces fit. Even then, its progress was always precarious. I will describe here some of the influences that led to the bill's passage.

Consecutive Introductions Provided Public Education

In all, nine different versions of the the gay rights bill were aired at annual public hearings. After drafting, proponents secured council members to sponsor and introduce the legislation. The majority leader then referred the bill to the General Welfare Committee. The committee hearings and the meetings, demonstrations, and lobbying they spurred were the most effective route to the pressure politics of constituen-

Marilyn Laguerre and Marsha Neal.

© Morgan Gwenwald

cies. With representatives arguing the merits and demerits of the bill, the hearings were consistently a major media event. As such, they provided an important means for the gay and lesbian community to reach the general public—an outlet customarily denied or limited by the mainstream press.

Through these often marathon thirteen-hour, day-long hearings, a "rhetoric of repetition" took charge. Again and again, year after year, the hearings neutralized the "imminent dangers" presumably posed by these terrible homosexuals. When the terrible homosexuals stood in front of you and told their stories of discrimination and societal hate, the vague, faceless stereotypes disappeared. When others stood alongside them, their place in the world became real: They had families, children, neighbors, and ordinary lives. Extremist fears, reiterated year after year, sounded more and more ludicrous; the sensational became boring.

Society was slowly changing while the hearings seemed to stand still in time.

The Gay and Lesbian Community Became Increasingly Visible

Gay and lesbian people formed important, influential organizations. Two in particular were especially effective for the legislation in its final years: the Coalition for Lesbian and Gay Rights, which mobilized community pressure and lobbied persistently for votes, and FAIRPAC, a political action committee that raised money for local candidates supportive of gay rights. The Gay Activists Alliance, the Mattachine Society of New York, Lesbian Feminist Liberation, and the National Gay Task Force and NYPAC played critical roles in the bill's early years.

The growth of the gay press alerted community members to developments regarding the bill and became an important educational and political tool. Community members learned to ask their council members where they stood on the bill and to support them accordingly.

Documentation of Discrimination Expanded

In 1985 the city's corporation counsel, Frederick A. O. Schwarz, spoke to the heart of the matter when he said, with considerable exasperation, that

"you don't need a microscope or a telescope to know there is discrimination based on sexual orientation in this city."

In 1973 the City Commission on Human Rights conducted a small survey of employment discrimination with the help of the Gay Activists Alliance. Later, beginning in 1979 and culminating in a report in 1981, the commission forwarded its data and discussion to the city council. The National Gay Task Force contributed additional data comparing patterns of discrimination in New York to other parts of the country.

New York took two important steps in 1983 and 1985 to illustrate the nature and extent of antigay bias that would later prove invaluable during the council hearings. In 1983 the mayor established the AIDS Discrimination Unit at the Human Rights Commission. When complaints regarding AIDS were reported, the investigators separately noted any sexual orientation aspects of the cases. Thus they were able to address the gay-AIDS cases through provisions that defined AIDS as a handicap (and therefore covered by law) and catalog the other gay-related complaints for later publication. They publicized this effort with brochures and community presentations, asking anyone experiencing discrimination to file a complaint in the areas that the prospective law would address: employment, housing, and public accommodations. Though these reports were attacked as unsubstantial when originally released in 1985 and 1986, the press highlighted the pain and suffering in its 376 accounts and underscored that the report represented only a fraction of the actual number of cases.

In 1985, shortly after the Human Rights Commission issued its first report, the New York City Police Department added "sexual orientation" to the scope of their special Bias Incident Investigating Unit. This provided more official recognition of the oppressed status of gay people. The high-powered Bias Unit then conducted special investigations of gay-motivated cases along with crimes motivated by race, religion, or ethnicity.

Leadership in the City Council Changed

When Edward I. Koch first campaigned for mayor in 1977, he said that any mayor who wanted the gay rights bill passed could get it passed. He became mayor in 1978 and quickly regretted that statement. The political reality was that the majority leader of the city council appoints committee members and by those choices can stall a bill indefinitely. Tom Cuite, council member and majority leader for an unprecedented seventeen years, did just that. State and national commander of the Catholic War Veterans, he was determined to protect the city from the gay rights bill. Cuite learned a lesson in 1974 when the bill was comfortably voted out of committee and went to the full council for a vote. A major political press was necessary to defeat it by the narrow margin of 22–19. Never before in the history of the city council had a bill passed in committee and been defeated on the floor. The bill did not get out of committee again while Cuite headed the council. He retired in 1985.

Through the efforts of FAIRPAC and gay political organizations in each of the boroughs, the election of 1985 brought primarily gay-sensitive elected officials into the council. Tom Cuite's district replacement, Steve DiBrienza, for example, supported the gay rights bill. Also important, the new majority leader, though not a supporter, agreed not to stack the committee against the bill in order to leverage backing for his appointment.

Traditional Fronts of Opposition Were Weakened

Over the years, the major forces of opposition have been the Roman Catholic church, Orthodox Jewish groups, and the uniformed service agencies (police and fire). They cast the bill as an endorsement of homosexuality and a threat to the family, children, and society. The scriptures, religious leaders argued, condemned homosexual behavior as immoral and contrary to natural law.

While the Fire Department formally opposed the bill "because of the unique housing arrangements for on-duty personnel"—a public position that also led them to oppose female firefighters—the Uniformed Fire Officers Association (UFOA) was more blatant. The UFOA ran full-page ads in the news dailies directing readers and "all concerned straight citizens" to defeat a bill that would "force an employer to hire a pervert. . . . Expose our children to the influences of sodomites. . . . Impose the will of a few deviates on the majority of our citizens. . . . Make the small home owner rent to sex

deviants. . . . Destroy the teamwork tradition of Fire Fighting. . . . Subvert the laws of our nation and negate police enforcement."

Lobbying by religious groups took on many forms. The general counsel for Catholic Charities of the Archdiocese of New York wrote to all city council members in opposition to the legislation. Sermons were delivered from the pulpits, instructing parishioners to call or write their council members. Schoolchildren were coached to secure letters of disapproval from their parents.

But opposition by police, firefighters, and religious organizations was seriously weakened by the implementation of two mayoral executive orders, both seeking to provide some relief from discrimination and set a tone of tolerance in the city. The orders had been a long time in coming.

Leaders of the Gay Activists Alliance, formed in late 1969, had pressed then-mayor John Lindsay for an executive order banning discrimination in employment in city agencies. Although he did not issue the order, Lindsay did eventually issue a personnel policy statement in January 1972 directing agencies to assure equal opportunity including sexual orientation "in the processing of appointments and promotions in the civil service (except where restrictions are established pursuant to law)." But this statement, directed only to civil service with no enforcement provisions, was virtually worthless. Also, since consensual sodomy remained a crime until 1980, its parenthetical exception provided a key escape clause.

Along with promises to get the city bill passed, Ed Koch pledged during the 1977 mayoral campaign to issue an executive order forbidding city agencies to discriminate on the basis of sexual orientation in employment and the provision of city services. The Human Rights Commission would be the enforcement agency. Less than three weeks after taking office in 1978, he issued Executive Order 4. The Police and Fire Departments' opposition to the city bill became largely irrelevant, since the policy directing their hiring practices was now in place.

Mayor Koch's second executive order affecting gay rights, issued in 1980, presented a more complicated situation for the conservative religious organizations. Executive Order 50 required agencies contracting with the city for $50,000 or more in goods and services to sign a provision indicating that they did not discriminate in employment on the basis of sexual orientation. Since the city does billions of dollars' worth of contracting for goods and services, thousands of companies and agencies were affected.

In 1984, Catholic Charities, the Salvation Army, and Agudath Israel sued the city, threatening to withdraw service contracts totaling nearly $100 million unless they were exempted from the order on religious grounds. The case went on for eighteen months, dominating the press each time the legal process moved to the next step. Ultimately, the city lost the case when the highest court in the state ruled that the mayor had exceeded his executive authority by establishing a policy that forbade discrimination on a ground not covered by existing legislation. However noble the intention, the court concluded, the law must first be passed.

None of the religious institutions wanted to be cast as hating homosexual people or denying them employment or services. So publicly and legally, they went to great lengths to emphasize that they "didn't discriminate" and that their suit was primarily over jurisdictional matters.

The publicity stirred up by Executive Order 50 weakened the opposition to the annual airing of the gay rights bill. It served to put the religious agencies in a less flexible posture as to how the issue was framed. Having characterized themselves as nondiscriminating, how could they then object to a law that provided penalties for others less honorable? The churches' role in the final hearings and voting was considerably tamer than in previous years: no front page story in *The New York Times* asking the council to defeat the bill, no pulpit politics, no blatantly orchestrated mass efforts.

Conclusion

For gay rights protections, community members and their allies must battle a force of resistance centuries in the making. Gay rights laws will slowly pass because they are needed and because they are right. But it will not be without the push of visible gay men and lesbian women. The pressure is mounting for all gay people to "come out." Some pressure will be positive—the development of registered partnerships enabling unmarried persons living together to obtain various insurance and work benefits.

Additional tensions in the gay and lesbian community will increase between those in the closet and those out—with less understanding for those with double lives. AIDS taught our community the starkest possible truth: Gay people are an expendable population whose deaths did not rally a nation.

It had taken fifteen years for this law to pass: fifteen frustrating, demeaning, bitter, hostile, angry years. Now the gay rights bill stands as a testament to the integrity of a people, the reality of their differences, and the dignity that comes from honorable actions to protect minorities from disabling prejudice.

Legal Planning for Lesbian Couples

May Glazer, Esq.

This article will address the legal issues that arise when two women decide to live together in a committed and intimate relationship with the expectation that the relationship will endure for a long time. Since a lesbian partnership does not have the traditional economic, financial, and societal guidelines of a heterosexual marriage, the best means of ensuring that the desires of the life partners are carried out is a written contract. In the first blush of new love, discussions about the terms of a contract may not seem very romantic, but the benefits of thought and discussion at the beginning of the relationship far outweigh the disadvantages.

Initially, the partners should be urged to obtain separate attorneys. This may be costly, but partners have adverse as well as common interests. Separate representation will also insure against errors in favor of one of the partners or charges of misrepresentation or fraud. Getting one's own attorney is the safest course.

The next step is a statement, by each party, of all material facts. These statements should include a schedule of each partner's assets and the concerns, intentions, and expectations of each regarding the present and future of the relationship. Finally, a list of possible provisions to include in such a contract should be drawn up.

One subject the contract can address is whether present separate financial and property holdings should remain separate. If such assets are to continue as separate property, the question arises as to how the income from that property should be treated. Assets are often combined; even if one party has greater assets than the other, she may be

Alice Krause and Sally Cowan.

© 1989 Morgan Gwenwald

willing to combine equally. If that is the case, state that explicitly in the contract, so that no question of misrepresentation will arise later. Commingling of assets has advantages and problems, and both should be considered carefully.

This kind of contract can deal with personal as well as financial issues. However, not all personal provisions are enforceable by a court or subject to arbitration. Thus a paragraph concerning who will walk the dog and when, though helpful in setting guidelines, may not become the subject of a lawsuit.

Methods of enforcing the contract should also be considered. Even if the relationship is not about to end, problems of interpretation often arise. If the partnership is about to end, impartial third parties can be very helpful. To avoid litigation, the use of arbitration, or alternative dispute resolution, has become increasingly popular. If the parties prefer to have other lesbians or gay men arbitrate, each party may select one person she respects. Then the two arbitrators may select a third person to participate. These alternative methods of dispute resolution can be incorporated into the contract.

If the parties have decided to combine their assets and income, the pitfalls and benefits of jointly held assets should be considered. Assets may be held in "joint tenancy," or as "tenants-in-common." While both partners are living, the characteristics of these two types are essentially the same: Absent a requirement that each partner agrees, either may exercise complete control over the entire asset. At the first partner's death, however, the character of the asset changes. In a joint tenancy, the survivor acquires the whole asset by operation of law, without the need for a will. In a tenancy-in-common, the survivor retains her one-half interest and the *estate* of the first to die is the owner of the other one-half. The contract might include a provision as to what must be included in each partner's will, provided the partners are still together at the time of the first partner's death.

The contract being contemplated should address every aspect of the lesbian relationship while it is ongoing, as well as its conclusion by death or divorce. The contract can be renegotiated, modified, renewed, or revoked. It is a viable instrument that can guide the partners toward a stronger and happier relationship. And once the contract has been signed, it can be put in a drawer and forgotten until it is needed.

Listed below are suggested contract provisions, with a brief explanation of each suggestion. Not every contract requires the inclusion of each item on the list and certain items will require separate documents. If you don't have a pet or any expectation of getting one, don't agonize over that item. If there is no real possibility of having or adopting children, skip that item also.

1. The contract should specify a time period. This gives both parties the chance to rethink and reevaluate their goals and desires. In the absence of any modification, at the end of the time period the contract could provide that it is deemed to be automatically renewed for a similar period. Of course, property that has already been commingled or acquired jointly retains that form of title unless both parties agree otherwise.

2. The contract should include a schedule of each party's assets and liabilities, stating which assets shall remain separate and which shall become joint. The same rule would apply to liabilities.

3. A provision requiring a joint household checking account should be considered. This account should maintain a sufficient balance to pay about three months' expenses. It should not retain large sums of money and it should not be a repository for excess joint income. Any excess joint income should be deposited in a savings or brokerage account requiring two signatures or joint control, thereby protecting these assets from destructive divorcers. The death or disability of one of the partners may be handled by other provisions.

4. The most significant asset acquired by lesbian partners is generally a co-op, condo, or a house, for which a tenancy-in-common is the recommended form of ownership. The contract should include provisions regarding how title is to be held, how a mortgage will be obtained, the proportions of the partners' contributions to the down payment and the monthly carrying costs, and how much either person may spend on improvements without the approval of the other party. The most critical problem arises at the end of the relationship, if both partners want to keep the property but do not wish to continue the relationship. That problem can be partially resolved by the inclusion of a buy-sell provision in the contract. Buy-sell means that a fair market value for the asset has to be established, and one party must either buy the other party's share or sell her own share to the other party. The procedure of the buy-sell, the terms of sale, and the assumption of the mortgage liability should all be included in the contract.

5. To cover the possibility of a partner's becoming disabled in the future, the partners should exchange powers of attorney, which respectively appoint the other as "attorney-in-fact," with the authority to handle the financial affairs of the other. If the partners want that authority to continue even if the appointing party becomes incompetent, the power of attorney is called "durable." These powers of attorney should be separate documents, but the direction to execute them should be included in the contract.

6. A health care proxy has also become a popular separate document. The health care proxy appoints another person, called a health care agent or surrogate, to make medical decisions, including decisions about withholding life-sustaining treatment. Like a will, the document does not become active as soon as it has been signed; rather, the authority to make health care decisions is granted only when it has been determined that the person who has given the proxy lacks the capacity to make such medical decisions. The benefit is obvious. If a catastrophe occurs, a health care proxy may be used to overcome the intrusion of parents, siblings, or adult children into an already difficult decision-making process.

7. A living will, sometimes called a health care directive, is used to state a person's own instructions as to the kind of health care she would want to receive, should she become incompetent to make such decisions. The living will can indicate whether a person wishes to refuse medical treatment, including life-sustaining medical treatment. A living will may also be combined with a health care proxy so that the health care agent can be provided with the guidance necessary for making appropriate decisions about the granting or withholding of medical care.

8. A last will is probably the single most important document to consider drawing up. Using a will, one can dispose of all of one's assets, name an executor who will implement the testator's desires, arrange for probate, collect and protect assets, file tax returns, pay taxes and debts, and finally, distribute the assets according to the desire of the testator.

9. Parenting, the formation of a family either by biological means or by adoption, is an important new dimension to consider. Protecting and avoiding the possibility of disruption of that family is a very complex issue, and absolutely requires the assistance of counsel experienced in this area of the law.

10. For a woman with significant assets, a revocable living trust is an efficient way to pass along assets to her partner and to ensure that her partner will handle her affairs in the event of incapacity. The trust is subject to the claims of creditors, but it is a possible means of saving money through the avoidance of probate and court fees. On the other hand, a trust is costly to create and requires that all assets be transferred to that trust. Frequently, people forget to add assets to the trust as they are acquired. The result is that those assets not transferred still require probate.

Because a committed lesbian relationship does not automatically grant its partners the same protections of a heterosexual marriage, each lesbian partner must outline her wishes explicitly in legally binding documents. The legal issues that occur in the course of a lesbian partnership must be considered and addressed before critical situations arise. Drawing up some of the documents discussed in this article is the best means of ensuring that the desires of both partners are recorded, agreed to, and implemented.

VIII

The Spectrum of Lesbian Experience

Blacks and Gays:

Healing the Great Divide

Barbara Smith

(Editor's Note: The following was edited from an article published in Gay Community News, *October 1993.)*

Perhaps the most maddening question anyone can ask me is "Which do you put first: being Black or being a woman; being Black or being gay?" The underlying assumption is that I *should* prioritize one of my identities because one of them is actually more important than the rest or that I have been *forced* to choose one of them over the others for the sake of acceptance in one particular community.

I always explain that I refuse to do political work and, more importantly, live my life in this way. All of the aspects of who I am are essential, indivisible, and pose no inherent conflict. They only seem to be in opposition in this particular time and place, living under U.S. capitalism, a system whose functioning has always required that large groups of people be economically, racially, and sexually oppressed and that these potentially dissident groups be kept divided from each other at all costs.

As a Black lesbian feminist, I've devoted many years to making the connections between issues and communities and to forging strong working coalitions. Although this work is far from finished, it has met with some success. In 1993, however, two essential aspects of my identity and two communities whose freedom I've always fought for were publicly defined as being at war with one another.

For the first time, the relationship between the African American and gay communities is being widely debated both within and outside of movement circles. One catalyst for this discussion has been gay leaders' cavalier comparison of lifting the military ban with racially desegregating the armed forces following World War II. The NAACP and other Black civil rights organizations' decisions to speak out in favor of lesbian and gay rights and to support the 1993 March on Washington have met with protests from some sectors of the Black community and have also spurred the debate.

Ironically, the group of people who are least often consulted about their perspective on this great divide are those who are most deeply affected by it: Black lesbian and gay activists. Contradictions that we have been grappling with for years are suddenly on other people's minds: homophobia in the Black community, racism in the gay community, and the need for both communities to work together as allies to defeat our real enemies. Because Black lesbians and gays are not thought of as leaders by either community, this debate has been framed largely by those who have frighteningly little and inaccurate information.

Thanks in part to the white gay community's own public relations campaign, Black Americans view the gay community as being uniformly wealthy, highly privileged, and politically powerful—a group that has suffered nothing like the centuries of degradation caused by U.S. racism. Civil rights activists maintain that gays are not subject to water hoses and police dogs, denied access to lunch counters, or prevented from voting. Most Blacks have no idea, however, that we are constantly threatened with the loss of employment, housing, and custody of our children, and are subjected to violence ranging from verbal abuse to gay-bashing and death at the hands of homophobes. This interpretation also fails to acknowledge those lesbians and gays who have been subjected to all of this racist abuse, because we are both Black and gay.

Because we are rendered invisible in both Black and gay contexts, it is that much easier for the Black community to oppose gay rights and to express homophobia without recognizing that these attacks and the lack of legal protections affect its own members.

The racism that has pervaded the mainstream gay movement only fuels the perceived divisions between Blacks and gays. Single-issue politics, unlike the gay organizing that is consciously and strategically connected to the overall struggle for social and economic justice, do nothing to convince Blacks that gays actually care about eradicating racial oppression. At the very same time that some gays make blanket comparisons between the gay movement and the Black civil rights movement, they also assume that Black and other people of color have won

Oris D'Amil, Big Apple Corps, New York City, 1988.

© Kathryn Kirk

all our battles and are in great shape in comparison with gays.

Andrew Sullivan, editor of the *New Republic,* asserted the following in *The Advocate:* "The truth is, our position is far worse than that of any ethnic minority or heterosexual women. Every fundamental civil right has already been granted to these groups: The issues that they discuss now involve nuances of affirmative action, comparable pay and racial quotas. Gay people, however, still live constitutionally in the South of the 1950s." Other gay and lesbian leaders have asserted that gays are the last minority group unfairly legislated against in the United States. This assertion overlooks the fact that legislation that negatively affects people of color, immigrants, disabled people, and women occurs every day, especially when court decisions that undermine legal protections are taken into account.

This assertion also ignores that quality of life is determined by much more than legislation. Joblessness, poverty, racist and sexist violence, and the lack of decent housing, health care, and education make the lives of women and minorities supposedly protected by legislation into a living hell.

Affluence, male and white privilege often protect many members of the gay community from these injustices.

Lesbians and gay men of color have been trying to push the gay movement to grasp the necessity of antiracist practice for nigh onto twenty years. Except in the context of organizing within the women's movement with progressive white lesbian feminists, we haven't made much progress.

I'm particularly struck by the fact that for the most part queer theory and queer politics, which are currently so popular, offer neither substantial antiracist analysis or practice. Queer activists' understanding of how to deal with race is usually limited to their including a few lesbians or gay men of color in their ranks, who are expected to carry out the political agenda that the white majority has already determined, and/or to their sleeping with people of color.

One lesbian organizations's appropriation of the term "freedom ride" offended some lesbians of color from Albany, New York. We pointed out that the organization had not demonstrated involvement in antiracist organizing and had made no links with people of color, including nonlesbians and gays in the communities they planned to visit. Even when we explained that calling themselves "freedom riders" might negatively affect the coalitions we've been working to build with people of color in Albany, the group kept the name and simply made a few token changes in their press release.

These divisions are particularly dangerous at a time when the white right wing has actually targeted people of color with their homophobic message. As white lesbian activist Suzanne Pharr points out in the excellent article "Racist Politics and Homophobia" (*Transformation*, July/August 1993):

Community by community, the religious Right works skillfully to divide us along fissures that already exist. It is as though they have a political scismograph to locate the racism and sexism in the lesbian and gay community, the sexism and homophobia in communities of color. While the right is united by their racism, sexism, and homophobia in their goal to dominate all of us, we are divided by our own racism, sexism, and homophobia. (Emphasis mine.)

The Right's divisive strategy of enlisting the Black community's support for their homophobic campaign literally hit home for me in June. A Black lesbian who lives in Cleveland, Ohio, where I grew up, called to tell me that a group of Black ministers had placed a virulently homophobic article in the *Call and Post*, Cleveland's Black newspaper.

Entitled "The Black Church Position Statement on Homosexuality," the ministers condemned "HOMOSEXUALITY [including bisexual as well as gay or lesbian sexual activity] as a lifestyle that is contrary to the teachings of the Bible." Although they claim to have tolerance and compassion for homosexuals, their ultimate goal is to bring about "restoration," in other words, changing lesbians and gays back into heterosexuals in order "to restore such individuals back into harmony with God's will." One of the several sources they cite to prove that such "restoration" is possible is the *Traditional Values Talking Points, 1993,* a publication of the Traditional Values Coalition.

The ministers also held a meeting and announced their goal to gather 100,000 signatures in Cleveland in opposition to the federal gay and lesbian civil rights bill, HB 431, and to take their campaign to Detroit and Pittsburgh. A major spokesperson for the ministers, the Reverend Marvin McMichol, is the minister of Antioch Baptist Church, the church I was raised in and of which the women in my family were pillars. Antioch was, on a number of levels, one of the most progressive congregations in Cleveland, especially because of the political leadership it provided at a time when Black people were not allowed to participate in any aspect of Cleveland's civic life.

McMichol states, "It is our fundamental, reasoned belief that there is no comparison between the status of Blacks and women, and the status of lesbians and gays." He explains that being Black or being female is an "ontological reality . . . a fact that cannot be hidden," whereas "homosexuality is a chosen lifestyle . . . defined by behavior not ontological reality."

When I first got news of what was going on in my hometown I was emotionally devastated. It would have been bad enough to find out about a major Black-led homophobic campaign in any city in this country, but this place wasn't an abstraction, it was where I came from. It was while growing up

Turtle Bear at Seneca Women's Peace Encampment, New York, 1983.

© Shoshana Rothaizer

in Cleveland that I first felt attraction toward women, and it was also in Cleveland that I grasped the impossibility of ever acting upon those feelings. I wanted to get out even before I dreamed of using the word *lesbian* to describe who I was. College provided my escape. Now I was being challenged to deal with homophobia, dead up, in the Black community at home.

I enlisted the help of NGLTF (National Gay and Lesbian Task Force) and Scot Nakagawa who runs their Fight the Right office in Portland, Oregon, and of members of FAN (Feminist Action Network), the multiracial political group to which I belong in Albany. Throughout the summer we were in constant contact with people in Cleveland. FAN drafted a counterpetition for them to circulate, and in early September several of us went there following NGLTF's and Stonewall Cincinnati's Fight the Right Midwest Summit. Unfortunately, by the time we arrived, the group that had been meeting in Cleveland had fallen apart.

We had several meetings, primarily with Black lesbians, but found few people who were willing to confront through direct action the severe threat in their midst. The desire to remain closeted, a reluctance to deal with Black people in Cleveland's inner city, and the fact that Cleveland's white lesbian and gay community had never proven itself to be particularly supportive of antiracist work were all factors that hampered Black lesbian and gay organizing. Ironically, racial segregation seemed to characterize the gay community, just as it does the city as a whole. The situation in Cleveland was very familiar to me, however, because I've faced many of the same roadblocks in attempts to do political work against racism and homophobia in my own community of Albany.

I cannot say that our efforts to support a visible challenge to the ministers in Cleveland were particularly successful. The right wing's ability to speak to the concern and to play upon the fears of those it wishes to recruit, the lack of visionary political leadership among both Black and white lesbians and gays both nationally and locally, and the diffi-culty of countering homophobia in a Black context, especially when it is justified by religious pronouncements, makes this kind of organizing exceedingly difficult. But we had better learn to do it quickly and extremely well if we do not want the Christian right wing to end up running this country.

Since returning from Cleveland, we have been exploring the possibility of launching a nationwide petition campaign to gather at least 100,000 signatures from Black people to support lesbian and gay rights. One Black woman, Janet Perkins, a heterosexual Christian who works with the Women's Project in Little Rock, Arkansas, has already spoken out. In a courageous article entitled "The Religious Right: Dividing the African American Community" (*Transformation*, September/October 1993), Perkins takes on the ministers in Cleveland and the entire Black church. She calls for Black church members to practice love instead of condemnation. She writes:

These African-American ministers fail to understand they have been drawn into a plot that has as its mission to further separate, divide and place additional pressure on African-Americans so they are unable to come together to work on the problems of the community. . . .

What is needed in our community is a unity and a bond that can't be broken by anyone. We must see every aspect of our community as valuable and worth protecting, and yes, we must give full membership to our sisters and brothers who are homosexual. For all these years we have seen them, now we must start to hear them and respect them for who they are.

This is the kind of risk-taking and integrity that makes all the difference. Perkins publicly declares herself as an ally we can depend on. I hope in the months to come the gay and lesbian movement in this country will similarly challenge itself to close this great divide, which it can only do working toward an unbreakable unity, a bond across races, nationalities, and classes that up until now this movement has never had.

Latina Lesbians in Motion

tatiana de la tierra

I'm Hispanic and so are my parents. They came from the old country, Hispania, which was a little island in the Caribbean next to Caucasia. But when my parents were young, they had one dream: to move to North America because, like most Hispanics, they love to ski.

—Marga Gomez, comedienne

When I arrived in this country at seven years of age, I was Colombian. The next day, I became "Hispanic." Fifteen years later, right around the time I came out as a lesbian, I became "Latina." Today, out of respect for my specific breed, I consider myself a Colombian-Miamian lesbian. But for simplicity's sake I am a Latina lesbian, part of a complex community in this country that is undocumented in the textbooks, alienated from the dominant white lesbian culture, and often internally segregated and isolated.

One thing Latina lesbians aren't is "Hispanic." That's the federal government's favorite term for our people. It lumps those of Spanish, Portuguese, and Latin American origin into one convenient category, a square on government forms to be checked off. That's the oversimplified and inaccurate identity that Cuban–Puerto Rican lesbian comedienne Marga Gomez so deftly illustrates as ridiculous.

Being a Latina lesbian is a complicated endeavor. The first critical consideration is the definition of this term. Who is a Latina lesbian? Is it a lesbian who was born in Latin America and emigrated to the United States? Is it one whose parents or grandparents are Latin born? What if she's got Latin roots but doesn't speak Spanish and is "Americanized"? What about a Chicana? What if she's a North American who lived in Latin America as a child and knows in her soul she is Latina? What percentage lesbian and Latin does one need to be a Latina lesbian? And who decides who is a Latina lesbian? There is no "official" formula or response to these identity questions, and the term *Latina lesbian* is never defined. One standard measure is self-identification.

Latina lesbians rooted on U.S. soil bask in our differences. We speak English, Spanish, Spanglish, Portuguese. Our homelands span continents and dot the oceans in between. We are Chicanas from Aztlán on U.S. soil. We come from small Caribbean islands, remote mountainous villages, and bustling metropolises. Our countries are famed for tropical fruit, *guerrilleros*, coffee, cocaine, sugarcane, *chiles*, carnivals, colonies, democracies, and dictatorships. We slice plantains at particular angles. We drink *tinto* from little porcelain cups, dark syrupy *coladas* in white paper shot glasses, and *café con leche* just like everyone else.

The list of words for *lesbiana* in our countries' languages begins with *tortillera* and goes on to include *cachapera*, *marimacha*, *trola*, *arepera*, *jota*, *maricona*, and *manflora*. Our blood is thick with

Sandra Rovira, attorney.

© Donna Gray

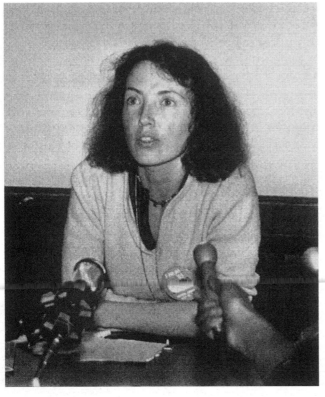

© 1991 Ann Meredith

Claudia Hinajosa at a lesbian press conference, Nairobi, 1985.

cumbias, bombas, salsa, son, mariachis, vallenatos, rancheras, merengue, baladas, valses, and *musica guajira.* Our skin tones are bronze, mother of pearl, tangerine, earth, and coal. We worship Yemaya, Isis, Maria, Ochun, God, la Virgen de Guadalupe.

We don't necessarily agree on anything in particular. We are Democrats and Republicans and socialists and communists and anarchists. We coalesce with "white" Anglo-Saxon lesbians. We have nothing to do with them. We're in solidarity with our gay Latin brothers. We're separatists. We are "out" to our families. We are totally in the closet. We dance Latin. We don't dance Latin. We are patriotic to our homelands, and we are apolitical.

Perhaps the element that unifies us is the shared experience of being the "other" in this society. We know discrimination, racism, and the colonization of our people firsthand. We learned the institutional shame we were taught in school. We see other Latinas as glitter among a crowd. A visible Latina lesbian is one who's prioritized her sexual preference along with her ethnic and cultural identity. We are those who don't separate ourselves within. We recognize that our power is inherent in being whole. And we look to each other to be with ourselves.

Latina lesbian is a generic term that we embrace to embrace us all. As members of this community we have been organizing nationally for decades in spite of invisibility and a lack of resources to express and develop our culture. There has been minimal documentation of our communities, and our work has been fragmented by the very nature of our identity. As individuals, we often live isolated from each other and alienated from the heterosexual Latino communities because we are lesbians. And we are on the fringe of the dominant lesbian culture because we are Latinas.

This dual estrangement has been the impetus for Latina lesbians to organize themselves as entities apart from all other gay groups since the Stonewall riots in New York City in 1969. Latin lesbians and gays played crucial roles in this uprising; butch Latina lesbians and gay Latino transvestites were among those who resisted the police raid with bottles and anything that could be transformed into a weapon on the spot. Among the hundreds arrested as a result of the week-long riots was an undocumented Argentinean gay who flung himself from the police station's third floor and was mortally impacted when he landed on a steel rod. Given the racism that exists within gay and lesbian culture, it's not surprising that the gay movement's first martyr remains unnamed and unheralded to this day.[1]

Latin lesbian and gay organizations evolved in the years following the Stonewall riots, just as North American lesbian and gay organizations did. The initial groups formed in the early seventies were cogender. Among these groups were El Comite de Orgullo Homosexual Latinoamericano (New York City), Greater Liberated Chicanos (Los Angeles), Gay Latino Alliance (San Francisco), and Comunidad de Orgullo Gay (Puerto Rico). They formed to celebrate gay liberation, to confront the Latin community's homophobia, to strategize within, and to support Latin lesbians and gays who were unacknowledged by the North American gay and lesbian community.

Cogender Latin groups continue to form part of the national Latina lesbian and gay identity. Among these groups are Gay and Lesbian Latinos (Los Angeles), La Gente Unida (Denver), Austin Latina Lesbian and Gay Organization (Austin), Gay and Lesbian Hispanics Unidos (Houston), Gente Latina de Ambiente (San Francisco), VIVA! (Los Angeles), ENLACE (D.C.), National Latina/o Lesbian and

Gay Organization (D.C.), and la Coalición de Lesbianas y Homosexuales (Puerto Rico). Newly established groups include LLANY (NYC), Latinos en Acción (Atlanta), La Guía (Colorado Springs), Entre Amigos (Orange County), and the national Coalición Popular de Ambiente.

By and large, these mixed groups are dominated by gay interests; the majority of Latina lesbian energy is funneled through Latina lesbian organizations, which began to appear in the early eighties. Support groups for Latina lesbians developed across the nation because of a need to have our own sense of home in the gay life. We exist with inherent disadvantages. Most of the organizations lack an infrastructure that allows for maximum access to resources. Many, for instance, do not have nonprofit status with the federal government, nor are they directly affiliated with the general North American lesbian community. We exist as a subculture within a subculture.

The organizations' focuses fluctuate, reflecting their local political climate. One common conflict within the groups is the social-versus-political aim. Hundreds show up for parties. Far fewer attend community organizing meetings. At the very least, the groups meet several times a month to discuss topics such as family, spirituality, dating, addictions, erotica, immigration, human rights, and coalition building with other women of color. The groups' "official language" might be Spanish or English or both. Some have annual retreats and occasional picnics, sporting events, cultural presentations, and dances. A few publish newsletters, and others bring Latina lesbian visibility into mainstream Latino communities by marching in Latin parades.

Among the most established Latina lesbian organizations are Lesbianas Unidas (Los Angeles, 1983–present); Las Buenas Amigas (New York City, 1986–present); and ELLAS (San Antonio, 1987–present). One group no longer in existence that had an impact in its time was Mujerio (San Francisco, 1988–1992). Currently active groups that formed in the early nineties include Las Salamandras de Ambiente (Miami); Lesbianas Latinas de Tucson (Tucson); Lesbianas Latinas de Dallas (Dallas); Nosotras (Austin); and Ellas en Acción (San Francisco).

Linkages between Latina lesbians on a national and international level have been mostly attributed to individual participation in the Latin American and Caribbean lesbian feminist *encuentros* (encoun-ters), which have been happening since 1987. These gatherings, which are an offshoot of the older Latin American feminist ones, have been held in Mexico, Costa Rica and, most recently, Puerto Rico. The third *encuentro* was organized by members of Puerto Rican lesbian organizations Aquelarre, Colectivo de Lesbianas Feministas, and Teatreras Donde Quiera. Held in 1992, this gathering attracted a significant number of Latina lesbians who live in the United States. But the rooted conflict between Latinas who reside in Latin America and those who don't impeded international coalition. "Official" interaction between these groups is infrequent. The next *encuentro* will be held in Argentina in 1995. The organizers, Frente de Lesbianas de Buenos Aires, have invited Latinas who live in the United States to attend the event. This attitude may signal a change in the conflict that's marred the gatherings until now and could result in establishing international dialogue.

National coalition among Latina lesbian organizations is a relatively recent phenomenon, and these groups are in the process of identifying a national agenda. In the fall of 1994, Lesbianas Latinas de Tucson hosted *Adelante con Nuestra Visión: the First National Latina Lesbian Self-empowerment and Leadership Conference.* Representatives from most Latina lesbian groups attended this historic event, as well as individuals linked with a variety of cogender Latin organizations. This conference comprises the beginning conversations as a "movement." Some of the topics of discussion at this gathering included health, immigration, erotica, publications, safe sex, leadership, lesbian mothers, intimacy, spirituality, and the documentation of our history.

National visibility for Latina lesbians has been practically nonexistent in traditional avenues of the mainstream Latin and North American communities, as well as in the gay media. This began to change in 1991 with the birth of *esto no tiene nombre*, the first national Latina lesbian magazine. Based in Miami, *esto* published features, short stories, international news, reviews, and poetry about and by Latina lesbians in Spanish, English, and Spanglish. When *esto no tiene nombre* ceased publishing in 1994, *conmoción, revista y red revolucionaria de lesbianas latinas*, was created to continue the work. Besides celebrating Latina lesbian existence, *conmoción* created an international information network that includes a writers' *telaraña* (web) and a national resource directory for Latina lesbians. Our writers, activists, artists, musicians, and organizations are featured in *conmoción* and all the material published is written and edited by Latina lesbians. *conmoción* is also spearheading the next national Latina lesbian gathering, planned for Miami.

Latina lesbians' writings were first included in a variety of groundbreaking women of color anthologies in the eighties. Among the first "out" Latina lesbians to publish personal writings were Cherríe Moraga and Gloria Anzaldúa, both of whom continue to write, edit, and shape the visible Latina lesbian experience. The Latina lesbian voices that hummed in the eighties formed a chorus in the nineties. Included among these writers are Ibis Gómez Vega, Carmen de Monteflores, Kleya Forté-Escamilla, Luz Maria Umpierre-Herrera, Mariana Romo-Carmona, Alicia Gaspar de Alba, Terri de la Peña, and Achy Obejas. Also in print are dozens of Chicana lesbians in Carla Trujillo's anthology, as well as those writers whose work was published in *esto no tiene nombre* and later in *conmoción*. "Out" lesbians from Latin America who also published lesbian-laced novels include Rosamaria Roffiel, Silvia Molloy, Cristina Peri Rossi, Sara Levi Calderón, Nancy Cardenas, and Sabrina Berman. Some of these lesbians' writings have been translated into English and are distributed in the United States.

Seeing ourselves in print is proof of our existence. Another notable resource for our community in the Lesbiana Latina Archives, created by Chicana herstorian Yolanda Leyva. These important archives document the Latina lesbian community; without them, it appears that we don't exist. It is clear that Latina lesbian visibility lies in our own hands.

And visibility is not a given for us. A handful of musicians, vocalists, and artists work their craft while being true to their roots and lesbian nature, often in unsupportive environments. Due to economic survival or internalized *lesbophobia,* a much larger number of our entertainers squelch their Latina lesbian selves. We have dozens of heard-it-through-the-grapevine Latina superstars but no k. d. lang to look us in the eye. And we have comediennes like Monica Palacios, Carmelita Tropicana, and Marga Gomez, who decorate their performances with Latina lesbian sensitivity, exaggerating stereotypes, and bullet-holing identities.

Today, twenty-five years after the historic Stonewall rebellion, Latina lesbians are joining forces, strengthening local organizations. The emergence of a national coalition is imminent. We are strategizing the future of our community. *La lucha* (the struggle) continues, up uncharted terrain, down abandoned slopes, across familiar valleys.

Notes

1. This information is from "Abriendo Caminos, Nuestra Contribución," by Gonzalo Aburto in LLEGO's Stonewall Twenty-fifth Commemorative program, 1994.

Resources

Las Buenas Amigas, c/o the Center, 208 West 13th Street, New York, NY 10011, 201-868-7816 (newsletter).

conmoción, revista y red revolucionaria, 1521 Alton Road #336, Miami Beach, FL 33139, 305-751-8385 (magazine and membership information network).

ELLAS, P.O. Box 681061, San Antonio, TX 78268-1061, 210-435-5750 (newsletter: "ELLAS Dicen").

Ellas en Acción, c/o the Women's Building, 3543 18th Street, Box 16, San Francisco, CA 94110, 415-552-8944.

Lesbianas Latina Archives, 408 West Simpson, Tucson, AZ 85701, 602-620-1087.

Lesbianas Latinas de Dallas, 107 S. Edgefield #D, Dallas, TX 75208, 214-946-7108.

Lesbianas Latinas de Tucson, 404 N. 4 Ave., Box 139, Tucson, AZ 85705, 602-624-0428.

Lesbianas Unidas, P.O. Box 85459, Los Angeles, CA 90072, 818-282-6093.

Nosotras, 1501 Robert Weaver Ave., Austin, TX 78702.

Las Salamandras de Ambiente, P.O. Box 520554, Miami, FL 33152-0554, 305-380-8585.

Further Reading

Anzaldúa, Gloria. *Borderlands/La Frontera.* San Francisco: Aunte Lute, 1987.

Anzaldúa, Gloria, ed. *Making Face, Making Soul: Creative and Critical Perspectives by Women of Color.* San Francisco: Aunt Lute, 1990.

Castillo, Ana. *The Mixquiahuala Letters.* New York: Doubleday, 1992.

Colorlife! the Lesbian, Gay, Two Spirit and Bisexual People of Color Magazine. 301 Cathedral Pkwy. #8M, New York, NY 10026.

conmoción, revista y red revolucionaria de lesbianas latinas. 1521 Alton Road #336, Miami Beach, FL 33139, 305-751-8385.

Forté-Escamilla, Kleya. *Nike Airs and the Barrio Stories.* San Francisco: Aunt Lute, 1994.

Gaspar de Alba, Alicia. *The Mystery of Survival.* Tempe, Ariz: Bilingual Press, 1993.

Gómez, Alma, Cherríe Moraga, and Mariana Romo-Carmona, eds. *Cuentos: Stories by Latinas.* Latham, N.Y.: Kitchen Table, 1983.

Gómez Vega, Ibis. *Send My Roots Rain.* San Francisco: Aunt Lute, 1991.

Levi Calderón, Sara. *The Two Mujeres.* San Francisco: Aunt Lute, 1991.

Silvera, Makeda, ed. *Piece of my Heart: A Lesbian of Color Anthology.* East Haven, Conn: Sister Vision, 1991.

de Monteflores, Carmen. *Singing Softly/Cantando Bajito.* San Francisco: Aunt Lute, 1989.

Moraga, Cherríe. *Loving in the War Years.* Boston: South End, 1983.

Moraga, Cherríe. *The Last Generation.* Boston: South End, 1993.

Moraga, Cherríe. *Heroes & Saints & Other Plays.* Albuquerque: West End, 1994.

Moraga, Cherríe, and Gloria Anzaldúa, eds. *This Bridge Called My Back: Writings by Radical Women of Color.* Latham, N.Y.: Kitchen Table, 1981.

Obejas, Achy. *We came all the way from Cuba so you could dress like this?* Pittsburgh: Cleis, 1994.

Paravisini-Gebert, Lizabeth, and Margarite Fernández Olmos, eds. *Pleasure in the Word, Erotic Writing by Latin American Women.* Fredonia, N.Y.: White Pine, 1993.

de la Peña, Terri. *Margins.* Seattle: Seal Press-Feminist, 1992.

de la Peña, Terri. *Latin Saints.* Seattle: Seal Press-Feminist, 1994.

Peri Rossi, Cristina. *Evohe.* Washington, D.C.: Azul Editions, 1994.

Ramos, Juanita. *Compañeras: Latina Lesbians.* (1987; reprint New York: Routledge, Chapman, and Hall, 1994).

Trujillo, Carla, ed. *Chicana Lesbians.* Berkeley, Calif.: Third Woman, 1991.

Umpierre-Herrera, Luz María. *The Margarita Poems.* Berkeley, Calif.: Third Woman.

VIVA Latina Lesbian and Gay Arts Quarterly. 4470-107 Sunset Blvd. #261, Los Angeles, CA 90027.

Asian Pacific Lesbian

a.k.a. Dead Girl, China Doll,

Dragon Lady, or the Invisible Man

Kitty Tsui

I remember the year I turned twenty-one. I was enrolled in the creative writing department at San Francisco State in the peaceful years that followed the riotous student strikes demanding the establishment of ethnic studies. I remember that year because I came out as a lesbian. Desperately seeking other women like myself, I frequented coffeehouses, bookstores, bars, political rallies, rap groups, and rock concerts. To no avail. I felt alone and isolated; I thought I was the only Chinese lesbian in the world.

When I came out to my mother she told me it was just a phase. She said I always had to be different, wanted to be a bad girl. What, going out with black men and all! But I've been a lesbian for over two decades now. And a happy one at that!

The first gay bar I frequented was Bojangles on Polk Street. I went there on weekend nights with my best friend Diana, an artist who had married a bi-sexual black man. With the exception of a clique of Filipino butches with their femmes, I was the only Asian woman in the bar. A veritable exotic flower, white and black women alike clustered around me.

It wasn't until a year later that I met my first Asian lesbian. It was Halloween, Tuesday, a school night, and Diana had to work extra hard to persuade me to go with her to Peg's Place, a local lesbian hangout. The place was packed wall to wall with women dressed in costumes, mustachioed, and in high drag, in black-seamed stockings and fuck-me heels, in outfits fit to kill. Marvin Gaye crooned "Let's Get It On." Laughter trilled in the smoke-filled air. Couples bumped on the dance floor or ground their groins together in the dark corners of the bar.

When a heterosexual couple, both Asian, walked into the bar, Diana and I had a good laugh. I stopped laughing when the androgynous man walked over and asked me to dance. I realized that he was a she. Her name was Jen and she was mending a broken heart. Jen became my first Chinese woman lover. When I first came out as a lesbian, loving women seemed so natural, as natural as breathing. Along with that feeling came a great sense of freedom of being released from gender roles. In addition, when Jen and I got together, our wardrobe doubled.

In 1977 Anita Bryant, the spokesperson for Florida orange juice, launched a highly publicized campaign against the first gay rights ordinance to be passed by a Southern city, Miami. Six months later, the ordinance was repealed by voters. I was busy working on my master's degree and commuting to Lake Tahoe on weekends to sleep with Jen's best friend's girlfriend.

A year later, Proposition 6, which resolved to bar gays or anyone "advocating a gay lifestyle" from teaching in the public schools, was spearheaded by

Canyon Sam, San Francisco tradeswoman, activist, writer, performing artist.

conservative California State Senator John Briggs. In November it qualified for the state ballot. In this virulently antigay climate, the gay and lesbian community organized to fight.

It was around this time that the first Asian women's group was formed. Ranging from a handful to two dozen women, the group met occasionally to talk about issues, and sometimes just to socialize and share a potluck meal. At first, the group Asian American Feminists had included both straight and lesbian women, then the composition changed, and it became mostly lesbian. In my mind, this is the incident that precipitated it: At one particularly lively potluck, amidst the platters of chicken adobo, pansit noodles, cha siew and roast duck, fried rice and curry, was a plate of pitted dates filled with sweet butter brown with hashish. Satiated with good food and pleasantly high, the roomful of women began a game of "spin the bottle." The straight women left.

As an Asian American lesbian in the gay and lesbian community, I felt invisible and very much in the minority. The women's movement nurtured women's presses and many pioneering women writers living in the San Francisco Bay Area, but Willyce Kim was the lone Asian lesbian in print.

In 1979 a group of Chinese American women writers, frustrated at the lack of Asian voices, decided to present a reading of individual work. The event was so wildly successful that we formed a group called Unbound Feet, comprised of Nancy Hom, Genny Lim, Canyon Sam, Merle Woo, Nellie Wong, and myself. We were three lesbians and three married women.

The success of the group and the enthusiasm with which we were received illustrated vividly the dearth of work by Asian American women. We traveled and toured with Unbound Feet for two years. Unfortunately, political differences split the group. Three of us wanted to focus solely on creative work. The other three believed that our writing and our politics were inseparable. The latter group, Merle, Nellie, and myself, resolved to continue and we did for a time as Unbound Feet Three.

Growing up in Hong Kong, I heard all around me mothers yelling at their children: "Say nui, mo no, mo yung!" Dead girl, no brain, no use. We were not just brats or bad girls. Worse, we were dead girls. No brain. No use. Confucius wrote: "The aim of female education is perfect submission, not cultivation and development of the mind."

In *Between Worlds, Women Writers of Chinese Ancestry*, Amy Ling writes that "in order for a Chinese immigrant woman to write and publish a book in English, she must be something of a rebel, for writing, an act of rebellion and self-assertion, runs counter to Confucian training. Also she has to possess two character traits: an indomitable will and an unshakable self-confidence."

It is difficult to develop self-confidence in a world without role models. It is difficult to trust in your creativity when there is no validation for it. It is difficult to believe in your work, indeed in your *self* when you are rendered invisible. And it is doubly difficult to be a lesbian and a person of color living in a racist, misogynist society surrounded by advertising images celebrating white privilege, power, and attractiveness.

This was a time when Asian American lesbian writers were excluded from both anthologies of works by writers of color and anthologies of works by gays and lesbians, or included merely as a token gesture. In 1983 when my book, *The Words of a Woman Who Breathes Fire*, was published, I joined Willyce Kim and Barbara Noda as one of only three Asian American lesbians with books in print. All three books were published by small presses.

In 1983 on the East Coast, a handful of Asian American lesbians felt their invisibility so intensely that when *The Words of a Woman Who Breathes Fire* was finally published, they were moved to action. They organized to become Asian Lesbians of the East Coast (ALOEC). A decade later, the group has a mailing list of 120 members. On the West Coast, the Asian women's group went through many changes. People came and went. A newsletter was printed that went out to a handful of readers. In 1986 the Asian Lesbian Network (ALN) was formed to gather resources and organize to give voice and visibility to Asian lesbians in countries all over the world.

In 1987 the first Asian lesbian retreat took place at the Valley of the Moon in Sonoma, California. There, I met eighty women of Indian, Vietnamese, Thai, Malaysian, Filipino, Korean, Chinese, Japanese, Pacific Islander, and mixed-heritage descent. It was truly an incredible experience to look around and see all those beautiful Asian American lesbians together in one place. Fourteen years previously I had thought I was the only one! In 1989 a second Asian/Pacific lesbian gathering took place in Santa Cruz, California, with approximately 185 lesbians attending.

Anne Mi Ok Bruining.

At the 1987 March on Washington for Lesbian and Gay Rights, the seeds were sown that became the networking group Asian/Pacific Lesbian Network (ALPN). The following year, Asian/Pacifica Sisters (APS) was born in San Francisco. Now there are a thousand on the mailing list, and the organization is a vibrant presence in the social and political landscape of the community. Groups were forming in Canada, the largest being Asian Lesbians of Vancouver (ALOV). Overseas, the first Asian lesbian conference was held in Thailand in 1990. The second Asian Lesbian Network conference took place in Tokyo in 1992, with 160 Asian lesbians from thirteen countries attending.

As Asian American women we still face the challenge of debunking many stereotypes. In the popular culture, there still exists the dragon lady/China doll dichotomy versus the servile, demure, long-suffering Madame Butterfly. We are either the conniving, sex-hungry Dragon Lady or the submissive sex slave/geisha girl. By virtue of our skin color and our Asian faces, we will never be accepted as anything other than alien, although we may have been born in the United States.

Though the political climate in this country is changing, things look much the same for Asian Americans and Asian/Pacific lesbians. Anti-Asian sentiments are high, as evidenced by the growing number of violent incidents against us. The brand of racism that labeled us the "model minority" relegates us to the closet as invisible. We are still plagued by the lack of role models in every segment of society and in the arts.

Pick up any anthology, magazine, journal, or resource guide. Attend a film festival or conference. Count the number of panelists, presenters, participants, journalists, filmmakers, actors, artists, or authors who are Asian American. Even at people of color events, Asian Americans seldom have a voice.

Surprisingly, in a city like Chicago (where I currently reside), with an Asian American population of 104,118, many bookstores do not have an Asian American section. We are a people who have been part of this country since the mid-seventeenth century, yet we have a token month, May, dedicated to our history. In some places it is designated as Asian American Heritage week, in others, not at all. As recently as August 1992, an article appeared in a local gay newspaper entitled, "Are There Really Only Two Asian Lesbians in Chicago?" A good question indeed. Am I one of the two or one of the invisible ones?

For me as an Asian American lesbian, the invisibility is twofold. In the Asian American community, I am not acknowledged as a lesbian. In the gay and lesbian community, I am not acknowledged because of the color of my skin or, conversely, acknowledged solely because of the color of my skin.

Reader, you are probably wondering how, if there are Asian and Asian/Pacific lesbian groups on both coasts and around the world, are we invisible? In this case, visibility in numbers still translates to invisibility if there is no recognition or acknowledgement of who we are as Asian/Pacific lesbians in the community and in the world. San Francisco and New York may have a large Asian lesbian presence, but many other cities do not. And although smaller cities may all have Chinatowns, an Asian American lesbian may well be the only one in town.

As a feminist movement, we have the rhetoric down pat. Parlance and vocabulary are tools that we have learned to use well. We juxtapose words like diversity and difference with justice, equality, and human rights. Yet the reality for Asian/Pacific lesbians

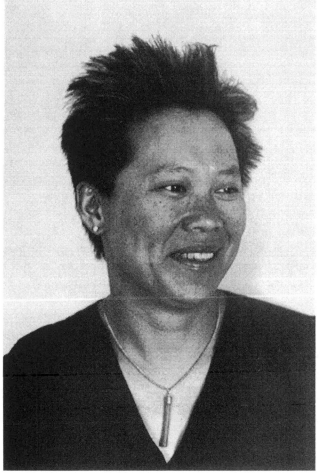

Kitty Tsui.

voices to break silence, to shatter stereotypes and to tell our stories.

In *Homecoming,* Willyce Kim writes: "first asian woman/I lay my head/upon your thigh/you are all the women/that I have ever feared/. . . you are my mother's daughter/bone of my bone/throat arching like a curve of the moon."

For me as an Asian/Pacific lesbian, silence is not an option. It is imperative for me to continue to speak out. To ensure that we Asian/Pacific lesbians be acknowledged as who we are. Women with a history. Women with a culture. Women with voices. Women who talk story. Women who live and breathe and sing. Women who survived being dead girls. Women who can turn the heritage of silence and oppression into strength, solidarity, and sunshine.

Resources

Asian Lesbians of the East Coast (ALOEC), P.O. Box 850, New York, NY 10002, 212-517-5598.

Asian Pacific Lesbian and Bisexual Network (APLBN), P.O. Box 460788, San Francisco, CA 94146, 510-814-2422.

Asian/Pacifica Sisters (APS), P.O. Box 170596, San Francisco, CA 94117.

Phoenix Rising Newsletter, a publication of Asian/Pacifica Sisters, same address as APS.

Further Reading

Asian Women United of California, eds. *Making Waves, an Anthology of Writings by and about Asian American Women.* Boston: Beacon Press, 1989.

Him-Ling, Sharon, ed. *The Very Inside: An Anthology of Writings by Asian and Pacific Islander Lesbians and Bisexual Women.* East Haven, Conn.: Sister Vision Press, 1994.

is that we are not included, we are not invited, we are not acknowledged. We are still invisible. We are not part of the community. Racism has excluded us from the fabric of the rainbow quilt.

As Asian American women we must use our own voices to create our visions and to forge our identities. We are women of many identities. We come from many lands. We speak in many tongues. We are American born and foreign born. We must use our

No Apologies:

A Lakota Lesbian Perspective

Barbara Cameron Nation Shield

If sage and sweet grass are not part of your culture, why are you burning it?

For many years, the lesbian and gay movement has been in full swing. And Native lesbians and gay men have been organizing, as such, since a gay Native man and I cofounded an organization in the mid-seventies to meet the social needs of our community in San Francisco. Fortunately, our effort also was felt in Indian country, giving courage to Native lesbians and gay men to organize throughout the United States and Canada.

In many respects, the coalescing of Native lesbians and gay men has proven beneficial for our community. Some of the isolation we experience is mitigated. For several years, an annual gathering has been held in a different area of Indian country. An informal network exists as a result of the gatherings. Various organizations have formed. Several notable spokespersons, in addition to myself, have gained recognition, such as Chrystos, Beth Brant, Richard LaFortune, Curtis Harris, and James Abrams. The slow but steady return to traditional acceptance of Native lesbians and gay men in Indian country has been encouraging.

As the mainstream lesbian and gay movement gains strength and visibility, racism remains a strong factor of the movement. Leadership positions and spokespersons are predominantly white. There are deliberate but surreptitious actions by the cartel of the lesbian/gay community to undermine and politically neutralize people of color. These tactics, either through direct attacks or by lack of consistent and meaningful support of our projects and social concerns, seemingly have tacit approval of the community. If we make mistakes, we are never forgiven and it's never forgotten, in contrast to some white lesbian and gay leaders who get promoted and obtain even more support *because* of their mistakes. And some of these leaders have attained almost godlike reverence even though they are openly racist.

Progress of the lesbian and gay movement is measured by how many lesbians and gay men get elected, the passage of domestic partnership laws, successful lesbian custody cases, and other significant achievements. But it is never measured by whether a strong, consistent, and communitywide commitment to addressing racism is maintained.

A political and social environment such as described in the preceding paragraphs is unattractive to Native lesbians, particularly when the lesbian and gay movement does not embrace, let alone acknowledge, those issues important to Native people.

Not only are Native issues disregarded, but instead there is an obscene practice of cannibalizing Native cultures. *Anyone* living in the United States can claim to be Native American. You, too, can be a Native American lesbian. Within the U.S. lesbian community, Native American/American Indian/Alaska Native cultures, religious ceremonies and icons, music and art are purloined. Even the institutions of our grandmothers and great grandmothers are quarry. (The procreation rate of Cherokee princesses is astounding; the whopping numbers of their descendants who claim to be "part Cherokee" attests to that.) The "pioneer spirit" of lesbian pillagers is horrific; Shivington and Custer would have admired their moral righteousness.

Not surprisingly, for merely suggesting a hint of the iniquitousness of the appropriation of Native lives and cultures, birthright Natives are severely chastised by those whose "Native" identities are driven by opportunism and personal greed.

The "rights" of instant Indians have usurped the cultural tradition of those of us who are Native. In the meantime, "neo-Native Americans" pad their bank accounts selling fake, inferior "Native art," obtain employment listing a Native American identity, pretend to experience intergenerational stress, and make a premeditated effort to discredit those of us raised as Indians. Their sage is purchased from feminist, new age, or gay/lesbian bookstores, where it is already trivialized, and burned sacrilegiously. Sundance, for them, is a vacation spot while their parents play golf over Native cemeteries. A few, who have been successful in cajoling tribal officials to enroll them as tribal members, flash their tribal enrollment cards as a source of their legitimacy. Some contemporary writers, resplendent with their "Indian names," steal our words, make our truth their lives, charging thousands of dollars for hokey, earth-mother workshops.

As discussed by Native lesbians over the years, there is evident disinterest of many people of color, including lesbians of color, toward us. In their lives, we are just as invisible as we are to whites, although, at various times, lesbian/gay Asian Americans and Native lesbians and gay men have forged alliances for several reasons. Asian Americans experience a similar invisibility, and Asian and Native women are stereotyped as worthless, quiet, and subservient. And everyone else refers to both groups as "other." Clearly absent is a vibrant interaction with Natives by some people of color who claim they are part Native American. Angst poetry bemoaning a lost identity is one of the manifestations of this blatant opportunism, and serves as their only "connection" to us. Moreover, the invisibility of Native women, in particular, is evidenced by the fact that the only U.S. press for women of color, in its thirteen-year history, has yet to establish a strong commitment to Native women writers. And that is one of the reasons Chrystos and I are creating a press for Native women exclusively.

A tremendous disservice is done, by the cultural opportunists and pioneer-spirited lesbians, to the difficult struggles of those persons who are attempting to reintegrate into Native cultures. The thoughtless trendiness of instant Indians, in effect, makes a mockery of those Native people who were unable to grow up Native due to adoption into non-Native homes or removal from their families and cultures because of the difficult social conditions that Native people exist in, or for any number of reasons. Identity issues within Native communities are complex and painful; feckless neo-Native Americans/instant Indians add unwelcome layers of suspicion and mistrust.

The troubling attachment to and appropriation of Native cultures by pioneer lesbians is undeniably an act of hatred and violence against us; it is an element of the silent violence that Chief Fools Crow accurately assessed as the primary menace to our health and well being.

Oddly, members of the non-Native lesbian/gay communities seem to possess more knowledge about Native lesbian and gay male pre-European and pre-Spanish invasions (berdache societies, etc.) than about those of us who live now. This speaks to several truths: They believe the lie that Native people have been exterminated; they prefer relating to dead Native Americans; they romanticize our lives, denying that we are real people with very serious problems. Reaching to our past Native traditions of accepting lesbians and gay men to underscore non-Native lesbian/gay political agendas while virtually ignoring present-day Native lesbian and gay voices is simply crude.

In the present day, resisting the covert pressure to become "racially neutral" in the lesbian/gay community (the racial equivalent of androgyny) is an additional stress for Native lesbians and gay men who must also withstand assimilation into mainstream U.S. culture. (A racially neutral person is nonthreatening, ethnically safe, but still exotic.) Nationwide statistics are maintained on hate speech incidents perpetrated against lesbians and gay men. But similar acts perpetrated by white lesbians and gay men against Natives and people of color are not documented. If such a program were developed, white lesbians and gay men would probably be outraged, but I believe such a program is needed.

The situation of Native Americans is very unique and the nationwide hatred of us is very deep. Native American lesbians and gay men fully understand this. A blatant example of the worth of Native American lives to the nation is the fact that if the Washington Redskins had been named the Washington Niggers, the entire nation would have worked feverishly to change the name. Instead, only a few non-Native persons support Native efforts to change racist team names. So-called "harmless" phrases such as "long time no see," "hold the fort," "bottom of the totem pole," "the wild west," "the new world," are ingrained in daily language.

Gentle racism tells us we'll never get our land back, our treaties will never be honored. Clearly, the message is don't bother me with these unimportant issues and do not remind me that I have acquiesced to illegal and immoral acts of the U.S. government. The muffling of Native-related issues is clear evidence that even the most politically astute lesbian does not escape the hatred of Native people that goes to the earth's core, deep and fiercely burning.

The news regarding lesbian and gay support of

Native issues is bleak. There has been some recent support of benefits for Leonard Peltier and Norma Jean Croy. It's not possible to name any well-known lesbian and gay leader, on a local or national basis, who advocates for our treaties to be honored (and does so because it's the right thing to do, not as an exchange of political favors). *Honoring of our treaties goes to the heart of the majority of Native Americans. We really care about this.*

It's important to understand the previous paragraphs because it's a map of how you can support Native lesbians and gay men. And to understand that so much of what Native lesbians and gay men care about, what many of our needs are, are often not separate from the rest of Indian country. We love our aunties, uncles, grandmas, grandpas, cousins, and would not disrespect them by calling them names like breeders, etc.

Of course there is homophobia and violence against Native lesbians and gay men, especially on reservations. But more and more Native health organizations are holding seminars about homophobia and about the lives of Native lesbians and gay men.

The silent violence is also a world of agonizing decisions for many Native lesbians and gay men who choose to leave the rural reservations, pueblos, and Native enclaves to live in urban areas. We, unlike other lesbians and gay men, are forced to disrupt clan, tribal obligations, and very particular family responsibilities that sustain and define us. We leave behind those special places on the prairies, in the mountains and the desert, far from the reaches of city lights. The seasonal ceremonies that nourish our spiritual lives are left behind; at best we make trips home when we can. Whether we like it or not, to be openly lesbian or gay often means being away from homelands and deep extended family structures that hold us together as Native people.

Leaving the isolation of reservations to locate to areas with visible lesbian and gay communities and then finding isolation within that community is truly ironic. Isolation, pervasive racism, poverty, a short life expectancy, suicide, life-threatening and life-disrupting diseases, and invisibility create a multitude of psycho-social problems for Native lesbians and gay men. But there are virtually no culturally relevant programs and services that specifically meet the needs of Native lesbians and gay men. These programs will come about soon as a natural outcome of the growth of our movement, and will be organized by Native lesbians and gay men.

One of the most important truths to understand is, regardless of whether we interact politically and socially with non-Native lesbian/gay communities, we generally do not view ourselves as separate from heterosexual Natives. It's also important to know that there are over five hundred tribes and nations; we are truly one of the most diverse groups of people. And we have been voicing Native issues and concerns for several decades; if you still must ask how you can support us, you haven't been listening.

The things being done to the Indians today might best be called silent violence. It is not necessary to have armed confrontations or to destroy with fire and guns in order to have violence. The silent violence is what is crushing the Indian people today.
—*Chief Fools Crow, Lakota Nation*

Further Reading

Mails, Thomas E. *Fools Crow.* Lincoln, Neb.: University of Nebraska Press, 1979.

Jewish Lesbians:

A Conversation with

Irena Klepfisz

Interviewed by Ginny Vida

Irena Klepfisz.

Linda Eber

You write in your book, *Dreams of an Insomniac: Jewish Feminist Essays, Speeches and Diatribes*, about being an immigrant and a Holocaust survivor. What was the experience of you and your family?

I was born a Jew in Warsaw, Poland, during the war, and my parents placed me in a Catholic orphanage for my protection. My father, who was a member of the Jewish resistance, was killed in the Warsaw Ghetto uprising. My mother was on the Aryan side.[1] After the uprising, she got me from the orphanage and we were in hiding for the rest of the war. A year later we went to Sweden and waited for three years for visas to the United States. We entered the States in 1949. We lived in the Bronx. I attended public and Yiddish school there.

After high school, I went to City College, then took a year off to go to Europe and Israel. When I returned, I went to graduate school and got my Ph.D. in English from the University of Chicago. I taught for four years on the Brooklyn campus of Long Island University. It was the only full-time academic job I've ever had. I was instantly on terminal contract because the school was experiencing enrollment drops. After four years I lost my job in what had become a very tight academic market.

When did you begin to deal with your attraction to women?

In 1973, right after I was laid off, I had my first relationship with a woman. I was thirty-three and took that year off and lived in Montauk, Long Island. During that period I collected unemployment and fulfilled a dream of mine, which was to live by the ocean and write. While I was out there I sort of mulled over what this affair meant to me. By the time I got back to Brooklyn I knew this was the direction I was going to go in. It took me a year to decide. I do not know whether that is long or short. To some people it would seem very short, since some agonize for a lifetime.

In many ways I was very lucky, because some of the first lesbians I met were Blanche Cook and Clare Coss, who got me in touch with Joan Larkin. Joan was forming a writing support group, which I joined. Jan Clausen was a member, and through her and Joan I met Elly Bulkin. As a result of those encounters, we created what was initially a fictitious publishing company, Out & Out Books. In the first year, Joan, Jan, and I each self-published our own poetry collections and Joan and Elly published *Amazon Poetry*. This was in 1976. Later, Joan made

Out & Out Books into a real press that issued books, pamphlets, broadsides, and a record by such writers as Audre Lorde, Adrienne Rich, Blanche Cook, Honor Moore, and others.

Almost immediately after the initial four books, Elly, Jan, Rima Shore, and I founded *Conditions* magazine. We felt very strongly that there needed to be an ongoing alternative outlet for creative writing, politics, and book reviews that supported the exploding feminist and lesbian feminist movements. We wanted to give ourselves and other lesbians space to publish. Of course, *Sinister Wisdom* was already around, and there were *Chrysalis* and *Heresies*, but we felt more outlets were needed.

Strictly speaking, *Conditions* was not a lesbian magazine. The original subtitle was *A Magazine of Women's Writing with an Emphasis on Writing by Lesbians*. This reflected our commitment to publishing not only lesbians but also women of color and poor and working-class women. I stayed with *Conditions* for five years, and the magazine lasted another seven with changes in collective members.

I believe it was a very important journal. It published a lot of people we now take for granted, but who in the late seventies and early eighties were really just beginning their careers—people like Barbara Smith (who was coeditor of *Conditions Five: The Black Women's Issues*—which ultimately grew into *Home Girls*), Dorothy Allison, Jewelle Gomez, Cheryl Clarke, Minnie Bruce Pratt. We also published established writers like Adrienne Rich and Alice Walker and also Audre Lorde, who was certainly already known, but still did not have the reputation she had when she died.

Did you have any problem reconciling your Jewish and lesbian identities?

Coming out had enormous repercussions on me, in terms of my connection with the Jewish community as well as with the heterosexual community. Dealing with my lesbian identity in the Jewish community was very hard. By the time I was thirty-three I was already an oddity because I was not married. I was an only child, and I was the last of my father's family. Particularly as a survivor I felt an unstated, enormous pressure to get married and have children. As a community, Jews had lost 6 mil-

lion people during the war. I had grown up with the idea that the next generation—meaning *my* generation—had an obligation to rebuild the community—demographically, that is. And here I was unmarried and childless. Coming out as a lesbian made me even more of an oddity, to say the least. It was very hard when I encountered Jewish homophobia. I had always relied on Jews—particularly survivors, people who were most like me and shared my experience—for total understanding. Suddenly, I was an outsider.

My mother, aside from what she felt personally—and she was really upset about it—was really worried about the danger: "They don't like you already because you are a Jew. You don't have to add something else onto this that they are not going to like."

How was it in the non-Jewish world—straight and lesbian?

My work and social life were rooted in a mixed Jewish and non-Jewish world. I don't think I kept any of my heterosexual friends after I came out. I don't know whether that was my fault or theirs. The lesbian movement was very defined in the seventies and eighties and, though many of us were *not* separatists in our ideology (in fact we often argued vehemently with separatists), we were quite separate in how we organized our lives. I simply didn't know how to interact socially with heterosexuals. And I don't think they knew how to interact with me. Today some may find that hard to imagine, but then it was a very, very different time.

I think I felt even more confused because I came out at the same time that I lost my job. I was someone who had grown up poor. Academia was supposed to be a way out. Most of my friends were academics and we all defined ourselves by our work. After I was laid off, when people asked "What do you do?" I didn't know what to say. So in addition to other people's responses to me, I had to deal with my own shock of doing office work again, something I thought I'd left behind in graduate school.

But it was also hard for me in the lesbian community. I did not have enough political sophistication to analyze some of the things I was experiencing, particularly around money and class. Downward mobility was in vogue, something I didn't understand at all. It was so against my own experience. I did *not* want to do office work. I wanted to teach. I'd been raised a socialist and thought it was important to improve the material conditions of people. It was just a question of not improving them at someone else's expense. But the economic inequalities among us lesbians were something that neither I nor for that matter anyone else I was associated with at the time was ready to deal with—not even just by naming them. It was essentially dishonest. Money and class were, for me, really painful issues, particularly as a Jew. I have to say, it's the one political area that I don't think has improved much—in theory or practice.

But at the same time, the lesbian movement liberated me in an important way—a Jewish way. I had spent most of my twenties dealing psychologically with myself as a survivor, dealing with the war. A close friend of mine, a child survivor who had been orphaned, committed suicide. I had to come to terms with that. So that's what I was preoccupied with. I was just trying to figure out how I would get past 1945. Coming out as a lesbian was very important because it helped pull me into the present. As a writer, I had always been worried that I would never write about anything but the Holocaust. So, after I came out, I realized there are things to write about besides the Holocaust. I saw that my present life was important, that there are political issues that are very, very immediate.

You have written that Jewish lesbians have tended to downplay their Jewishness in the context of the lesbian feminist community.

In the lesbian community anti-Semitism was complicated, because some of it was subtle and unstated. No one called me a "kike." It wasn't anything like that. It was very complicated in terms of politics, particularly around Israel and Zionism and anti-Zionism. In 1981 I wrote my first analysis of this, called "Anti-Semitism in the Lesbian/Feminist Movement," which appeared in *Womanews*. The essay tries to deal with the subtleties of what many Jewish lesbians were experiencing. By June of 1982, when *Nice Jewish Girls: A Lesbian Anthology* was published and Israel had invaded Lebanon, it seemed impossible for a lesbian to say that she was Jewish without someone asking her about her position on the Palestinians. There was nothing comparable. I knew Israeli dykes who were afraid to admit they were Israelis in lesbian and feminist groups.

It was a very complicated issue and I was basically uneducated both about Israel and the Palestinians. Jewish lesbians had to become educated and it became a real struggle. Some of the criticism of Israeli policy was sincere and some of it veiled anti-Semitism. It created real strains between Jewish and non-Jewish lesbians. But attitudes toward Israel also created chaos among Jewish lesbians. We had bitter fights, and people ended up not speaking to each other for years. Elly Bulkin documents in detail much of this history in her extended essay in *Yours in Struggle*.

There were other questions we faced in the lesbian community, such as: Where do Jews fit in? Are they white? Are they nonwhite? None of them very different than questions raised outside the Jewish community. As Jewish lesbians began to focus on Jewish culture and discuss assimilation, Jewish history, and anti-Semitism, we understood we belonged in multicultural coalitions. But often we were rejected on the basis of race (which assumes all Jews are European and white), and sometimes on the basis of class (which assumes all Jews are rich).

Though Jews are often perceived as a monolithic group, we are an international, multicultural, and multiracial people. Jews have lived all over the world and don't even look alike. Take the Jews in Israel. Some came from Eastern Europe, some from Arab countries and Africa. They look like other people who come from those areas.

Also the stereotype that Jews run everything made it difficult for Jewish lesbians to feel good about their achievements. It was, and still is, hard to take pride in them, and we always felt we had to tone it down. So there were multiple reasons why Jewish dykes had trouble asserting their Jewishness within the movement.

Did that change at all? How?

One of the things that helped to change attitudes within the lesbian movement was the emergence of an Israeli Women's Peace Movement. When that occurred, the stigma around Israel and Israeli lesbians began to fade. Many Jewish lesbians worked in support of that Israeli movement. I was one of the cofounders of the Jewish Women's Committee to End the Occupation of the West Bank and Gaza. In a way, Jewish lesbians and Jewish feminists in the United States became more accepted and legitimized within the broader movement as a result of the Israeli peace movement. Today there is a book of interviews in English with Israeli lesbians, *Lesbiot*. It's the first book of its kind. I don't think that book would have been possible ten years ago.

I think there are other signs that things have improved, such as the Jewish feminist magazine *Bridges*. That journal is much more secular and approaches issues with what I would call "seventies politics." It's not a lesbian journal, but a number of the collective members are dykes and it publishes a lot about Jewish lesbians. It's ironic, though, that *Bridges*, with its seventies politics, would not have been possible in the seventies. At that time most dykes (Jewish and non-Jewish) didn't have the consciousness to support such an endeavor and heterosexual feminists (Jewish and non-Jewish) hadn't worked through enough of their homophobia to support anything that gave significant visibility to lesbians.

Within the Jewish Community there has certainly been more visibility through the lesbian-gay synagogues. I am not in that group, because I am not observant. I'm much more active in trying to integrate lesbians into the secular Jewish community. But certainly within the more organized Jewish community, the Jewish gay and lesbian synagogues are very visible. We don't have total acceptance by any means, but we now have gay and lesbian rabbis.

In your book you mention parallels between gays and Jews. Could you elaborate on this?

I think Jews and lesbian and gay people have a lot in common. Neither group is bound by race, class, or ethnicity. That is one similarity. There is a whole class issue on how lesbians and gays are perceived, especially gay men, in terms of having money. This is very similar to the way Jews are always perceived as having money and being in control. Also, gay and Jewish sense of "outsidedness" is very similar.

I think that at various moments throughout history there has been a convergence of Jew hatred and gay and lesbian hatred. I think of the periods of the Black Plague, witch burning, the Inquisition, and so on. The Holocaust, too, but lesbians were not so much the victims as were gay men. There is a kind of "pariah" status that both groups have that should make us allies, which would make us stronger, but which unfortunately hasn't been realized on a large scale. I'm always baffled how when I go into one group I experience one prejudice, and when I go into another group I experience another prejudice. But I think that on both sides there has been movement toward dealing with these problems—of course, not enough.

Today there is a rise in anti-Semitism, in homophobia, and in racism. None of these is individual—it's a package deal. I can't imagine, for example, someone who hates Blacks or Latinos who would like Jews and gays. And I can't imagine someone who despises Jews who would like Blacks or gays. Isolated prejudices don't exist. That's why it's depressing to meet lesbians who think their only threat is homophobia and Jews who think their only threat is anti-Semitism. It's a cliché, but it's true: No one's safe until we're all safe. And if we personally are not being threatened at a specific moment in a specific situation, we shouldn't assume that we're secure. What we should assume is that they haven't gotten around to us yet.

As I said, in terms of individual communities, things have changed and improved for lesbians. But in some ways, despite the improvement, I think it's harder for lesbians and gays because we *appear* to have such greater acceptance in the mainstream and, as a result, the movement is less coherent. Without a coherent, visible, organized movement it's hard to struggle effectively against the right.

I know there are younger lesbian writers, for example, who have only published with mainstream presses. I often wonder if that's really the way to go. At one point we had so many presses, journals, and bookstores. As the mainstream has picked up gay writers, we've lost our own institutions. Is that good? Yes, things are better—but there's been a price. Jewish lesbians' experiences mirror everyone else's experiences. I don't know if it's gotten better for everybody or whether it's gotten better only for individuals. It's sort of hard to gauge. I personally believe in alternative institutions. I regret that lesbian institutions have dwindled.

People always put down tokenism, and I do, too. I don't like being a token, but I think tokenism is a step in the process. I just wish it were a shorter step.

For lesbians and gays, I think there is more tokenism within the Jewish community than before. I hate to say it, and other people will also say it: AIDS has played a part in this process. It has opened up many communities to gays. How deep the tolerance is, that's another question.

My measure of tolerance is yes, you'll tolerate a sick gay person, but what would you do if one of your children announced that he or she was gay or lesbian? That is always the test. Or are you comfortable with having gay or lesbian teachers in your children's school? I'm sure some of these areas have gotten better, but many of them haven't moved at all. A couple of years ago there was enormous controversy around the proposal to include lesbian-gay issues in the Rainbow Curriculum in the New York City schools. The curriculum was never implemented. And in December 1995 two lesbian activists in Oregon were murdered. It's scary.

Still, I was a keynote speaker at a major Jewish feminist conference in San Francisco last month, and I've been invited to speak at a Jewish conference in Toronto. At both I was invited as an "out" lesbian, and they don't seem to have a problem with it. I think it still depends on the organization. Some still won't tolerate it, beyond helping someone who has AIDS—if they tolerate that. Other organizations will be very supportive.

Also, I just helped organize a conference, "*Di Froyen*: Women & Yiddish," sponsored by the National Council of Jewish Women, and there were a lot of lesbians present. We had a workshop on Jewish lesbian identity that was listed in the advance program. At this conference there were about ten or twelve "out" lesbians whose bios reflected their lesbian identity. The National Council of Jewish Women New York Section is a progressive organization within the Jewish mainstream that is doing very important work and is obviously comfortable with lesbian programming.

What contributions have Jewish lesbians made to the Jewish community?

Here's an example: For the past five years, I have been going to a week-long gathering called "Klezkamp," a Yiddish arts festival originally founded around klezmer music, Jewish music that stems from Eastern Europe. Klezkamp is essentially a straight event attended by about 450 people. But a lot of lesbians and gays come to this festival; when we have a gay and lesbian party, it draws about fifty people.

This year it was very interesting, because the featured performer was Sarah Felder, who appeared in her two-act one-woman show *June Bride: A Traditional Jewish Lesbian Wedding*. And what she describes in this hour and twenty-five minute play is the process of her and her lover getting married. The performance was seen by about 450 people. It was the only event going on at that time. Sarah was truly remarkable. At Klezkamp there are sometimes tensions around lesbian and gay visibility. Some people are unprepared for it. But this year Sarah got a standing ovation.

Sarah's play *June Bride* is a very creative contribution to Jewish cultural life. It enriches the whole community and transforms Jewish consciousness. A magazine like *Bridges* is very important because it helps to change the Jewish landscape. Jewish lesbians also strengthen feminism and Jewish feminism. They are not moving away from the community, they are moving into it—and in the process changing it.

I've been pushed into more Jewish work by the lesbian feminist movement than I would have ever expected. I'm not sure if I hadn't come out, I would be doing this. For example, I wrote an introduction for an anthology of Yiddish women writers, *Found Treasures*. It took a kind of lesbian militancy to push me in that direction. I am not sure I would have done it, nor pushed to that degree, had it not been for my own lesbian feminism. This is enriching all the way around.

Note

1. "Aryan side" refers to any place outside the Ghetto.

RESOURCES

Bridges: A Journal for Jewish Feminists and Our Friends. $15 for two issues a year. Jewish art, poetry, fiction, political essays, reviews. POB 24839, Eugene, OR 97402.

Dreams of an Insomniac: Jewish Feminist Essays, Speeches and Diatribes, Irena Klepfisz (Eighth Mountain, 1990).

Exile in the Promised Land: A Memoir, Marcia Freedman (Firebrand, 1990).

Hemshekh: Feminist Institute for Secular Jewish Cultural Continuity. Plans educational, cultural, bilingual, political materials for adults and young people. POB 879, Veneta, OR 97487.

Jewish Women's Committee to End the Occupation of the West Bank and Gaza (JWCEO). Papers archived as Document Group 179, Swarthmore College, Peace Collection, 500 College Avenue, Swarthmore, PA 19081 (610) 328-8557.

Jewish Women's Call for Peace: A Handbook for Jewish Women on the Israeli/Palestinian Conflict, eds. Rita Falbel et al. (Firebrand, 1990).

Lesbiot: Israeli Lesbians Talk About Sexuality, Feminism, Judaism and Their Lives, ed. Tracy Moore (Cassell, 1995).

Nice Jewish Girls: A Lesbian Anthology, ed. Evelyn T. Beck (Persephone Press, 1982; Beacon Press, 1988).

Speaking for Ourselves: Short Stories by Jewish Lesbians, ed. Irene Zahava (Crossing, 1990).

The Tribe of Dina: A Jewish Women's Anthology, eds. Melanie Kaye/Kantrowitz and Irena Klepfisz (Sinister Wisdom, 1986; Beacon Press, 1989).

Twice Blessed: On Being Lesbian, Gay and Jewish, eds. Christie Balka and Andy Rose (Beacon, 1989).

Yours in Struggle: Three Feminist Perspectives on Anti-Semitism and Racism, Elly Bulkin, Minnie Bruce Pratt, Barbara Smith (Long Haul, 1984; Firebrand, 1986).

Young Lesbians:

Monique and Nicole

Joan Jubela

(Editor's Note: The following self-portraits of Monique Gonzalez and Nicole Charles have been excerpted from Homoteens, *a documentary video about gay and lesbian youth compiled and directed by Joan Jubela and the young people themselves. The video portrays the realities lesbian and gay teenagers face in their daily lives, documenting their struggles to assert their identities in a homophobic society.*

Monique Gonzalez is a twenty-year-old Latina lesbian living in New York City who left home and dropped out of school when she was fifteen. She saw the move as the only possible way to preserve her identity amidst the hysteria that resulted when she told her family she was a lesbian.)

MONIQUE: When I first came out I was actually very feminine. I had long hair and wore big earrings and wore pink all the time. And I ended up in a hall with this butch and she was coming on to me and I was like "No I'm sorry," and she said, "What's the matter, you don't like women like me?" And I said, "No, I don't," and she said, "Well, honey, you'd better change your clothes and change your hair if you want to get any other woman." So I did.

I called up everyone in my immediate family and I told them I wanted to meet with them, and they all came up with the idea that I was pregnant, which was pretty hysterical, when I came out and said I was a lesbian. Actually, I don't think I said I was a lesbian; I said I was gay. I think at that point I wasn't comfortable with saying "lesbian" yet.

There was the yelling and the tears, and my mother crying and my aunt telling her that it was all her fault because she didn't give me the right upbringing. And my cousin, who was in college, was like "Wow, can't you at least be bisexual?" My grandmother was like "What's wrong, Moe? You want to be a boy?" "No, Grandma. I don't want to be a boy. I know who I am, I just love other women." She just looked at me like I was a total freak.

This past year I moved four times. It's really annoying. When I moved at fifteen (when I left home), I just had a suitcase already packed up because I had a feeling I would have to be leaving suddenly or very soon.

I had a friend of mine over who was straight, who I had just come out to, and she was in my room and we had the door closed, and they totally freaked out. They thought I was doing something with her, so they were banging on the door, like "Open the door, open the door!" Then they started yelling at me and yelling at her to get out of the house. I was really embarrassed. This was just a straight friend, who I had just come out to, so she was already a little freaked out, and then they were accusing her of messing around with me.

Then me and my aunt got into a little bit of a physical fight, and my cousin came walking in and grabbed my suitcase. Then she just drove me off, drove me away. And that was it.

I guess I didn't have all the experiences fifteen-year-olds have, you know, because I had to work, but I was happy anyway, because I was able to be who I was, and that was what was most important to me.

The high school I went to was a Catholic, all-girl high school—uniforms, the whole bit. I dropped out of school because I knew I would be harassed, and I just couldn't deal with it. I didn't want to deal with it. I wanted to just be me, and go do what I needed to do. And I did.

I'm the coat check at the Clit Club. I have contact with 80 to 90 percent of the women who come to the Clit Club, especially on Friday nights, so there's an opportunity right there for them to strike up a conversation if they find me attractive, and to tip me very well, you know. . . . When I was seventeen, eighteen, my friends used to call me Don Juan and all these other names.

I was ecstatic about being a lesbian, and everyone else was freaking out and being really negative. Just loving another woman was so incredible. It was just such an incredible feeling; it was so real, it was so right. I never, ever, ever felt anything like that when I was going out with boys.

It's really strange, because I can't believe I dropped out of high school, and that I didn't even get my GED, and that I haven't been to college, because I just feel like my mentality is beyond that. There are a lot of important things in my life right now: independence, freedom. I need to spend a lot of time by myself. I need to stop messing around with all these women. I just have to get things straight in my life. I need to go to school, to do a lot of things for me.

(Nicole Charles is a nineteen-year-old African American lesbian living in a group home in New York City. Her sexual orientation runs contrary to her religious upbringing as a Jehovah's Witness, and as a result of it, she is no longer welcome in the church. But Nicki is no victim. She asserts that she is "a normal teenager going through the normal day-to-day thing. I'm in love. It's not a man, so what!")

NICOLE (sitting on the Christopher Street pier): I used to come here every day when I first came out. When I hit thirteen, I knew, I mean, I always knew, but it was thirteen [when I first came out]. And then, I started going out with guys. [I thought] still, maybe I could change, maybe I just needed that one good piece of beef, like everybody says, or that one good man to really change me. And when I did get that guy, still, something felt incomplete in the relationship. And I knew what it was, I knew it, but I just couldn't . . . I didn't want to accept it, because I was like, "Oh my god. Will I start looking like a man? How will I react? How will I view life?" And it seems like since I came out, I view life so much more positively, even when things are down. I know who I am, which, to me, a lot of people can't say they know who they are. At least I know my sexuality, which is the biggest thing.

I'm out of the closet. Two of my ex-boyfriends live in my house. For one of them, it took a really long time to get used to me, but now we're good friends, and he accepts it. I didn't even tell him, he heard it through the grapevine, and the reason why I didn't tell him is because I know how men's pride is and that he's really homophobic. We would sit up in the room, and he would be saying "faggots this and faggots that." I couldn't tell him because I knew he was going to be upset.

I still keep some of my Jehovah's Witness doctrines, because that's what I was born with; that's how I think. I kind of excommunicated myself, but if I was still in the faith, and going to the Kingdom Hall and everything, they would disassociate me out of the organization until I changed. Yeah, it hurts, because most of my friends were all Jehovah's Witnesses and I considered those my true, true friends, but they don't talk to me now, because I don't go to the Kingdom Hall. So you know, if I told them I was a homosexual, how they would re-act to that. And that's the biggest thing; that is a sin beyond a sin. I'm another Sodom and Gomorrah, you know.

When I was younger, being with guys, I used to want to kill myself every single day. I was scared to accept my feelings of who I was. Since Maria [her lover], I've come more out of the closet than before. When I [first] saw Maria, I was like "Oh my god, she's so hot." It was a lust thing when I first saw her. We see each other every day. We've missed two days in a month and two weeks.

I've had so many people since I've come out tell me that it's a phase, and then trying to brainwash me to be a different way. I'm just a normal teenager going through the normal day-to-day thing. I'm in love. It's not a man, so what!

Midlife as a Creative Time for Lesbians

Barbara E. Sang, Ph.D.

When I turned forty, I felt the need to reassess my life—where I had been, where I was going. Curious to know whether other midlife adults were having the same conflicts and experiences, I turned to books and articles. Most of the midlife literature was about men, but as a result of the women's movement, there was a growing body of research on midlife women. To my surprise and disappointment, however, there was no mention of midlife lesbians. I was able to identify with some of the issues and changes reported for heterosexual women at this time of life, but, on the whole, these findings did not speak to me. I wondered if midlife lesbians as a group had their own unique experience.

This led me to interview my midlife lesbian acquaintances and friends, and to run a number of workshops and discussion groups with my colleague, Joyce Warshow. Certain themes began to emerge which eventually led me to do research in this area.[1] I also coedited an anthology with Joyce Warshow and Adrienne Smith on different aspects of lesbian midlife such as health, menopause, sexuality, body image, relationships, spirituality, and finances. Although our findings may not necessarily apply to all lesbians, the main thread that ran through these different areas was that midlife is a creative time for lesbians—hence the title: *Lesbians at Midlife: The Creative Transition.* In what follows I will discuss what it is about the lives of lesbians that makes this a creative time.

The time period in which today's midlife lesbians grew up was a particularly oppressive one for women. Women who had careers, interests outside of the home, or were athletic were considered to be abnormal. Women were encouraged to support their husbands' work and creativity but not their own. Lillian Rubin's research on middle-aged women suggests that for many heterosexuals, mid-life is a time in which women are searching for their own identities, separate from those of their children and husbands. Many of them are working for the first time, or getting in touch with what interests them.[2]

In contrast, many of the lesbians I have spoken with in the course of my research on lesbians in midlife became self-supporting in their twenties and have continued to work and to develop their numerous interests over time. They have also spent a lifetime fighting to express themselves, and they feel that this has contributed to their having developed a strong sense of self. Ravenna Helson,[3] a researcher who is known for her studies on creative women, has found that women who are impulsive, rebellious, and rejecting of outside influence, as many lesbians are compelled to be simply to express their identity, are likely to show creative achievement.

It appears that many lesbians were nontraditional for girls of their age. While most heterosexual women are reported to have "traditional life dreams" in adolescence, that is, becoming a wife and mother,[4] many lesbians dreamed of careers and adventure.[5] Lesbians also described themselves as bookish and physically active as adolescents. Because lesbians seem to have been self-directed and multifaceted in earlier years, it is likely that they have many more resources to draw from at midlife.

In addition to the importance of work or career, it has been noted that lesbians have many personal interests and hobbies, for instance, gardening, painting, gourmet cooking, sports, concerts, politics, and spirituality.[6] Not only may lesbians live a creative lifestyle, but the diversity of their interests probably also enhances creativity in their work and relationships. Mary Bateson makes the case that individuals having multiple commitments or roles are more creative—more open to complexity and new possibilities, compared to the traditional male focus on a single goal.[7]

Lesbians in midlife are in their prime; they have been working most of their adult lives and therefore have a great deal of experience with independence and with meeting their own needs. Their work itself often becomes easier, less stressful, and more satisfying. They feel less of a need to push themselves than they did in their twenties and thirties. Many women also express a desire to have more fun and to be less achievement-oriented. Paradoxically, what seems to be happening is that as these women are "pushing" less, they are in a better position to be

creative, which helps them to perform better in their careers or in outside interests.

Having developed their work, relationships, and special interests throughout their adult lives, at midlife many lesbians feel a need for rituals and symbols that express that knowledge and maturity. In our culture, the status of wise person has traditionally been reserved for men. "Croning Celebration,"[8] a party to honor the importance of women's transition into aging, is one way in which contemporary midlife women, particularly lesbians, have acknowledged the wisdom that comes with age.

Lesbians who are at midlife today have had few role models for aging, and are therefore pioneers, in that they had to invent and create their own lives as they went along. Several lesbians at midlife told me of their wish to share their experience with younger women, and to serve as role models. It is also the lesbians who are now in midlife who have been instrumental in creating social change.

The lesbians I have spoken with state that at midlife they have become less concerned with what people think of them and with pleasing others. For these women, midlife is a time to be oneself, to be more spontaneous and inner-directed. One woman declared that "from a young age I felt that I had no control over my life, but lived it the way others expected me to. Now I live the way I want to, knowing who I am and being able to do the things that are important to me, and it does not matter to me what other people think." This demonstrates that there is a relationship between personal authenticity and creativity. When a woman is able to be herself, she is free to take risks and to be more open, playful, and flexible.

Although the lesbians I spoke to reported midlife to be the best time in their lives, many also indicated that they had what might be called a "midlife crisis." A crisis could be a relationship breakup, an illness, or a recognition of one's own limitations. What seemed to characterize a crisis for these women was their lack of control over both the crisis-provoking event and the way in which it was perceived. But a crisis need not have a negative outcome, especially since at midlife we are in a better position to deal with whatever life has to offer.

Other lesbians I spoke with indicated that they had deliberately made changes in their lives at midlife such as changing careers, "coming out," or leaving a relationship that was not working. Both a "crisis" and a deliberate change force the individual to reevaluate her needs and priorities, which stimulates the process of growth and development. One woman who discovered she had cancer got in touch with her need to live in the country and to spend more time working with her hands. Now, for the first time in her life, she is making pottery and feels a sense of joy. She has also found a more suitable community for friendship and support. This change in lifestyle has been a rebirth for her.

Another kind of change that often takes place in midlife is a letting go of "shoulds," or beliefs about the world or possessions one has outgrown. This "letting go" frees the individual to see things in new ways. Midlife is a time to integrate and transform many aspects of the self. Interests or pursuits that may have been abandoned become important again. For example, one woman who had not written poetry since adolescence is getting in touch with her creative side by beginning to write again at midlife.

A prevalent theme for lesbians in midlife is balance: the need to balance relationships, work, family, outside interests, community participation, and spirituality. They struggle to find a place for the various aspects of their lives, which is difficult, but revitalizing. Once again, the lesbian is put in a position of actively shaping her life and defining her priorities.

Lesbians at midlife are in their prime. This time can be the best time in their lives because of the freedom it brings. With a considerable amount of work and life experience under the belt, and with greater self-confidence and self-awareness, this is a time to be creative.

Despite the fact that the subject of midlife development has become an extremely popular one over the last decade, lesbians as a group continue to be invisible in this area. We are never mentioned in midlife women's newsletters, such as *Hot Flash* or *Midlife Women's Network*, nor are we included in most of the midlife health research. Currently, we know very little about the lives of women who have both worked and had relationships throughout most of their adult lives, and who therefore bring their own unique experience to midlife. At this time, we also know very little about the ways in which variables such as motherhood, race, abledness, and class affect the midlife lesbian experience. Clearly, there is much we can learn about women's adult development by studying women who have not taken a traditional path. It is my impression that midlife lesbians are a resourceful, creative, and fulfilled group of women.

Notes

1. Barbara Sang, "Moving Toward Balance and Integration," in B. Sang, J. Warshow, and A. Smith, eds., *Lesbians at Midlife: The Creative Transition* (San Francisco: Spinster, 1991), 206–11.
2. Lillian Rubin, *Women of a Certain Age: The Midlife Search for Self* (New York: Harper & Row, 1979).
3. Ravenna Helson, "Women Mathematicians and the Creative Personality," *Journal of Counseling and Clinical Psychology* 36 (1972): 210–20.
4. Priscilla Roberts and Peter Newton, "Levinsonian Studies of Women's Adult Development," *Psychology and Aging* 2 (1987): 145–63.
5. Barbara Sang, "Reflections of Midlife Lesbians on Their Adolescence," in E. Rosenthal, ed., *Women, Aging and Ageism* (Binghamton, N.Y.: Haworth Press, 1990), 111–17.
6. Martha Kirkpatrick, "Lesbians: a Different Middle-age?," in J. Oldham and R. Liebert, eds., *New Psychoanalytic Perspectives: The Middle Years* (New Haven, Conn.: Yale University Press, 1989), 135–48.
7. Mary Catherine Bateson, *Composing a Life* (New York: Plume, 1990).
8. Jacqueline Gentry and Faye Seifert, "A Joyous Passage: Becoming a Crone," in B. Sang, J. Warshow, and A. Smith, eds., *Lesbians at Midlife: The Creative Transition* (San Francisco: Spinster, 1991), 223–33.

Aging Lesbians

An Interview with Buffy Dunker

I came out when I was seventy-two years old. I had been playing softball with a group of women, and there was a gathering of them at a friend's house. One of the women, who was very attractive, very interesting, full of life and energy, was paying attention to me. We began to date, we fell in love, and it was wonderful. That was thirteen years ago.

I also came out publicly. I was interviewed for an article that appeared on the front page of the Living Section of the *Boston Globe*. This was both amusing and uncomfortable. But it's been fine because I've met so many wonderful friends in the lesbian community—though I'm not now as active as I was some years ago.

The woman I fell in love with is now my best friend. The intensity of the sexual relationship didn't last very long. She was nonmonogamous, and I was pretty unsophisticated about lesbian relationships. Now I see her nearly every day. We share a dog together, and when she's working, I get the dog. I rely on her; we do a lot of things together.

It's really important, I think, for old lesbians to keep alive with friends. It's easy to let oneself get isolated. Our own contemporaries die off, it's harder to make new friends, and younger people don't pay much attention to us. It's the isolation that all old people face. But the isolation is greater for lesbians, because they tend to want to be only with women. This cuts down on the number of friends they have. Heterosexuals are not so exclusive.

I get along easily with people younger than myself. I taught high school age kids for quite a number of years, so I've been connected with younger people most of my life. I'm fortunate, too, to have enjoyed good health through the years. And I also have a large number of descendants.

(*Editor's Note: The following excerpts are from "Aging Lesbians: Observations and Speculations," by Buffy Dunker, in* Lesbian Psychologies: Explorations and Challenges, *the Boston Lesbians Psychologies Collective, eds., [University of Illinois Press, Urbana and Chicago, 1987], 72–82.*)

Defining "old" as being more than sixty-five means that all of us older lesbians were born before the 1930s. We've lived through some tremendous economic, scientific, social, and political changes.... But we are still struggling with the same old oppressions of ageism, sexism, poverty, and racism, and we're still at the bottom of the economic pile.

During the late sixties and early seventies, the power of the women's movement, the slowly growing social acceptance of homosexuality, and the appearance of lesbian and gay communities in some of the big cities made it possible for some older lesbians to come out publicly. That was also a time when quite a number of older women left their marriages. We can assume that many of them were lesbians, because a high percentage of older lesbians have been previously married. Still, a lot of us who had early on accepted and honored our sexuality knew that coming out to others carried too great a risk, socially and economically.

Many older lesbians are now retired, and perhaps some are financially secure enough so that the strong economic reasons for staying hidden aren't so overriding.... So why not come out?

It is hard to change at any age, and for old people it is often harder.... For many, whose relatives and close friends have never known of their secret, the risks are too great, especially the risk of exposing their deception to people who love them as they have always known them.

The lesbian has had to be self-supporting, and the conventional married woman has not. The old lesbian, especially the lesbian of color, has had to deal with the hazards of oppression, exclusion, and prejudice. The wife has held an honored although secondary position in a society with many heterosexual privileges. The lesbian has had to seek her own friends, lovers, and communities. The wife took her place in the well-established society of couples. The lesbian has been in charge of her life, making choices of work, recreation, and companions as she wished. The wife has had to please others in most areas; even the kind of meals she prepared and the way she brought up the children often had to conform to her husband's wishes.

One aspect of aging that's hard for many women is the way the body changes. Skin loses its elasticity, and wrinkles, bulges, and flab appear. Hair goes gray or white, and muscles and joints get stiff. The conventional woman often accepts the male stereotypes of beauty and youth, and either mourns or fights the change.... Lesbians can reject the male standards. We can appreciate the quality of our own changes as we see what's happening to the faces and figures of the women we love. Our ideas of beauty aren't necessarily subject to male fantasies.

It's still common for women to stick with their husbands in spite of incompatibilities.... But for lesbians, there is less pressure to stay together if the relationship isn't mutually fulfilling. They can separate (and often become good friends) and perhaps find new partners. Moreover, they can look for younger partners as well as older.... Age differences aren't so important for a lesbian....

Heterosexual women are by definition confined to men for the expression of their sexuality. As they age they usually face an imbalance of sexual interest.... No such problem arises for lesbians. We change and develop pretty much according to the same pattern, so our sexuality can be as varied and as satisfying as we want.

The possibilities of enjoying the advantages and privileges of age and at least mitigating its inevitable disadvantages are greater for a woman who has been in charge of her life during most of it. Old lesbians are in a good position for that.... We can ignore the stereotypes and take risks: climb mountains, start a new career, go on bike trips, take cello lessons, become an actor or painter, learn to ski, write a book, adopt a protégé. We can even throw our Puritan consciences out the window and loaf. We can be peculiar, cranky, and funny, and we can dress as we like.

Previously married old lesbians have had some special concerns. Most of us married young ... and had our children while we were still in our twenties.... We had to deal with long-established habits of dependency, few marketable and emotionally satisfying skills, diminished income, and a dwindling circle of friends and family.... We had to accept the loss of heterosexual privileges and face up to the usual homophobic prejudice and exclusion. Instead of (or along with) the problem of coming out to parents, we had to come out to our children.

If we are going to live the last part of our lives to the full, it's essential to plan ahead; lesbians younger than sixty-five must be involved in the necessary planning.... We will have to be creative about new

Daniel H. Erlich

Buffy Dunker.

kinds of living arrangements such as congregate housing, shared living, projects with populations of differing age and economic levels. In a rural area, a few old lesbians might find a large house where they could live together for support, protection, and good times.

Good legal protection is vital so that a lesbian can be sure that her property goes where she wants it to, and not to others who may feel they have a right to it. It's essential to make a will, including instructions for funeral and other plans. A Living Will can state decisions about extraordinary medical procedures to prolong life. Insurance policies and wills can be specific, drawn up well enough to withstand any protests. We have the right to die as we have lived, with dignity and independence.

Old lesbians have few role models, and it's clear

that we'll have to fill that function for younger ones.... It's imperative that older lesbians find younger friends. They need us, too. The old crone, the wise woman, the witch have always been valued in many cultures. We can ensure that they are valued here, as well.

Lesbians with Disabilities

Janet Weinberg

(Editor's Note: The following was edited from an interview.)

My name is Janet Weinberg, and I've been a member of the lesbian community for seventeen years. I'm an occupational therapist. I also have a physical disability that causes me to have mobility problems. I'm in a wheelchair. I usually work with adolescents and young adults, many with disabilities. I'm also on the board of a group called Education in a Disabled Gay Environment (EDGE) and also serve on the board of the Center for Independence of the Disabled of New York (CIDNY). It's one of the independent living centers. I've been fairly active in the issues since I became disabled three and a half years ago. I'm thirty-five, so it's still new to me—how to get around and what I do. I still have anger because of structural barriers. I see people who are born with a disability, or who have been disabled longer than I, accept the fact that there are places we can't get into. Acceptance comes with time, and I haven't had that much time yet.

I have a disability called autonomic neuropathy. I literally spent twelve hours at work one day, came home, sat down, stood up again, and the next thing I knew I was on the floor. I was taken to the hospital with a skull fracture and fractured nose. It took a long time to diagnose my ailment; nobody quite figured out why I had blacked out. I spent many months getting diagnosed, and in the meantime, I was getter sicker. I have a brother who's a physician and he told me, "All your symptoms have to be related. Don't let them discharge you and don't let them tell you that you have four different medical problems." It was good advice because finally one doctor was able to diagnose the syndrome.

I had been an occupational therapist and had worked in hospitals. To be bedridden and see it from the reverse was a frightening experience. As a lesbian, it was also frightening. I had been involved

© Natt Nevins

Janet Weinberg on the Brooklyn Bridge.

walking is like because I don't want this damned thing." I tested my limits over and over again, and each time I would fall. At some point I said, "Enough." But I'm a fighter, and my instinct was, "Damnit, I'm not going to be shut in," and I started racing the wheelchair. Now I race about five miles, and that's my answer in saying, "No, I'm never going to be a shut-in." It's questionable whether the exercise is good or bad or indifferent for me. It's a safety valve for me. I'm happy doing it. It balances some of the difficulties of my life.

One difficulty was that my relationship of seven years ended. My partner had said to me, "I really have a difficult time handling physical difficulties." And, of course, I spent months in the hospital. She couldn't take it. It was I who finally said, "This is not good for either one of us, and maybe it's time to say this can't work." And it didn't.

The flip side is, I work with mobility impaired adolescents, and I feel as though I get through to them because they see me in a chair. All of them tell me I'm the first person in a wheelchair they've ever seen who's functioning. They examine my car. They're fascinated by the hand controls. I have a real sporty-looking wheelchair so they all try it out. It's nice to see kids who are not always vocationally geared say, "Gee, maybe I really should think about the fact that I have a life. It's not over."

Another flip side is that I have friends. A nice thing that has transpired out of this is that because my own apartment is inaccessible I'm living with friends in Brooklyn—a woman I met through EDGE and my two Brooklyn friends. They're trying to help me sell my apartment and get my feet back on the ground. After three and a half years, I can see where my pieces have started to pick up again. I'm beginning a new relationship with somebody and would certainly think about moving into my own wheelchair-accessible apartment. I'm very lucky, too, that my job was never threatened. I'm able to work the kinds of hours I need in order to have financial security, doing the same kind of work I did before my illness: working with disabled kids.

Besides this job, it's an exciting time to be around. The American Disabilities Act was passed in 1990, which means that public buildings must be made wheelchair-accessible. Right now, I see it only on paper because of the financial problems the country faces at this time. It will take a long time to get the financial backing, but at least there's an awareness of the need. More and more organiza-

with a woman for seven years, and she had a great deal of difficulty not being acknowledged by the hospital staff, as spouses are when one goes through these types of problems. Staying a little bit later, coming a bit earlier, getting medical information—this was not available to her. Fortunately, I was transferred to a hospital in Philadelphia where the head nurse was a lesbian and did my intake personally. She and her lover befriended me, knowing that I was hundreds of miles from home, and that my support system wasn't coming down so easily. I appreciated that sisterhood; it's very special and wonderful.

My medical condition is never stable because of a cardiac involvement, and because any positional change can cause me distress. My condition is more stable than it was because I have accepted the fact that I have to be in a wheelchair. In the beginning my attitude was, "Well, I'll just get up and see what

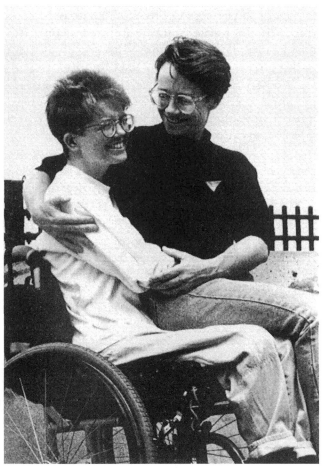

© 1989 Morgan Gwenwald

**Susan Buchanan and Jeanne Sullivan,
New York City.**

Another issue that hits the gay and lesbian community is that people with AIDS have a variety of disabilities. Some end up in wheelchairs. As a result, we see more of the community in need of structural building changes. I see ACT UP getting concerned when they see me going into the building and recognize that it's not just me who needs a ramp. So changes are occurring, but they're expensive. The price quoted for an elevator for the Gay and Lesbian Services Center was about $100,000.

I think, though, there's another kind of sensitivity that needs to be developed in the lesbian community. Frequently I see that lesbians pay attention to the physical needs of their disabled sisters. They are concerned that the lighting is right, the ramps are out, that one toilet is accessible. But there seems to be a tremendous fear of getting emotionally involved, a fear of what disability is. If I'm approached, it's always done with caution—or with so much concern that you almost feel your mother is standing there over you. Sometimes someone will be angry. I've been at crowded events and I can remember one where a woman tripped over my chair and looked at me as though it were *my* fault. Of course, there are some people who are unsure about offering assistance. Believe me, an offer is always appreciated. Offer the assistance, but accept when somebody says, "No, thank you."

There are all kinds of disabilities—physical, emotional, hearing, visual, respiratory, and cardiac, to name some. Not all disabilities are apparent. If there's a claim of disability, you have to take that person's word for it. Former mayor David Dinkins is probably the first public figure to say, "Ability is a temporary state of being." Ability isn't permanent; it can be taken away at any given time.

tions are popping up, and old organizations are becoming more outspoken. The lesbian and gay community in New York City has EDGE representing the interests of disabled gays and lesbians, and we're very vocal.

Down on the Farm:

Lesbians in Prison

Tatiana Schreiber

(Editor's Note: Tatiana Schreiber interviewed lesbian inmates at the Ohio Reformatory for Women in Marysville, Ohio, for a radio documentary about women behind bars. These interviews took place over a six-month period in 1985. This article originally appeared in the Lesbian Prisoner Supplement of Gay Community News, August 23–September 5, 1986. The Marysville prison was once a farm when it was a reformatory for delinquent girls.)

There's been a mistake. Although these interviews were scheduled weeks in advance and I received written confirmation from the superintendent, the guard at the gate says he doesn't have clearance to let me in. I've just driven sixty miles across the flat winter white corn and soy fields of northern Ohio to this place—these old gray brick buildings set in the middle of open empty land. It looks like an enormous farm, perhaps . . . but driving along the highway towards Marysville, there's this ten-foot-high chain-link fence with angled barbed wire across the top.

At the gate there's a large sign warning visitors that they are subject to search. . . . There's a little white boxlike house for the guard with his walkie-talkie. I've been waiting here almost an hour, parked near the gate, listening to the wind and the call of a few birds. Maybe I should just go home, back to my safe little apartment, back to my comfortable job, where being a lesbian is almost cool. Oh, here comes the guard. He says the interviews have been confirmed. I can drive in as soon as I fill out this form . . . nature of my visit, driver's license number, name and number of inmate I'm going to visit.

The giant gate swings open with a mechanical whir and I drive through the prison yard.

As I'm being ushered down a long hall, women, both black and white, all wearing similar dark clothing, are washing the floor, scrubbing the doors, or just standing around. Some stare at me. I try to look them in the eye and smile, but I'm about ready to turn and run. Why did I ever think these women would trust me? I can walk out anytime. Who do I think I am?

But after coming back to the Ohio Reformatory for Women many more times, until I was barred by the superintendent who was sure I had gathered more than enough material for my project, my feelings changed. I felt honored, entrusted with stories that need to be told, glad that I have had the opportunity to do so here, on the radio, and in other forums. The question is—has anybody heard?

My first thought when I tried to imagine life in prison was that it would be horribly lonely. You've lost your family, your home, your pets, your friends, your job. Everything. So my first question to the women I met in Marysville was, "How do you deal with loneliness?" Sharon is a big, white woman in her late twenties, and Renee is a tall black woman who was twenty-three when we met. She had been in prison since she was a teenager.

Sharon: There's two types of loneliness. You're never *lonely* here. There's a thousand women! You kind of wish for alone time . . . but, not being able to be alone with somebody that you love very, very much and you want to . . . you want to touch them, or hold them, or be with them. I miss that a lot.

Renee: I don't get lonely very much. (She laughs a good, deep laugh.) I'm pretty comfortable with me. I've been in institutions so long that . . . no, I don't get lonely. I find pretty much the comfort I need within me.

Now, in being gay, and being, you know, a rather highly affectionate individual, ah (laughs softly), I find that to be a problem . . . it becomes frustrating. I *do* express myself. They know I'm gay and I don't pull any punches with it. However, I do find it difficult . . . say, for instance, your lady is in another cottage. There are certain times you can meet, certain places, and you have to program yourself to be in the mood to talk, to be in the mood to be nice, from seven to nine in the evening, when you may feel that way at one in the afternoon, but there's nothing, absolutely nothing you can do about it. The frustration sometimes . . . it hurts.

Though relationships in prisons between lesbians can be strong, they are necessarily limited by regulations prohibiting contact. Lights are often left on all night long so prisoners can be watched; exercising in the dorms was disallowed in Marysville because a corrections officer (C.O.) thought it could be seductive; prisoners are not supposed to "expose" themselves to each other, and any kind of "closeness" is a crime.

Paula is a young white woman who had been in prison about a year when we met. I'm speaking to her and Claudia, a white woman in her forties. They refer to the guards as "sergeants" and "officers" because Marysville uses these military terms to assign rank to the staff.

Paula: How is anything going to work out here? You have very little privacy. If you end up going into the bathroom for a few minutes with someone, if you're lucky enough to have a C.O. in the cottage who will look the other way, you still have to watch out for a sergeant coming through one of the doors, or for an inmate running to the "police" saying "so-and-so" is in the bathroom with "so-and-so." Even having a platonic relationship, you're being watched. There's always somebody, a C.O. or an inmate, who's jealous of the relationship.

Claudia: This system is supposed to be dehumanizing. That's the whole idea. It's supposed to keep us from having relationships. We're supposed to be punished.

Paula: They provide religious services here where they encourage you to practice "brotherly love" and show compassion for one another, and then they punish you for it. The first ticket I ever got was because a friend of mine had borrowed my sweater. We both got a "lending and borrowing" ticket out of it, and "state clothes restriction," and then the C.O. tells me maybe I don't know the difference between compassion and passion. They throw you together in close quarters and then they expect you to get along, and when you do, they're suspicious of your getting along.

Claudia: This life in here is not conducive to mental health. It's not conducive to emotional health. It's not conducive to relationships. You're lucky if you get out of here intact.

With all the noise, confusion, and frustration of being locked up, it seems like it would take all your resources just to stay sane. How could anyone have room left over to care for anyone else, whether as lover or friend?

Renee: At home I've noticed that you have a wall from what's inside of you, what's really down inside of you, deep down. Being here makes you vulnera-

ble. It kind of strips that wall away, involuntarily sometimes, and to a person who's sensitive, it adds to a relationship. We try to give each other a little strength, talking about it, finding new ways to handle this place.

Sharon: I think being able to share those moments of frustration with somebody helps the relationship. Also, you do come from different backgrounds. You get to bring two different lives together under the same circumstances.

All the women I talked with were gay before they came to Marysville. These "real" lesbians are as much a minority "inside" as they are "outside," and they told me that it's often hard to trust prison "turn-outs"—women who say they're gay inside, for one reason or another, but maintain relationships with boyfriends while in prison, and will go back to being straight when they get out.

Renee: It's hard trusting people because there's so many people who just do it for the hell of it . . . do it to pass the time, do it to get what they can out of it . . . and they use love like it's saying "hi." They just see somebody and it's "Hey, I love you," and to me, that's (love is) real deep. You can't meet one day and the next day you're telling me you love me. I can't get into that.

Sharon: You just don't know. Maybe I like a woman who's going to leave here tomorrow, and I really love this woman, and she didn't love me. That puts bitterness there and when she goes home and doesn't write and doesn't contact me again, I get into another relationship and I carry this bitterness into that one. Some of them want compassion any way they can get it and they turn out. They're playing games with themselves more than they are anybody else. Some of them, it's because they're young and they need affection, or because it's the only way they could get by. Some are small and need protection. Different reasons for different people.

Despite the obvious pain of these situations, Claudia and Paula and Sharon and Renee seemed ready to give anyone the benefit of the doubt . . . but they advise any newcomers to keep a low profile and "watch your associations."

Claudia: It might look like use and abuse, but it does not necessarily have to be true. It could be 'cause you are so frustrated with not being able to let your feelings out and have some kind of sexual release, that you dropped someone, just because it was too hard.

Renee: Granted, it should have taken all my belief away from women, away from being gay, but I believe in feeling what I feel for women, and in dreams, and trying, and faith. . . . I have to go through all the pain, cry, sometimes in the middle of the night. I have to go through all this because I know it's gonna come and it's gonna be all right. Eventually I'm gonna get what I'm after whether it's gonna be in here or out there.

As for their relationships with the prison guards, the lesbians I met told me that occasionally, but only occasionally, the barriers of keeper and caged break down, and relationships bordering on friendship develop. For the most part, though, the guards' role as enforcer of the rules, combined with homophobia, internalized homophobia, or racism make real human contact impossible.

Renee: In this institution, some of the C.O.'s or guards that come up here, some of *them* are gay and in order to cover all that up, they're harsher on the ones that are gay. Male guards have a bad tendency to look at homosexual women as trying to take their place, and I try to let them know I didn't leave a man to be a man, and that's where I get my respect from.

Sharon: There's a few C.O.'s that understand [gays] better because there's a few that *are.* But as a whole, no. It's like "I don't want to understand anything that isn't me, that's not normal, that's not God's law." But, like Renee said, there's some staff members that, if you treat it [homosexuality] with respect, if you don't flaunt it or play games with it, they treat *you* with respect. Then you have a few that simply are not going to accept that you look like a butch . . . they say you're trying to be a man and they're gonna ride you like a man.

Renee: Any contact between staff and "inmate" is dangerous. I think they hold that like a bible in here, and I think that's one of the main problems. They don't try to sit down and say "Well, hey, you're human and let's talk about it." They'll come out of [the role] just to play you into something, to play you into getting angry . . . but as far as saying "I care," no, it's nothing like that. But you *know* which ones care. They'll hold their position, but you can feel that they care.

Sharon: If there's ever any coming out of that role between staff and inmates, it's dangerous for both parties. The first job I had here on this farm, my supervisor was a very sweet woman. She came out of the staff role and she was more like a friend. Due to that it was turned around that I was having an affair with the woman, which I was not. I was removed from the job. Just because she had been friendly enough to say "hi" or something that wasn't staff-oriented, it's dangerous, and not many do come out of that role. I can understand why. I wouldn't want to lose my job.

I met both black and white women in Marysville, and I had the feeling the numbers were about half and half, with a few Latinas. I wondered if racism was worse inside than outside, and if guards used racism to keep women apart.

Renee: The discrimination is within being here, period. There's a white and a black thing, sure enough, but there's an inmate thing more. You got caught. You're here. You ain't shit whether you're white, black, purple, green, or whatever. There *are* a lot of prejudiced C.O.'s as far as color goes. Some of them are real snotty to you, but personally, I don't have the time to deal with that. They have the keys! There's nothing I can do to change it so I don't let it get next to me.

Sharon: Maybe she's strong enough that she doesn't let it get to her, but there's a lot of people who aren't and it creates a problem. They have a problem with white and black relationships, and they tend to come down on that a lot. They don't like any of it, but they get real upset over white and black relationships. It depends on who the officers are, how prejudiced they are.

We have one officer on our cottage right now who is creating an extremely high tension between the inmates because of her bias. She's not coming out and making the statement, but she is taking white inmates off and talking to them. I don't like being put in the position of being called a honky because of what staff members do. It creates problems between me and my friends.

Renee: There's some C.O.'s that's working at this place right now that just have the attitude that, you know, you're nothing. The hell with you! Of course I'm something! Not only because I'm bigger than you are, and not only because I'm more educated than you are, but because I'm human. Now just because the color of my skin is a little darker than yours, don't mean that I'm made of dirt, and I will not expect for you to put a little water on me and make me into a mudpie. I won't have it, you know, from nobody.

Now the minute you step out of line and call yourself checking me because I'm black, or checking me because I'm gay, then I'm going to check you back, but I'm going to check you with the intelligence, the class, that you can't even write me a ticket for it. I'm so tired of all that ticket junk.

Renee and Sharon then talked with me about how the tenuous relationship between lesbians in prison and those outside could be improved.

Renee: If we could possibly find a way to let more women know that we're not exactly underground, that we're not exactly monsters of some sort, that we're alive, well, learning, growing, feeling, and going through life, even in here. . . . If they could find a way to find that out more, I think we could have a little bit more support.

Sharon: I think another reason why lesbians on the street aren't as much into women in here as they could or should be is—how would you like to have a relationship with somebody you've never met who's in prison? How would you like to offer support to somebody that you don't know? I can write articles for the newspaper, and people respond, but they don't know me. They don't know if I'm telling the truth or if I'm a wacko case, so why would you want to risk the lesbian movement for an unknown situation?

I think we need more publicity about what it's like in here, that we are people, we are women, we are for the lesbian movement, we are for gay rights, lesbian rights, we want a part in that. That's part of our world, our culture, our beliefs. We need to be informed from the outside, and they need to be informed from the inside, so it's a joint effort. Let them know what we are, who we are, who we represent, and we want to know what they're doing out there. If they're doing something out there that I don't agree with, as part of the lesbian movement, I want a voice in that, but they don't know me. If I stand up from in prison, that takes away from what I have to say. So get to know me as a person and what my beliefs are, and we'll discuss it. More publicity is needed, more representation.

IX

Lesbian Culture

Lesbian Literature:

A Continuation

Bonnie Zimmerman

When Bertha Harris wrote "Lesbian Literature: An Introduction" for the first edition of *Our Right To Love*, she argued that to have "a body of work that can be immediately perceived as a 'literature' . . . there must first exist cultural *identity:* A group or a nation must know that it exists *as a group* and that it shares sets of characteristics that make it distinct from other groups." From this the group gains "an explicit sense of 'realness.' " Between the time of Sappho and that of Natalie Barney and Renee Vivien, lesbians were denied any "sense of historical continuity" and therefore a culture and literature of their own. Barney and Vivien, at the turn of the century in France, created both a lesbian "sensibility" and "the precarious base for present lesbian literary expression." That precarious base was given a firm grounding through the change of consciousness brought about by feminism, resulting in the beginnings of a lesbian literature that expresses "a calm assumption of an independent female principle as a *reality.*"

Harris ended her 1976 review at the threshold of what has since become an industry beyond anyone's wildest dreams. In the 1990s it is almost amusing to read her words that "we have gone from a starvation diet to a feast." If we were feasting in 1976, today we are gorging ourselves at Roman banquets. Lesbian writers have been so prolific that it is no longer possible to identify only a few outstanding works. In the past two decades, they have produced *hundreds* of novels, anthologies, autobiographies, short story collections, and volumes of poetry. Dozens of literary journals have lived and died, including one, *Sinister Wisdom*, that has published continuously since 1976. Lesbians have established alternative presses, distribution networks, archives, and bookstores to ensure that when we write, we get read. After millennia of being defined by others, or having our words suppressed and destroyed, we are taking care that we leave a record and vision to the lesbians who come after us.

Lesbian literature is the collective voice of what has been called "the lesbian community," itself birthed out of the black, gay, and women's liberation movements of the sixties and early seventies. From the very beginning, lesbians understood that through writing we could shape a lesbian culture and establish the imaginative boundaries of what Jill Johnston first named "Lesbian Nation."[1] If lesbian oppression is characterized by silence and invisibility, then resistance to oppression lies in telling our stories, creating our own values and visions, and naming ourselves as we are or as we would like to be. By controlling and defining images and ideas, we "reconstitute the world."[2]

Thus the first lesbian writers were strongly political in both *what* they wrote and *why* they wrote. They imagined an independent literature by and for women, with lesbian love a central but not exclusive part of their vision. Influenced by the revival of feminism, they believed that lesbians and heterosexual women could work together to change society. Many of the novels published during the radical era of the early 1970s—June Arnold's *The Cook and the Carpenter* (1973) and *Sister Gin* (1975), Elana Nachmann's *Riverfinger Women* (1974), Rita Mae Brown's *In Her Day* (1973), and Monique Wittig's *Les Guérillères* (1971)—re-created the political events, language, and ideals of the women's liberation movement. Similarly, poets like Judy Grahn and Pat Parker invented an incantatory poetry that drew its subject matter and language from the everyday experience of those—street dykes and working-class women of all races—who had been shut out from poetic expression. At that time, a radical lesbian analysis extended to form as well as content; as Arnold and Harris argued, an experimental and audacious lifestyle like lesbianism demanded an equally experimental and audacious literary style.[3] Thus, the first half of the 1970s was not only a golden age of political literature but, especially with the fiction published by Daughters, Inc., a golden age of experimentation, culminating in Harris's inventive and joyous *Lover* (1976).

Daughters published its last book in 1978, a symbolic end to an era. By that time, most politically active lesbians had split off from other groups to form a separate lesbian movement or community. In the last line of her "21 Love Poems" (a lesbian sonnet cycle), Adrienne Rich wrote, "I choose to walk

May Sarton, author.

here. And to draw this circle."[4] In a sense, these words symbolize the development of lesbian culture through the seventies and into the eighties. Lesbian literature continued to develop practically, if not ideologically, as a separatist institution. Many writers began to "draw this circle" for an emerging lesbian audience that was starved for fiction and poetry expressing a lesbian point of view. So new presses—first Naiad and Persephone, and later Spinsters, Aunt Lute, Firebrand, Kitchen Table, Seal, New Victoria, and others (including some, like Crossing and Alyson, that are not exclusively feminist or lesbian)—emerged to give material form to the lesbian voice. Whereas only a half-dozen or so novels were published each year during the 1970s (the number of poetry chapbooks is harder to determine), that number doubled in 1982 and 1983, and exploded from 1984 on.

The kinds of stories that lesbians wrote in abun-dance during the late seventies and early eighties were the explicitly *lesbian* tales—the coming out stories, romances, and utopias—established by the first wave of lesbian-feminist writers. The immensely popular *Rubyfruit Jungle* set the standard for many other how-I-came-to-be-a-lesbian novels from Nancy Toder's *Choices* (1980) to Jeanette Winterson's *Oranges Are Not the Only Fruit* (1985). *Patience and Sarah* became the model for the countless girl-meets-girl love stories that carry on the tradition (but with a sharply feminist and prolesbian twist) of the pulp paperbacks of the fifties and sixties. And *Les Guérillères,* an epic tale of warrior women overcoming the rule of men and establishing a new society, inspired both the vision of alternative female worlds that achieved its best expression in Sally Gearhart's beloved fantasy, *The Wanderground,* and the many novels that show disparate women overcoming their mistrust in order to create one strong and vibrant lesbian community. Moreover, our poets created a uniquely lesbian system of ethics and values, or what Mary Carruthers calls "a truly civilized and social vision of being."[5]

Despite the popularity of the separatist perspective (even among lesbians who strenuously rejected the politics of separatism), other lesbian writers created a more inclusive world. Jane Rule in *Contract With the World* (1980) and Sheila Ortiz Taylor in *Faultline* (1982), for example, imagined women and men, both gay and straight, uniting together in open and loving human families. Others, perhaps sobered by the right-wing politics of the 1980s, revived the political novels that had for a time faded in popularity. Strikes, demonstrations, campaigns, even terrorism—all figure in novels published in 1981 and 1982, such as Barbara Wilson's *Ambitious Women,* Maureen Brady's *Folly,* and Valerie Miner's *Blood Sisters.* Although characters are pulled apart by political differences, each novel does conclude with the hope that together women can heal the wounds inflicted by patriarchal society. The ideal of women or lesbians creating a community in which we feel at home pervades all lesbian literature, whether separatist, feminist, or humanist.

Necessarily, then, our literary community is uniquely open and democratic. Unlike the dominant society, lesbians do not believe that you have to have special dispensation from the gods to be an artist. We value honest storytelling, immediate emotion, and accessible language. We desperately want to hear every woman's story. It all starts for us in the coming-out tale, in the sharing of the tales of our lives. From there to a novel, a poem, short fiction, or a play is a very short step. And because we control our own means of production, through our alternative presses and journals, literally hundreds of women have had the ability to seize the power of the word. Thus, lesbian poetry, prose narrative, and even fiction may be transparently autobiographical, or as Elly Bulkin puts it, "a direct statement of *personal* experience."[6] Lesbians often begin to write as a political, not literary, project: to give other lesbians a literature that expresses and validates what we believe to be our reality as well as to uncover aspects of the self that have been silenced by oppression. Lesbian poetry typically avoids obscurity and allusion; lesbian fiction values realism and a close identification of author and character. As Bulkin further explains, the strength of much lesbian literature lies in the way it projects a sense of one woman, the writer, communicating directly to another, the reader.

This democratization has its consequences, to be sure. A lot of very bad literature does get published. In the seventies and early eighties, in particular, lesbians tended to be suspicious of "standards" and "quality," or anything else that suggests "elitism," such as formal experimentation, irony, and satire, or literariness (a tendency that, fortunately, has diminished in the nineties). Community standards also may be so narrowly drawn that writers consciously or unconsciously censor what they are willing to write about—and if they do not, their more "politically correct" critics may take them to task. On the other hand, antielitism also means that no one version of the lesbian story or lesbian culture can ever dominate for long. It means that you need not have credentials of any kind to be published. Readers have the opportunity to learn how the world appears to and is experienced by lesbians of all backgrounds and all points of view. What we lose in sophistication and polish we make up in raw power and authentic emotion.

But the battle for a truly democratic lesbian literature has been hard fought and the struggle is not yet ended. Lesbian literature reflects the community in and for which it is created, which has been predominantly white and middle class. In the 1970s, only a few writers—Parker, Grahn, Ann Allen Shockley, Sharon Isabell, and Red Arobateau among them—published explicitly working-class and/or black lesbian works. The poetry published in newspapers like *The Furies*, *Ain't I A Woman*, and *Azalea* did reflect a more diverse community, but, by and large, lesbian literature, like the community itself, was dominated by the perspective of white and middle-class women, a perspective that stressed the *commonality* of all women without regard for the very material *differences* that make unity a goal to be worked for, not a premise to be taken for granted.

Hence, one of the most important developments in the short history of lesbian feminist literature has been the impact of the politics of identity and diversity. Through the 1980s, writers and critics like Audre Lorde, Barbara Smith, Cherríe Moraga, Paula Gunn Allen, Jewelle Gomez, Gloria Anzaldúa, and Leslea Newman (to name just a few) have both raised consciousness about and given literary form to the many forms of difference—race, class, age, ethnicity, physical ability—among women. This literary "renaissance" has resulted in collective works, such as *Nice Jewish Girls* (1982), *This Bridge Called My Back* (1981), and *Chicana Lesbians* (1991) that include poetry, theory, narratives, and fiction. It also encompasses individual works like Moraga's *Loving in the War Years* (1983) and Anzaldúa's *Borderlands/La Frontera* (1987), that cross the boundaries between genres. And it includes extraordinary works of fiction or autobiography (the distinction between the two is often deliberately blurred) that are among the most eloquent of lesbian texts: Lorde's "bio-mythography" *Zami: A New Spelling of My Name* (1982), Allen's *The Woman Who Owned the Shadows* (1983), Alice Bloch's *The Law of Return* (1983), and Michelle Cliff's *Abeng* (1984). If we further compare the literary journals from 1976 with those in the 1990s, we can see to what extent Lesbian Nation has changed from a tight white island to a cosmopolitan archipelago.

Early in the third decade of lesbian literature, we find writers working in all literary genres: We have our lyric poetry and our epic poetry, our fiction and our autobiography. We have a small but growing body of lesbian drama. We have a few poets whose names are familiar beyond the boundaries of Lesbian Nation, and myriads of others whose words reach us through the pages of local lesbian newspapers. Lesbian novelists have appropriated every form of escapist fiction: mysteries, westerns, coming-of-age novels, science fiction and fantasies, gothics and regencies, historical romances, erotica, and *endless* love stories. Although many of the most popular novelists still project that rose-colored vision of idealized lesbians falling together into eternal bliss, the most satisfying and serious create detailed and realistic representations of everyday life, including our everyday hopes, fears, dreams, and anxieties. For example, the "problem novel"—which explores such social issues as substance abuse, violence against women, and homophobia—became a popular format in the late eighties. Writers are also re-creating the lesbian communities of the past and present, exploring the parameters of lesbian sexuality, imagining new forms for lesbian families, dissecting the difficulties of sustaining relationships and the ways they end, and satirizing the foibles and excesses of our shared lesbian culture. Whatever your reading tastes, there now exists a literature for you.

In a sense, lesbian literature in 1990 has grown out of its youthful idealism and now struggles with the complexities and compromises of adulthood. As a result, lesbian fiction and poetry is no longer just about how we came to be lesbians, but also about how lesbians see *everything* in the world. Being a lesbian is not necessarily the subject of the work, but it is always its premise and ground. To some extent lesbian literature is no longer the separatist endeavor it once was, as we can see in the current trend toward "mainstreaming." In the early 1970s, commercial publishers, recognizing a sizeable market for lesbian titles, eagerly published paperback editions of Monique Wittig, Isabel Miller, Rita Mae Brown, Ann Allen Shockley, and Kate Millett. As lesbianism ceased to be "fashionable," publishers ceased to be interested in lesbian writers. A few isolated works were published after 1976, but only recently have lesbian writers—most notably, perhaps, Jeanette Winterson, Sarah Schulman, and Dorothy Allison—once again crossed over to the mass marketplace. It may be that the success of novels with lesbian themes by women who are not themselves lesbian-identified (such as Alice Walker's *The Color Purple*) has encouraged publishers to once again look kindly on lesbian fiction. But history should remind us that it would be a big mistake to rely upon their generosity. Another important development is that lesbian literature is no longer an exclusively American phenomenon. Although a few European writers—Monique Wittig, Verena Stefan, and Michelle Roberts, for example—were known in this country prior to about 1984, since then international lesbian literature, par-

ticularly in Great Britain and Australia, has truly proliferated. Some novels from Latin America have already appeared in translation, to be followed, no doubt, by works from Africa and Asia.

Lesbian literature of the past two decades was united by a clearly *feminist* vision and ideology that took as its central task the naming and exploring of an authentic and inclusive lesbian experience. In the 1990s, lesbian writers place themselves at all points on the political spectrum of women-loving-women: from lesbian feminist to womanist, gay activist to queer theorist. Despite local differences, however, I believe all lesbian writers are motivated to some degree by what Adrienne Rich calls "a politics of *asking women's* questions, demanding a world in which the integrity of all women—not a chosen few—shall be honored and validated in every culture."[7] In addition to validating lesbianism as a sexual *behavior* (for our literature has become intensely and satisfyingly erotic), lesbian writers articulate a lesbian *perspective:* a particular way of seeing and understanding the world. With a lesbian perspective, we emphasize connections and bonding among women; we recognize the eroticism, sexuality, and passion in women's relationships; we suppress or invert conventional gender categories; we esteem separation from or critical analysis of patriarchal institutions; and we take up a position at the margins of society—"outside the law"—from which we develop our own ethics and values. Each individual lesbian text, of course, may not incorporate all these characteristics. But whoever is writing lesbian literature, and however she does it, all lesbian writers, to one degree or another, do share in a communal project: the creation of imaginative renditions of uniquely lesbian experiences and lesbian points of view.

Notes

1. *Lesbian Nation: The Feminist Solution* (New York: Simon & Schuster, 1973).
2. Adrienne Rich, "Natural Resources," *The Dream of a Common Language* (New York: W. W. Norton, 1978), 67.
3. June Arnold and Bertha Harris, "Lesbian Fiction: A Dialogue," *Sinister Wisdom* 1, no. 2 (1976), 42–51.
4. Rich, *Dream*, 36.
5. "The Re-Vision of the Muse: Adrienne Rich,

Audre Lorde, Judy Grahn, Olga Broumas," *The Hudson Review* 36, no. 2 (Summer 1983), 321.

6. "Introduction" to *Lesbian Fiction: An Anthology* (Watertown, Mass.: Persephone Press, 1981), xxvi.

7. "Foreword: On History, Illiteracy, Passivity, Violence, and Women's Culture," *On Lies, Secrets, and Silence* (New York: W. W. Norton, 1979), 17.

Further Reading

Coss, Clare, ed. *The Arc of Love: An Anthology of Lesbian Love Poems.* New York: Scribner, 1996.

Cook, Blanche Wiesen. "Female Support Networks and Political Activism." *Chrysalis* 3 (autumn 1977). Reprinted in Nancy Cott and Elizabeth Pleck, eds. *A Heritage of Her Own.* New York: Simon & Schuster, 1979.

© Natt Nevins

Deborah Glick, celebrating her 1990 election to the New York State Assembly.

Lesbian History:

Recovering Our Past

Karen Krahulik

To live without history is to live like an infant, constantly amazed and challenged by a strange and unnamed world. There is a deep wonder in this kind of existence, a vitality of curiosity and a sense of adventure that we do well to keep alive all of our lives. But a people who are struggling against a world that has decreed them obscene need a stronger bedrock beneath their feet.

We need to know that we are not accidental, that our culture has grown and changed with the currents of time, that we, like others have a social history comprised of individual lives, community struggles, and customs of language, dress, and behavior—in short, that we have a story of a people to tell. To live with history is to have a memory not just of our own lives but of the lives of others, people we have never met but whose voices and actions connect us to our collective selves.

—Joan Nestle, *A Restricted Country,* 1987

Archival collections as well as less formal community-based history projects provide us with our sources—the voices, letters, images, and narratives by lesbians about their lives and the media, medical, and legal accounts and records of these lesbians as heterosexual societies saw and constructed them. What intrigues me the most, however, about lesbian history is not only that we were everywhere and that we can now, by searching faithfully, bring to light women who have been "hidden from history," but also that we can deploy strategic methods to research and write lesbian history—to tell and retell lesbian stories. Historians, trained professionally and more creatively, have enabled us to see how lesbians lived in the past, how different societies represented, accepted, and condemned women's same-sex relationships and how these women both fought back successfully and in defeat.[1]

This field of inquiry has developed significantly

over the past two decades. Perhaps the seminal article that changed the way historians write about lesbians was Carroll Smith-Rosenberg's "The Female World of Love and Ritual," first published in 1975. Smith-Rosenberg investigated the diaries and correspondences of women and men from thirty-five middle-class families from 1760 to 1880, including hundreds of letters from women to other women. She suggested that a distinct and separate homosocial, female world developed during the late eighteenth and nineteenth centuries in which women freely and unapologetically expressed their love for each other. Men, she suggests, were mostly if not entirely absent from these women's relationships. Smith-Rosenberg analyzed the intimate and erotic nature of women's letters and concluded that the women in these romantic friendships were "lovers—emotionally if not physically." Her view of women's same-sex relationships contradicted Freudian psychosexual interpretations that had dominated the field of lesbian history and analysis since the early 1900s and which posited that women's intimate attachments—those of the "homosexual"—could only be understood as psychopathic. Smith-Rosenberg contextualized women who may or may not have had genital sex by removing them away from the realm of psychopathology and locating them within their social and cultural worlds—the ones in which they were truly present.

Smith-Rosenberg paved the way for other historians such as Lillian Faderman to write about middle-class women's same-sex relationships as erotic friendships without referencing the authority of psychopathology. Faderman, in *Surpassing the Love of Men: Romantic Friendship and Love Between Women from the Renaissance to the Present* (1981), traced the female world Smith-Rosenberg described, suggesting that its origins could be found during the Renaissance era. In her overview of women's romantic friendships from the sixteenth to the early twentieth century, she found in these "friendships" not only emotional and erotic relationships between women, some of whom declared, for example, "to remain 'faithful' forever, to be in 'each other's thoughts constantly,' to live together and even to die together,"[2] but also societies that accepted and even condoned these relationships as long as neither woman took on the appearances or mannerisms of men. It was not, Faderman argued, lesbian *sex* that worried these early "heterosexual"

societies; it was the usurpation of male power and privilege. If both women at least seemed feminine, their same-sex relationship was often approved as a precursor to heterosexual relationships. A pleasant foray into the lives of these women who "surpassed the love of men" will lead one to heartfelt sentiments expressed in letters, such as one written by Sarah Orne Jewett to Annie Fields in the late nineteenth century:

Here I am at desk again, all as natural as can be and writing a first letter to you with so much love, and remembering that this is the first morning in more than seven months that I haven't woken up to hear your dear voice and see your dear face. I do miss it very much, but I look forward to no long separation, which is a comfort.[3]

Faderman also touched upon the problem of locating a different kind of lesbian in history—that of the "passing" woman or the woman who dressed and passed as a man in order to marry, live with, and share a life with another woman. A "passing" woman who cross-dressed usually did so, however, to gain employment so that she might economically support another woman. The act of "passing" has recently been analyzed as a working-class strategy of resistance against a society that condemned women for their erotic choices or inclinations and attempted to prevent them earning a "living wage."

Jonathan Ned Katz was one of the first historians to begin locating "passing" women from the annals of history. *Katz's Gay American History* (1975) presented evidence of nearly twenty women who "passed" at some time between 1782 and 1920. Katz also introduced new methodology in his historical analysis. He presented his material on "passing" women as an argument against the limiting and essentialist stereotypes of "masculinity" and "femininity," suggesting instead that historians must expose the ways in which the categories male and female are historically contingent and socially constructed. Katz was in conversation with the lesbian-feminist debates about lesbian sexuality and identity—did "butch" women and their "femme" girlfriends simply mock male and female roles, or were their relationships more complex? While this heated debate exploded in the early 1980s and is still heard today, Katz recognized in the mid-1970s that we must look beyond these stereotypes to capture

Mabel Hampton.

the full significance of passing women's lives. Katz also liberated "passing" women from the frequently used terms "transvestite" and "cross-dresser." Such categories, he argued, bound women to roles and analyses that focus exclusively on their costumes rather than on their chosen occupations, vocabularies, voices, gestures, and erotic attachments. Although most of the "passing" women Katz located were from the working class, such as cooks, factory workers, bellboys, innkeepers, and several soldiers, he also found middle- and upper-class women who "passed," for example, three doctors and a "society gentleman."[4]

In the early 1980s, John D'Emilio in *Sexual Politics, Sexual Communities: The Making of a Homosexual Minority in the United States, 1940–1970* (1983), furthered Katz's and other scholars' arguments that the "homosexual" and the "lesbian" are social and historical constructs rather than essential gender identities.[5] D'Emilio also suggested that while the Stonewall rebellion in 1969 was a pivotal moment, it was not as the beginning of the gay liberation movement but rather one part of an evolving gay protest tradition which had its origins in the sexual and political subcultures that emerged following the Second World War. D'Emilio chroni-

cled the formation of the early homophile organizations and the working-class bar cultures, which have been critical to our understanding of Stonewall and the modern gay liberation movement. The reader looking for lesbians will learn about the Daughters of Bilitis (DOB) and emerging working-class bar cultures; however, she will want to supplement this narrative with primary sources such as DOB's newsletter, *The Ladder,* which is now available in many libraries nationwide as well as at the Lesbian Herstory Archives in New York City. And for the voices of the butches and femmes who helped to shape the emerging working class, lesbian bar cultures—which were vital foundations for later gay and lesbian political and social formations—one can turn to Joan Nestle's *Persistent Desire—A Femme Butch Reader,* as well as to *A Restricted Country* (1987).

In her extensive book, *Odd Girls and Twilight Lovers: A History of Lesbian Life in Twentieth-century America* (1991), Lillian Faderman placed in historical context the various working- and middle-class lesbian subcultures—from bourgeois romantic friendships in the early 1900s, to the sexologist and medical "invert" theories of the 1910s, the bohemian and Harlem subcultures of the 1920s, the WACS (Women's Army Corps) during World War II, the sexologist and medical literature, the butch-femme bar cultures of the 1950s and 1960s, the lesbian-feminist revolution in the early 1970s, and even the phenomena of lipstick lesbians—the "Ladies of the Eighties." Faderman's work, a wonderful resource for women seeking an overview of lesbian life in this century, contains many intriguing photographs.

Building on these earlier projects of locating communities, several gay and lesbian historians recently have completed works on more specific gay and lesbian communities. Under the rubric of social history and communities studies, these scholars have enriched an otherwise homosexually vacant field of research. The project for these historians was to make the invisible visible *and* to explore more thoroughly the distinct nature of gay and lesbian communities—how they formed, at what specific historical moments, and why in certain urban spaces. One of the first within this genre was Allan Berube's *Coming Out Under Fire: The History of Gay Men and Lesbians in World War Two* (1990). Although Berube's project covers gay male GI life more extensively than gay women's, his interpretation makes for an interesting read of lesbian life as a WAC or a WAVE (Women's Navy Corps).

One of the most exciting community studies is Liz Lapovsky Kennedy and Madeline Davis's *Boots of Leather, Slippers of Gold: The History of a Lesbian Community* (1993). This project focused on the working-class, butch-femme community in Buffalo, New York, from 1940 to 1970. The authors described this community in detail with its intricacies and relationships and positioned it as central to the origins of the modern gay liberation movement—as opposed, for example, to the central focus that historians like D'Emilio placed on middle-class homophile communities. Kennedy and Davis, on the other hand, reclaimed and rewrote the history of working-class butches and femmes—whom many lesbian feminists had denounced in the early 1970s as unenlightened and "retro."[6] Kennedy explained, "I was hoping to correct the assumption of my students that lesbian history consists of Sappho, Gertrude Stein, and gay liberation," while Davis stated, "I also wanted to write an accurate and compassionate chronicle of the lives of these brave women who had cared for me so generously when I came out in the mid-1960s."[7] Kennedy and Davis claimed that butches and femmes developed strategies of resistance and survival to stake out space in a heterosexist and homophobic society as they came out in working-class bars. The authors detailed butch-femme behaviors, gestures, sexual expressions, and meanings, and they suggested how some of these behaviors and meanings changed over time. Kennedy and Davis produced their own sources for this project on working-class lesbians—since few exist—in the form of oral histories. They provided rich quotes and anecdotes from the forty-five narrators they interviewed who spoke about lesbian life, death, survival, and sex, and offered fascinating material on butch and femme voices and lives. "Arlette," a black femme from the 1950s, remarked, for example, on her sexuality:

I enjoy the feminine role better due to the fact it's not as much hard work; see, being a stud, that's a lot of work. I have a tendency to be kind of lazy. So I'd rather stay fem. Every once in a while I might want to act a little boyish and say "Lay down girl, it's my turn tonight," but I couldn't stand a steady diet of that. No, that's kind of hard work. If [she's] anything like me, they gonna have a job. You just

can't snap your fingers on me, boy. So I'm gonna stay like I am . . . a lady.[8]

Another community study with intriguing voices and anecdotes about lesbian life in the mid twentieth century is Ester Newton's *Cherry Grove: America's First Gay Resort Town* (1993). Newton argued that Cherry Grove was a place where lesbians found the freedom, in an extremely homophobic era, to express themselves openly without fear or repercussions. Newton's project spoke widely to the gay male community, which was in the majority, yet she also explored the 1930s, middle-class "gay ladies," and the 1960s working-class lesbians who found Fire Island increasingly accessible. *Cherry Grove* is especially interesting for its discussions of the relationships between gay men and their reactions to the influx first of middle-class lesbians, and then of working-class lesbians, into their homosocial, homosexual space. Newton also examined how the racism, sexism, and economic factors embedded in Cherry Grove's culture prevented many lesbians from experiencing this world.

In addition to these and other individual projects that examine lesbians in history are two exceptional anthologies, *Hidden from History: Reclaiming the Gay and Lesbian Past* (1989), edited by Martin Duberman, Martha Vicinus, and George Chauncey, Jr., and *The Lesbian and Gay Studies Reader* (1993), edited by Henry Abelove, Michele Aina Barale, and David M. Halperin. Included in *Hidden from History* is an article by Paula Gunn Allen about women's same-sex erotic and spiritual relationships in American Indian cultures. Gunn reclaims both lesbian and Native American history while urging historians to examine lesbians in Native American cultures within a broader social and spiritual framework so that individual cases of cross-dressers or *berdache* are not taken as ahistorical aberrant examples. Also in this anthology one will find a discussion of women's sexuality in Medieval Europe by Judith Brown and a study by Shari Bernstock tracing early twentieth-century Parisian lesbian cultures. Bernstock argues against romanticizing these turn-of-the-century coteries and suggests instead that we look at how class privilege helped to shape these lesbians' political assumptions and ideologies.

The Gay and Lesbian Studies Reader is, similarly, an excellent resource for exploring issues of lesbians in history. The articles in this anthology are largely theoretical rather than historical, speaking to the issues and methodologies of writing about the lesbian as subject. Gloria T. Hull, for instance, argues in " 'Lines She Did Not Dare': Angelina Weld Grimke, Harlem Renaissance Poet," that we must look at Grimke's work and life not just as a black poet or a woman poet but also as a lesbian poet. And Martha Vicinus explains in " 'They Wonder to Which Sex I Belong': The Historical Roots of the Modern Lesbian Identity," why historians need to consider not only the most obvious lesbian identities in history such as the dyke, witch, or amazon, but also those who seem more obscure, such as the femme, androgyne, and women who only occasionally participated in lesbian relationships. Vicinus also invokes the inspiring work, *This Bridge Called My Back: Writings By Radical Women of Color* (1981), which made a critical intervention in the early 1980s by raising the issue of racism within feminist scholarship and the lesbian-feminist movement, and thus urging historians to begin questioning the elusive "lesbian" in history and focus more on the diversity of lesbians everywhere. Charlotte Furth, in this same anthology, provides an exceptional study of Chinese gender benders in her essay, "Androgynous Male and Deficient Females: Biology and Gender Boundaries in Sixteenth- and Seventeenth-Century China." Furth examines late Ming accounts of sexual transformation and finds that "strange" or anomalous men and women helped to define the social and biological meanings of "normal" male and female categories.[9]

Theory, by and about lesbians, has increasingly affected the ways historians are currently researching and writing lesbian history. Its most recent incarnation, in the form of "queer" theory (a theoretical movement whose origins lie with the literary-based poststructuralists and gender theorists), insists that gay and lesbian historians should focus more on central rather than marginal topics, read events not as occurrences but as texts with embedded political and cultural meanings and messages, move away from categories such as gay and lesbian, which continue to "naturalize" or claim authentic gender identities, and look not to make the invisible visible but rather to analyze historical power relations, strategies, conceptualizations, narratives, and imaginations to see how these systems worked to maintain or disrupt the dominant order. Furthermore, queer theorists urge historians to refrain from reporting on the linear,

heroic, and romantic progress of lesbian history without also paying attention to its setbacks, limitations, pitfalls, and tragedies.[10]

While queer theory often neglects the importance of empirical-based research and strains to make its claims politically strategic, several historians are writing about lesbians in history using queer theorists' suggestions and engaging with the debates offered by queer theorists while also retaining necessary empirical strategies. Lisa Duggan, for example, has explored the Alice Mitchell case (1892)—a middle-class woman who planned to marry her female lover and then pass as a man to support her, but who killed her instead when their plans went awry. Duggan theorizes about lesbian identities, experiences, representations, and desires while also examining empirical sources, such as newspaper accounts, sexology reports, and court narratives. Duggan aims, by using these sources in this way, to locate the different ways stories about Alice and her lover were told in relation to racial, regional, material, and social networks. She demonstrates how historians can thus use queer theory to enrich our understanding of lesbians in history while retaining empirical strategies. She also decenters the authority of late-nineteenth-century sexologists by retelling the pathologizers' tale. Furthermore, Duggan shows how the Mitchell case disrupts the celebratory and romantic stories historians tell about middle-class romantic friendships and the heroic tales of working-class "passing women," which marginalize other stories and only wield certain types of narratives. Alice Mitchell, for example, was engaged in an accepted, bourgeois romantic friendship but was denounced when she desired to use a working-class, "passing" strategy.

Jennifer Terry, "an archivist of deviance," also demonstrates a provocative method for locating and reading lesbian voices from the past. In "Theorizing Deviant Sexuality," Terry explores a 1930s medico-scientific study of homosexuals in New York City, published as *Sex Variants: A Study of Homosexual Patterns,* and "reads against the grain" to see how lesbians were constructed as deviant subjects by the researchers. She also identifies the ways in which the lesbians in this study spoke against this flawed construction. Terry refers to this process as "vengeful countersurveillance"—a balancing or reinterpreting of authority, how it is constructed, assumed, and disrupted. Terry "queers" history here by showing how lesbian subjects disrupted heteronormativity and exploded rigid binary classifications such as masculine and feminine. She analyzes the responses of several lesbians, such as Ursula, who explained to the researchers:

I found Frieda, the grandest person in the world. She's tiny and very feminine, a fine artist, very virile and aggressive, my equal in aggressiveness and not at all possessive. . . . Love is a form of madness—every part of the body becomes beautiful—caressing and kissing all parts of the body. This is the greatest love of my life. . . . My sex life has never caused me any regrets. I'm very much richer by it. I feel it has stimulated me and my imagination and increased my creative powers.

Terry interprets Ursula's response to direct questions about sex by arguing that "Ursula refuse[d] the standard opposition between femininity and aggressiveness . . . refused the centrality of genitals, thereby territorializing the lesbian body as capable of polymorphous desire and satisfaction."[11] Moreover, Terry suggests that Ursula's response challenged common sexologists' assumptions about lesbian desires by relating her desires to creative rather than psychopathic energy.

In addition to the latest works by queer historians, the avid reader of lesbian history will not want to miss Blanch Wiesen Cook's recent biography, *Eleanor Roosevelt*, which retells the story of Eleanor, this time including her passion, energy, sex, power, and intimacy. Cook examines Eleanor's political and strictly social relationships and friendships as well as her romantic involvement with reporter Lorena Hickock. Noteworthy passages for the starstruck, love-struck lesbian reader include: "ER" to "Hick," March 5, 1933, "Hick, my dearest—I cannot go to bed without a word to you. . . . You have grown so much a part of my life that it is empty without you, even though I'm busy every minute." And a note by Hick, "Only eight more days. . . . Funny how even the dearest face will fade away in time. Most clearly, I remember your eyes, with a kind of teasing smile in them, and the feeling of that soft space just north-east of the corner of your mouth against my lips."[12]

Researching lesbian history has taught us that we have traditions of courage, dignity, wit, and romance that date from Sappho's time and are still honored today. Historians have demonstrated the methods by which lesbians represented themselves and were represented in the past—how they struggled to shape their identities and futures, how they triumphed and failed. The field of lesbian history has changed over time as historians continue to seek out and debate creative and strategic methods to locate lesbian voices and to construct a lesbian past. Archival collections, community-based history projects, oral histories, and queer tactics of researching and imagining represent and hold our most invaluable sources. We must continue the courageous work of collecting and producing as we retell our stories, reshape our futures, and rewrite history as we know it.

Notes

1. For a discussion of gay and lesbian archives, community-based research projects, and the financial problems faced by researchers and professional historians, see Lisa Duggan, "History's Gay Ghetto: Contradictions and Growth in Lesbian and Gay History," in Lisa Duggan and Nan D. Hunter, ed., *Sex Wars: Essays in Sexual Dissent and American Politics* (New York: Routledge, 1995).
2. Lillian Faderman, *Surpassing the Love of Men: Romantic Friendship and Love Between Women from the Renaissance to the Present* (New York: William Morrow, 1994), 16.
3. Faderman, *Surpassing the Love of Men*, 201.
4. For a sourcebook of primary documents about "passing" women and other women engaged in relationships from 1607 to 1740 and 1880 to 1850, see Jonathan Ned Katz, *Gay/Lesbian Almanac* (New York: Carroll & Graf, 1994).
5. Especially noteworthy for laying the groundwork to this conceptualization was the article, "The Homosexual Role," by Mary McIntosh, in *Social Problems* 16 (1968): 182–92. For a summary of historical approaches to sexuality see "Matters: On Conceptualizing Sexuality in History," *Radical History Review* 20 (Spring/Summer 1979).
6. For a history of the feminist movement, including lesbian feminist organizations such as the Radical Lesbians and the Furies, see Alice Echols's *Daring To Be Bad: Radical Feminism in America, 1967–1975* (Minneapolis: University of Minnesota, 1989). For discussion and debates

about the roles of butches, femmes, lesbian-feminists in terms of sexuality, desire, and power—inspired by the conversations at the Scholar and the Feminist IX Conference, Towards a Politics of Sexuality (April 1982) at Barnard College—see Carol Vance, ed., *Pleasure and Danger: Exploring Female Sexuality* (New York: Routledge and Kegan Paul, 1984). Especially pertinent is Joan Nestle's "The Fem of Question," in which the author states as a working-class femme of the 1950s, "I wasn't a piece of fluff and neither were the other fems I knew. . . . I could tell you stories . . . about the twenty-year-old fem who carried her favorite dildo in a pink satin purse to the bar every Saturday night so her partner for the evening would understand exactly what she wanted." Nestle also notes, "The message to fems throughout the 1970s was that we were the Uncle Toms of the movement." See also Ann Snitow, Christine Stansell, and Sharon Thompson, *Powers of Desire: The Politics of Sexuality* (New York: Monthly Review Press, 1983), especially Amber Hollibaugh and Cherríe Moraga, "What We're Rollin Around in Bed With: Sexual Silences in Feminism," and Lisa Duggan and Nan D. Hunter, eds., *Sex Wars: Essays in Sexual Dissent and American Politics.*

7. Liz Lapovsky Kennedy and Madeline Davis, *Boots of Leather, Slippers of Gold: A History of a Lesbian Community* (New York: Routledge, 1993), xvi.

8. Ibid., 209.

9. For more essays reflecting the diversity of lesbians in history, see Laura Engelstein, "Lesbian Vignettes: A Russian Triptych from the 1890's," *Signs* 15 (1990), for a discussion of what appears to be the only study of lesbianism in Russia during the late 1800s. The author finds that "extradomestic" sexual relationships between women were not necessarily considered to be abnormal. See also Judith C. Brown, *Immodest Acts: The Life of a Lesbian Nun in Renaissance Italy* (New York: Oxford University Press, 1986), and Joan Nestle's recently published excerpts from an oral history with Mabel Hampton, a courageous working-class African American lesbian who was a founding member of the Lesbian Herstory Archives.

10. For a provocative discussion of queer theory and lesbian history, see Henry Abelove, "The Queering of Lesbian/Gay History," and Donna Penn, "Queer: Theorizing Politics and History," in *Radical History Review* 62 (Spring 1995), and Lisa Duggan, "The Discipline Problem: Queer Theory Meets Lesbian and Gay History," *GLQ,* forthcoming.

11. Jennifer Terry, "Theorizing Deviant Sexuality," *Differences* 3 (Summer 1991).

12. Blanche Wiesen Cook, *Eleanor Roosevelt,* vol. I (1884–1933) (New York: Penguin, 1992), 479, 497–98.

Building Cultural Memories:

The Work of the Lesbian Herstory

Archives

Deborah Edel

The work of the Lesbian Herstory Archives is about collective memory, about self-empowerment, about definitions of self and sexuality in changing and often difficult times. It is a grassroots, cultural project whose beginnings were in the mid-1970s, a time of rapid growth in the lesbian and gay communities. Recognizing how quickly the stories of their foremothers and their own lives and activities were being lost in the flow of time, and viewing lesbians as a people with their own cultural history, a group of lesbian women made a commitment to themselves and to the community that from then on, there would always be a place to gather and preserve the records and history of lesbian lives and activities. It was to be a place open to all lesbians, a place to take pride in the diverse history collected, and a place where any lesbian, by her own choosing, could add a message from her own life to the growing pool of history.

Over the twenty years since its inception, the Lesbian Herstory Archives has become just that, a cultural institution that, although it plays a dynamic role in the lesbian community, is, at its core, a safe, nurturing environment, a mixture of a library and a family album. It is a place where women come, some to use the resources, others just to visit, sit, and explore. Some come seeking specific information, searching for a book difficult to find in mainstream collections, a journal needed for an article, reference material for a term paper, sources for a book, connections in other cities. Others come on personal searches to read about coming out, about making love, about health problems and solutions, about work, about relationships. Yet others come to read the biographies of our foremothers, the paperbacks of the 1950s and 1960s, the collections of unpublished poetry and short stories, the small press novels of today hard to find in local bookstores. Still others come to look: at the work of lesbian artists and photographers on the walls and on slides, at the snapshots sent in from lesbians all around the world, pictures of individual faces, of couples, of teams, of friends, of children, of women working and playing and making love and relaxing. Women come to use the archives for as many different reasons as there are visitors.

The archives, however, is not just a passive place to preserve and cherish our history. It is an active place where the history already collected has been an important resource for filmmakers and authors to create new lesbian culture in the form of movies, books, plays, journals, and much more.

The Lesbian Herstory Archives began in a small back room in an apartment on the Upper West Side of New York City in 1974. The collection started with the amassing of parts of the personal libraries of the founders and supporters. Word about the archives grew and a newsletter was introduced to help maintain ties with those who had visited and to share information and cultural history with a broader audience. The archives grew over the years from those early days in the little room. By the mid-1980s the archives filled almost an entire large West Side apartment in New York City, leaving only two bedrooms for the women who lived there. The collection poured into storage lockers for duplicates, equipment, and the film collection, which needed special temperature controls for preservation. The archives grew from the early days of index cards to a computer for cataloging, cross indexing, and compiling mailing lists. Recognizing that the collection had outgrown its original space, the women of the archives began a building fund drive in 1986. In December 1991, with the purchase of a town house in Brooklyn, that dream became a reality.

Today the collection is housed in its own building, with the elegance and dignity a collection of lesbian history and culture deserve. Presently, file cabinets of subject files, biographical files, conference files, organizational files, unpublished papers, short stories and poetry, endless shelves holding books and periodicals, artwork, slides, photographs, graphics, audio and video tapes, buttons, clothing, special collections of manuscripts, diaries, letters and personal papers, and other representa-

Cofounders of the Lesbian Herstory Archives in New York City: Joan Nestle, Mabel Hampton, Deborah Edel, and Judith Schwarz.

tions of lesbian lives and activities fill two floors of the house and the basement. The top floor, a caretakers apartment, helps sustain the security of the collection.

The archives has always been staffed entirely by volunteers, from the earliest days when the cofounders put in endless time and money to develop the archives, to today, when a large core group of lesbians meet regularly to try to keep up with the daily needs of archiving, including the cataloging and filing of materials, answering letters, updating the mailing list, and attending to visitors. In addition to volunteers from the community, the archives has had interns from college programs who, because of their time, have been able to work on more extensive projects.

Though it is known informally to this day as the archives or LHA, the archives was formally incorporated as a not-for-profit institution in 1979 as the Lesbian Herstory Educational Foundation, Inc., an information service.

In addition to the core of the collection—the resource center—the archives continues to produce a newsletter and sponsors educational and cultural events, including forums, readings, concerts, slide shows, and dances. Over the years, responding to requests for speakers, women from the archives have presented slide shows about lesbian history to lesbian and gay groups, student and community groups. They have participated in workshops and panels both around the country and internationally, and have written articles for the lesbian, gay, feminist, and mainstream presses.

The archives continues to grow through the donation of materials and funds from individuals within the lesbian community and the broader gay and feminist communities. Some grants from nontraditional funding sources have made possible the acquisition of such basic equipment as a photocopy machine, a tape duplicator, a microfilm machine, a reader printer, and two computers. Some materials have been acquired by purchase. However, the most essential elements of the collection, the diaries, letters, photographs, the bits and pieces of daily lesbian life, come through personal donations from individual women during their lifetimes or in their wills.

The following principles have shaped the growth and direction of the archives, making sure it is an institution greater than the lives of the individual women who run it:

• All women are welcome. No one shall be turned away from using the archives and there shall be no charge for access to information.
• The collection will never be sold and will never become part of a larger public or private mainstream institution such as a university library.
• All lesbian lives are important and should be collected at the archives. We are all part of the next generation's history. The archives must therefore aim to collect material reflecting the full diversity of lesbian experience.
• The archives is dedicated to building intergenerational and cross-community connections through education and respect.

The Lesbian Herstory Archives is about all of us. Come add your voice to the historical record. Come visit the archives.

For more information about the Lesbian Herstory Archives, write: LHEF, Inc., P.O. Box 1258, New York, NY 10116 or call us at 718-768-3953.

Lesbian Books:

For Love and for Life

Barbara Grier

My love affair with lesbian publishing started very early, when I began to collect every written word I could find having to do with lesbian lives. This love affair produced a great many informational columns and book reviews for *The Ladder*, the singular and significant lesbian publication in the United States during the years 1956 to 1972. It also produced a bibliography—the first edition of *The Lesbian in Literature,* published in 1967. I became editor of *The Ladder* in 1968.

Two pioneering retired women, who had helped with *The Ladder* until its demise, came to me and my partner, Donna J. McBride, and proposed creating a lesbian/feminist publishing company. They lent Donna and me $2,000 of their retirement funds as seed money.

In 1973 the Naiad Press was born, with myself and Donna as managing partners. In 1974 *The Latecomer,* the fine and enduring novel by Sarah Aldridge led off as our first published book, and Naiad Press became part of the turbulent history of our emerging lesbian nation in the 1970s.

Allied finally with the growing women's movement, the lesbian nation was discovering its voice, first in women's music, and then in women's publishing, as fledgling publishers fought to establish and maintain a precarious economic beachhead.

The 1978 edition of *Our Right To Love* listed nine lesbian/feminist book publishers. Yet, one by one, they perished—all save one. Why did only Naiad Press survive the struggles of those early days?

We survived through the most careful nurturing of our resources. And through fierce determination.

We did not draw a dime of salary during Naiad's first nine years of existence; we funneled all of Naiad's income and all of our energy into establishing our publishing identity, into making the name Naiad Press synonymous with books by, for, and about lesbians. We allied ourselves with the core of hardy feminist bookstores digging toeholds all around the country, bookstores run by women as determined as we to disseminate lesbian presence and culture. Slowly, tenaciously, we expanded our mailing lists and our visibility to an audience tantalizingly difficult to reach because of entrenched homophobia. We began to build quality, to find and develop the authors who would, at long last, portray in well-written books the truth and beauty of lesbian lives.

Several milestone events combined to create the impetus that became explosive growth for Naiad Press in the 1980s. One milestone was *Outlander,* brought to us by prestigious Canadian writer Jane Rule, the first of eleven of her superb works that would be proudly issued by Naiad in the ensuing years, culminating in original publication of the great *Memory Board* in 1988, and *After the Fire* in 1989.

Faultline by Sheila Ortiz Taylor came out in 1982, a luminous comic literary classic that deservedly drew large sales and wide review attention.

The author tour for *Faultline* resulted in another milestone. At Sisterhood Bookstore in Los Angeles, a woman walked up to say that she had a manuscript of possible interest to Naiad Press—a not uncommon occurrence for us. But this was an uncommon writer and surely an uncommon manuscript—the author was Katherine V. Forrest and the manuscript was *Curious Wine,* the first of the ten best-selling books that would make her Naiad's most popular author and the most popular lesbian author in America.

In 1985 *Lesbian Nuns: Breaking Silence* burst into national prominence, a blockbuster international best-seller that launched numerous television appearances for its two editors, translations of the book into all Western European languages, and reviews in hundreds of newspapers and magazines as well as foreign publications. In 1986 Jane Rule's *Desert of the Heart* became the movie *Desert Hearts,* leading to renewed best-selling status for a classic novel originally published in 1964.

By the mid-eighties we were, routinely, scheduling twelve-thousand-copy print runs even for first novels for which we projected the most modest of sales.

That Naiad Press had arrived as a real and astonishing success first came home to me personally one day in 1986 when Donna and I were rushing through the Jacksonville, Florida, airport to catch a connecting flight to a booksellers conference. Out of the cacophony of that airport I heard in the harsh static of a loudspeaker something that sounded like "paging Barbara Grier" and realized, unbelievingly, that indeed my name was being called. With the greatest imaginable pride, I recognized then that Naiad Press had become so important that I had to be paged in the caverns of an airport to conduct its business—and that we had accomplished something unprecedented and spectacular in the history of our lesbian world.

The 1980s saw great expansion in the field of women's publishing, with new companies constantly stepping into the publishing scene with the clear resolve to focus on lesbian and gay material. David Wilk, founder of Inland Book Company, the largest small press distributor in the United States, told the New England Booksellers Association in the fall of 1986, "If I were going into publishing today, I'd go into genre publishing and the genre I'd choose is gay and lesbian fiction because it is the wave of the future."

How did we achieve our leadership role in gay and lesbian publishing? How is it that we continue to build and consolidate our success? What differentiates us from mainstream presses who today also seek to tap into this burgeoning lesbian market? I believe that the vitality and substance and heart of women's small press publishing spring from a clear philosophy: the profound belief that the strength of lesbian writing lies in its diversity, accessibility, and continuity.

It has always been the plan of Naiad Press to present a mix of books with appeal to the broadest spectrum of lesbian readership, and we have accomplished this goal. Today's lesbian reader can see herself reflected in an array of books written by lesbians and intended for lesbians: literary novels, coming-of-age stories, cartoons, short stories; works of fiction in every genre—mysteries, science fiction, spy novels, fantasy, westerns, Regencies, ghost stories, vampire tales, light romances; essays and poetry and nonfiction conveying every possible aspect of lesbian life—coming out, sex, relationships, commitment patterns and ceremonies, former relationships, having or not having children, and so on and on. And Naiad Press has returned to print classic works that are a part of the lesbian heritage—books by such legendary writers as Gertrude Stein, Gale Wilhelm, Claire Morgan (Patricia Highsmith), and Ann Bannon.

Naiad Press, as part of its philosophy, seeks where possible the entire body of work of any given author and will strive to maintain those books in

The founders of Grand Books, Jackson, Wyoming.

print in perpetuity. This two-value system, virtually unheard of today in the establishment press, is inordinately successful for any lesbian/feminist and gay small press in reaching an audience whose needs far exceed the supply of available material.

Many authors can make as much or more money if they place their work in the hands of lesbian and gay publishers who distribute books through a worldwide network of distributors, to bookstores throughout the United States and Canada, and through their own extensive mailing lists. In her essay collection, *A Hot-Eyed Moderate,* Jane Rule said of Naiad Press: "They fill orders the day they receive them. They go to every feminist and lesbian conference, every book fair, and the books they sell are never allowed to go out of print. . . . They want their books not only in the stores but in the classrooms, easily and continuously available to everyone who wants them. They want to make a living for themselves and for their writers. . . . Playing with the women instead of the big boys is an ambition I hope the writers of coming generations will recognize and fulfill."

Increasingly, authors have realized that they can come to a small press and get the perks that only publishing with a small press provides. Naiad Press (and many of its companion lesbian-feminist and gay presses) is a throwback to the era before literary agents ran interference between author and publisher, to those days of loyalty and honesty and shared information between publisher and author.

Our desire is for a personal and lasting relationship with our authors, and we offer full disclosure of the details of publishing, marketing, and royalty payments. We provide editorial cooperation and support, not editorial interference. We sell our authors' work in a hands-on marketing approach that involves aggressive pursuit of all domestic and international markets, and constant contact with the distributors worldwide who carry our books. And we *call* those hundreds and hundreds of bookstores who deal with us directly, who have loyally served the lesbian nation's desire to know its literary past and present.

Many people know the rags-to-riches story of *Rubyfruit Jungle* by Rita Mae Brown, originally published by a small press, and Isabel Miller's self-published *Patience and Sarah*—both novels bought by mainstream publishers. In the 1980s that did not happen, and such events seem far less likely to happen as lesbian and gay small presses become more commercial and more viable and even more successful in the competitive world of publishing.

Small press lesbian publishing has produced its own forms of success and best-sellers, and in a surprising number of ways. A brief list of the lesbian and gay presses' recent successes includes the optioning by film companies of *Monarchs Are Flying* by Marion Foster, Jane Rule's *Memory Board, A Room Full of Women* by Elisabeth Nonas, and *Murder at the Nightwood Bar* by Katherine V. Forrest. The selling of specifically lesbian material to be made into mainstream movies will most assuredly continue.

Articles appearing in the publishing trade media have been proclaiming since the late seventies the coming death of conglomerate trade publishing and the rise of the small press. Nowhere is that more evident than in the incredible success of lesbian and gay publishing.

Today, in place of the nine original women's presses, fifty-four small press publishers have risen to contribute to a robust lesbian literature. Naiad Press is not only the oldest and largest, but, interestingly, one of the few publishers extant with an exclusively lesbian list.

Of these fifty-four current publishers, the twenty-seven largest and most active in producing lesbian materials range from entirely women-owned companies to mixed-gender companies to collectives, to gay male–operated businesses. Mixed genre publishers, such as Alyson and Banned Books, are swelling too the availability of lesbian books that appeal to the popular reading public by including genre fiction, historical romances, and milder erotica on their lists. A handful of active and very important presses are based in Canada and Great Britain.

Lesbian fiction is indeed the most popular field, and gay male fiction that reflects the reading levels and interests of the most popular lesbian fiction has grown fast as well. Purely feminist fiction and nonfiction still attract a lot of lip service but in fact little attention; the real thrust in publishing is more clearly a reflection of the changes in the feminist movement and is mainly lesbian.

As managing editor of Naiad Press, a dream of mine continues to be that some day every woman who discovers her lesbianism will be able to walk into a bookstore, any bookstore, and find books that say, in effect, "Yes, you are a lesbian and you are wonderful." Today's lesbian and gay presses are, indeed, moving toward making that dream come true. I am proud of my lifetime work, and of Naiad Press's achievements and place in the history of lesbian literature.

Women's, Lesbian, and Gay Publishers

All publishers mentioned in this list will provide catalogs on request. For a more complete listing of publishers in these fields, see Andrea Fleck Clardy, *Words to the Wise: A Writer's Guide to Feminist and Lesbian Periodicals and Publishers*, rev. 4th ed. (Ithaca, N.Y.: Firebrand Books, 1993).

Alyson Publications, P.O. Box 4371, Los Angeles, CA 90078, 213-871-1225.

Aunt Lute Foundation, P.O. Box 410687, 223 Mississippi St., San Francisco, CA 94107, 415-558-9655.

Calyx Books, P.O. Box B, Corvallis, OR 97339, 503-753-9384.

Cleis Press, P.O. Box 8933, Pittsburgh, PA 15221, 412-731-3863.

The Crossing Press Feminist Series, P.O. Box 1040, Freedom, CA 95019, 408-722-0711.

The Feminist Press at the City University of New York, 311 E. 94th St., New York, NY 10128, 212-360-5790.

Firebrand Books, 141 The Commons, Ithaca, NY 14850, 607-272-0000.

Kitchen Table: Women of Color Press, P.O. Box 908, Latham, NY 12110, 518-434-2057.

Mother Courage Press, 1533 Illinois St., Racine, WI 53405, 414-634-1047.

The Naiad Press, P.O. Box 10543, Tallahassee, FL 32302, 904-539-5965.

New Victoria Publishers, P.O. Box 27, Norwich, VT 05055, 802-649-5297.

Rising Tide Press, 5 Kivy St., Huntington Station, NY 11746, 516-427-1289.

Seal Press, 3131 Western Ave., #410, Seattle, WA 98121, 206-263-7844.

Spinsters Ink, 32 E. 1st St., Ste. 330, Duluth, MN 55802, 218-727-3222

Third Side Press, 2250 West Farragut, Chicago, IL 60625-1802, 312-271-3029

Melissa Etheridge:

Yes She Is

Val C. Phoenix

(Editor's Note: The following article appeared in Deneuve *magazine, November/December 1993.)*

It was an exciting time when Bill Clinton was sworn in as President. The air was ripe with promises and hope. Melissa Etheridge was one of many revelers at the lesbian and gay Triangle Ball sharing in the victory celebration, and in that spirit she made a little proclamation of her own, telling the crowd, "I'm proud to have been a lesbian all my life."

With that sentence Etheridge joined the select group of out recording artists on major labels. One month later she won a Grammy for best hard rock vocal performance, and in April she performed at the March on Washington to ecstatic cheers. Now the record-buying public has its say, as her latest release, *Yes I Am*, hits the stores.

All this seems very far away when we meet on a hot, dry summer's day in Los Angeles. Removing her shades, Etheridge settles down at a table for the lunchtime interview. The restaurant, which serves health food, is one she frequents, though she's perplexed as to which veggie burger to order. Dressed in a black cotton shirt with cut-off sleeves, jeans, and cowboy boots, ornamented by a labyris earring and some jangly bracelets, she seems tanned and healthy, if a bit tired. But, once her food arrives, she seems to perk up, offering to share some of her hummus quesadilla. Punctuated by throaty chuckles and guffaws, her manner is brisk and authoritative, yet still friendly and accessible.

Titling her post-coming-out album *Yes I Am* might seem to be a defiant challenge to homophobes, but, in fact, it's not. "It's because I think it's a powerful statement. I think it's motivating, you know, 'Yes I Am.'" She gestures firmly with her hand. "It's all nothing to do with me comin' out at all, which is the first thing everybody asks. I decided to do that before I came out. So, you know, maybe there's a bit of a sense of humor in that, possibly, but, eh, it's a real powerful statement."

This powerful statement is number four in a line of releases going back to her self-titled debut in 1988. Originally from Leavenworth, Kansas, Etheridge, 32, was discovered by Island Records' founder Chris Blackwell when she played the lesbian bar Que Sera in Long Beach, California. Before that, she'd had her demo tape rejected by Olivia Records, a fact which gives her a chuckle now.

Yes I Am marks a return to form for her, a back-to-basics approach after some stylistic wandering on 1992's *Never Enough*. The new record was mostly recorded live, Melissa's preferred approach, and it sticks to rock shouters and ballads. The album's title track is a slow burn that builds up to the climax of the chorus: "To the question your eyes seem to send, 'Am I your passion, your promise, your end?' I say I am. Yes I am." As such, it is the latest in a series of Melissa's patented "my-hormones-are-out-of-control songs," steeped in unfulfilled desire: "Like the Way I Do," "Bring Me Some Water," and "Meet Me in the Back."

Occasionally, she does step outside herself to observe someone else's experience. "All American Girl" records the work-a-day life of an average American woman, one whose dreams have been beaten down and who, Melissa sings, "will live and die in this man's world, an all-American girl."

Melissa explains, while chewing thoughtfully, that the song meant several things to her. "It's a song where I'm totally outside myself, third person, singing about things I've observed and feel looking at other women. But, also, I felt like in rock 'n' roll women don't have a powerful American anthem. You know, we have 'Born to Run' or 'Born in the USA.'

"I like singing about women's issues. I don't think in rock music that they're ever addressed or ever brought up. I like putting it in a strong rock 'n' roll vehicle where you can move to it. And that's what I wanted to do with that," she says.

Another new song, "Silent Legacy," was inspired by the story of a man who threw his teenage daughter out of the house when he caught her having sex. Etheridge is indignant. "How come we, in this day and age, just say, 'Don't do it,' when we know what we went through as teenagers? *We* know how hard it is. *We* know how the world seems and feels, and how our parents never talked to us about anything. And why do we pass this on? It just—it makes me crazy! I grew up in the Midwest where nobody talked about it, and you just learned it as you went along, and in this day and age that's dangerous." The song, which she sang in D.C. before the March, declares, "The legacy stops here."

Melissa started writing songs when she was ten, then moved on to playing in churches around town, but she says she was never religious herself. "I was never of the mind that I believed what was going on. I thought it was very curious, the organized religion, but I felt that there was a greater spirituality than these rules and this judgment that these people were laying down. And I still have a real hard time with organized religion. I think that it's the root of a lot of our problems." She leans over her meal and adds grimly, "As the Christian right is proving right now."

Those early songwriting efforts were pretty simple and not really true to her. "I was copying, you know. I would write about love, and I didn't know love, you know, 'cause I hadn't had an experience. I would just sort of write what I thought people would write songs about. Wasn't 'til I was about (chuckles) 17 or 18 that I really started writing about personally what was going on."

That year coincided with another auspicious occasion. "I, uh, had my first lesbian experience when I was 17. Now, I never told anybody about it, you know," she says with a laugh. "I never came out. Not 'til I moved to Boston when I was 18."

After studying music in Boston, she returned to Kansas with some news for the folks. "I moved back and told my parents and kind of came out and just drove out here. I told 'em like the week before I left. They knew anyway. It was very obvious. Very clear. They were fine. You know, long as I'm happy. That sort of thing."

Her songs now frequently address relationships and the search for fulfillment, a subject she knows well. "Lust is just searching—I think as human beings we are searching for, you know, what's gonna make us feel better, what's gonna take that pain away. And, um, a lot of people go drinking and taking drugs to try to numb the pain. I found it in physical relationships. I wrote a lot about that, because I was fascinated and absorbed in that. I mean I basically sang and had a relationship, you know, or relationships. That was basically in my 20s, what I was doing, which is where the first two albums and half of the third album comes from—is that inner growth, is that experience, is trying to find relief," she chuckles. "Or security or whatever you look for in a relationship that you don't know that you're looking for."

What she was seeking relief from was a whole host of nagging, inner demons. "Loneliness. Fear. You know: 'Why didn't my mother love me enough?' You know, the things that were missing, that I hadn't found in myself yet, that I couldn't fill up in myself. So, I was looking for someone else to fill them up."

Now settled in a four-year relationship with Julie Cypher, Melissa is happy to list what she looks for in a woman. "I think I'm attracted to strength," she says with a smile. "Independent ability, you know, to have their own career, have their own things that push them on, wicked sense of humor. 'Course I'm just describing my girlfriend is what I'm doing, so . . ." Her voice trails off with a chuckle. "Intense and willing to challenge and grow and push themselves and me. Yeah," she finishes.

Okay, so where would she rate herself on the butch-femme scale? She doesn't even pause. "Well, you know, being a Gemini I can go from one into the other real quickly. Just lookin' in my closet it's like how do I feel today, so I think because of my work and because you know, it's rock 'n' roll and all that, I tend to be more butch. I tend to put on a much more strong outward push. My, I'm just a little femme inside, so. . . . And I actually don't like to categorize anyone. I think a woman can be many things, whatever she wants."

What Melissa wants to do now is get in touch with her body. Sitting at the table, she isn't hefting anything heavier than a veggie burger, but, in fact, she's been working out this year. It's a decision influenced by her turning thirty. "That was when I first started going, 'You know what? I think I'm gonna start taking care of my body.'" With a mock-butch growl, she shows off the results by flexing her arm, revealing, well, if not a grapefruit-sized bicep, then at least one the size of a small peach. "Ah, well," she sighs. "I'm not really working out to be impressive-looking. I'm working out just to be stronger, 'cause what I do is really hard."

She'll have to be in shape when she gets back on the road to play live. Etheridge's dynamic with her audience is intense and fraught with sexual energy. The stage, she says, "is a place where I can really let loose. It's a safe place for me to let some energy out that I might not let out one-on-one. I really enjoy pulling an audience in. And, yeah-h. There's a lot of energy. There's a lot of sexual energy there. It's that sort of passionate energy, that other kind of energy that I don't think women get to express a lot, you know. And I enjoy doing it, and I enjoy my audience: women and men, and you know, straight and gay, and all of them together just, you know, hollerin'. I love it."

Having observed her mixed audiences, Etheridge sees similarities in their responses and says, "That's what I think we as a community should try to get across: That's the same passion. It's the same desires, you know. It's just whom you're deciding to direct that towards. And that's why I enjoy seeing straight and gay sitting next to each other feeling the same energy, because it *is* the same."

Though sexually exuberant, Etheridge has resisted being marketed as a boy-toy sex symbol. Fierce, unrestrained, defiantly unsvelte, she has had one of the most distinctive images of women in rock, and one not calculated to appeal to men. Of her record company she says, "I never let them market me as a sexy symbol, or you know, for men. They knew better than that."

So, it was a bit of a surprise to many longtime fans to see the glamorous, slick photos of a heavily made-up Etheridge that accompanied *Never Enough*. She has gotten some grief over the photos and says a bit testily that they were entirely under her control. She has no time for suggestions that they undercut her strength by molding her to the corporate image of women in rock: a slim, blonde, processed sex bomb. "I don't think that being pretty means you're not strong or you can only be pretty for men. I was being pretty for my lover." The underlying issue of just what constitutes "pretty" remains unexamined. Ah, well. Perhaps that's best left to *The Beauty Myth* to explain.

Etheridge has undergone a political awakening in the last couple of years, speaking out as a feminist and performing on behalf of concerns from gay rights to AIDS to reproductive choice. In January she canceled a performance in Colorado to protest the passage of Amendment 2. "I started looking around a bit, and my eyes were just opened a bit. And I started realizing that this has a lot to do with me. Women's rights, gay rights have everything to do with me," she declares.

In awakening as a feminist, she says, "I was realizing that I was, um, undermining myself as a feminist entity and not taking a hold of that power, not saying, 'You know what? There's not equality.' So,

there's a lot of power in saying I'm a feminist. And I think that the backlash of the eighties was to make feminism a bad word, and I just think that takes so much power away from us, and feminism is a beautiful word."

Etheridge's coming out as a lesbian was partially prompted by an awkward magazine interview in 1992, in which the interviewer prodded her to be a role model for gay youth. Unpleasant though it was, the experience got her thinking. "I was like, 'You know what? I want to come out. I want to find the right way to do it.' k. d. [lang] did it great in *The Advocate*. Boom! There it was," she recalls.

"And there I was at the Triangle Inaugural Ball and k. d. said something and she introduced me, and I just said, 'Well, you know, I'm really proud to have been a lesbian all my life,' not realizing that what I was doing," she says chuckling, "was coming out. I was just stating the fact. You know, there's the community and the friends, and I kinda walked off stage and went, 'You know what? I *th-think* I just came out.' Boom! It was out then. So, it was an incredible moment for me. I really couldn't have asked for better."

There is still cause for concern in the attitudes of the record industry, which hasn't historically been kind to out lesbian and gay artists. Warner Bros., k. d. lang's label, tried to censor the interview with *The Advocate* before it was published. Etheridge fired her own publicist this year, after discovering she was cutting the singer off from the gay press. "I really had a big, big change-up in my company and in the way that they handled things. I think they were more homophobic than I ever knew." She now sees every request for an interview that comes in to insure that it doesn't happen again. "It's much better now."

Having worked in the industry for five years, she says, "See, the thing is that I think that the business part of it—the record company part of it, the management part of gay artists—is that they're just afraid that somewhere there's gonna be a huge backlash. That all of a sudden the whole middle part of America, the big record-buying public, is gonna burn records and not support their artists. And it needs to be proved otherwise, and that's what artists like k. d. and myself are trying to do—to prove that one can be successful and it doesn't matter, and even people in Idaho and Missouri and Arkansas are gonna buy our records." And Kansas? "And Kansas! Well. Yeah," she says chuckling, "Kansas." That's an all-American girl talking, so America would be wise to listen.

Lesbian Outdoor Festivals

Robin Tyler and Torie Osborn

(Editor's Note: The first section of this article is authored by Robin Tyler. The second is authored by Torie Osborn.)

There were three times in my life when I "came out." One was in 1959 when, at age sixteen, I realized I was gay. My second coming out was over a decade later, when I joined the women's movement and began to identify as a lesbian feminist. Yes, I was a woman-loving woman, and in those days, one did not have to eat tofu or wear a crystal to qualify. "New Age" was every birthday, and the only witch I knew was in *The Wizard of Oz.* Our roles were simpler then, and we thought a twelve-step program was a dance class and leather was shoes, not a political issue. Feminism at that time was so "in" that even ABC television signed our feminist comedy team of Harrison and Tyler, and we starred on national network TV.

The third, and final, rebirthing was almost two decades from my first coming out, when I discovered that not only did I love women, but I was an Amazon, a lesbian warrior . . . and that the straight show business establishment world that I came from would never, never again be able to dictate what I should look like, what I should wear, if I should shave my legs, and what my weight should be.

That final coming out happened in 1978 when I attended the Michigan Women's Music Festival. Like thousands upon thousands of other dykes who have attended festivals, that experience totally changed my life.

After I'd been to Michigan that year, I knew that I could no longer continue in establishment show business. Women's music, no matter whether folk or jazz or rock or classical, was about the changing lives of women, of lesbians—and listening to it, being immersed in the huge dynamic lesbian village out in the woods was a totally transformative experience.

At that time, in the mid-seventies, women's music had become an important political and spiritual thread binding together the more daring wing of the women's movement. Lesbian feminists had boldly built a thriving alternative cultural, economic, and political network—a mini music industry of twenty record companies (Olivia, Redwood, Pleieades, and others), forty-five production companies, thirty full-time record distributors (called W.I.L.D., the Women's Independent Labels Distributors)—all helping to support the work of about forty lesbian recording artists singing out proudly about emerging lesbian identity.

This women's music circuit was the feminist equivalent of the folk circuit of the sixties. The blossoming women's music and the accompanying network were a kind of spiritual force behind women's liberation not unlike the gospel music and churches behind the civil rights movement.

On well-worn LPs by Cris Williamson, Margie Adams, Meg Christian, Alix Dobkin, and others, shared by lesbian lovers and friends in living rooms and bedrooms across the country, a bright new voice had burst forth—singing of self-discovery, empowerment, and bold, open pride in lesbian love. Concerts in clubs, women's coffeehouses, and church basements became political/spiritual experiences, with women linking arms with strangers and friends alike, and singing our hearts out, feeling the enormous surge of our collective power as lesbians for the first time in history.

But that power and force needed an even bigger and more total arena, an environment that could contain its expansive and enormous force. The outdoor, women-only music and culture festivals became that arena of the richest explorations and expressions of the burgeoning lesbian politics and culture.

The first Michigan Women's Music Festival was held in the summer of 1976 in the woods near Mt. Pleasant, Michigan. By that time there had been a few other outdoor gatherings, and one campus-based festival (the National Women's Music Festival at Champaign-Urbana, Illinois), but the timing, location, and strong need for lesbian-only space created a special spirit, and Michigan was born.

The first festival had one simple stage and was held on farmland with no amenities. But this event was historic: It was done by women, for women, and about women, and those women were virtually all lesbians. Building from nothing but raw land, the first city of lesbians in the modern age had a magnetic and pioneering sense of empowerment. Hundreds of women were free to be outdoors together without clothes, if they chose, and without the built-in caution and fear of male threat, male violence, male control that permeates women's existence normally. Free from daily battle with the patriarchy, the Amazon warrior could be reborn . . . and the lesbian nation formed.

In the nineteen years of its existence, Michigan has grown from a small, unsophisticated production into a major, internationally renowned event. Women save money and vacation time, sometimes for years, to travel across half the world to attend. In 1984, after years of various forms of organization, Lisa Vogel, one of the original organizers, and Barbara Price, an original producer and key shaper of women's music, formed a partnership to own and produce the festival. Now, eight thousand women gather annually every August at this Amazon Woodstock, making it the largest gathering of lesbians in the world.

The original lesbian separatist vision of women's music, which predominantly defined lesbian culture in the mid-seventies, was expanded in 1980 by the birth of Michigan's first daughter, The West Coast Music and Comedy Festival. Its owner/producer, Robin Tyler, and director, Torie Osborn, had come from diverse backgrounds: Robin emerged from professional, establishment show business as well as the feminist movement; Torie was a political organizer, shaped by the New Left and grassroots women's liberation politics of the sixties and early seventies. These women's influences reshaped women's festival history. Because of Robin's extensive theatrical background, from its inception, the West Coast Festival included, in addition to the music, three separate stages featuring comedy, theater, and films. Because of both Robin and Torie's political backgrounds, there was a major emphasis on political workshops. This multidimensional vision in turn influenced all successor festivals, as well as the mother festival, Michigan, which responded by expanding its production. Over the past fifteen years, the West Coast Festival has grown to thirty-five hundred women, making it the second-largest festival. A variety of new and diverse festivals sprang up in later years, including Campfest in New Jersey, New England Women's Music Festival in Massachusetts, and urban, noncamping festivals such as those sponsored by Redwood Records in Berkeley, and Sisterfire in Washington, D.C.

After Michigan and the West Coast, the Southern Women's Music and Comedy Festival is the next largest event of this kind. Begun in 1986 also by Robin Tyler, it is held near Cleveland, in White County, Georgia, an extremely reactionary area. It was started on a dare. A lesbian from California dared Robin Tyler to try to create a gathering of thousands of lesbians in the Deep South. Robin immediately bought an airline ticket, a book on southern campgrounds, and was off.

The Southern Festival is unique in that as well as having three stages—for music, comedy, and politics—there are cabins for five hundred, a lake, and tennis courts. It has gained a reputation as a "luppie" (lesbian upwardly mobile professional) and distinctively southern festival. Grits as well as granola are served for breakfast, and barbecued chicken, black-eyed peas, and other regional specialties are served, in addition to tofu and tempe; square dancing is a favorite event. This festival has been a major catalyst to lesbian/feminist political organizing in the South. The first women's bookstore in Mississippi came out of this festival, as well as the initial seed money of thirteen thousand dollars for the main stage rally for the 1987 Gay and Lesbian March on Washington. In 1989 this festival of lesbians participated in the AIDS candlelight memorial, joining hundreds of cities around the world.

Despite the evolution and increasing diversity over the years, all the women's festivals create a fundamentally similar and radical lesbian experience of empowerment and change. An intricate village is made from raw land by the labor, energy, and creativity of hundreds of women working together free from the constraints of regular lives infested with patriarchal dangers and damage. A work crew of 150-plus arrives a week early for the Southern; 200 arrive two weeks early for the West Coast; and 600 arrive months earlier for the Michigan Festival. These crews come to the land to put together the myriad services for a city of thousands upon thousands of women: health care, wheelchair ramps, circus tents, stages, lighting and sound systems, gigantic coordinated kitchens, toilets.

Women with varied professions or skills—doctors, carpenters, healers, electricians, stagehands, cooks, and others—come together to build these "cities of women." It is not unusual to see a lawyer flipping burgers at concessions or a doctor helping

K. D. Dickinson,
Mary Wildeman,
and Boo Dawson
in Montana.

with plumbing problems. For this is "Camp Run A Dyke," and the communal sense of participation toward a common and positive goal is overwhelming. The building of these festivals is one of the most rewarding parts of the events because it creates an ongoing community of lesbians.

The incredible range of expertise lesbians have is brought together in a cooperative, creative environment. From carpenters to child care workers, from acupressurists to aikido trainers, for a few short days, women come together from across the country and the world to build our own vision of what the world should be: accessible to all, inclusive of our rich diversity, responsive and caring, and wildly, powerfully creative. Women who have never met work cooperatively around the clock for a month to prepare this minicity in the woods, so that when the festival participants arrive, systems are in place and the fun can begin!

The essence of any festival is a chaotic, spontaneous spirit of creativity; and safety, healing, and inclusiveness are the touchstone concepts: Twelve-step programs and "chemical-free space" abound; differently-abled access is everywhere. Women dance and sing and make costumes and play together in the outdoors, making mud dances in the rain and circles in the sun. Thousands bring their

own instruments and percussion, and music jam sessions blossom like flowers everywhere. The rigors and rigidness of ordinary life explode into a rich, unrestrained exploration of ourselves, our potential, our culture.

Women's crafts booths display hundreds of womenmade goods; physical activities range from aerobics and tai chi classes to long walks in the magical woods. Eroticism and sensuality are everywhere, and absolute freedom abounds for all varieties of women—young and old, teenagers and grandmothers, fat and skinny, brown, black, and white. Moving stories of personal liberation are made and told every day: The woman who has had two mastectomies proudly taking her shirt off in the sun; the twelve-year-old who is learning to conga-drum rhythmically pulsing away personal pain and lack of self-confidence.

Festivals are also a time for serious networking and for intense discussion of all major issues in the lesbian community: incest, battering, S/M, pornography, insemination, lesbian ethics, class dynamics, fat oppression, racism and anti-Semitism, sobriety, self-defense, and women's roles in male politics, in global politics.

As a vibrant microcosm of lesbian culture in general, all the political debates have been played out at the festivals, including the early feminist tendency toward purism and "political correctness." At one festival an S/M group was (briefly) outlawed, creating an outcry. At several, spirituality was attempted to be entirely defined by feminist witchcraft. But, over time, the tendency toward extremes and toward correctness has loosened and the principle of inclusiveness has prevailed.

Women's outdoor festivals have helped launch not only cultural giants like Holly Near, Cris Williamson, and Teresa Trull, but women who have moved out into the mainstream. For example, the West Coast and Southern women's outdoor festivals introduced Danitra Vance and Melissa Etheridge on the main stage.

In important contrast to the lesbian utopian experience created at these festivals have been the real-world legal and political barriers faced by festival producers in obtaining and keeping permanent and stable homes for these outdoor events. The very idea of a large lesbian gathering is, of course, a significant threat to the established powers who own and control the land. Michigan faced a homophobic backlash after several years when its land's owner became a "born-again" Christian. The organizers finally bought their own land.

The West Coast Festival was thrown off its original site, a camp owned and operated by the presumably unhomophobic city of San Francisco. Years later, in depositions during a lawsuit brought by Robin Tyler, city representatives admitted the reason was the lesbian nature of the event. (The lawsuit brought against the city was dismissed on a technicality.) Two other West Coast sites were lost for the same reason, and its current site near Yosemite has been able to charge exorbitant rates.

The ACLU and NOW had to help the Southern Festival secure an ongoing site, due to homophobic response to media attention in its second year. Political and legal pressure finally forced the board of directors of the camp to back down. The East Coast Festival (NEWMR) has been turned off land again and again. The organizers have canceled the festival twice, including the 1989 festival.

The Southern Festival, which is produced by Robin Tyler, has run into another problem. They were not allowed to rent the campground near Cleveland, Georgia, called Camp Coleman. Although the camp is owned by the Union of American Hebrew Congregations, to which most gay and lesbian synagogues belong, the camp, after eight years of hosting the festival, succumbed to the political pressure of the local tax board, who said that if the festival continued, the camp's taxes would be raised. The festival is trying to bring a lawsuit against both the county and the Union of American Hebrew Congregations, whose alleged "nondiscrimination policy" does not extend to the southern lesbian community.

Wanda and Brenda Henson, who produce the SisterSpirit festival, have had numerous articles written about their campground in Ovett, Mississippi. They have been subjected to threats and harassment, both by individuals and the town, to the point that Attorney General Janet Reno tried to send a federal mediator to help work out the problem. The town of Ovett refused to meet with the mediator.

Yet another southern festival also lost its land, after four years in the South. Thousands of lesbians gathering is not a "right" in a homophobic country. It is something that has had to be fought for again and again.

Despite periodic attempts by the patriarchy to outlaw or outmaneuver lesbians' attempts to create these annual Sapphic cultural rituals in the woods, there seems little way to stop us. The festivals continue, undaunted, year after year, with no signs of diminishing: thousands upon thousands of women gathering to camp and play and organize and create worlds of our own making, free at last to expand our vision and our art.

Acknowledgments

Special thanks to Barbara Price, one of the original shapers and producers of women's music, and co-owner/producer of the Michigan Women's Music Festival.

Resources

For information on all festivals: Send S.A.S.E. to Robin Tyler Productions, 15842 Chase St., Sepulveda, CA 91343 (Tel: 818-893-4075, 9–5 Mon.–Fri. Pacific Standard Time; Fax: 818-893-1593).

Lesbians in the Arts

Jewelle L. Gomez

In 1988 the *New York Post,* a daily newspaper in Manhattan, ran a cover story and subsequently a series of articles denouncing the New York State Council on the Arts for its support of gay arts projects which "promoted" the homosexual way of life. One of the prominent grant recipients named was *Conditions* magazine, among the oldest lesbian literary journals in the country. While the attack on the arts council caused flurries of indignation, confusion, outrage, and a special legislative hearing in Albany, it was simply one in a series of periodic attempts by conservative forces to undermine funding of arts projects.

With the citation of *Conditions,* ignoring other women's projects that are not as lesbian-identified, it could be said that lesbian arts have arrived. Finally lesbian artists are visible enough to be considered for use as a public relations club against a state funding agency. (In fact the National Endowment for the Arts stopped funding the magazine several years earlier with the excuse that it was more lesbian than literary despite the publication of work by noted writers of international acclaim.) In spite of the backhanded nature of the compliment, there is something to be said for being too threatening to fund.

Two years later this ill wind turned into a typhoon as the National Endowment for the Arts itself was attacked by Jesse Helms and other members of Congress for funding provocative (or in their words "obscene") art. Helms specifically named three lesbian writers, Audre Lorde, Minnie Bruce Pratt, and Chrystos, as endowment award winners whose work was suspect.

In an attempt to divert attention from First Amendment issues, the executive director of the Endowment, John Frohnmayer, refused to allow awards, which had been approved by the endowment's review panel, to four performance artists, three of whom were lesbian or gay. The fourth was a self-identified feminist, which in some circles is still synonymous with being a lesbian.

The offering up as sacrifice to conservatives of four performance artists dramatically shifted the atmosphere for artists in the lesbian and gay community. The prickly questions of the previous decade—whether or not one's work was created just for the women's community; how "out" an artist is in the general art world—took on larger than simply philosophical dimensions. The politics and economics of being an out lesbian artist were thrown into sharp relief against a background of a conscious effort by conservatives to relegate openly lesbian and gay art to the realm of illegitimacy alongside child pornography. For the first time many artists who had not felt it necessary to articulate their lesbianism in their work began to see not only the dangers of being out but also the political power of uniting with other lesbian artists.

As a poet and a journalist over the past ten years, I've felt exhilarated by the range of arts activities women have explored and developed not only in New York City or San Francisco, the "gay centers," but also around the country—places where survival as a lesbian is a primary issue and art might seem to be simply something you do on those few, short days you spend at the Michigan Women's Music Festival.

Without denying the difficulty of making a living from day to day as an open lesbian, many of us have still actively pursued the development of the numerous art forms to which we are devoted.

The significance of the emergence of lesbian artists as a political focus should not be undervalued historically or sociologically for a number of reasons. Women have always expressed themselves, often through noninstitutional or non-Western art forms such as quilting or cornrowing of the hair. It is comforting to know that lesbians continue to value those types of outlets, because as our foremothers knew, the satisfaction of creating something in this world is one that cannot be equaled or destroyed.

Sociologically, the evolution of a lesbian cultural community and in turn an identifiable lesbian art (using art in the broad sense) is more significant than certainly the *New York Post* reporter was smart enough to know. As anthropologists would tell us, the establishment of an arts community is a great step in the solidification of a group's identity and a positive indicator of that group's impact on the surrounding culture. It is prophetic that probably the best known and most ancient lesbian figure

Kate Clinton, comedienne.

is not a buffalo tracker, stockbroker, or track star but a poet, Sappho of Lesbos.

When looking at the arts of the lesbian communities (and there have certainly been a number of communities defined by race, class, sexual habits, professions, among other criteria), we see that the written word has been the most prominent expression we have chosen. Names such as Adrienne Rich and Pat Parker have been the rallying points for the past decades. This is an odd choice in some ways since the production of books and magazines is so expensive. It is perhaps the result of the pervasive resistance of mainstream publishers to positive work by lesbians about lesbians (as opposed to work by straight women about lesbians or by lesbians about everything else but lesbians).

From the first presses such as Diana and Cleis and magazines such as *The Ladder*, the market has grown to include visual arts magazines, politically polemical magazines, esoteric philosophy journals, and erotica. The printed word has remained a most powerful tool, as if we defy anyone to again attempt to expunge us from history. We have used it collectively, individually, politically, and commercially from the dynamic self-publication of Harlem poet Sapphire to the national success of a publishers like Firebrand Books (publisher of both Audre Lorde and Minnie Bruce Pratt), Naiad Books, Spinsters Book Company, and Seal Press; as well as the international growth of *Hot Wire,* a magazine of women's music and culture. This past decade even witnessed the founding of the first press run by and for women of color—Kitchen Table—publishing and distributing fiction, poetry, nonfiction, and organizing pamphlets.

With the success of Alice Walker's *The Color Purple,* which featured two women entering into an explicitly lesbian relationship, and the well-received film version of Jane Rule's lesbian classic, *Desert of the Heart,* commercial publishers began to recognize the financial possibilities presented by lesbian fiction. But as in the days that produced *The Well of Loneliness,* commercial publishers appear interested primarily in white lesbians, characters who are alienated from other women.

But other mediums have also flourished. From the production and marketing of postcards to videos, lesbians have left no artistic stone unturned. It is significant that the other field that developed as quickly as poetry (which is an oral tradition and has always been the art of choice in a revolutionary culture) was music. Witness the small city that the Michigan festival has become as well as the New England Women's Music Festival and the West Coast Music and Comedy Festival.

It is in the arena of "women's music" that those prickly questions can be clearly examined. The success of lesbian music artists exemplified by the continuing music festivals and the growth of Olivia Records (success that includes the sponsorship of an annual cruise just for women) would indicate that there is an audience willing to support lesbian musicians. But this success had led to very little crossover popularity.

In music as in other arts disciplines, a lesbian artist who does not articulate her lesbianism either in her work or in interviews has a chance of being perceived as "universal" enough to warrant mainstream support. Like the "don't ask, don't tell" policy of the military, silence sometimes prevails. One young singer/songwriter burst upon the national music scene through an almost serendipitous series of social connections after being sustained by the devotion of the lesbian community. Her extraordinary talent and brilliant music brought her critical acclaim, yet the inequities she decries in her socially conscious lyrics do not yet include homophobia.

After Grammy Award–winner k. d. lang had avoided the "L" word in the national media for a while, she chose to come out nationally. Despite the music awards, lang does not get the level of radio airplay she might. Although this limited exposure may have slowed her record sales in some audiences, her openness made those who were already fans even more loyal. Rocker Melissa Etheridge also made the big step out of the closet, with few ill effects to her career.

Phranc, with her delicious crewcut and complete openness about her lesbianism, appeared to be embraced by the new music scene, but still remains somewhat of a specialty act for the record-buying public. Women's music festival veteran Holly Near has had substantial crossover success, primarily in the leftist, folksinging arena rather than among general audiences. Unequivocally out lesbian performers such as Alix Dobkin and Linda Tillery continue

to sustain successful careers with a new generation of audiences, even without the radio airplay they deserve.

There are a number of artists with national and international recognition who have chosen not to articulate their lesbian identities either in their work or in interviews. It seems pointless to demand that they slit open their personal lives to be picked over by the sensation-seeking media; yet because a good deal of their initial support has come from lesbians there is the sense that their coyness contributes to the myth that art with universal appeal is devoid of ethnic, gender, or sexual identity. In reality this standard is only raised by critics if the ethnicity, gender, or sexual identity isn't white, male-identified, and heterosexual (or at the very least pansexual).

For artists not using explicit language or images such as jazz composers, abstract painters, or even choreographers, the question may be somewhat philosophical, but certainly one to be pondered as personal contacts and connections are as much a part of success in the world of the arts as in the busi-

Jewelle Gomez.

© Ann E. Chapman

ness world. Artists nurtured in a lesbian social context have to figure out how to break through homophobia in order to make contacts in the other communities in order to promote their work.

The discussion of lesbian culture and the acceptance of lesbian artists in the mainstream has a somewhat antithetical angle to it, though. The development of a feminist/lesbian culture would seem to be a collective experience growing out of a unified political or social activity, such as a music festival, while the nature of artistic achievement is usually solitary, individualistic—forged from personal skill or genius. But the reason that lesbian artists have progressed this far can be attributed to an insistence on our right to create as open lesbians.

We have exercised an individual right and a collective right simultaneously. Unlike most gay men, who had access to commercial publishers, producers, and filmmakers, and chose to participate simply as men within the mainstream culture, lesbians made a space for ourselves, made an art for ourselves. It is this art that is a threat and that is our greatest treasure.

And it is invisibility that is our greatest enemy. In addition to providing a forum for lesbian musicians, festivals have often been an open marketplace for visual artists. Painters, sculptors, as well as weavers, jewelrymakers, and other craftspeople have made the festival circuit an important part of their survival. But the spectrum of visual artists remains broad: Myriam Fourgére is French Canadian–born and one of the founders, with Lin Daniels, of the new East Coast Lesbian Festival (the first to actually include the "L" word in its name!). She is also a sculptor of delicate cuntal images, blurring the lines between woman and the natural land and seascape to create art for both display and wear. Diane Edison, Afro-American oil painter, has chosen to paint a series of women of color who are lesbians. She is working on large canvases—five by six—a format that directly assails the notion of our invisibility.

Out of the great tradition of lesbian newspapers have come other artists in the visual tradition—cartoonists such as Alison Bechdel and Andrea Natalie, and a number of photographers. Until recently, newspapers seemed the only outlet for the work of people like Tee Corinne, JEB (Joan E. Biren), or Sharon Farmer. But the urge to do away with invisibility has led to greater deliberate documentation of lesbian life and the display and publication of that work. Books such as *Ceremonies of the Heart: Celebrating Lesbian Unions*, edited by Becky Butler, are designed explicitly to document the individual and personal elements of which a community is constructed. Veteran photographer Jill Posener is the creator of "refacement," that is, photographing sexist billboards enhanced by political graffiti. Her most famous is the Fiat car ad, which originally read "If it were a lady, it would get its bottom pinched." Sprayed across the bottom of the billboard was "If this lady was a car she'd run you down." Posener's work is now available in two collections from Pandora Press.

The Lesbian and Gay Community Center of New York City held an exhibit in 1989, curated by a coalition of lesbian artists. It featured four rooms of paintings, sculptures, collages, photographs of every definable approach from the old festival favorites of labial derivation to multidimensional, abstract assemblages of found objects. No longer is the lesbian artist content with simply the earth mother wonder image, but rather exploring the full spectrum of images that fill our lives.

But in spite of increasingly explicit and sexual imagery in the work of visual artists, the art that seems to have attracted the most direct attacks from conservatives seems to be that of performance artists like Holly Hughes, one of the artists whose award was rescinded by the national endowment director and who says her work is homosexual with a capital HOMO. What is a performance artist? And why would a lesbian want to be one? I think it's a poet gone public. Not simply reading in public but opening up ideas, following them to their theatrical conclusion. It's not being a stand-up comedian—turned TV star—like Sandra Bernhard, who lent Madonna the aura of lesbian chic by squiring her about.

When Marty Pottenger performs her work (shows such as *The Construction Stories* and *What It's Like to be a Man*), she becomes a series of characters who enact parts of their lives for you. The work is sometimes humorous, as when the adolescent rites of a teenage boy are seen to be as draconian as they really are. It is sometimes wistful as she demonstrates the installation of a lock paralleling the instructions with the description of the end of a seventeen-year relationship with her lover. It is perhaps this intimate and active linking of lesbian life with things considered ordinary that makes performance art so immediate and so threatening to conservatives.

The experience is three-dimensional. When characters created by Holly Hughes or Marty Pottenger or The Five Lesbian Brothers speak, the audience is acutely aware of both their attempt to write a person who is specific and real and of their presence as a lesbian interpreting the character.

The removal of the fourth wall is endemic to the process of performance art. For those who enjoy their fourth wall the New York–based WOW Cafe remains an important theater institution for women in this country. Founded in 1976, it has provided a home for a variety of productions like the classic *Cinderella,* fractured hilariously by playwright Cheryl Moch. It has been the home of cofounders Peggy Shaw and Lois Weaver, who have used the traditional theatrical conventions to revitalize literary classics such as Isabel Miller's *Patience and Sarah.*

Most recently they have been touring in the two-character piece, *Dressed Suits To Hire,* a play written by Holly Hughes that they helped to develop. The play has the traditional elements of theater yet uses the mythology of film noir, detective novels, and dyke drama to whip up two larger-than-life characters living in what feels like a claustrophobic fishbowl that's teetering on the edge of a rickety table. Although the form can be said to be traditional, it is the audacity of both the writer and the performers that makes this lesbian art. They've digested all the stereotypes and spit them back at us with an irony that is rooted in performing on a public stage as an out lesbian. After all, it was only a few decades ago that the subject of lesbianism was forbidden by law to be portrayed on the Broadway stage.

Film is another arena that has not welcomed the presence of lesbians and one in which our space has to be taken. While making theater has long since lost the simplicity of those mythical days when the kids in the neighborhood threw a blanket up in a barn and had themselves a show, the process of raising money to make a film has become even more arcane. Yet the number of lesbians who follow the pursuit continues to grow. Not so many years ago I knew only one lesbian filmmaker—Greta Schiller, who directed *Before Stonewall,* for which I did research and interviews. And *Born In Flames,* directed by Lizzie Borden, which foretold a mythic lesbian revolution complete with weaponry and explosives, was hotly debated among women. The Lesbian and Gay Film Festivals in New York and

© 1991 JEB (Joan E. Biron)

Stormé Delarverié and Michelle Parkerson.

California now feature 20 to 40 percent films by lesbians and have spawned the annual Lesbian and Gay Experimental Film Festival and the Lesbian and Gay Video Festival. The offerings run the gamut from the deleterious drama of Sheila MacLaughlin's *She Must Be Seeing Things,* a sexy examination of what happens when a woman lets her jealous imagination run away with her; to Su Friedrich's *Damned if You Don't,* a darkly sensual glimpse at the seduction of a young nun by her woman neighbor woven through with the narratives from the 1947 Deborah Kerr film, *Black Narcissus* and *Immodest Acts: The Life of a Lesbian Nun in Renaissance Italy.*

In the same festival, pioneer lesbian filmmaker Barbara Hammer premiered her newest film, *Optic Nerve.* The short piece, while maintaining her visually experimental style, was one of her most personal statements. She overlays primal and electronic images underscored with penetrating sound (by Helen Thorington) to depict a visit to her grandmother in a nursing home. Hammer is able to explore a very particular relationship—lesbian to foremother—in an intuitive way that experimental film is always striving for.

More traditional explorations of who we are on film are still being made. Michelle Parkerson, who lives in Washington, D.C., has, along with her books of poetry, been making documentary films for a number of years. Her latest documents the life of Stormé Delarverié, a singer who was the only woman in the integrated, male drag show, The Jewel Box Revue, in the 1950s.

In the popular culture there is Pop Video run by Lil Pitcaithly and Joyce Compton in Washington, D.C. They have produced *Heroines,* a collection of film clips of women athletes; *Lesbianage,* a full-length comedy thriller; and *Lesbian Tongues,* a series of light-hearted interviews with a variety of lesbians from across the country. The popularity of the VCR and the commercial sale of lesbian videos has had a powerful impact in the past decade because lesbians—whether living in urban, suburban, or rural areas—can have unifying experiences on a national scale, something generally not provided lesbians by the mass media.

In fact, such a lack has given rise to the lesbian soap opera, *Two in Twenty,* produced in Somerville, Massachusetts. It is a comic parody of the suds that fill the daily airwaves, using the complications of a number of lesbian relationships from the one who's in love with the one who's still married, to what if your daughter would rather live with her straight father.

Comedy is an abiding element for lesbians in our expressions of art. For me it has always been the hinge upon which I've hung all of my tough emotional stuff. Perhaps because my grandmother was such a comic storyteller, perhaps because the irony of being a black lesbian is such that there is no other way of expressing it.

Danitra Vance, a black lesbian stand-up comedian and actress who died in 1995, brought that irony to the stage in a way that was more biting than performance art, drama, film, or video had previously been. She had some success doing performances around the country, including benefits for community organizations such as Kitchen Table Women of Color Press. She was even a regular for a year on NBC's *Saturday Night Live.* But her open lesbianism and feminism seem to have made her taboo on talk shows.

Because Vance spoke directly to the audience from within herself, she could bend reality much the same as one can do when writing a poem. But because so much humor relies on our ability to make fun of ourselves, the charge of self-hatred or bitchiness will never be easy to sidestep. Our best comedians—Pat Bond (who died just at the end of the decade), Robin Tyler, Kate Clinton, Karen Williams—have not been afraid of pushing those boundaries as far as they can. When a Vance character pulled her hat down over her eyes and told us in a deep voice how she became a transsexual when she accidentally OD'd on her birth control pills, the "Thought Police" must have rustled in the audience. But others remembered those dial-a-day dispensers and laughed, happy that another lesbian was unafraid to remember those days out loud. Vance balanced being an activist and artist. In the same year in which she won an Obie Award for her Off-Broadway performance in Zora Neale Hurston's *Spunk,* she also led a demonstration against The Philip Morris Company for their support of Jesse Helms. The conservative religious Right, under the auspices of many national organizations, most with the words "family" and "values" prominently displayed in their names, began to put much of their influence behind whipping up fear of openly lesbian and gay people. Yet the media has selectively embraced lesbian comedians—both the profoundly profane Lea Delaria and the elegant Marga Gomez brought their comedy to national television despite the political climate.

Speaking out loud about our sexuality, past or present, has been made even more difficult than usual by the recent growth of a segment of the feminist movement focusing on defining what is and is not politically correct in women's sexual lives and thoughts. Ironically, this faction's efforts provided the platform for right-wing conservatives such as Jesse Helms while simultaneously being an impetus for lesbians' recognition of the pivotal role of our sexual desires, whatever they might be. Following a number of public attacks on lesbian writers—Dorothy Allison, Amber Hollibaugh, and Joan Nestle—who spoke openly about the relationship of sexuality to their lives and work, the market for explicitly lesbian erotica boomed in the women's community. In response to censorship efforts the production of erotic magazines, books, and videos by women increased tenfold. Because the artist, whether comedian or essayist, is also a social critic, the attacks from the *New York Post,* conservative feminists, and Jesse Helms can be received as compliments.

For lesbian artists, being out will always be a dilemma. We all know the rumors about which movie star, which comedian, which actress, which director is a lesbian. And we know the fear that artists have of their work being dismissed once their lesbianism is known publicly. Who's going to cast someone as a movie love interest if everyone knows she's a butch? This is why the development of a lesbian arts community has been so crucial. In observing and participating in this development it's striking to notice how closely the arts parallel political developments. In many ways our arts and arts audiences are integrated—when I do poetry readings my audience is multiethnic; the cast of *Two in Twenty* is integrated; Firebrand Books publishes the work of Asian, Hispanic, Native American, Afro-American, as well as white writers. But often, except for incidents of convenient cultural imperialism,[1] the communities do remain as separate as our social patterns.

Yet the multiethnic nature of the women's community can never again be ignored. The 1989 Feminist Book Fair in Montreal was rocked by Native American women who challenged white feminists who profited from the appropriation of Native American religion. The 1991 conference of the National Women's Studies Association was canceled amid complaints by black members of ongoing racism. When Audre Lorde was given the Bill T. Whitehead Award by the predominantly white, gay professional association, The Publisher's Triangle, she refused to accept the cash offered and insisted it be used to promote lesbians and gay men of color who are struggling to be published. Asian, Latina, and Native American lesbians still remain "the other" in the eyes of many members of the lesbian community. Yet *Companeras,* the first anthology of Latina lesbian writing was edited and published by Juanita Ramos and Mariana Romo-Carbona; Asian Lesbians of the East Coast continues to raise money to fund its traveling cultural/history slide show, and in 1990 for the first time an official Native American contingent marched in the New York City Gay Pride march. Lesbian artists who've felt the pressure of being out in their own ethnic communities, yet have not felt welcomed by the lesbian community, have begun to make their own mark, insuring that the lesbian cultural landscape will never be as Caucasian dominated as women's music festivals were once perceived to be.

The past decade has found lesbian artists less naive and a little shopworn by both internal struggles and external attacks. Collectivity is no longer universally worshipped and identity can never be taken for granted. The work that lesbians create can no longer be defined simply with catch words such as "nurturance" or "gentleness." But passion, political and legal savvy, and endurance must be included to get closer to an accurate description of the life and work of lesbian artists.

The ability to embrace all the varied threads that make up the lesbian cultural tapestry is ultimately our greatest strength. The impulse to create is the impulse to comment on the human condition, to make our presence felt. Those of us who leave our mark as lesbian artists will have helped to insure the future for us all—artist and audience alike. Years ago Meg Christian celebrated the arrival of "the leaping lesbians" in song. It's still a great coda—there are just more of us now.

Notes

1. The author notes that whites have absorbed, imitated, and popularized black art forms. For example, black drag queens have been "vogueing" or moving in a particular manner for a long time. When Madonna adopted this movement,

vogueing came to public notice and gained acceptance.

Resources

Belle Lettres, a review of books by women, 11151 Captain's Walk Ct., Gaitherburg, MD 20878

Born in Flames, dir. by Lizzie Borden.

Buffalo Hide, a lesbian and gay Native American newsletter, Suite 141, Zeckendorf Towers, 111 E. 14th St., New York, NY 10003

Damned If You Don't, dir. by Su Friedrich, 1988. Distributed by Filmmakers Coop, 175 Lexington Ave., New York, NY 10016

Firebrand Books, 191 The Commons, Ithaca, NY 14850

Hot Wire, journal of women's music and culture, 5210 North Wayne, Chicago, IL 60640

Immodest Acts: The Life of a Lesbian Nun in Renaissance Italy, by Judith C. Brown (New York: Oxford University Press, 1986).

Kitchen Table: Women of Color Press, P.O. Box 908, Latham, NY 12110

Lesbianage and *Lesbian Tongues,* dir. by Joyce Compton, POP Video, P.O. Box 60862, Washington, DC 20039

The New Festival; Lesbian and Gay Films, 568 Broadway, Rm. 1104, New York, NY 10012.

The New Phoenix Rising, an Asian Pacific newsletter, P.O. Box 31631, Oakland CA 94604

Optic Nerve, dir. by Barbara Hammer, 1988. Distributed by Women Make Movies, 225 Lafayette St., New York, NY 10012, 212-925-0606.

Outlook, a magazine of lesbian and gay culture and politics, P.O. Box 246430, San Francisco, CA 94114-6430

She Must Be Seeing Things, dir. by Sheila MacLaughlin, 1988. Distributed by Women Make Movies.

Storme, dir. by Michelle Parkerson, 1988. Distributed by Women Make Movies.

Two in Twenty, P.O. Box 105, Somerville, MA 02144

WOW Cafe, 59 E. 4th St., New York, NY 10003

Directory of National Lesbian Organizations

Compiled by Karol D. Lightner

For many years, annual guides have been published that list services, organizations, bookshops, accommodations, and bars for lesbians. They usually cover the United States, Canada, Mexico, and Puerto Rico, but there are also international guides for the world traveler. These guides can be mail ordered or purchased in most alternative or women's bookstores. For a more complete and regularly updated listing of national and international resources, we suggest you consult one of the following travel guides:

Ferrari's Places of Interest for Women: Guide to Women's Travel, P.O. Box 35575, Phoenix, AZ 85069, 602-863-2408. An international guide, covering Africa, Asia, Europe, Middle East, Pacific Region, Canada, Caribbean, Latin America, and the United States.

Gay Yellow Pages: The National Edition, P.O. Box 533, Village Station, New York, NY 10014-0533, 212-674-0120.

Inn Places, Worldwide Accommodations Guide, Ferrari Publications, P.O. Box 37887, Phoenix, AZ 80569, 602-863-2408

Women's Traveller, P.O. Box 422458, San Francisco, CA 94142-2458, 415-255-0404. (Also publishes *Damron Address Book,* which is a gay men's guide, but can be used if no women's guides are available. In general, most men's guides can be used in a pinch.)

If you do not have access to a guidebook or contacts in a given area, here are some tips on finding the community you seek:

1. Check the telephone directory to look for lesbian or gay service centers, organizations, and/or hotlines. Be aware that the names of some organizations may not have gay/lesbian names for reasons of protection, or because of hassles with a local phone company.

2. Visit or call a local college campus. Check bulletin boards in student or women's centers. Many colleges have lesbian, gay, and bisexual organizations and activities. Their bookstores will probably carry lesbian and gay titles and perhaps local newspapers.

3. Look in the phone directory for any bookstore with a "curious" name that may possibly carry alternative titles, as well as have information and listings of organizations and events. By "curious," I mean this: Alternative bookstores tend to be named after famous gay men, lesbians, feminists, or an event or book title familiar to those communities; some stores may have a New Age feel to their names, and many have names familiar to the women's community (examples: Sisterhood Books, A Woman's Place, Lavender Books, Lambda Rising, Pink Pyramid, Oscar Wilde Memorial, Gertrude Stein Memorial, Beyond the Closet, Giovanni's Room, Full Circle Books, Different Drummer, or any store with "Pride" or "Out" in the title). If you are in doubt, just call and ask. What's the worst that can happen? Someone may slam the phone down! Then, at least you will know.

4. Another good resource, and sometimes the only one in a given area, is the Metropolitan Community church (MCC), which will be listed in the phone directory by name, whereas movement or service organizations may be less obvious for survival purposes. MCC staff may be able to direct you to other resources. Check out Unitarian and Quaker resources: Both churches have been not only accepting of our communities for decades, but also sponsor lesbian/gay activities. Dignity, for lesbian and gay Catholics, may have a chapter in the area.

5. Parents and Friends of Lesbians and Gays (PFLAG) have many chapters and may be listed in the phone directory. If they do not know where lesbians socialize, they should be able to put you in contact with those who do.

6. The National Organization for Women (NOW) has chapters around the country and will be listed in the phone book. Someone there may know where to go (or at least know someone you can call). Women's centers, alternative health clinics, or an

AIDS center/task force may be good resources. Many women's centers can be found on college campuses.

7. Another possible contact, and one quite necessary for those lesbians in twelve-step programs, is Alcoholics Anonymous (AA), Narcotics Anonymous (NA), or Overeaters Anonymous (OA). These organizations are found all over the world: Many cities have gay or lesbian AA, OA, or NA groups.

8. Check out the local bars if you have the time and energy. Be aware that, in many parts of the country, there will only be one gay bar and both men and women will frequent it. Usually, if you are in a bar for more than a few moments, you can tell if it's straight, gay, or mixed. Or you can just call and ask.

9. Check out local publications, especially freebies. Many restaurants, coffeehouses, bookshops, and merchandise stores catering to alternative clients, may carry local gay and lesbian periodicals. These publications will have listings and advertising for bars, organizations, and happenings around town.

At the end of this article is a small, national listing of those organizations, religious groups, services, bookstores, and publications that might be helpful to the lesbian who wishes to make contact with lesbian and gay communities around the country. If one name of an organization or resource in a given area is acquired, just a phone call is all it usually takes to enable the lesbian traveler to find her sought-after community.

In my research, I discovered that in some areas of the United States, resources are few and far between. I found this especially so in the far Northwest of Minneapolis to east of Spokane and Portland—and in some areas of the South. Generally speaking, the closer one is to a large metropolitan area, the easier it is to find lesbian, gay, and bisexual resources. In smaller towns and rural areas, little or nothing may be found, and the lesbian who lives in or is visiting those areas may have to travel to find activities and community.

One of my gutsier friends found her way around a strange city by walking up to two "obvious" lesbians at a flea market and asking them where the action was! While I do not advocate walking up to a stranger and "outing" her in a public place, you might, if your dyke antenna is up and you suspect that she is a "sister," ask her if she knows where women's events or groups are held, or if she knows of a women's bookstore in town. Believe you me, if you find the bookstore, you'll know within minutes where every lesbian event in town is held and probably receive directions on how to get there to boot!

My friend Diana and I once found ourselves in Tucson, Arizona, without a guidebook, and wanted to see if any lesbian events might be taking place and/or the whereabouts of a lesbian bar. We had no names to go by, but Diana had heard there was a feminist bookstore there; alas, we didn't know the name. We looked in the phone directory. There were a number of bookstores listed, but one bore the name "Antigone Books." I knew that Antigone, in classical Greek literature, was the lead (female) character in the oldest play in the world dealing with civil disobedience. "That has to be it," I said—and it was.

If dozens of bookstores are listed, and classical literature is not a topic you ever got around to studying, a phone call to a large bookstore might reveal a knowledgeable clerk who would be happy to refer you to an alternative bookstore.

A friend I know tells me that when she was in New York, she asked a taxi driver where the lesbian bars were—and he knew. (I would only do this, however, if someone else was with me in the cab. I know of at least two lesbians who have had nasty encounters with male taxi drivers in similar circumstances.)

I knew a lesbian couple who lived in a rural area in New England and were quite isolated. Then, one day they discovered there was a local women's softball team. Guess what!?

Remember—all you have to do is make one good contact and, within minutes, you will more than likely know every organization, event, and bar in town!

The following entries were compiled from a mailing list provided by the *Gay Yellow Pages*, and also from networking. Only those organizations that responded to our mailings and phone calls are listed. I am grateful to *Feminist Bookstore News*, San Francisco, for supplying us with the very valuable addresses of women's and alternative bookstores all over the United States and Canada, and also San Diego's *Obelisk, the Bookstore* for allowing me to do some last-minute bird-dogging.

I would personally like to thank those individuals, good friends, and significant others who assisted me in the original compiling and mailing of this directory: Diana Denoyer, Tory Seger, and the late Rickey Dattile. Thank you all, dear friends.

National Organizations

Able-Together, P.O. Box 39752, Los Angeles, CA 90039. Publication for disabled and nondisabled gay and lesbian people who want to meet or correspond. Quarterly publication.

Affirmation/Gay & Lesbian Mormons, P.O. Box 46022, Los Angeles, CA 90046, 213-255-7251. Educational and support group for lesbian and gay Mormons. Publishes *Affinity*.

American Gay and Lesbian Atheists, Inc. (AGLA), P.O. Box 66711, Houston, TX 77266-6711, 713-880-4242; Fax and office 713-862-3283. Regular activities. Devoted to constitutional principal of separation of state and church. Offers forum for lesbians and gay atheists to meet, exchange ideas, uphold civil rights of atheists. Publishes *The American Gay and Lesbian Atheist* monthly.

Bisexual Resource Center, P.O. Box 639, Cambridge, MA 02139, 617-338-9595. Publishes the *International Directory of Bisexual Groups*.

Brethren/Mennonite Council for Lesbian and Gay Concerns, P.O. Box 65724, Washington, DC 20035-5724, 202-462-2595. Answering machine. Provides support for Brethren and Mennonite gay people and their parents, spouses, relatives, and friends. Publishes *Dialogue*, BMC newsletter, free. Topical newsletter to encourage dialogue with churches, among lesbian and gay members.

Conference for Catholic Lesbians (CCL), P.O. Box 436, Planetarium Station, New York, NY 10024, 718-680-6107. Evenings, weekends. Leave message. Write for membership. A national organization of women who recognize importance of Catholic tradition in shaping lives and who seek to develop and nurture a spiritual life that enhances and affirms lesbian identity and who proclaim existence as Catholic lesbians. Twenty CCL groups around the country.

Dignity, USA, 1500 Massachusetts Ave., N.W., Ste. 11, Washington, DC 20005, 202-861-0017; Fax 429-9808. Organization of lesbian, gay, and bisexual Catholics working toward development of a sexual theology for acceptance of gays and lesbians in the Catholic church. Has a hundred chapters throughout the United States. Publishes *Dignity Newsletter* monthly, price included with membership.

Dykes, Disability & Stuff, P.O. Box 6773, Madison, WI 53714-8773. Quarterly with news, verse, articles, and views of, by, and for lesbians with disabilities.

ELLAS, P.O. Box 681061, San Antonio, TX 78268-1061. Network for Latina lesbians, provides cultural, social, and political alternatives for and by lesbian Latinas to affirm identity, recognize lesbian Latina herstory. Annual retreat held. For lesbian Latinas only.

Feminist Bookstore News, P.O. Box 882554, San Francisco, CA 94118, 415-626-1556; Fax 626-1556. Hours: Mon.–Fri., 9–5 P.M. Trade magazine for the women-in-print movement and women who care passionately about lesbian literature; acts as center for networking and support of feminist booksellers. Publishes bimonthly trade journal for feminist booksellers; includes over two hundred announcements and reviews of books plus lots of information on women-in-print movement. Send for updated list of women's bookstores.

Gay & Lesbian Advocates and Defenders (GLAD), P.O. Box 218, Boston, MA 02112, 617-426-1350. Serves New England. Publishes *GLAD Briefs*.

Gay & Lesbian Alliance Against Defamation (GLAAD), Inc., 150 W. 26th St., Ste. 503, New York, NY 10001, 212-807-1700; Fax 807-1806. Works for fair, accurate images of lesbians and gay men in the media. Publishes *GLAAD Bulletin*.

Gay & Lesbian Hispanics Unidos, P.O. Box 70153, Houston, TX 77270-0153, 713-523-1140. Twenty-four hours. A social and political organization for Latinos and Latinas. Meets second Monday of month, other information may be obtained by calling phone numbers given above. Social, cultural, and educational organization created to motivate, educate, and instill pride in all gay and lesbian Hispanics. Largest organization of its kind in Texas and the nation. Publishes *Noticias* monthly.

Gay & Lesbian History Stamp Club, P.O. Box 230940, Hartford, CT 06123-0940, 203-653-3791. Activities: three times yearly in New York City in conjunction with local stamp shows. Promotes and fosters interest in collection, study, and dissemination of knowledge of worldwide philatelic material depicting gay and lesbian history on stamps. Publishes *Lambda Philatelic Journal,* quarterly.

Gay/Lesbian Legal Referral Service, P.O. Box 421983, San Francisco, CA 94101-1983, 415-621-3900.

Gay and Lesbian Parents Coalition International (GLPCI), P.O. Box 50360, Washington, DC 20091, 202-583-8029; Fax 202-783-6204. Provides support to gay/lesbian parents and others in a child nurturing situation. Educational outreach to gay and straight communities. Publishes *Network* bimonthly.

Gay & Lesbian Task Force, American Library Association, c/o O.L.D.S., 50 E. Huron St., Chicago, IL 60611. Directory of bookstores specializing in gay, lesbian, and feminist books—$2.00; directory of publishers—$1.50; professional groups of gays and lesbians—$1.50.

Gaylaxians International, P.O. Box 675, Lanham-Seabrook, MD 20703-0675. Holds workshops, social parties at various science fiction and fantasy conventions. An international organization for gay people and their friends interested in science fiction and fantasy. Publishes *Gaylactic Gayzette,* quarterly. Promoting Gay/Lesbian/Bisexual Sci-Fi worldwide.

Heresies: A Feminist Publication on Art & Politics, P.O. Box 1306, Canal Street Station, New York, NY 10013, 212-227-2108. Heresies Collective, Inc. Hours: Wed.–Thurs., 10–6. Publishes twice yearly. Thematic centered on arts and politics within a theme, focused on women.

Human Rights Campaign, 1012 14th St., N.W., Ste. 607, Washington, DC 20005, 202-628-4160; Fax 202-347-5323. Hours: Mon.–Fri., 9 A.M.–6 P.M. Nation's largest political action committee for lesbian and gay rights and responsible AIDS policy with largest independent political action committee in the United States. Lobbies legislators, contributes to campaigns of pro-gay politicians, educates constituency on gay politics. Publishes *Momentum; Capital Hill Update.*

International Association of Lesbian/Gay Pride Coordinators, 746 14th St., Ste. 1, San Francisco, CA 94114, 415-861-0779.

Jewish Lesbian Daughters of Holocaust Survivors (JLDHS), P.O. Box 75, Hadley, MA 01035-0075. Semiannual meetings, intensive weekends of networking, and support. Outreach, networking, and support to Jewish lesbian daughters of Holocaust survivors and their partners. Lesbian only.

Lambda Youth Network, P.O. Box 7911, Culver City, CA 90233. Lists referral services for gay and lesbian youth, under age twenty-three. For details, send S.A.S.E., give age and state. Lists talklines, newsletters, pen-pal programs, and other services.

Latina Lesbian History Project, P.O. Box 678, Binghamton, NY 13905-0678.

League for Gay & Lesbian Prisoners, 1202 Pike St., Ste. 1044, Seattle, WA 98122-3934. A support and resource network for gay, lesbian, bisexual, and transgender prisoners and people in their support systems.

Lesbian Herstory Archives/Lesbian Herstory Educational Foundation, Inc., P.O. Box 1258, New York, NY 10016, 718-768-3953. The archives exists to gather and preserve records of lesbian lives and activities so that future generations of lesbians will have access to materials relevant to their lives. Publishes *Lesbian Herstory Archives News.*

Lesbian Mother's National Defense Fund, P.O. Box 21567, Seattle, WA 98111, 206-325-2643. Voice and TTY. Twenty-four-hour answering service. Weekly meetings. To support lesbian mothers in their parenting decision and maintenance of parenting role; to include just decisions in child custody and visitation disputes, eliminating sexual orientation as consideration in these decisions. Offers prelegal advice, personal and emotional support, referral system, quarterly newsletter, and alternative conception and adoption information. Publishes *Mom's Apple Pie.*

The NAMES Project Foundation, A National AIDS Memorial, 310 Townsend St., #310, San Francisco, CA 94107-1607, 415-882-5500. Created a quilt as memorial to those who have been lost to AIDS. Provides positive and creative means of expression for those whose lives have been touched by the epidemic. Publishes *NAMES Letter,* the NAMES Project newsletter.

National Center for Lesbian Rights (NCLR), 1663 Mission St., #550, San Francisco, CA 94103, 415-621-0674 (formerly the Lesbian Rights Project). Only organization in the country whose priority is defending the rights of lesbians. Public interest law firm provides no-fee legal service and law reform litigation for men and women who have experienced discrimination based on their sexual orientation; nationwide telephone advice and counseling program; publishes *Quarterly Newsletter* and distributes materials about legal effects of antigay discrimination.

National Coalition for Gay, Lesbian, and Bisexual Youth, P.O. Box 24589, San Jose, CA 95154-4589, 408-269-6125; Fax 269-5328.

National Coalition of Black Lesbians and Gays, c/o 505 8th Ave., 16th floor, New York, NY 10018, 212-563-8340. Addresses the needs and concerns of black lesbians and gays. Information about black lesbian and gay issues and lifestyles.

National Gay and Lesbian Domestic Violence Victim's Network, 3506 S. Ouray Circle, Aurora, CO 80013, 303-266-3477.

National Gay and Lesbian Task Force, 1734 14th St., N.W., Washington, DC 20009, 202-332-6483. Hours: Mon.–Fri., 9 A.M.–5 P.M. Membership $30. Publishes *Task Force Report* quarterly. Free with membership. NGLTF is a national gay rights organization with an activist agenda for social change.

National Organization for Women, 1000 16th St., N.W., Ste. #700, Washington, DC 20005, 202-331-0066. Largest women's rights organization in the United States; members actively involved in every issue relating to full equality for women in our society. Publishes *National NOW Times*.

National Women's Mailing List, P.O. Box 68, Jenner, CA 95450, 707-632-5763. Maintains a feminist mailing list consisting of sixty thousand individual names, approximately half of which have requested mail of interest to lesbians. List of over five hundred gay and lesbian organizations.

National Women's Music Festival, P.O. Box 1427, Indianapolis, IN 46206-1427, 317-927-9355.

off our backs, 2423 18th St., N.W., Washington, DC 20009, 202-234–8072. A women's newsjournal. Hours: 5 days/week, 10 A.M.–6 P.M. Publishes eleven times/year. Longtime feminist newsjournal with news, reviews, commentary, announcements, letters.

Open Hands, 3801 N. Keeler Ave., Chicago, IL 60541, 312-736-5526; Fax 736-5475. Resources for ministries affirming diversity of human sexuality.

Parents and Friends of Lesbians and Gays (PFLAG) National Office, 1012 14th St., N.W., Ste. 700, Washington, DC 20005, 202-638-4200. Offers family support, support of gays and les-

bians, advocacy for rights, education. Chapters and contacts all over the world. Publishes *Federation Newsletter* quarterly.

Partners Task Force for Gay & Lesbian Couples, P.O. Box 9685, Seattle, WA 98109-0685, 206-935-1206.

Radical Women. National office: 523-A Valencia St., San Francisco, CA 94110, 415-864-1278. Call ahead. Public and educational meetings held. An international socialist feminist organization in front line in the war against racism, sexism, antigay bigotry, and labor exploitation. Order form of publications available.

Section on Gay/Lesbian Legal Issues, Association of American Law Schools, c/o Professor Arthur Leonard, New York Law School, 57 Worth St., New York, NY 10018, 212-431-2156. Annual meeting during convention of AALS. Educates law teachers about lesbian and gay legal issues and provides support for lesbians and gay men in law teaching. Publishes newsletter once per semester.

Sex Information & Education Council of the United States (SIECUS), 130 W. 42nd St., Ste. 25FL, New York, NY 10036-7901, 212-819-9770. Publishes *SIECUS Reports*.

Sinister Wisdom, Inc., P.O. Box 3252, Berkeley, CA 94703. Journal for the Lesbian Imagination in the Arts and Politics. Publishes three to four times/year. Literature, arts, political analysis, essays, songs, plays. Work by and for lesbians.

Spinsterhaven, P.O. Box 718, Fayetteville, AR 72702. Women planning a retirement haven for both older women and women with disabilities.

United Church Coalition for Lesbian/Gay Concerns (UCCL/GC), 18 N. College St., Athens, OH 45701, 614-593-7301. National organization related to the United Church of Christ providing support, education, and advocacy for lesbian/gay rights in church and society. Publishes WAVES quarterly.

Universal Fellowship of Metropolitan Community Churches (MCC), 5300 Santa Monica Blvd., Ste. 304, Los Angeles, CA 90029, 213-464-5100. Publishes *Alert and Keeping in Touch*.

Wages Due Lesbians, P.O. Box 14512, San Francisco, CA 94114, 415-626-4114. Please call answering machine. International network of lesbian women of different races, nationalities, occupations, ages, dis/abilities, organizing in the international wages for housework campaign to get women's unwaged work counted and paid for. Publishes pamphlet "Out of the Closet, Into the Workhouse."

Wishing Well, P.O. Box 71390, Santee, CA 92072-3090, 619-443-4818. Publication for women-loving women to write and meet each other.

Women and AIDS Resource Network, 30 Third Ave., Ste. 212, Brooklyn, NY 11217, 718-596-6007; Fax 596-6041.

Women's Motorcyclist Foundation, 7 Lent Ave., LeRoy, NY 14482, 716-768-6054. Answering machine. Networking foundation to help women bikers find each other, ride together, and inspire other women to ride; hosts a biannual motorcycle rally. Publishes *Chrome Rose's Review* biannually, newsletter/directory.

Womyn's Braille Press, P.O. Box 8475, Minneapolis, MN 55408, 612-822-4352. Evenings and weekends, leave message. Provide books and periodicals on tape and braille, for loan or purchase, to blind and print-handicapped womyn. Publishes *W.B.P. Newsletter* quarterly.

World Congress of Gay and Lesbian Jewish Organizations, P.O. Box 3345, New York, NY 10008-3345.

Annotated Bibliography

Wendy Caster

Twenty years ago, when Karol Lightner wrote the bibliography for the first edition of *Our Right To Love*, it was possible to catalogue every single existing lesbian-written and lesbian-focused work in a handful of pages. The past two decades have brought a thrilling explosion in the publication of lesbian writing, and it would now take hundreds of pages just to list all the lesbian books that are out there. This bibliography samples lesbian titles from presses big and small, from writers famous and little known, and from many genres and points of view. (These books can be mail-ordered from Lambda Rising [800-621-6969] and A Different Light Bookstore [800-343-4002].)

(Note: I researched this list both at bookstores and through *Books in Print* on CD-ROM, which is the industry standard. Sometimes the years of publication given in the books themselves differed from those on *Books in Print;* in addition, sometimes *Books in Print* listed books under their authors but not under their titles. To confuse matters more, *Books in Print* occasionally spelled an author's name in different ways; for instance, some of Rita Mae Brown's books were listed under "Brown, Rita Mae," while others were listed under "Brown, Rita M." Therefore, if someone at a bookstore tells you that a title is out of print, suggest other ways it might be listed.)

Prolific Multigenre Authors

Allison, Dorothy. *Bastard Out of Carolina* (NAL/ Dutton, 1992). National Book Award–nominated novel. *Skin: Writing About Sex, Class & Literature* (Firebrand, 1994). Essays. *Trash* (Firebrand Books, 1988). Short stories exploring the love and violence of a southern childhood. *Two or Three Things I Know For Sure* (Dutton, 1995). Autobiography. *The Women Who Hate Me* (Firebrand, 1983). Poetry.

Grahn, Judy. *Another Mother Tongue: Gay Words, Gay Worlds* (Beacon Press, 1984), *Blood,*

Bread, & Roses: How Menstruation Created the World (Beacon Press, 1994), *The Queen of Swords* (Beacon Press, 1987), *The Queen of Wands* (Crossing Press, 1982), *The Work of a Common Woman* (Crossing Press, 1978), and more. Strongly lesbian poetry, fiction, essays, and history.

Lorde, Audre. *The Black Unicorn* (Norton, 1978/1995), *A Burst of Light: Essays* (Firebrand, 1988), *The Cancer Journals* (Spinsters/Aunt Lute, 1980), *From a Land Where Other People Live* (Broadside Press, 1973), *Marvelous Arithmetic of Distance* (Norton, 1994), *Our Dead Behind Us* (Norton, 1994), *Sister Outsider* (Crossing Press, 1984), *Undersong* (Norton, 1992), *Zami: A New Spelling of My Name* (Crossing Press, 1983), and more. Fiction, essays, poetry, biomythology— African-American, lesbian, and feminist oriented.

Newman, Leslea. *Every Woman's Dream* (New Victoria, 1994), *Fat Chance* (Putnam, 1994), *The Femme Mystique* (Alyson, 1995), *Gloria Goes to Gay Pride* (Alyson, 1991), *Heather Has Two Mommies* (Alyson, 1991), *In Every Laugh a Tear* (New Victoria, 1992), *A Letter To Harvey Milk* (Firebrand, 1988), *Remember That* (Houghton Mifflin, 1995), *Too Far Away to Touch, Close Enough to See* (Houghton Mifflin, 1995), *Writing From the Heart: Inspirations and Exercises for Women Writers* (Crossing Press, 1993), and more. Novels, short stories, children's books, a writing how-to, and anthologies.

Rich, Adrienne. *Blood, Bread, and Poetry: Selected Prose 1979–1985* (1986/1994), *Collected Early Poems, 1950–1970* (1993), *Diving into the Wreck: Poems 1971–1972* (1973/1994), *Dream of a Common Language: Poems 1974–1977* (1978/1993), *Of Woman Born: Motherhood as Experience and Institution* (1986), *On Lies, Secrets, and Silence: Selected Prose 1966–1978* (1978), *Time's Power: Poems 1985–1988* (1989), *What Is Found There?* (1994), *A Wild Patience Has Taken Me This Far: Poems 1978–1981* (1981), and more (all published by Norton Press). Poetry, essays, extended nonfiction, much lesbian-oriented, all feminist.

Sarton, May. *As We Are Now* (1992), *At Seventy* (1993), *Collected Poems: 1930–1993* (1993), *Coming Into Eighty* (1994), *Crucial Conversations* (1994), *Encore: A Journal of the Eightieth Year* (1993), *Journal of a Solitude* (1973/1992), *Kinds of Love* (1994), *Mrs. Stevens Hears the Mermaids Singing* (1965/1974), *Selected Poems* (1978), *The Silence Now* (1988), *The Small Room* (1961), and more (all published by W. W. Norton). Essays, poetry, journals, novels, some lesbian-oriented, some not, all with a very personal point-of-view.

Fiction and Poetry

Alther, Lisa. *Other Women* (NAL, 1985). Perhaps the first mainstream best-seller to feature a lesbian protagonist; an exploration of the relationship between a newly out lesbian and her straight therapist.

Arnold, June. *Sister Gun* (Feminist Press, 1989). Reprint of the 1975 classic.

Bannon, Ann. *Beebo Brinker* (1962), *I Am a Woman* (1959), *Journey to a Woman* (1960), *Odd Girl Out* (1957), *Women in the Shadow* (1959) (all published in new editions in 1986 by Naiad Press). Pulp novels depicting the New York butch-femme bar scene of the 1950s and 1960s; once sold amid trashy novels in drugstores, these books were a lifeline for many of the closeted lesbians of their day.

Boyd, Blanche. *The Revolution of Little Girls* (Random House, 1992). Lambda Literary Award–winning fiction.

Brown, Rita Mae. *Bingo* (Bantam, 1988), *High Hearts* (Bantam, 1986/1988), *In Her Day* (Bantam, 1976/1988), *Murder at Monticello* (Bantam, 1994), *Rubyfruit Jungle* (Bantam, 1973/1988), *Six of One* (Bantam, 1978/1988), *Southern Discomfort* (Bantam, 1982/1988), *Venus Envy* (Bantam, 1994), and more. Early novels with strong, positive lesbian characters; later novels often focus on straight people.

Califia, Pat. *Macho Sluts* (Alyson Publications, 1988). Erotic short fiction, including S/M, leather, and even men.

Coss, Clare, ed. *The Arc of Love: An Anthology of Lesbian Love Poems.* New York: Scribner, 1996. With an introduction

Donnelly, Nisa. *The Bar Stories: A Novel After All* (St. Martin's Press, 1989). Stories of lesbian survival in a world more hostile than tolerant.

Dreher, Sarah. *Bad Company* (1995), *Gray Magic* (1987), *Other World* (1993), *Something Shady* (1986), *Stoner McTavish* (1985) (all from New Victoria). Stoner McTavish mysteries.

Forrest, Katherine V. *Amateur City* (1984), *The Beverly Malibu* (1989), *Curious Wine* (1983/1989), *Daughters of a Coral Dawn* (1984/1989), *Dreams and Swords* (1987), *An Emergence of Green* (1986/1987), *Flashpoint* (1994), *Murder at the Nightwood Bar* (1987/1989), *Murder by Tradition* (1993) (all published by Naiad Press). Novels and short story collections ranging from coming out tales to detective stories to science fiction, all lesbian-oriented.

Gearhart, Sally Miller. *Wanderground* (Alyson, 1979/1984). Feminist Utopia.

Gidlow, Elsa. *Sapphic Songs: Eighteen to Eighty, the Love Poetry of Elsa Gidlow* (Booklegger Press, 1982). Poetry.

Gomez, Jewelle. *The Gilda Stories* (Firebrand, 1991). Lambda Literary Award–winning tales of a lesbian vampire.

Grae, Camarin. *Edgewise* (1989), *Paz* (1989), *The Secret in the Bird* (1988), *Slick* (1990), *Soul Snatcher* (1985), *Stranded* (1991), *Wednesday Nights* (1994), *Winged Dancer* (1983/1986) (all published by Naiad Press). Magical lesbian adventures.

Hacker, Marilyn. *Going Back to the River* (Vintage, 1990). Lambda Literary Award–winning poetry. *Love, Death, and the Changing of the Seasons* (Norton, 1986/1995). The story of a relationship, told in poetry.

Hall, Radclyffe. *The Well of Loneliness* (Doubleday, 1928/1990). Although now outdated, *the* lesbian classic for many years.

Katz, Judith. *Running Fiercely Toward a High Thin Sound* (Firebrand, 1992). Lambda Literary Award–winning fiction.

Kaye-Kantrowitz, Melanie. *My Jewish Face & Other Stories* (Spinsters/Aunt Lute, 1990). The coming of age and coming out adventures of a daughter of the Jewish left.

Lynch, Lee. *Cactus Love* (1994), *Home in Your Heart* (1986), *Morton River Valley* (1992), *Old Dyke Tales* (1984/1988), *The Swashbuckler* (1985/1986), *That Old Studebaker* (1991), *Toothpick House* (1986) (all published by Naiad Press). Novels, many set in the present and recent past, all with many lesbian characters.

Martinac, Paula. *Home Movies* (Seal Press, 1993). A lesbian writer deals with the AIDS-related death of her uncle. *Out of Time* (Seal Press, 1990). Lesbian ghost story.

Miller, Isabel. *A Dooryard Full of Flowers* (Naiad, 1993). Short pieces, including a sequel to *Patience and Sarah*. *Love of a Good Woman* (Naiad, 1986). A married woman falls in love with her sister-in-law during World War II. *Patience and Sarah* (Fawcett, 1969/ 1994). Two young women fall in love in nineteenth-century New England.

Morgan, Claire. *The Price of Salt* (Naiad Press, 1952/1984). Early lesbian fiction, written under a pseudonym, by famous mystery writer Patricia Highsmith.

Pratt, Minnie Bruce. *Crimes Against Nature* (Firebrand, 1990). Poetry.

Rule, Jane. *After the Fire* (1989), *Against the Season* (1971/1988), *Contract With the World* (1982/1990), *Desert of the Heart* (1985), *Memory Board* (1987/1988), *Outlander* (1981/1989), *Theme for Diverse Instruments* (1990), *This Is Not For You* (1970/1988), *The Young in One Another's Arms* (1977/1984), and more (all published by Naiad Press). Mostly fiction, some essays, all deeply lesbian.

Salvatore, Diane. *Benediction* (Naiad, 1991). A coming of age story. *Love, Zena Beth* (Naiad, 1993), *Not Telling Mother: Stories from a Life* (Naiad, 1993), *Paxton Court* (Naiad, 1995).

Sappho (trans. by Josephine Balmer). *Sappho: Poems and Fragments* (Meadowland Books, 1988). Poetry by the Ancient Greek poet—considered by some to be the best who ever lived.

Schulman, Sarah. *After Dolores* (Plume, 1988), *Empathy* (NAL, 1993), *Girls, Visions, and Everything* (Seal Press, 1986), *People in Trouble* (Dutton, 1990), *The Sophie Horowitz Story* (Naiad Press, 1984). Novels including lesbian adventure, excitement, mystery, and sex on New York's Lower East Side.

Silva, Linda Kay. *Storm Shelter* (1993), *Taken by Storm* (1991), *Weathering the Storm* (1994) (all from Paradigm). Delta Stevens mysteries.

Stein, Gertrude. *Lifting Belly* (Naiad Press, 1989; edited by Rebecca Mark). Stein's erotic poetry.

Taylor, Valerie. *Journey to Fulfillment* (1964), *Return to Lesbos* (1963), *World Without Men* (1963) (all reprinted by Naiad in 1982). The Erika Frohmann series; follows the life and loves of a lesbian concentration camp survivor.

Wilson, Barbara. *The Dog Collar Murders* (1989), *Murder in the Collective* (1984), *Sisters of the Road* (1986), *Trouble in Transylvania* (1993) (all published by Seal Press). Detective stories and other fiction.

Winterson, Jeanette. *Oranges Are Not the Only Fruit* (Grove/Atlantic, 1987). Growing up and coming out in an evangelical family. *Written on the Body* (Random House, 1994). The story of a consuming affair.

Nonfiction and Essays

Adelman, Marcy, ed. *Long Time Passing: Lives of Older Lesbians* (Alyson, 1986). Old lesbians discuss their lives and loves and their experiences being gay pre-Stonewall. Includes information on health, social services, and legal matters.

Barrett, Martha Barron. *Invisible Lives: The Truth About Millions of Women-Loving Women* (Harper & Row, 1990). What it's like to be a lesbian in the United States, based on interviews with 120 women.

Becker, Carol S. *Unbroken Ties: Lesbian Ex-Lovers* (Alyson, 1988). How and why lesbians break up, mourn, and invent new relationships with their ex-lovers.

Berzon, Betty. *Permanent Partners* (NAL, 1988/1990). How to make a relationship last; with emotional, psychological, financial, and legal advice. *Positively Gay* (Mediamix Associates, 1979/1984). A primer for newly out lesbians (and gay men). Covers family, mental health, religion, relationships, aging, politics, etc.

Borhek, Mary V. *Coming Out to Parents* (Pilgrim Press, 1983/1993). Written by the mother of a gay son; offers useful insights on parents' points of view and on the coming out process in general.

Butler, Becky, ed. *Ceremonies of the Heart: Creating Lesbian Unions* (Seal Press, 1990). Personal stories.

Califia, Pat (illustrated by Tee Corinne). *Sapphistry: The Book of Lesbian Sexuality* (Naiad, 1980/1988). Lesbian sex manual. *Sensuous Magic* (Richard Kasak Books, 1993). S/M handbook.

Cammermeyer, Margarethe (with Chris Fisher). *Serving in Silence* (Viking, 1994). Autobiography of the highest-ranking officer ever to be kicked out of the military for being homosexual.

Card, Clauda. *Lesbian Choices* (Columbia University Press, 1995). Essays exploring the meaning of being a lesbian.

Caster, Wendy. *The Lesbian Sex Book* (Alyson, 1993). Lesbian sex manual.

Cavin, Susan. *Lesbian Origins* (Ism Press, 1985). Examines lesbian origins in a heterosexist world, focusing on sex devolution, Amazon origin theories, sex ratio theories, high female societies, cross-cultural lesbianism, and more.

Cook, Blanche Wiesen. "Female Support Networks and Political Activism." *Chrysalis* 3 (autumn 1977). Reprinted in Nancy Cott and Elizabeth Pleck, eds. *A Heritage of Her Own.* New York: Simon & Schuster, 1979.

de Acosta, Mercedes. *Here Lies the Heart* (Ayer, 1960/1975). Autobiography of the reputed lover of both Marlene Dietrich and Greta Garbo!

Donoghue, Emma. *Passion Between Women* (HarperCollins, 1993). History of British lesbian culture from 1668 to 1801.

Faderman, Lillian. *Odd Girls & Twilight Lovers* (Penguin, 1991). History of lesbian life in twentieth-century America. *Surpassing the Love of Men* (Morrow, 1981/1994). Love between women from the Renaissance to the present.

Feinberg, Leslie. *Stone Butch Blues* (Firebrand, 1993). The story of "growing up differently gendered in a blue-collar town in the 1950s."

Gidlow, Elsa. *Elsa, I Come With My Songs* (Booklegger, 1986). Autobiography.

Hoagland, Sarah Lucia. *Lesbian Ethics: Toward New Value* (Institute for Lesbian Studies, 1988). In-depth analysis of how lesbians interact and live now and how they might interact and live in a world based on lesbian ethics and free of sexist, racist, and heterosexist assumptions.

Jo, Bev, Linda Strega, and Ruston. *Dykes-Loving-Dykes: Dyke Separatist Politics for Lesbians Only* (Battleax, 1990). Detailed discussion of separatism and lesbianism, including heterosexism, butch hatred, S/M, motherhood, and the patriarchy.

Johnson, Susan E. *Staying Power: Long-term Lesbian Couples* (Naiad, 1990). The stories of 108 lesbian couples who have been together for ten years or longer—and what can be learned from them.

Kiss & Tell (Persimmon Blackbridge, Lizard Jones, & Susan Stewart). *Her Tongue on My Theory: Images, Essays, and Fantasies* (Press Gang Publishers, 1994). Lesbian sex theory.

Klaich, Dolores. *Woman Plus Woman* (Naiad, 1974/1989). An exploration of lesbianism through interviews, questionnaires, and discussions of such "historical lesbians" as Colette, Sappho, and Gertrude Stein.

Lesbian and Gay Media Advocates. *Talk Back! The Gay Person's Guide to Media Action* (Alyson, 1982). How to make your opinions matter to the media.

Lewin, Ellen. *Lesbian Mothers* (Cornell University Press, 1993). A discussion of lesbian motherhood in the United States.

Loulan, JoAnn. *Lesbian Sex* (Spinsters/Aunt Lute, 1984) and *Lesbian Passion* (Spinsters/Aunt Lute, 1987). *Lesbian Sex* examines what lesbians do in bed, through information, quotes from lesbians, and "homework exercises." *Lesbian Passion* focuses on sexual and nonsexual passion. Questionnaire results from sixteen hundred lesbians are included. *The Lesbian Erotic Dance* (Spinsters, 1990; with Sherry Thomas). Discusses "butch, femme, androgyny, and other rhythms" of lesbian sexuality and romance.

Moraga, Cherríe. *Loving in the War Years* (South End Press, 1983). Essays, stories, and poems exploring being a Chicana and a lesbian in the United States.

Muller, Ann. *Parents Matter* (Naiad Press, 1987). About coming out to parents.

Navratilova, Martina, and George Vecsey. *Martina* (Fawcett, 1986). Autobiography of the tennis great.

Near, Holly. *Fire in the Rain . . . Singer in the Storm* (Morrow, 1991). Autobiography of the singer, songwriter, and political activist.

Nestle, Joan. *A Restricted Country* (Firebrand, 1987). Essays on lesbian herstory of the fifties and sixties, butch-femme relationships, lesbians and prostitutes, the right to fuck, and more.

Pharr, Suzanne. *Homophobia: A Weapon of Sexism.* (Chardon Press, 1988). Aimed at lesbians and straight women, *Homophobia* examines how homophobia stops feminism, its similarities to racism and sexism, and how lesbians can set ourselves free of internalized homphobia.

Pratt, Minnie Bruce. *Rebellion: Essays 1980–1991* (Firebrand, 1991). Essays.

Rafkin, Louise. *Queer and Pleasant Danger: Writing Out My Life* (Cleis, 1992). Fiction and essays.

Schulman, Sarah. *My American History: Lesbian & Gay Life During the Reagan/Bush Years* (Routledge, 1994). Updated essays by novelist and activist Schulman.

Segrest, Meg. *My Mama's Dead Squirrel* (Firebrand Books, 1985). Essays on southern women writers, religion, feminism, gay-baiting, and more.

Slater, Suzanne. *The Lesbian Family Life Cycle* (Free Press, 1995). A discussion of the stages in lesbian couplehood.

Starr, Victoria. *k. d. lang: All You Get Is Me* (St. Martin's Press, 1994). Biography of the openly gay singer.

Stein, Gertrude. *The Autobiography of Alice B. Toklas* (Random House, 1933/1990).

Thompson, Karen, and Julie Andzrejewski. *Why Can't Sharon Kowalski Come Home?* (Spinsters/Aunt Lute, 1988). In 1983, Sharon Kowalski was seriously injured in a car accident. In 1985, the court awarded Sharon's father sole guardianship of Sharon, ignoring the rights, commitment, and love of her partner of many years, Karen Thompson. Here, Thompson tells their story. Also includes information on durable power of attorney.

Weiss, A., and G. Schiller. *Before Stonewall* (Naiad Press, 1988). Lesbian and gay history, pre-1969 in the United States.

Whitbread, Helena, ed. *No Priest But Love: The Journals of Anne Lister From 1824 to 1826* (NYU Press, 1992). The actual diary of a lesbian in nineteenth-century Europe.

Whitlock, Katherine (for the American Friends Service Committee). *Bridges of Respect: Creating Support for Lesbian and Gay Youth* (American Friends Service Committee, 1989). A Quaker-produced resource book; includes much practical information of use to young and old, gay and straight people.

Zimmerman, Bonnie. *The Safe Sea of Women* (Beacon Press, 1991). A critical survery of popular lesbian novels from 1969 to 1989, with a focus on the connections and reflections between lesbian fiction and lesbian life during that period.

Zipter, Yvonne. *Diamonds Are A Dyke's Best Friend* (Firebrand, 1989). A social, personal, and historical look at the lesbian love affair with softball.

Anthologies and Collections

Barber, Karen, ed. *Afterglow: More Stories of Lesbian Desire* (Alyson, 1993), *Bushfire: Stories of Lesbian Desire* (Alyson, 1991). Erotic short fiction.

Beck, Evelyn Torton, ed. *Nice Jewish Girls: A Lesbian Anthology* (revised and updated edition; Beacon Press, 1989). A collection of essays, stories, poetry, autobiography, and photographs exploring all facets of Jewish lesbians' lives.

Boston Lesbian Psychologies Collective, ed. *Lesbian Psychologies* (University of Illinois Press, 1987). Twenty psychology-based lesbian-focused essays, covering such topics as sexuality, aging, power, race, socialization, coming out, alcoholism, weight, and spirituality.

Brown, Susan E., Debra Connors, and Nanci Stern, eds. *With the Power of Each Breath: A Disabled Women's Anthology* (Cleis Press, 1985). Poetry, essays, journal entries, interviews, autobiography by and about disabled women; some lesbian representation.

Card, Claudia, ed. *Adventures in Lesbian Philosophy* (Indiana University Press, 1994). Essays on lesbian creativity, the sex wars, constructing "lesbian," lesbian community and responsibility, and reclaiming lesbian herstory.

Curb, Rosemary, and Nancy Manahan, eds. *Lesbians Nuns: Breaking Silence* (Warner Books, 1985). The first-person stories of lesbians who were—and some who still are—nuns.

Faderman, Lillian, ed. *Chloe Plus Olivia* (Viking, 1994). An anthology of lesbian literature from the seventeenth century to the present.

Forrest, Katherine V., and Barbara Grier, eds. *The Erotic Naiad* (Naiad, 1994), *The Romantic Naiad* (Naiad, 1993). Love stories by Naiad Press authors.

Freedman, Estelle, Barbara C. Gelpi, Susan L. Johnson, and Kathleen M. Westen, eds. *The Lesbian Issue: Essays From Signs* (University of Chicago Press, 1985). Essays focusing on lesbian identity and survival.

Holoch, Naomi, and Joan Nestle. *Women on Women 2* (Plume, 1993). Short stories.

Jay, Karla, and Joanne Glasgow, eds. *Lesbian Texts and Contexts* (New York University Press, 1990). Critical discussions of lesbian writing explore identification, meaning, and interpretation.

McKinley, Catherine E., and Joyce L. Delaney. *Afrekete: An Anthology of Black Lesbian Writing* (Anchor, 1995). Fiction, nonfiction, and poetry; contributors include Michelle Cliff, Jewelle Gomez, Audre Lorde, and Sapphire.

MacPike, Loralee, ed. *There's Something I've Been Meaning to Tell You* (Naiad Press, 1989). First-person stories of lesbian and gay parents coming out to their children, plus a section on the political and legal implications of coming out.

Moraga, Cherríe, and Gloria Anzaldúa, eds. *This Bridge Called My Back* (Kitchen Table, 1984). Writings by radical women of color.

Morse, Carl, and Joan Larkin, eds. *Gay & Lesbian Poetry in Our Time* (St. Martin's Press, 1988). Extentive collection of poetry by contemporary lesbians and gay men.

Nestle, Joan, ed. *The Persistent Desire* (Alyson, 1992). A femme-butch reader.

Nestle, Joan, and Naomi Holoch. *Women on Women* (NAL, 1990). Short stories. Lambda Literary Award winner.

Pace, Anita L., ed. *Write From the Heart:*

Lesbians Healing From Heartache (Baby Steps Press, 1992). Includes personal stories and advice.

Penelope, Julia, and Susan J. Wolfe, eds. *The Original Coming Out Stories: Expanded Edition* (Crossing Press, 1980/1989). Poems and personal narratives by women, famous and not, who have come out over the past forty years.

Pollack, Sandra, and Jeanne Vaughn, eds. *Politics of the Heart* (Firebrand Books, 1987). Collection of essays, autobiography, poetry, fiction, and interviews about lesbian motherhood.

Portillo, Tina, ed. *Dykescapes* (Alyson, 1991). Short stories.

Rafkin, Louise, ed. *Different Daughters* (Cleis Press, 1987). Twenty-four mothers talk about their reactions to having lesbian daughters. *Different Mothers* (Cleis, 1990). Thirty-eight "children" (five to forty years old) talk about growing up in lesbian families.

Ramos, Juanita, ed. *Companera: Latina Lesbians: An Anthology* (Routledge, 1994). An anthology of writings by Latina lesbians.

Reti, Irene, and Shoney Sien, eds. *Cats (and Their Dykes)* (Herbooks, 1991). Cat-related fiction, essays, and photos.

Roger, Susan Fox, ed. *Sportsdykes* (St. Martin's Press, 1994). Stories from on and off the field.

Samois. *Coming to Power: Writings and Graphics on Lesbian S/M* (Alyson Publications, 1982/1987). Essays, poetry, fiction, and how-to for sadomasochistic lesbians.

Silvera, Makeda, ed. *Piece of My Heart: A Lesbian of Colour Anthology* (Sister Vision Press, 1992). Essays, stories, poetry, letters, and more.

Singer, Bennett L., ed. *Growing Up Gay/ Growing Up Lesbian: A Literary Anthology* (New Press, 1994). Contributors include Jeanette Winterson, James Baldwin, Rita Mae Brown, Paul Monette, Audre Lorde, and many more.

Snitow, Ann; Christine Stansell, and Sharon Thompson. *Powers of Desire: The Politics of Sexuality* (Monthly Review Press, 1983). Essays on gay rights, abortion, pornography, and the political meanings of sex, sexuality, and liberation by both men and women.

Stevens, Robin, ed. *Girlfriend Number One: Lesbian Life in the 90s* (Cleis, 1994). Essays, stories, cartoons.

Swallow, Jean, ed. *The Next Step* (Alyson, 1994). Essays and interviews about lesbians in long-term recovery from addictions.

Trujillo, Carla, ed. *Chicana Lesbians: The Girls Our Mothers Warned Us About* (Third Woman Press, 1991). Poetry, essays, and journal entries by and about Chicana lesbians. Lambda Literary Award winner.

Wild, Mara, and Mikaya Heart, eds. *Lesbian Adventure Stories* (Tough Dove Books, 1994). Lesbian adventure stories.

Wilton, Tamsin, ed. *Immortal Invisible: Lesbians and the Moving Image* (Routledge, 1995). Essays on lesbians in film.

Woodrow, Terry, ed. *Lesbian Bedtime Stories* (Tough Dove Books, 1989) and *Lesbian Bedtime Stories 2* (Tough Dove Books, 1990). Lesbian short stories, with a focus on warmth, love, humor, and happy endings.

Zahava, Irene, ed. *Lesbian Love Stories* (Crossing Press, 1989) and *Lesbian Love Stories, Volume 2* (Crossing Press, 1991). Lesbian love stories. *Speaking for Ourselves* (Crossing Press, 1990). Short stories by Jewish lesbians.

Other

Aurora of Santa Cruz. *Lesbian Love Signs: An Astrological Guide to Women Loving Women* (Starstruck Enterprises, 1975/1984). Find out if you and your lover are compatible according to the stars.

Bechdel, Alison. *Dykes to Watch Out For* (1986), *Dykes to Watch Out For: The Sequel* (1992), *More Dykes to Watch Out For* (1988), *New, Improved! Dykes to Watch Out For* (1990), and *Spawn of Dykes to Watch Out For* (1993) (all from Firebrand). In continuing stories told in cartoons, Bechdel both records and gently satirizes contemporary lesbians and their worlds and beliefs.

Caminos, Jane. *That's Ms. Bulldyke to You, Charlie!* (Madwoman Press, 1992). Cartoons.

Chambers, Jane. *Last Summer at Bluefish Cove* (1982), *A Late Snow* (1970/1989), *My Blue Heaven* (1982/1986) (all published by JH Press). Lesbian plays.

DiMassa, Diane. *Hothead Paisan: Homicidal Lesbian Terrorist* (Cleis Press, 1993). The cartoon adventures of a highly caffeinated murderous lesbian and her sidekick cat/conscience, Chicken.

Dreher, Sarah. *Lesbian Stages* (New Victoria, 1988). Five plays, with topics ranging from jealousy to child abuse to war to reconciliation, all with a lesbian perspective.

Foster, Jeannette. *Sex Variant Women in Literature* (Naiad Press, 1985). Bibliography.

Grey, Morgan, and Julia Penelope (with illustrations by Alison Bechdel). *Found Goddesses: Asphalta to Viscera* (New Victoria Publishers, 1988). A dictionary of newfound dyke goddesses, including Cuddles and Chocolata. Who says lesbians don't have senses of humor?

Natalie, Andrea. *The Night Audrey's Vibrator Spoke: A Stonewall Riots Collection* (Cleis, 1992), *Rubyfruit Mountain: A Stonewall Riots Collection* (Cleis, 1993). Cartoons.

Richards, Dell. *Lesbian Lists* (Alyson, 1990). Where else can you find twelve Lesbian Actresses, fourteen Famous Switch-Hitters, eighteen Alleged Causes of Lesbianism, fourteen Epithets for Lesbians, and seven Masturbatory Objects, Real or Alleged?

Roberts, Shelly (illustrated by Yani Batteau). *The Dyke Detector: How to Tell the Real Lesbians From Ordinary People* (Paradigm, 1992). Humor and cartoons.

Silva, Rosemary. *Lesbian Quotations: Reflections on Life and Love, Politics, and Culture, From Sappho to Modern Times* (Alyson, 1993).

West, Celeste. *A Lesbian Love Advisor* (Cleis, 1989). A tongue-in-cheek yet practical book of advice, covering topics such as flirting, love, breaking up, safe sex, and partnership rituals.

Index

Page numbers in *italics* refer to illustrations.

Grier, Barbara, 10, 61, 272–75
Griffin, Pat, 10–11, 21, 163–68
Griffin, Susan, 113, 115
Griffith, Mary, 158
guardians, 195–96
Guérillères, Les (Wittig), 259, 260
Gurumayi, 113
gynecology, 55, 74

Halakhah, 180
Hale, John P., 154
Hammer, Barbara, 288
Hampton, Mabel, *265, 271*
Hard to Get: AIDS in the Workplace,
    11
Hardwick, Michael, 192–93
"Harlem Ghetto, The" (Baldwin),
    240
Harris, Anne, 11, 108–11
Harris, Bertha, 259
Harris, Curtis, 234
Harris, Elise, 11, 151–57
Harris, Sherry, 19
Harvard University, 104, 161
Harvey Milk High School, 11, *152*
Hate Crime Act, 125, 134
Hawaiian Islands, 194
Hawkins, Yusuf, 151–52
Hazeldine, Patty, 26
headache, healing of, 116
healing, 67, 111, 112, 115–17
    distance, 116
    hands-on, 116–17
    lesbian, 117
    psychic, 11, 21, 41, 42, 116–17
    visualization in, 116
Health and Human Services Depart-
    ment, U.S., 156, 201
health care:
    caregiving networks and, 41–43
    gay and lesbian affirmative programs
        in, 102–4
    holistic and spiritual, 42, 67, 111,
        112, 115–17
    homophobic practices and, 97
    and screening of lovers, 94
    sexual history and, 94, 98
    see also specific diseases
health care proxy, 218
health insurance, 41–42
heart attacks, 94
Heart of the Matter, The, 109
Heather Has Two Mommies (New-
    man), 151, 157
Hebrew Union College, 14, 180
Heiman, Julie, *77, 78*
Helms, Jesse, 128, 151, 283, 288, 289
Helson, Ravenna, 245
Hemingway, Mariel, 143
Henderson, Rob, 15, 22

Henson, Brenda, 282
Henson, Wanda, 282
hepatitis B, 93, 94, 146
herbalism, 111
Hernandez, Aileen, 125
Heroines, 288
Hetrick-Martin Institute for the Pro-
    tection of Lesbian and Gay
    Youth, 12, 156
Heyward, Carter, 113, 114
Hickock, Lorena, 268
*Hidden from History: Reclaiming the
    Gay and Lesbian Past,* 266
Hill, Marjorie J., 11, 25–29
Hinajosa, Claudia, *226*
Hiroshima International Film Festival,
    11
Hitchens, Donna, 125
HIV, 11, 20, 61, 93, 97, 98, 137
    health care advocacy and, 21, 61, 63,
        108–11, 145–47
    heterosexual transmission of, 100,
        137
    intravenous drug use and, 93, 108
    testing for, 54, 94, 100, 101
    woman-to-woman transmission of,
        94, 108, 110
    women's infections associated with,
        109, 110
Hoaglund, Sarah, 162
Hodgkin's disease, 96
holidays, 55
    stress of, 27
Hollibaugh, Amber, 108–11, 289
Holocaust, 179, 237, 238, 240, 241
Holy Book of Women's Mysteries, The
    (Budapest), 182, 184
Holy Union celebration, 34
Homecoming (Kim), 233
*Home Girls: A Black Feminist Anthol-
    ogy* (Smith, ed.), 13
homophobia, 19, 20, 39
    AIDS and, 128–29, 146, 204
    decreases in, 19, 20, 47–48
    education and, 57, 125
    fighting of, 18, 21, 60
    hostility and rejection of, 20–21, 25,
        27, 44, 48, 50, 53, 62
    internalization of, 19, 25, 27, 57, 63,
        102, 114
    racism and, 49–50, 51, 53, 154,
        221–24, 226
homosexuality, 44, 45, 141
    education on, 151–56
    government security concerns and,
        121, 125
    education on, 151–56
    new definitions of, 124
    religious definitions of, 172, 175,
        223

Homoteens, 242
Hooker, Evelyn, 25, 124
hormones, 56, 96, 98
hospitals, 116
    gay/lesbian inpatient rehab facilities
        in, 93
Hot-Eyed Moderate, A (Rule), 274
Hot Flash, 246
Hot Wire, 284
housing, 133, 134
Housing and Urban Development De-
    partment, U.S., 201
Huberman, Barbara, 151
Hudson, Lee, 11, 22, 212–15
Hughes, Holly, 286, 287
human papilloma virus (HPV), 97, 98
Human Rights Commission, N.Y.,
    AIDS Discrimination Unit at, 213
Human Rights Commission, San Fran-
    cisco, 11
humor, 107
Hungry The, 143
Hunt, Mary, 176
Hunter, Joyce, 152
Hunter, Tim, 143
Huntington chorea, 146
Hurston, Zora Neale, 288
Hurwitz, Howard, 154
husbands, 39, 166
    coming out to, 48–49
Hyde, Susan, 19

Illinois, University of, 39
illness:
    care-giving and, 41–43
    legal documents and, 195–96
    sexuality and, 81
*Immodest Acts: The Life of a Lesbian
    Nun in Renaissance Italy,* 288
immunization, 93, 94
Impellizzeri, Irene, 154, 155
incest, 75, 93
Indian Family Preservation Act, 134
Indigo Girls, 138
infertility, 54
Inland Book Company, 273
Innis, Roy, 155
Institute for Advanced Study of Hu-
    man Sexuality, 11–12
Institute on Native American Health
    and Wellness, 9
Integrity, 124, 173
intercourse, 72, 73, 100
intestinal parasites, 94
intrauterine insemination (I.U.I.),
    100–101
Islam, 171
*Is the Homosexual My Neighbor? An-
    other Christian View* (Mollenkott
    and Scanzoni), 12

Congregation for the Doctrine of the Faith in, 175
lesbians in, 10, 21, 174–76
Romo-Carmona, Mariana, *37*, 228, 289
Roosevelt, Eleanor, 268
Roseanne, 19, 143
Rosenberg, Dale, *59*
Rovera, Sandra, *225*
R-SAC, 43
Rubin, Lillian, 244–45
Rubyfruit Jungle (Brown), 162, 260, 274–75
Rule, Jane, 260, 273, 274, 275, 284
RuPaul, 136

sadomasochism, 93, 281, 282
Safe is Desire, 95
Safe Sea of Women, The: Lesbian Fiction 1969–1989 (Zimmerman), 14
Sagaris, 131
Salvation Army, 178, 215
Sam, Canyon, *230, *231
Samaritan College, 13, 178
Sanchez Vicario, Arantxa, 137
San Diego State University, 14
San Francisco, City College of (CCSF), 10, 161
San Francisco Chronicle, 124
San Francisco Ethics Commission, 14
San Francisco State University, 10, 230
San Francisco Unified School District, 156
Sang, Barbara E., 13, 244–46
Sapphire, 284
Sappho, 121, 259, 266, 284
Sarton, May, *260*
Satanism, 184
"Say Not the Struggle Naught Availeth" (Clough), 173
Scanzoni, Letha, 12
Schiller, Greta, 287
Schmiege, Karen, *160*
Schreiber, Tatiana, 13, 252–55
Schulman, Sarah, 141, 143, 262
Schwartz, Frederick A. O., 213
Schwartz, Judith, *271*
Schwerner, Michael, 240
Second Sex, The (Beauvoir), 241
Seelman, Katherine D., 13, 41–43
self-esteem, 11, 25, 28, 30, 73, 107, 174
self-love, 40, 129
Senate, U.S., 19, 128
Seneca Women's Peace Encampment, 223
Senior Action in a Gay Environment, 12
Serving in Silence (Cammermeyer and Fisher), 9, 22, 210–11
sex clinics, 74, 76
sexism, 25, 125, 128

sex therapy, 74, 76–77
sex toys, 80, 81, 85, 93, 94
sexuality, 19, 69–89
aging and, 81, 247
attraction and, 28, 29, 33, 79, 88, 107
children's questions about, 46–48
communication and, 71, 75–76, 81, 84
disabilities, illness and, 81
diversity and range of response in, 71–72, 75, 77, 86, 93
education on, 44, 151, 153, 155, 156
fear and guilt in, 75
foreplay and, 38–39, 73, 80, 84, 85
heterosexual vs. lesbian, 72, 73, 74, 88
insecurity about, 71–72, 73, 75, 77–78
laws and, 191–93, 205
love and, 28, 74, 81
male authorities on, 71
multiple partners and, 94, 97, 98
myths of, 71, 72, 74, 75, 76
orientation to, 44, 45, 105
outside standards and, 71, 72, 74
parental attitudes and behavior bearing on, 44, 46, 77
rejection of, 73–74, 75
role-playing and, 73, 80
safe sex practices and, 21, 81, 94, 98, 180
satisfaction and pleasure in, 28, 31, 33, 36, 37–39, 71–72
secret affairs and, 31, 77
techniques of, 21, 71, 73–74, 79–85
vasocongestive component of, 72, 73
sexually transmitted diseases (STDs), 94, 97, 98, 110
Sexual Politics, Sexual Communities: The Making of the Homosexual Minority in the United States (D'Emilio), 265
sexual problems, 29, 71–78
anger and, 75–76, 77, 78
causes of, 74–76, 77
communication failure and, 74–75
disparity of desire and, 74
inhibition and dysfunction as, 71, 72–74, 75
intrapsychic conflict and, 75
organic pathology and, 74
phobias and rigidity as, 73–74
religious and social taboos and, 75
traumatic experience and, 75
treatment of, 74, 76–77
shamanism, 183
Shaw, Peggy, 287
Sheedy, Charlotte, 15, 22
Sheldon, Lou, 158
She Must Be Seeing Things, 288
Shibley, Gail, 19

Shockley, Ann Allen, 261, 262
"Silent Legacy," 276–77
Silver-Tongued Sapphistry, 9
Sinister Wisdom, 259
Sisterly Conversations: Current Concerns Among Lesbians of Faith, 173
Sloan Kettering Memorial Hospital, 42
Smith, Adrienne J., 13, 30–32, 244
Smith, Barbara, 13, 221–24, 261
Smith, Freda, 178
Smith, Liz, 138
Smith College, 10
Smith-Rosenberg, Carroll, 264
smoking, 98
cessation of, 94
disease risk and, 94, 97
social service organizations, 61, 62, 63, 291–96
Society for Individual Rights (SIR), 124
Society for the Psychological Study of Lesbian and Gay Issues, 13
Sodom and Gomorrah, 20
sodomy, 151, 153
laws against, 192–93, 205
Sojourner, 13
solar power, 66
"Song of Bilitis" (Louys), 121
Southern Baptist Convention, 172
Southern Women's Music and Comedy Festival, 280, 282
speculum, 100
Spender, Stephen, 147
Sperm Bank of California, 12, 55
Donor Insemination Program (DIP) at, 99, 101–2
sperm banks, 12, 54, 55, 93, 99–102
sperm donation, 21, 54–56, 93, 99–102
AIDS and, 100
identity disclosure and, 55, 100, 101, 200
paternity claims and, 100, 200
preponderance of male children with, 56
see also artificial insemination
Spin, 9
Spiral Dance, The (Starhawk), 182, 184
spirituality:
alternative avenues of, 21–22, 111–115
healing and, 11, 21, 41, 42, 67, 111, 112, 115–17
self/no self paradox and, 113, 114
see also religion; *specific disciplines*
"Split at the Roots" (Rich), 237–42
Spong, John, 172

weight, 98
  excessive, 94, 96
Weinberg, Janet, 14, 249–51, *250*
Weindling, Elissa, 151
Weld, William, 155
Wellesley College, The Stone Center
  at, 113
Well of Loneliness, The (Hall), 284
West Coast Music and Comedy Festival, 280, 282, 284
wheelchair accessibility, 66, 251
wheelchair races, 250
White House Conference on Aging,
  12, 126
white light, 116
Whitman Walker Clinic Lesbian Services, 95
Wicca, 112–13, 171
  Burning Times and, 182, 184
  Celtic form of, 182, 183
  Dianic form of, 183, 184
  tradition and holidays of, 182–84
Wiener, Nancy H., 14
Wildeman, Mary, *281*
Wilk, David, 273
William Paterson College, 12
Williams, Karen, 288
Williamson, Chris, 279, 282
wills, 41, 196–97, 218, 248
Wilson, Barbara, 260
Wilson, Nancy, 178
Wimbledon Tennis Tournament, 137

Windows, 143
Winterson, Jeanette, 260, 262
witchcraft, 21, 111, 112–13, 182–84
Wittig, Monique, 259, 262
Women, Men and the Bible (Mollenkott), 12
Women-Identified Women, 162
Women of Brewster Place, The (Naylor), 143
Women of Faith in Dialogue (Mollenkott), 12
Women's Army Corps (WACS), 265,
  266
Women's Choice Clinic, 12
Women's Church Convergence, 176
women's health centers, 100–101
Women's Independent Labels Distributors (W.I.L.D.), 279
women's movement, 13, 61, 114, 125,
  240–41
  see also feminism
Women's Ordination Conference, 10
Women's Project, 224
Women's Review of Books, 10
Wong, Nellie, 231
Woo, Merle, 231
Woodson, Jackie, 141
Woolf, Virginia, 114
Wooten, Cynthia, 19
Word Is Out, The, 10, 207
*Words of a Woman Who Breathes Fire,
  The* (Tsui), 13, 231

work, 59–65
  alcohol abuse and, 106
  competition for jobs and, 62
  discrimination against lesbians at,
    59, 62–64
  dress codes and, 63, 64, 65
  equal pay for equal, 18, 125, 127
  free-lance, 42
  immersion in, 31
  loss of jobs and, 19, 62, 65, 106, 129,
    167
  retirement from, 42, 67
  searching for, 59, 63
  self-employed, 60, 62
  volunteer, 61, 63
  see also businesses; careers
Work, Eli, 205
World Council of Churches, 178
World War II, 221, 237, 265–66
WOW Cafe, 287

X rays, 96

Yale University, 161
Yes I Am, 276
Your Native Land, Your Life (Rich),
  12
Ywahoo, Dyani, 113

Zanotti, Barbara, 176
Zilly, Thomas S., 209
Zimmerman, Bonnie, 14, 22, 259–63